Religious Freedom and Conversion in India

Papers from the 4th SAIACS Academic Consultation

Religious Freedom and Conversion in India

Papers from the 4th SAIACS Academic Consultation

Edited by
Aruthuckal Varughese John
Atola Longkumer
Nigel Ajay Kumar

SAIACS Press
BENGALURU — INDIA

RELIGIOUS FREEDOM AND CONVERSION IN INDIA
Papers from the 4th SAIACS Academic Consultation

SAIACS Press
SAIACS, 363 Doddagubbi Cross Road
Kothanur, Bengaluru–560077, India
www.saiacs.org
saiacspress@saiacs.org

Copyright © SAIACS 2017

All rights reserved. No part of this publication may be reproduced, stored in a retrieval system, or transmitted in any form or by any means, electronic, mechanical, photocopy, recording, or any other, without the prior permission of the publisher.

ISBN 13: 978-93-86549-06-8

Cover and Book Layout: Nigel Ajay Kumar
(Cover image adapted from: Freepik)

Printed and bound by SAIACS Press, Bengaluru

SAIACS Press is the publishing division of
South Asia Institute of Advanced Christian Studies

Contents

Introduction vii

1. Religious Freedom, Minorities and the Concept of Religion: Critical Issues in Legislation on Conversion in India 1
   Sebastian Kim

2. Rights, Responsibilities and Rebirth: Balanced Biblical Christianity and Extremism 34
   Christopher D. Hancock

3. Is Secularism Compatible with Hinduism? 51
   Aruthuckal Varughese John

4. Freedom of Religion in India: Violated in Practice, Questioned in Principle 75
   Tehmina Arora

5. Contours of Democracy, Freedom and Faith in the Indian Context: A Brechtian Approach to 'Seeing' the Complexities Involved 95
   A. S. Dasan and Nalini Xavier

6. Reconstructing Early Christian Posture in Lucan Historical Writing from a Postcolonial Perspective 118
   Roji T. George

7. Reading John's Gospel as a Jewish-Christian Conflict Narrative: A Paradigm for Contemporary India 139
   Johnson Thomaskutty

8. An Indian Pentecostal Reading On Conversion 162
   Wessly Lukose

9. A Theology of Religious Freedom: An Engagement with the Odisha Freedom of Religion Act, 1967 186
   Nimai Charan Suna

10. Religious Freedom and the Church: Between Secularism And Religious Nationalism 212
    John Arun Kumar

11. Freedom and Tolerance: A Muslim Perspective on Religious Freedom and Conversion 235
    Farida Khanam

12. *Khrist-Bhakta* Model of Ecclesia. 255
    Cyril Kuttiyanikkal

13. Religious Freedom and Conversion in Sri Lanka: An Analysis 273
    G. P. V. Somaratna

14. Bollywood Spirituality and Audience Desires: Exploring the Theme of Religion and Conversion Through a Study of Popular Hindi Films 297
    Nigel Ajay Kumar

Introduction

A few weeks before the release of this book, various Indian Christian church leaders released an "Open Letter," expressing deep concern over the alarming situation of religious intolerance, the shift of India from a secular democracy to a "Hindu Rashtra."[1] The letter noted how over the past few years, incidentally since the current BJP government came to power, there had been a sharp rise in violence against minorities:

> The number of violent acts against Christians alone during the last 3 years (2014-2016) are over 600, including an increasing trend at social boycott that impinges on the right to life, food and livelihood. This includes physical violence, stopping of worship in churches, attacks on churches, arrests of pastors and their companions, and rapes of Nuns. The National Crime Records Bureau documented 47,064 acts of violence against Dalits in 2014, up from 32,643 in 2010. The violence against Muslims is reaching an alarming peak.[2]

The letter ended with a challenge for the Indian Church "to act before it is too late"; to "stand with the victims"; and also to "partner with civil society to spread the truth" by taking "action to prevent further erosion of… constitutional values." The letter promoted five steps that needed to be undertaken:

> 1. Based on the Biblical values of justice, rights, freedom, dignity and the well-being of every human being, the Christian community should be part of every civil initiative for truth, reconciliation and peace.
> 2. Any erosion, dilution, infringement or violation of Constitutional rights to life and liberty must invite a response from the Church, as it does from the people. Speaking out is often the one response that is needed. Saying "Stop" to an act of injustice can often prevent tragedy.

---

[1] Concerned Citizens of India, "Open Letter to Church Leaders," August 4, 2017.
[2] Concerned Citizens of India, "Open Letter."

3. Our educational institutions must assume their pristine role as crucibles for nation-building, as the Supreme Court has described them.

4. Our Theological institutions, Bible colleges, Formation Houses must in their pedagogy include familiarization with the rights and duties of citizens in international covenants and the Constitution of India to enhance knowledge and hone civic conscience.

5. In unison with members of all faiths, ideologies we should marshal India's tremendous spiritual resources in consolidating peace, resolving conflicts infusing a sense of values in the body politic.³

It is ironic that much of the same fears and need for action existed when the 4th SAIACS Academic Consultation was held in 2015. With its theme, *"Religious Freedom and Conversion in India Today,"* the Consultation aimed to address the growing threat against the multi-religious and secular fabric of India, from a multi-disciplinary perspective. The emergence of the BJP government and the aggressive Ghar Wapsi campaign had brought into light the very nature of "religious freedom" and "conversion" and it was an opportune time to invite critical discussion and clarity about secularity and democracy in the context of religion.

It is with some sadness we state that—in view of the current state of affairs—the papers presented in that Consultation still remain just as relevant and urgent today. Those papers spoke on numerous topics, from historical, legal, theological and cultural perspectives. As the "Open Letter" suggests, the Indian Church must continue to engage with these issues before it is too late.

The contents of this book are the result of that SAIACS Consultation, where each author not only submitted their presentation drafts, but went on to revise their work in view of the robust discussions by the participants of the Consultation. Most of the articles represented here are interdisciplinary, and so it was not possible to neatly divide them into separate sections. As editors, we tried to roughly group philosophical and political issues first, and then biblical, theological, missiological and contextual issues next. What follows is a brief summary of the articles in this volume.

---

³ Concerned Citizens of India, "Open Letter."

Sebastian Kim's keynote address on Religious Freedom and Minorities in India critically examines the legislation on conversion undertaken by certain states in the country, curtailing the rights of minorities. A key analytical position espoused by Kim is the discussion of the concept of "religion" from a theological and philosophical perspective that has its bearing on the different understandings of religion. Rather than legal measures against conversion, Kim argues for open discussion and mutual respect between the different religions marked by a code of conduct for Christian witness, as proposed in the document prepared by the World Council of Churches together with World Evangelical Alliance and the Pontifical Council for Inter-religious Dialogue.

In his paper "Rights, Responsibilities and Rebirth," **Christopher Hancock** warns against the dangers of "Christian exceptionalism" and "cultural elitism" when speaking about religious freedom within the language of rights. Cautioning against the snares of materialism, pessimism, and individualism, he provides "practical applications in relation to a Christian's primary and secondary 'rights' and 'responsibilities'."

Aruthuckal Varughese John examines how Indian secularism is different from the Western constructs. Engaging with diverse articulations on the question of compatibility of Hinduism with secularism, he concludes that it is hard to argue that Indian traditions provide sufficient grounding to establish the current success of secular democracy.

In her article "Freedom of Religion in India," **Tehmina Arora** examines the Freedom of Religion Acts enforced in various Indian states and the constitutional law that seeks to define religious freedom, especially in the area of religious conversion. She argues that the Freedom of Religion Acts undermine religious freedom rather than protect them, both in the way the laws are interpreted and in the way that it has emboldened divisive forces to target people of minority religions.

A. S. Dasan and Nalini Xavier jointly write on the "Contours of Democracy, Freedom and Faith in the Indian Context." They ask a fundamental question, "Can religious freedom mean absolute fundamental right to convert?" And their answer, using a Brechtian approach, is for the need for "enlightened dialogue, wherein shared wisdom prevails without discrediting other faiths."

Roji T. George's article, "Reconstructing Early Christian Posture in Lucan Historical Writing" uses the postcolonial approach to propose that Luke has often been misunderstood as writing simple "history" to help build Christians (and aid survival). When in fact, in view of the struggle for religious freedom, Luke's intent was a "discursive literary response of the early Christian subjugated community towards 'the Powers that Be'." Which is to say, Luke's writing not only helps the survival of Christian community, but is also an assertion for the continual call to mission in difficult times.

Exploring the techniques of *nimesis* and *deigesis* as employed in the Fourth Gospel, **Johnson Thomaskutty** brings a biblical analysis to the issue of religious freedom and conversion in India. Drawn from the *church-and-synagogue conflict* as presented by the narrator of John's Gospel, Thomaskutty values the rhetoric of difference rather than a rhetoric of distance developed in the Fourth Gospel. This reading of Johannine Gospel centres Jesus in the discussion on religious freedom.

Wessly Lukose in his article provides an "Indian Pentecostal Reading of Conversion," seeing it fundamentally as a function of the Holy Spirit. Using stories of conversion experiences from North India, he argues that the greatest motivation for conversion has been the miraculous intervention of God in the lives of people.

Nimai Charan Suna writes on the Odisha context, especially looking at the Odisha Freedom of Religion Act (1967). His study looks at government documents that discuss how the Act came about and makes the important conclusion that the document aims to "close the door of conversion from Hinduism" and move "forward towards a monolithic nationalism." He finds the Act "vindictive, biased and a punitive tool in the hands of the religious majority." And yet, Suna offers a theological response, of how as Christians we can and must act when the government and laws are against us.

"Religious Freedom and the Church: Between Secularism and Religious Nationalism" is the title under which **John Arun Kumar** explores the dilemma of freedom of religious expression and conversion to Christianity. Kumar situates the dilemma faced by Indian

Christians within the larger framework of global movements and documents pertaining to religious freedom as human rights. While critical of the Ghar Wapsi movement by the Hindutva group, Kumar provides a Christo-centric relevance of the term, in a call to return to God's family in restored relationship.

Writing on Religious Freedom and Conversion from an Islamic perspective, **Farida Khanam** argues that the Islamic view of conversion is not really "proselytization in the formal sense", but a "spiritual transformation."

G. P. V. Somaratna presents an analysis of the legal measures the government has taken to curb the freedom of religion in Sri Lanka. While Sri Lanka is a democratic republic with multi-ethnic and multi-religious population, Theravada Buddhism forms the majority of the population. The intolerance to religious freedom particularly towards Christians, and the discrimination based on religious adherence reveals an aspect of Buddhism some may not know.

Nigel Ajay Kumar's article on Bollywood and Religion ends this collection of articles. In it, Kumar looks at a few films that deal with "religious conversion" to show how mass media both reflects and shapes culture, and that the popular (mass) Indian view about "religious conversion" is negative. Yet mass media also offers a hope that within its own language it is possible to communicate a more positive view about religious conversion at a mass scale.

Apart from the chapters in the volume, there were some other important presentations covering critical topics and locations, such as Adivasis and Dalits. However, their revised drafts, in light of the consultation discussions, were not received for the present publication.

On the whole, the papers in this volume are rich and diverse representing several Christian traditions existing in the country. The perspectives and views presented are solely of the academics and theologians. As the host-institution, SAIACS is grateful to all the authors who participated in the Consultation, and especially to those who revised their presentation for this volume. While SAIACS as an institution might not share all the views represented here, we wholeheartedly believe in the free exchange of ideas, even those that we do not agree with.

Religious Freedom, Minorities and the Concept of Religion: Critical Issues in Legislation on Conversion in India

Sebastian Kim[1]

INTRODUCTION

Religious conversion is the most contentious issue between Hindu and Christian communities in India. This was demonstrated in the legal and political debates between Hindus and Christians that took place in the first half of 19th century Bengal, during the Constituent Assembly (1947-49), over the Niyogi Report on Christian missionary activities (1956), and around the introduction of the Freedom of Religion Acts in various states (1967-2006). There have also been debates between individual Hindu thinkers and Christian theologians, among Christian theologians and church leaders, and scholarly discussions on religious conversion.[2] This paper will discuss key disputes and events on legalisation of conversion activities, and Hindu and Christian responses to these. By examining the Hindu-Christian perceptions on religious conversion revealed in relevant literature and debates, this paper will then discuss three key areas of differing understandings between Hindu and Christian protagonists: first, the historical and contemporary interpretation of freedom of religion and its implementation in the Freedom of Religion Acts; second, the place of religious minorities in a democratic state and the interactions of minorities with wider society;

---

[1] Professor Sebastian Kim is the Executive Director of Korean Studies Centre, and Professor of Theology and Public Life, School of Theology, Fuller Theological Seminary, Pasadena, CA, USA. He is a Fellow of the Royal Asiatic Society and the Editor of the *International Journal of Public Theology*.

[2] For example, Rowena Robinson and Sathianathan Clarke, eds., *Religious Conversion in India: Modes, Motivations, and Meanings* (Delhi: Oxford University Press, 2007); Sebastian Kim, *In Search of Identity: Debates on Religious Conversion in India* (Delhi: Oxford University Press, 2003); and Rudolf Heredia, *Changing Gods: Rethinking Conversion in India* (Delhi: Penguin Books, 2007).

and third, the differing theological, philosophical and practical concepts of "religion" between the two religious traditions.

Disputes Over Legislation on Conversion in India

The legal attempt to deal with conversion issues goes back to the late 1820s and the beginning of the 1830s, when a number of young higher caste Hindus in Bengal converted to the Christian faith. These were mainly students of the colleges run by Alexander Duff and other missionaries, who aimed to raise up a body of educated converts through whom the ultimate conversion of the country would take place. From the missionaries' point of view, it was a major breakthrough that Indians were beginning to show a "measure of intellectual conviction reached before confession of faith in Christ,"[3] which showed that the Christian message had begun to make sense to Indian intellectuals. They regarded the conversions of these young people as the result of their sincere and religious quest not because of any "other motives" as the Hindu leaders claimed. They were of higher castes and had made the decision in spite of the social disadvantages and possible excommunication from the community resulting from it.

But Hindu leaders saw this new phenomenon as a threat to society and religion, and their anxiety was heightened by the Charter of 1833 which granted almost unrestricted permission for citizens of all nations to take up residence in British-controlled India. The Christian missions benefited greatly from this. Thus after 1833, the "missionary effort sprouted with great rapidity. When the country was opened up to European penetration, the missionaries entered in with very little delay."[4] And without doubt this change brought a confirmation of Hindu suspicions that it was the common

---

[3] Among them, in 1832, were: Mohesh Chunder Ghose, a student of the Hindu College; Krishna Mohun Banerjea, a Brahman who was the editor of *The Enquirer*, which attacked Hinduism for its superstition and corruption, and who later became a well-respected Christian leader; Gopinath Nandi, after a long search for moral truth. See Stephen Neill, *A History of Christianity in India, 1707-1858* (Cambridge: Cambridge University Press, 1985), 310-311.

[4] Neill, *A History of Christianity in India*, 177.

intention of both the missionaries and the British government to convert Indians to Christianity.

Since conversion was increasingly understood as renouncing one's caste and leaving the fold of Hinduism, new converts were rejected by family and caste, and thus had little choice but to leave their homes.[5] The missionaries were then compelled to provide shelter for them, especially in the case of youth converts. This was in turn seen by Hindu society as an intrusion on their system of family and culture; so they endeavoured to get their youth back from the custody of the missionaries. This led to a series of court cases against missionaries by the parents of the youth over guardianship of the children.[6] After investigation, the courts generally decided in favour of the missionaries and converts. This caused great anger in the Hindu community, who believed the courts were biased in favour of the missionaries.[7] On the other hand, the missionaries were doubly encouraged, first because they won the cases, and second because the court proceedings proved that the missionaries did not use unfair methods to convert these young Hindus since they all testified that it was their own conscious decision.

As a result of the futility of legal action, attempts were made to reclaim converts by forcible abduction by the parents or the relatives of the converts. In some cases missionaries brought court cases against them for this. By 1842, incidents of abduction were spreading so rapidly that the missionaries called on the government to interfere, but the government expressed its reluctance to engage in religious matters. The *Prabhakar*, along with the *Bengal Harkaru* and the *Englishman*—leading English language papers—objected strongly to the missionaries' attempts to obtain government

---

[5] See Duncan B. Forrester, *Caste and Christianity: Attitudes and Policies on Caste of Anglo-Saxon Protestant Missions in India* (London: Curzon Press, 1980), 25-27.

[6] The missionaries regarded 14 years as the legal age whereas the Hindus 18 years. The court cases of this nature in 1833, 1845, 1848 and 1851 are described in detail in Muhammad Mohar Ali, *The Bengali Reaction to Christian Missionary Activities 1833-1857* (Chittagong: The Mehrub Publications, 1965), 78-85.

[7] Whether or not there was bias in the courtroom, judgements in favour of the converts were in any case the likely result of the British legal system's concern with the rights of individual conscience.

intervention in the matter. They registered their opposition to the missionaries' "very mode of criticising the religion of the natives and seeking converts from them, thereby interfering with their religion." The *Prabhakar* went further and argued that Hindu abductions of converts were justified because it was the missionaries who had "abducted" them in the first place.[8]

But the physical return of the convert by abduction did not immediately set matters right for the Hindu community because of the harshness of the caste discipline against those who had converted. As early as the 1840s, as Christian converts were brought back to the Hindu community, there was felt a need to amend the Hindu *Sastras*.[9] In 1843, *Sambad Bhaskar*, a Hindu paper, announced that Shyamacharan Bose[10] had been received back to his own caste and that "this restoration of the Christian convert to caste, if adopted generally by the Hindus, will prove a great obstacle in the way of the spread of Christianity."[11] After much discussion over the issue, there was a large gathering of a few hundred high caste Hindu leaders and Pandits at the Oriental Seminary in Calcutta at which the issue of re-admission to the previous caste was discussed.[12] As the outcome of these efforts, the "Society for the Deliverance of Hindu Apostates" was founded in August 1852, for the purpose of re-introducing Hindu converts into Hindu society.

Yet another cause of concern over Hindu converts was the question of inheritance of property. The Regulation Law established in 1832 laid down that no person would be debarred from inheriting his ancestral property on the grounds of religion and race. But it was not properly implemented,[13] and it was suggested that the

---

[8] Ali, *The Bengali Reaction*, 91.

[9] Ali, *The Bengali Reaction*, 94.

[10] Bose was baptized in 1842 but later abducted by Hindu relatives. About a year later, he appealed in court and denied that he had ever been a Christian.

[11] *Calcutta Christian Advocate* (December 30, 1843), 422-423.

[12] Ali, *The Bengali Reaction*, 97-99. The *Friend of India* stated that the meeting was "one of the most important events that has occurred in India in the present century," June 5, 1851 in Ali, *The Bengali Reaction*, 99.

[13] Because the law was applied only in Bengal; because Calcutta was under the jurisdiction of the Supreme Court and not the Regulation Law; and because the Law was not applicable to property with religious purpose. Ali, *The Bengali Reaction*, 117.

law of the land (*Lex Loci*) should be amended by the Indian Law Commissioners in 1840. The missionaries wanted to ensure that the rights of the convert would be protected since, as the convert became out-caste, he was considered debarred from any share in his patrimony. This attempt caused a serious reaction from the Hindu community, which expressed anxiety that the amendment would lead to an open door to conversion and that "the Hindu religion will be brought to an end."[14] Over the years, the Draft Act (known as the Freedom of Religion Act or Caste Disabilities Removal Act) was written and revised several times, and missionaries and the Hindu community brought their responses on the Draft Act to the government. In 1845, a petition signed by Raja Radhakanta Deb and 32 other Hindu leaders was submitted to the government, in which it was stated that the Draft Act looked "very like a Government premium to conversion."[15] After years of discussion, drafts, petitions and responses,[16] the Act was passed in 1850, safeguarding the right of inheritance and property for the convert. The reaction from the Hindu community was so furious that almost all the Hindu journals made hostile comments. Ali observed that both missionaries and Hindus believed that the amendment of the law would lead to large-scale conversion and that, as the result of the amendment of *Lex Loci*,[17] Hindu suspicions that the government had "allied themselves with the missionaries in order to facilitate the process of conversion" were confirmed in their minds.[18]

[14] *Calcutta Christian Advocate* (February 6, 1841), II/323.

[15] Ali, *The Bengali Reaction*, 123.

[16] Details of the account are in Ali, *The Bengali Reaction*, 117-136.

[17] Also known as the Caste Disabilities Removal Act or the Freedom of Religion Act. See E. Daniel Potts, *British Baptist Missionaries in India, 1793-1837: The History of Serampore and Its Missions* (Cambridge: Cambridge University Press, 1967), 223.

[18] Ali, *The Bengali Reaction*, 125. Majumdar has pointed out that the British government in India had "no intention of encouraging, far less making, conversions to Christianity." He explains, "The Indians of the first half of the ninteenth century did not know what is fully known today, and it is difficult, therefore, to regard the fear and anxiety which the people felt as totally unjustified. In any case, there cannot be any doubt that such feelings not only did exist, but were deep-rooted, and provoked discontent, even hatred, of the people against the English." See "Discontent and Disaffection" in R. C. Majumdar, ed., *British Paramountcy and Indian Renaissance*, 3rd ed. (*The History and Culture of the*

As a result of the passing of the *Lex Loci*, the Regulation Law in 1832, and the amendment of it in 1850 (known as the Caste Disabilities Removal Act or the Freedom of Religion Act), the disadvantages caused by change of religion had been largely removed in British India.[19] However, this did not apply in the princely states, where Hindu or Muslim law was practised and, in the period before Independence, various restrictions concerning conversion were passed in these states. The Raigarh State Conversion Act of 1936 required that a person seeking conversion needed to obtain a certificate of conversion from the authorities, and disallowed preaching for the purpose of conversion. Similarly, the Patna State Freedom of Religion Act of 1942;[20] the Surguja State Apostasy Act in 1945;[21] and the Udaipur State Anti-Conversion Act in 1946;[22] all placed legal obstacles in the way of the would-be convert and the one propagating the message. Mahatma Gandhi, throughout his political career, made his strong objections against Christian conversion movements clear in the public.[23] He made the following statement in his interview with a missionary nurse in the context of growing tensions between Hindu and Christian communities due to "mass" conversion of Depressed Classes in the 1930s: "If I had power and could legislate, I should certainly stop all proselytizing. It is the cause of much avoidable conflict between classes and unnecessary heart-burning among missionaries."[24] Perhaps it was the clearest indication of an Indian political leader to express the prevention of conversion activities through legal means.

Indian People, vol. 9, part 1; Bombay: Bharatiya Vidya Bhavan, 1988), 423.

[19] Potts, *British Baptist Missionaries*, 222-223.

[20] See K. F. Weller, "Religious Liberty in Some Indian States," in *National Council of Churches Review* 66, no. 3 (March 1946): 80-81; Dhirendra K. Srivastava, *Religious Freedom in India: A Historical and Constitutional Study* (New Delhi: Deep & Deep Publications, 1982), 161; Donald E. Smith, *India as a Secular State* (Princeton: Princeton University Press, 1963), 176-181; Rajah B. Manikam, "The Effect of the War on the Missionary Task of the Church in India," *International Review of Mission* 36, no. 142 (April 1947): 175-190.

[21] *National Council of Churches Review* (*NCCR*) 66, no. 3 (March 1946): 87.

[22] *Report of the Christian Missionary Activities Enquiry Committee I* (*Niyogi Report*) (Nagpur: Government Printing, Madhya Pradesh, 1956), 12-13.

[23] See Kim, *In Search of Identity*, 23-36.

[24] *Harijan*, May 11, 1935.

The restrictions on conversion in the princely states and the comments by Gandhi led to anxiety among foreign missionaries and Indian Christians that their religious freedom would be severely limited and the rights of the Christian minority would be ignored in independent India. This was expressed by Christian leaders at the time of Independence, and especially during the Constituent Assembly debates on the inclusion of the word "propagate" in the clause on the fundamental rights in the Constitution.[25] In the proceedings of the Constituent Assembly, and in the Christian literature during and after it, the word "propagate" as used by Christians and Hindus was understood to include the right to seek the conversion of others.[26] The question then arises as to why Christians used the word "propagate" instead of "convert" at the time of the Constituent Assembly. One reason is that the word "conversion" was sensitive at that time so that the Christians would tend to avoid it in order to minimize the reaction from the Hindus. But more significantly, it appears to be the case that the Christians used "propagate" because they saw the right to propagate one's faith as the most fundamental right, and assumed that the right of an individual to convert to another religion was guaranteed by the clause "freedom of conscience" in the same article.

This Hindu attempt to legislate against conversion activities was reiterated in the findings of the Report of the Christian Missionary Activities Enquiry Committee (Niyogi Report), published by the Madhya Pradesh government in 1956.[27] On the basis of enquiry, the report recommended: first, that missionaries whose main object was conversion "should be asked to withdraw" and their entry to the country should be monitored. Second, that use of any professional services as a means of making converts should be prohibited by law. Third, that an amendment of Article 25 of the Constitution was needed, to limit the fundamental rights to Indian citizens only, and clarify that it does not include conversion brought about by undue means. Fourth, that suitable controls should be

---

[25] See Kim, *In Search of Identity*, 37-58.

[26] Sita Ram Goel, *History of Hindu-Christian Encounters, AD 304 to 1996*, (New Delhi: Voice of India, 1996), 240-241; Saldanha, *Conversion and Indian Civil Law*, 159-160; Srivastava, *Religious Freedom in India*, 153.

[27] See Kim, *In Search of Identity*, 60-73.

implemented on conversions brought about through illegal means and, if necessary, legislative measures should be enacted. Fifth, that distribution of literature for propaganda without the approval of the state government should be prohibited.[28]

There were various attempts by Hindus to prevent conversion by means of legislations. The Hindu laws and the withdrawal of special provisions for the Scheduled Castes amounted to what Christians saw as "discriminatory" measures against both caste Hindu and non-caste Hindu converts.[29] However the Freedom of Religion Acts represented direct Hindu attempts to prevent conversion and, as such, were vehemently challenged by Christians. There were several attempts to implement the recommendations of the report in Madhya Pradesh but it was in 1967 that the government of the neighbouring state eventually passed the Orissa Freedom of Religion Act, which was intended "to provide for prohibition of conversion from one religion to another by the use of force or inducement or by fraudulent means." This led to controversy and debate between Hindus and Christians in various court cases, during which both sides bitterly opposed each other's position on religious conversion. The main objections to conversion in the Act were that it undermines another's faith; that it is more objectionable when it is brought about through undesirable methods; and that it creates

[28] *Niyogi Report* I, 163-5.

[29] Hindu "personal laws" were made up of a series of acts passed in the mid-1950s, applicable only to Hindus, that though generally progressive as far as democratization and the status of women were concerned, had serious negative implications for conversion. Conversion would have far-reaching implications including loss of identity in Hindu society and loss of certain marital, parental and inheritance rights for converts and their children. The Hindu Marriage Act (1955) states that a partner ceasing to be a Hindu by converting to another religion gives legitimate ground for divorce. The Hindu Succession Act (1956) lays down that although a convert retains the right to inherit, the children born to that person after conversion and their descendants are disqualified from inheriting the property of their Hindu relatives unless the children remain or become Hindus. The Hindu Minority and Guardianship Act (1956) disqualifies the convert from being the guardian of his own child and from being the natural guardian of his wife if she is a minor. The Hindu Adoptions and Maintenance Act (1956) states that a convert does not have any say over his/her partner adopting a child, one parent can give his/her child in adoption without consent of the partner if he/she has converted, and no one can claim maintenance if he/she has converted to another religion.

"maladjustments in social life" and causes "problems of law and order."[30] The following year, the state of Madhya Pradesh adopted the Madhya Pradesh *Dharma Swatantrya Adhiniyam* (Freedom of Religion Act), which was almost identical to the Orissa Act but added clauses on the reporting of any conversion ceremony to the district magistrate.[31]

As a result of the enactment of the Orissa Act, the authorities arrested some Christians,[32] which resulted in others engaging in legal action against the Acts. The Catholic Union of India filed a case against the Orissa Freedom of Religion Act on the grounds that the Act violated the fundamental rights guaranteed in the Constitution, and that it was beyond the competence of the state legislature.[33] In their decision on October 24, 1972, the Orissa High Court acknowledged, on the basis of the petitioners' arguments, that "it is the religious duty of every Christian to propagate his religion" and as far as the scope of Article 25 (1) of the Constitution is concerned, "[c]onversion into one's own religion has to be included in the [fundamental] right so far as a Christian citizen is concerned." It therefore concluded that the Act was *ultra vires* the Constitution, that the term "inducement" was vague, and that the state legislature had no power to enact it since only parliament could act in matters related to religion.[34] The verdict was welcomed by the Christian community and effectively prevented other states from proceeding with similar Acts.[35] However, in the case of the Madhya Pradesh Act, Chief Justice P. K. Tare delivered a final verdict on April 23, 1974, which was in contradiction to the decision of the Orissa High Court. By arguing that the freedom of religion

---

[30] The Orissa Freedom of Religion Act, 1967. For the full texts of Orissa, Madhya Pradesh and Arunachal Pradesh Acts, see Mathai Zachariah, ed., *Freedom of Religion in India* (Kottayam: NCCI, 1979).

[31] The Madhya Pradesh *Dharma Swatantrya Adhiniyam*, 1968.

[32] These were a Catholic priest, three Catholic catechists and two Baptist evangelists. See *The Examiner*, January 4, 1969, 4. The Orissa Act became effective on January 9, 1968 and the Madhya Pradesh Act on October 10, 1968.

[33] For a detailed account of the Catholic campaign of legal action, see *The Examiner*, January 4, 1969, 4. For the Protestant campaigns, see *NCCR* 89, no. 4 (April 1969): 129.

[34] *All India Reporter (AIR)* 1973 *Orissa*, 116-123.

[35] *NCCR* 92, no. 12 (December 1972): 485-488.

should not "encroach upon similar freedom of other individuals," he concluded that the Act, far from violating Article 25 (1) of the Constitution, actually "guarantees equality of religious freedom to all."[36]

The contradictions of the verdicts of the Orissa High Court and the Madhya Pradesh High Court inevitably led to the case being brought before the Supreme Court, which gave its final verdict on January 17, 1977. This was to uphold the decision of the Madhya Pradesh High Court. On the matter of the charge that the Acts violated Article 25 (1) of the Constitution, the Court argued thus:

> [W]hat the Article grants is not the right to convert another person to one's own religion, but to transmit or spread one's religion by an exposition of its tenets.... there is no fundamental right to convert another person to one's own religion because if a person purposely undertakes the conversion of another person to his religion... that would impinge on the "freedom of conscience" guaranteed to all the citizens of the country alike.[37]

Since the Supreme Court is the final interpreter of the Constitution, the decision was of crucial importance to the Christian community. It not only authenticated the Orissa and Madhya Pradesh Acts but also paved the way for other states to enact such legislation if they so desired. The fears of the Christian community that the verdict of the Supreme Court would trigger the adoption of similar Acts by other state governments became apparent when the government of Arunachal Pradesh passed the Freedom of Indigenous Faith Act on May 19, 1978 (yet to be implemented).[38] It is important to notice that, although the Arunachal Pradesh Act is similar to the Madhya Pradesh Act, it specifies "indigenous faith" as "religions, beliefs and practices" which have been "sanctioned, approved, performed" by indigenous communities, and this, in their view, included certain forms of Buddhism, Vaishnavism, and "Nature worship." In this

---

[36] *AIR* 1975 *Madhya Pradesh*, 163-174.

[37] *AIR* 1977 *Supreme Court*, 908-912.

[38] Arunachal Pradesh Freedom of Indigenous Faith Act, May 19, 1978. This Act has not been implemented since the Rules governing the Act are yet to be framed.

way, many of the indigenous communities of the state were included under the umbrella of Hinduism. The presentation of an all-India Freedom of Religion Bill to the Lok Sabha by O. P. Tyagi on December 22, 1978 caused great anxiety among Christians and increased the Hindu-Christian debate. As the Lok Sabha session for discussing the new Bill drew near, the debates intensified, and both Hindus and Christians insisted on their own way and called for mobilization for action, especially during the months of May and June 1979, but this was rather abruptly called off and the Bill was never discussed due to the fall of the government in July 1979.[39] Similar Acts were introduced in various states: Chhattisgarh Freedom of Religion Act, 2000 (adopted from Madhya Pradesh); Tamil Nadu Prohibition of Forcible Conversion of Religion Act, 2002 (repealed in 2006); Gujarat Freedom of Religion Act, 2003; Rajasthan Dharma Swatantrya Bill, 2006 (yet to be enacted); and Himachal Pradesh Freedom of Religion Act, 2006.[40]

CRITICAL ISSUES IN CONVERSION IN INDIA

The issues relating to conversion have been a bone of contention between the Hindu and Christian communities in the history of modern India. As Shripaty Sastry put it, "in the whole of the Christian-Hindu strained relationship there has been no greater

---

[39] In *The Examiner*, July 14, 1979, the editor gave a detailed account of the party's division and suggested that one of the main reasons was that the party leadership had lost the confidence of its members because of the controversy over the Bill.

[40] For recent discussion on Freedom of Religion Acts, see Tehmina Arora, "Indian's Defiance of Religious Freedom: A Briefing on 'Anti-conversion' laws," *International Journal for Religious Freedom* 5, no. 1 (2012): 59-71; Saadiya Suleman, "Freedom of Religion and Anti Conversion Laws in India: An Overview," *ILI Law Review* 1, no. 1 (2010): 106-128; The Indian Law Institute, "A Study of Compatibility of Anti-Conversion Laws with Right to Freedom of Religion in India," 1-79. For the issue of law and violence towards Christian minorities, see Vrinda Grover, ed., *Kandhamal: The Law Must Change its Course* (New Delhi: Multiple Action Research Group, 2010); Chad Bauman, *Pentecostals, Proselytization, and Anti-Christian Violence in Contemporary India* (Oxford: Oxford University Press, 2015), 70-130. See also Tehmina Arora, "Freedom of Religion in India: Violated in Practice, Questioned in Principle," in this volume.

cause of friction than the Christian campaign of conversion."[41] As I have discussed, there have been various attempts, both Hindu and Christian, to legalize matters related to conversion: the Freedom of Religion Act (Caste Disabilities Removal Act) and the amendment of *Lex Loci* in 1840s and the Constituent Assembly (1947-49) put forward by missionaries and Christians; "anti-conversion acts" in princely states towards Independence, Hindu "personal laws" and special rights and privileges for Scheduled Castes in the 1950s, and the Freedom of Religion Acts in various states during 1967-2006 initiated by Hindus. In this section, I shall discuss the contentious areas of dispute in order to move forward and seek potential common grounds.

Freedom of religion as a fundamental human right or protection of traditional religion?

Christian arguments for conversion of Hindus in this period were largely based on the notion that the right of conversion was not only the kernel of the Christian faith but also a key issue in the matter of religious freedom, which Christians regarded as a vital part of fundamental human rights. The Christian arguments were met by counter-arguments of Hindus who consistently challenged the Christian position, not only on the basis of a Hindu understanding of conversion, but also on the basis of the problems involved in applying a universal understanding of religious freedom in multi-cultural contexts. The broader context of the issue of religious freedom and human rights was discussed widely at an international level and in Christian churches worldwide and so this needs to be considered in our study.

During the first half of the 20th century, and particularly toward the end of World War II, the Western nations raised concerns about human rights in international politics, especially in relation to communist countries and nationalist movements, and there was a consensus for an "International Bill of Rights," which would have a universal basis and be acknowledged by all nations.[42] Christians

---

[41] Shripaty Sastry, *A Retrospect: Christianity in India* (Pune: Bharatiya Vichar Sadhana, 1983), 6.

[42] See Theo C. van Boven, "Religious Liberty in the Context of Human Rights,"

in the West were actively involved in drafting the Bill and ensuring that religious freedom was counted as an integral part of human rights.[43] Some Christians also insisted that the freedom to propagate religion or persuade others to convert is part of religious liberty and that this right should be universally acknowledged.[44] As the outcome of these collective Anglo-American Christian efforts, the "Charter of Religious Freedom" in a statement on "Human Rights and Religious Freedom" (March 1947) affirmed that freedom of religion is an "essential and integral aspect of human freedom," and includes "freedom to choose... religious beliefs" and to "propagate and to persuade" others.[45] The British draft of the International Bill of Human Rights (June 1947) and the first Assembly of the WCC (August 1948) in its "Declaration on Religious Liberty" also affirmed this.[46] These Christian efforts to ensure religious liberty, were reflected in the formation of the United Nations Universal Declaration on Human Rights (December 1948), which declared, in Article 18, the universal right of the freedom to "change" and to "manifest" one's religion or belief in "teaching, practice, worship and observance."

However, the relationship of religious liberty with human rights came under strain within Christian churches, especially in the 1960s. First, there was increasing pressure from the non-Western world not to limit Christian concern for human rights to individual freedom only but to widen it to include economic, social and cultural rights. This was particularly in evidence in the WCC at the Uppsala Assembly (1968) and Nairobi Assembly (1975), where there was a shift from a "Western-civil-liberal view of human rights and the social rights of the human community to the eventual

---

ER 37, no. 3 (July 1985): 345-355.

[43] See Anton Houtepen, "From Freedom of Religion Towards Really Free Religion: Voices from Rome and Geneva," *Exchange* 27, no. 4 (October 1998): 295.

[44] See Cecil Northcott, *Religious Liberty* (London: SCM Press, 1948), 85; H. G. Wood, *Religious Liberty To-day* (Cambridge: Cambridge University Press, 1949), 5.

[45] "Human Rights and Religious Freedom" issued by the Joint Committee on Religious Liberty of Great Britain in Wood, *Religious Liberty To-day*, 133-134.

[46] World Council of Churches, *The Church and the International Disorder* (London: SCM Press, 1948) 229-232.

perception of the life-interests of the 'Third World'."⁴⁷ And this recognition was paralleled by a shift in understanding of conversion to encompass liberation from socio-economic and political oppression, which could be said to be the right of every human being regardless of their faith commitment.⁴⁸ Second, the challenge to the priority of religious freedom over human rights was also due to the objections raised by Orthodox and Catholic leaders against the proselytizing of their members by some Protestant groups, who justified their activities on the basis of religious freedom.⁴⁹ It is worth noting here that tension over the issue of religious freedom and proselytism caused much debate at ecumenical meetings in this period. Third, there were strong objections from adherents of non-Christian religions—Muslims, Jews and Hindus—against the inclusion of the right to change one's religion among universal human rights. In particular, they regarded the issue of religious freedom as part of a Christian missionary agenda to evangelize people of other faiths and insisted that the right to keep one's faith should also be respected.⁵⁰

As a result of these factors, the following clause was included as Article 18(2) in the UN International Covenant on Civil and Political Rights (1966): "No one shall be subject to coercion which would impair his freedom to have or to adopt a religion or belief of his choice." This addition was regarded as "protection both *for* the individual's right to change his religion and *against* zealous proselytizers and missionaries."⁵¹ In a similar vein, the strength of WCC pronouncements on religious liberty was much reduced during the fifth WCC Assembly in Nairobi (1975), which stated that the right to religious freedom "should never be seen as belonging exclusively

---

⁴⁷ Jürgen Moltmann, *On Human Dignity, Political Theology and Ethics*, trans. M. Douglas Meeks (Philadelphia: Fortress Press, 1984), 6.

⁴⁸ Jürgen Moltmann, "Christian Faith and Human Rights" in Alan D. Falconer, ed., *Understanding Human Rights* (Dublin: Irish School of Ecumenics, 1980), 184-185.

⁴⁹ Houtepen, "From Freedom of Religion," 296-302.

⁵⁰ Houtepen, "From Freedom of Religion," 291-293.

⁵¹ Martin Scheinin, "Article 18" in Asbjørn Eide and others, *The Universal Declaration of Human Rights: A Commentary* (Oslo: Scandinavian University Press, 1992), 267.

to the Church" and that the church has an "obligation to serve the whole community." In the report, the right to religious freedom was limited to "worship, observance, practice, and teaching."[52] Furthermore, the statement of the next Assembly at Vancouver acknowledged the complexity of human rights and the struggle for justice was emphasized.[53] Both in ecumenical Christian documents and in international politics, religious freedom now tended to be limited to freedom to maintain or to change one's own religion. In other words, the freedom to change one's own faith remained the fundamental human right, but the initial Christian insistence on the right to "propagate" one's faith in a way which involved the conversion of the other, proved increasingly unacceptable in both domestic and international law.[54]

When it comes to the debates in India, it is interesting to observe the debate between Mahatma Gandhi and E. Stanley Jones in 1931. While Gandhi argued against conversion by applying the principle of *swadeshi*,[55] Jones' argument was based on human rights and religious freedom. They also differed over the nature of religious identity. Gandhi considered that religion was embodied in the religious heritage of one's forefathers—thus a person is born into it. Since it is one's very identity, one needs to reform it rather than renounce it. Therefore conversion to another religion was not only religious apostasy but also a denial of the self and understood as a rebuff to Hindu society. But Jones believed that religion, like

---

[52] David M. Paton, ed., *Breaking Barriers: Nairobi 1975* (London: SPCK, 1976), 106.

[53] David Gill, ed., *Gathered for Life* (Geneva: WCC Publications, 1983), 138-140.

[54] See recent discussion on religious freedom and Christian mission, Hans Aage Gravaas, Christof Sauer, Tormod Engelsviken, Maqsood Kamil and Knud Jørgensen, eds., *Freedom of Belief and Christian Mission* (Oxford: Regnum Books, 2015).

[55] The *swadeshi* principle was the most powerful and most frequently used in Gandhi's arguments, that is, India needed economic, political and religious self-reliance—the fundamental right of any society as a people of dignity. His ideas on *swadeshi* had implications for three spheres of Indian life: religious, political and economic. In the religious sphere, he claimed that Hinduism was the "most tolerant [religion] because it is non-proselytizing" and, according to this spirit of *swadeshi*, a Hindu "refuses to change his religion" since he can improve it through reforms within.

ideology or scientific facts, could be separated from one's socio-cultural heritage. It is something that the individual may decide rather than something already decided by one's socio-cultural background. While Gandhi argued for the *duty* of Hindus to keep the identity they were born with, Jones argued for the *right* of the individual to select the religion of their choice. The key issue here is whether the priority of the freedom of religion should lie in individual choice or group solidarity—right to individuals to choose their religious affiliations and the right to share their faith with others, or right to keep or protect their traditional faiths from aggressive proselytization.

As I have mentioned earlier, after the Supreme Court decision of 1977, Christians could no longer claim that the word "propagate," based on their understanding of freedom of religion, justified their attempts to bring about the conversion of others. Although both Christians and Hindus continued to anchor their arguments in the right of freedom as defined by the fundamental rights of the Constitution, their concepts of freedom were mutually opposed: the right to propagate, for Christians, and right to retain one's own religion, for Hindus. The difficulty of respecting and safeguarding the conflicting Hindu and Christian interpretations of conversion, of reconciling the right to retain one's own religion and the right to try to persuade others to change theirs, is a major obstacle in any attempt to resolve the problem of conversion on the basis of human rights ideology. Although there were attempts to find a satisfactory theological basis for human rights,[56] this notion still derives from an Enlightenment liberal understanding of individual sovereignty over a domain of beliefs and behaviour, circumscribed only by the potential of that sovereignty to be exercised in a manner which invades the like sovereignty of other individuals. On these grounds, the attempt to marry Christian theology to human rights ideology has been challenged by scholars of other religious traditions and has also been questioned by Christians. Furthermore, in view of our studies on human rights, it seems quite clear that the Christian argument on religious freedom and human rights was not effective in debate with Hindus. Therefore the justification of Christian mission that includes the call to conversion is in need of an alternative foundation.

[56] For example, Moltmann, "Christian Faith and Human Rights," 182-195.

The place of religious minorities in a democratic state and the interaction of minorities with wider society

In the process of shaping the new India, the leaders of the nationalist movements not only had to arrange for the orderly transition of power from the British but also to channel in a common direction the widely differing views within the Hindu majority while keeping together the various "minority" communities of the country. Though it has been shown that the nationalist leaders were committed to a secular ideology throughout their campaign,[57] their bias toward the Hindu majority was equally evident. As the struggle with the British for independence neared its close, the struggles between different communities within India became apparent—particularly between the majority Hindus and the minorities. The nationalist leaders' objection to religious conversion was based on the view that it undermines the legitimacy of other religious traditions and disturbs the harmony of society. Therefore religious conversion was seen as incompatible with the pursuit of secular India, where all the religious communities "respect" one another's religious traditions and tolerate them.

The ideology of Hindutva strongly asserted that the rights of the majority Hindus must be respected as opposed to the Christian and moderate Hindu argument of the freedom of choice for individuals. As far as the rights of religious communities were concerned, several arguments were advanced by Hindus for giving Hindus preferential rights. First, in the context of the encounter between Christianity, which is actively proselytizing, and Hinduism, which is non-proselytizing, it is fair to give certain protection to the latter. Second, since Hinduism is the religion of the majority of Indians, in a democratic setting, the majority's interests should be respected and should determine the direction when it comes to a conflict of opinion with religious minorities. And third, because Hinduism is part and parcel of traditional Indian society and constitutes the very identity of Hindus, it should be given preferential treatment over against the other religions. Presenting this problem of conversion over against "Hindu rights," Ashok Chowgule challenged

---

[57] Bipan Chandra and others, *India's Struggle for Independence* (New Delhi: Penguin Books, 1988), 518-528.

Christians not only to accept the notion that "the Hindu's way of salvation is as valid as the way through Christ, and that salvation is possible in other faiths as well," but also to accept their position as a minority group and be conformed to the framework set by the Parivar.[58] Abhas Chatterjee explained the Parivar understanding of the term "minority" in the following terms: "the residents of this land who have alienated themselves from her national attribute—Sanatana Dharma—are no more part of this nation, but minorities" and not "nationals."[59] According to this way of thinking, people are defined not in terms of numbers but by their attitude toward Hinduism. And this is based on the notion that in India, Hindu ways should prevail and, just as within the territory of a secular state, one has to abide by its law. Therefore, in the Parivar's understanding, conversion lay "beyond being a communal issue" and was considered an attack on the Hindu nation "as it exists."[60]

However, Christians anchored their identity primarily on the individual right of conversion—the right to seek the conversion of others and the right of oneself to convert to another religion. This they regarded as fundamental to their faith and to their religious freedom. Christians also argued that as individuals have equal rights in a democratic country, religious communities should also have equal rights to maintain their notion of belief, rather than be forced to conform to the majority.[61]

The hallmarks of democracy could be identified as equality, freedom and the rule of law for all citizens, but when it comes to forming a collective concept of the meaning of these three aspects and their applications, the view of the majority is determinative and the opinion of a minority is often ignored or suppressed. Particularly during the second half of the 20th century, wide and increasing acceptance of liberal democracy in world state politics was demonstrated by the increase in the number of nations classified

---

[58] Ashok Chowgule, *Hindutva and the Religious Minorities* (Mumbai, HVK, 1997), 74-78. *Hindutvavadis* are proponents of *Hindutva*.

[59] Abhas Chatterjee, *The Concept of Hindu Nation* (New Delhi: Voice of India, 1995), 24-30.

[60] Chowgule, *Hindutva*, 7-8.

[61] See A. N. Dar, "The Hindu is Hurt," *Indian Express*, March 1, 1999.

as democratic,⁶² and was highlighted in the much-quoted, though heavily criticized, thesis that liberal democracy is the "end point of mankind's ideological evolution" and the "final form of human government."⁶³ Recently the problems of democracy have become more apparent. A feature article in *The Economist* (March 1, 2014) asked "What's gone wrong with democracy?" The authors raised a series of challenges to the "end of history" thesis and pointed to a "setback" in democracy developed in the world.⁶⁴ In addition, they drew attention to the serious problem of distrust towards politicians among voters in Europe and the USA, and yet, the issue concluded with some degree of optimism, employing James Madison and John Stuart Mill who regarded democracy as a powerful but imperfect system in need of constant care with checks and balances, and arguing that the most important part of the nurture and maintenance of a democratic system is its care for minorities:

> The most successful new democracies have all worked in large part because they avoided the temptation of majoritarianism—the notion that winning an election entitles the majority to do whatever it pleases.... the first sign that a fledgling democracy is heading for the rocks often comes when elected rulers try to erode constraints on their power—often in the name of majority rule.⁶⁵

How then do we maintain the freedom and autonomy of individuals, groups and nations, and yet protect vulnerable minorities in a society or in a nation? The question of "the problem of minorities," according to Jennifer Preece, is among the most contested issues

---

⁶² *The Economists* (March 1, 2014). By 2000 Freedom House, an American think-tank classified 120 countries or 63% of the world total, as democracies.

⁶³ Francis Fukuyama, *The End of History and the Last Man* (London: Hamish Hamilton, 1992), xi.

⁶⁴ They put forward a number of reasons for this, including the financial crisis of 2007-08 when people witnessed the incompetence of their political systems to police the workings of financial sectors and the way in which China, under the exclusive control of the Communist Party, had achieved economic success as well as apparent political stability. Editorial, "What's Gone Wrong With Democracy," *The Economist*, accessed August 2, 2017. http://www.economist.com/news/essays/21596796-democracy-was-most-successful-political-idea-20th-century-why-has-it-run-trouble-and-what-can-be-do.

⁶⁵ "What's Gone Wrong With Democracy," *The Economist*.

in political life because of "competing desires for freedom and belonging," especially when it comes to the issue of equality and freedom.[66] Freedom requires autonomy of action, promotes a variety of values, as well as innovation and diversity; whereas belonging requires certain constraints of freedom in order to maintain social relationships and social cohesion, and preserve common identity and certain uniformity. The issue of minority rights is not only a matter of government toleration but also of positive government action to promote diversity and to "affirm the dignity, esteem and mutual respect of all citizens whatever their religious, racial, linguistic or ethnic identities."[67] There are some difficulties of applying rights between individual and group rights and between human rights and minority rights. The former is applied to more political, economic and social areas of life whereas the latter is more to do with the cultural sphere. Preece insists that "what matters is not the content of the ideal but rather its ability to sustain a sense of solidarity towards other members that is not ordinarily extended to outsiders." Typical ways to deal with the "problem of minorities" in many states is by means of discrimination, assimilation, persecution, or separation, but she warns that these will not solve the problem since human diversity is "remarkably resilient."[68] Instead, Preece advocates the state recognizing diversity by setting moral and legal frameworks for it, such as the UN Declaration on the Rights of Persons Belonging to National or Ethnic, Religious and Linguistic Minorities (1992).

Bhikhu Parekh discusses the difficulties of recognizing and incorporating minority rights in a democracy. Minority groups such as gays and lesbians, women, ethnic and cultural minorities, and indigenous people demand that society should recognize their identities and take full account of these into laws and public policies, but many of these would face opposition from across the spectrum of political orientations.[69] He discusses the two distinctively differ-

---

[66] Jennifer Jackson Preece, *Minority Rights: Between Diversity and Community* (Cambridge: Polity, 2005), 5. See John Rawls, *A Theory of Justice* (Oxford: Oxford University Press, 1993), 277.

[67] Preece, *Minority Rights*, 8.

[68] Preece, *Minority Rights*, 183-186.

[69] See Bhikhu Parekh, "Redistribution or Recognition? A Misguided Debate,"

ent political approaches of "redistribution" and "recognition," and suggests that the best model for dealing with the issue should be an integral approach to the two since this is the most advantageous. In his proposal of a new theory of justice, he argues that differing views need to be acknowledged and understood and that the issues between them are not always issues of justice but rather to do with differing values and ideas. Therefore there is a need to negotiate with each other to seek a common solution.

How to deal with a minority in any society or nation is a vital part of the healthy conduct of democracy, but states, whether of liberal (individualistic) or social (communal or cooperative) orientation, often fail to address the issue due to the democratic nature of majoritarianism.[70] South African theologian John de Gruchy points out that the relationship between Christianity and democracy has been ambiguous in that, although he sees that Christian faith has provided democratic values, historically Christianity has often distanced itself from the system. However, he further comments that, especially after the experience of Nazism and Stalinist totalitarianism, most churches regard democracy as "essential to [their] vision of a just world order." De Gruchy employs Reinhold Niebuhr's argument for democracy and also the way it was expressed in the perception of ecumenical Christianity.[71] Throughout Christian history, although the church has often been on the side of the state endorsing its policies, nevertheless Christians have also been among the chief critics of state policies, particularly on the poor and marginalized by challenging its majoritarianism.

The ideology of *Hindutva* has been criticized not only by religious minorities but also by moderate Hindus for several reasons: first, it is a "majoritarianism" of power-driven "minority" high-caste Hindus over against the other sections of society;[72] second,

in Stephen May, Tariq Modood and Judith Squires, eds., *Ethnicity, Nationalism and Minority Rights* (Cambridge: Cambridge University Press, 2004), 199-213.

[70] See Jonathan Israel, *A Revolution of the Mind: Radical Enlightenment and Intellectual Origins of Modern Democracy* (Princeton: Princeton University Press, 2010), 1-36.

[71] John de Gruchy, *Christianity and Democracy: A Theology for a Just World Order* (Cambridge: Cambridge University Press, 1995), 9, see also 228.

[72] Sumit Sarkar, "Hindutva and the Question of Conversions," in *The Concerned*

it is "untrue both to Hinduism and to Indian nationalism" and, in defining "Indianness" along religious lines, it is fundamentalistic;[73] and third, whereas to the secularist, Indians should be defined on the "basis of common participation in the body politic known as India—regardless of their caste and religion," *Hindutva* thinking legitimizes social hierarchies that guard the privileges of the powerful.[74] The Parivar's pursuit of *Hindutva*, as David Ludden points out, is a "majoritarian idea that does not espouse communal conflict in principle" but sees communal conflict as a by-product of reactions from minority communities and secular forces in the course of their cultural and ideological search for Hindu national self-identity. And it may be argued that, in many cases of communal conflict in India, the problem did not entirely lie with the majority Hindus,[75] but the combination of this "majoritarian idea" with the politics of numbers, which in a modern democratic electoral system became so dominant that the religious minorities had limited space to locate their own self-identity, let alone to uphold any conflicting ideology against the dominant Hindu groups. Indeed, Robert E. Frykenberg questions whether India has ever had "a single, self-conscious, unified *majority* community" and regards the concept of "majority" as misused by some Hindu leaders for their political gain, at the expense of minorities.[76]

It is not surprising then that conversion in this context was understood as a way for Dalits and Adivasis to "protest" against what was perceived to be overwhelming ideological aggression. But

Indian's Guide to Communalism, ed. K. N. Panikkar (Viking, New Delhi: Viking, 1999), 101; A. J. Philip, "Hindutva, the Lexical Way," *Indian Express*, March 8, 1999.

[73] Shashi Tharoor, "Hindutva Assault on Hinduism," *Indian Express*, March 14, 1999.

[74] Teesta Setalvad, "A Warped Debate," *Communalism Combat*, Jan 1999, 8-10; Praful Bidwai, "The Congress's Dangerous Temptation," *Times of India*, February 6, 99.

[75] David Ludden, "Introduction–Ayodhya: A Window on the World" in *Making India Hindu*, ed. David Ludden (New Delhi: Oxford University Press, 2005), 15-16.

[76] Robert E. Frykenberg, "The Concept of 'Majority' as a Devilish Force in the Politics of Modern India," *The Journal of Commonwealth & Comparative Politics* 25, no. 3 (November 1987): 267-274.

for the Parivar, it was a stand against the affirmation of Hindu nationhood and struck at the very root of their vision of Hindu India. It is ironic that the Parivar, in their assertion that the self-identity of Indians must be founded on *Hindutva* over against any other ideology, not only failed to appreciate the struggle of other religious groups to define their own identities, but imposed their ideology on them as the only means of being part of the "Hindu nation." As they reject the universality of the Christian theology of salvation through Christ, the Parivar need to consider whether their ideology of *Hindutva* is necessarily applicable to all in India, regardless of their socio-religious understanding of Indianness.

In the context of systematic attacks on Christian communities in recent years,[77] Christians were bound to be suspicious of any Hindu argument and regard it as part of an aggressive Hindu "majoritarianism" that Christians could not yield to. The conversion issue then, for Christians, was not just a matter of the freedom to change religious affiliation but it was to do with whether to conform to a Hindu system of thought. The theological struggle for Christians was whether Christian faith provides "salvation" *outside* Hinduism so that one has to reject it, or *within* its boundaries so that one remains inside it. And Hinduism in this case signifies not so much the cultural boundaries of India as the ideological boundaries of Hindu identity. What Christians resented most was the pressure from dominant Hindu groups that sought to impose the rights of Hinduism over both the socio-cultural and the sacred space of Christians. Conformity to the former involved the adoption of the Indian socio-cultural heritage, in which Christians had made significant progress over the years, but conformity to the latter meant giving up Christian distinctiveness altogether. It was not only a question of whether salvation is in Hindu or Christian faith; it was to do with preserving Christian religious and communal identity. Christians asked Hindus to respect this in the same way as Hindus expected Christians to respect Hindu religion.

---

[77] Vijayesh Lal provided a glimpse of some of the recent violence against Christian communities in his presentation at the SAIACS Academic Consultation, 2015. See also John Arun Kumar, "Religious Freedom and the Church," in this volume.

The differing concepts of "religion" between Christianity and Hinduism

The Hindu-Christian debate on legislation of conversion helps us to see that interpreting religious conversion requires more than an examination of personal changes of religious commitment or the socio-political changes taking place in a community. Study of the debate exposes the religious complexity of the problem of conversion in India and suggests that it is also due to a clash of two radically different religious frameworks in Christianity and Hinduism. As we have discussed, the religious dimension is of vital importance in the Parivar's pursuit of *Hindutva* ideology, which is described as a "desire to restore the centre of faith of the Hindus."[78] It is ironic that both the Parivar and Christians accuse each other's practice of conversion as being politically motivated and lacking in spiritual dimensions, while both are clearly religious movements and their arguments are based on their own understanding of religious conversion. The theological dimensions of the problem imply that, though the debate is conditioned by the particular historical and socio-religious background of India, it is not unparalleled. Consequently debates arising from other contexts and the resulting theological formulations may be of relevance here.

The arguments of the Hindu nationalist movements against conversion were focused on presenting the supremacy of the Hindu philosophy of tolerance and persuading Christians of the "openness" of Hindu thought. This was expressed particularly starkly in the articles in the *Vivekananda Kendra Patrika* where the fundamental difference between Hinduism and Christianity was seen in the assertion that there is freedom of thought *within* Hinduism whereas Christianity has no freedom within it but confines its members to its particular doctrines. In other words, as Savyaksh argued, Hinduism "tolerates" other beliefs, modes of worship or codes of behaviour since it teaches that divine revelation must be understood in pluralistic terms. Therefore Hindus argued that Hinduism, having this ideology of the plurality of the truth, embodied a "philosophy of toleration" which exhibits a mature understanding of God and nature over against exclusive claims to the truth by

---

[78] Rakesh Sinha, "Nationalism Redefined," *Indian Express*, December 30, 1998.

Christians. In Hindu understanding, then, it is not necessary to convert to Christianity to find truth since within Hinduism there is built-in provision and scope for finding the truth in various religious forms and ways. Conversion confines the convert to one particular side of the truth, hindering his/her search for the whole truth.[79]

While Christians call Hindus to a conversion to Christianity—a particular religious tradition—regardless of race, gender, and caste, and as a result to affirm an identity distinctive from others who are not Christians, Hindus call Christians to conform to a particular Hindu view of the truth, regardless of the different history, doctrines and practices of Christian tradition, and as a consequence, to endorse values which can operate only within the Hindu worldview. Therefore, one cannot say that Hindus are tolerant and Christians are intolerant, because each has its own distinctive claim to truth and the ways to approach it—Hindus, at least on the conversion issue, are equally exclusive in their claims. The problem of conversion then does not lie in the supposed tolerance of Hindus and intolerance of Christians. It is rather the clash or mismatch of areas of tolerance between the two religions.

The enactment of the Hindu laws, the state benefits for the Scheduled Castes and the legislation against conversion made clear distinctions between Hindus and non-Hindus, between Hinduism and other religions. It is important to notice that these distinctions drew definite boundaries of Hindu religious affiliation, belief and practice. Both caste and non-caste Hindus were required to remain in their own fold, for there were now serious penalties for those who deliberately moved out through conversion to another religion. However, these boundaries were not completely closed from the other side, for those who were willing to assimilate into the wider Hindu family. For non-Hindus, to be associated with Hindus became an attractive option, as is suggested by the inclusion of various "indigenous faiths" in the Arunachal Pradesh Act.

Nationalist Hindus tried to show that Hinduism also gave an answer to the meaning of life and confidently asserted that Hindu religion provided an understanding of salvation differing from the

---

[79] The argument that Hinduism offers a superior way to Christianity was also that of the early 19th century *Pandits*. See Kim, *In Search of Identity*, 18-23.

Christian notion. The arguments against conversion put forward by the Parivar, perceived by Christians as socio-political ones, reflected this struggle to provide an answer to the Christian theology of salvation through conversion. In Hindu thought, keeping one's *dharma* is vital. Therefore conversion as change of religion (*dharma*) can only originate from outside one's religious sphere as a form of interference with one's right to pursue the religious quest defined by one's birth. The problem of conversion for Hindus runs deeper than concern about changes of religious affiliation; it is to do with the perceived incompatibility of the Christian call to conversion with the Hindu idea of keeping one's own *dharma*. In the course of the debate, comparison of Hindu and Christian understanding of the ways to achieve salvation was inevitable, and despite their ideology of "equality of religions," Hindus made unfavourable comparisons of Christianity with Hinduism. Paradoxically, while Hindus strongly objected to contemporary Christian attacks on Hinduism on the basis of religious tolerance, they also resorted increasingly to verbal abuse against Christianity. They asserted the superiority of Hindu religious thinking and attempted to discredit the Christian scriptures and the traditions of the church, as part of their attempt to win the battle over conversion. From their new yet fragile political strength, the Parivar promoted a Hindu ideology based on the traditional Vedic philosophy of tolerance in their encounter with other religions. However this tolerance was not applied within what was perceived to be Hindu territory. In other words, the Parivar defined a Hindu nation within which Indians are protected from what is seen as outside theological interference by other religions, such as Christianity or Islam. In such a Hindu nation, other patterns of thought could be tolerated only on the terms set by existing Hindu norms. Religious conversion was a threat to this concept of nationhood and the communities that promoted it were seen as subversive.

While Christians tended to approach the question of conversion from the perspective of human rights, Hindus insisted that conversion was against their notion of keeping one's *dharma* and therefore a challenge to Hindu tolerance. S. Radhakrishnan, the prominent Indian philosopher, portrayed tolerance as a hallmark of Hinduism and a sign of maturity, and insisted that it should be adopted "not as a matter of policy or expediency but as a principle of spiritual life" and a "duty" rather than a "concession." He saw tolerance as based on the belief that "every community has inalienable rights which others should respect," which resulted in "equal treatment for others' views."[80] Throughout the debate over conversion, Hindus described Christianity as intolerant and identified its insistence on the conversion of others to the Christian faith as the major cause of communal tension. For Christians, this question of truth and tolerance was an awkward one. Some Christians regarded tolerance as compromise with an alien doctrine and therefore to be avoided. Others were acutely aware that Christian history, including recent history in India, posed undeniable evidence of Christian intolerance. As George M. Soares-Prabhu comments, compared to the "aggressive, intolerant and powerful missionary religions" of Christianity and Islam, Hinduism certainly appeared tolerant and Christians were falling "between the intolerant truth [Christianity] professes and the unrestrained love it tries to live."[81] At the same time, we have seen the limitations of Hindu tolerance when it comes to conversion of Hindus to other religions in actions including the Hindu personal laws, withdrawal of concessions for Scheduled Castes and Tribes, Freedom of Religion legislation, and above all, physical attacks on Christian communities by the Sangh Parivar. As Lipner points out, although "a genuine doctrinal tolerance" is evident throughout traditional Hinduism, the orthopraxy of Hindus often shows otherwise.[82]

This paradox of "tolerant" Hinduism was well explained by P. D. Devanandan, first Director of the Christian Institute for Religion and Society in Bangalore, who saw that the tolerance of Hinduism had developed and was mainly operational *within* Hinduism. However, during the course of its encounter with other

[80] S. Radhakrishnan, *The Hindu View of Life* (New Delhi: Harper Collins, 1927), 21-36; "Hinduism" in A. L. Basham, ed., *A Cultural History of India* (Delhi: Oxford University Press, 1975), 70-72; S. Radhakrishnan, *Eastern Religions and Western Thought*, 2nd ed. (Oxford: Oxford University Press, 1940), 313-317.

[81] George M. Soares-Prabhu, "Religion and Communalism: The Christian Dilemma" in S. Arokiasamy, ed., *Responding to Communalism* (Anand: Gujarat Sahitya Prakash, 1991), 143-145.

[82] Julius Lipner, *Hindus: Their Religious Beliefs and Practices* (London: Routledge, 1994), 180-190.

religions, he argued, the tolerance that was manifested within its geographical and ideological sphere of influence, was not exhibited to other religions unless they also conformed to its framework.[83] Similarly, Ainslie T. Embree, writing on "the question of Hindu tolerance," provides a convincing argument that Hindu civilization has grown self-content through centuries of development and has established its own distinctive "endurance and persistence of its style and its patterns," and that the Hindu approach is not best described as "absorptive, synthesising, or tolerant" but that it "encapsulates" other cultural and religious traditions.[84] It is evident that the Hindu policy of toleration, which had developed over centuries within its geographical and philosophical sphere, was not equipped to accommodate the challenge of the "intolerant" doctrine and practice of conversion brought by Christianity. The debate over conversion between Hindus and Christians should not be seen as between "tolerant" Hindus and "intolerant" Christians. The problem is the mismatch in the scope and understanding of tolerance between the two religions.

In the process of the debate over conversion, many socio-political problems became attached to the issue of conversion. These included, for Hindus, the problem of its association with colonial power, ecclesiastical extension, political manipulation and social disturbance, and for Christians, its relation to social uplift, caste mobility, and the search for justice. The tendency was to blame the problem of conversion on the socio-political difficulties of India caused by colonial occupation and post-Independence power struggles; many religious leaders accused others of being politically motivated and therefore side-stepped the religious issue. Although all these socio-political factors contributed to the problem of conversion in India, and were therefore unique to India, nevertheless we have seen that the problem had more to do with a clash between two different and opposing religious systems.

Well aware of the limitations of Hindu toleration, at the time of Independence, Nehru and others set up the political scheme of

---

[83] P. D. Devanandan, "The Hindu Conception of Religious Liberty in the Melting-Pot," *ER* 13, no. 4 (July 1961): 439-449.

[84] Ainslie T. Embree, *Utopias in Conflict: Religion and Nationalism in Modern India* (Los Angeles: University of California Press, 1990), 19-37.

secular India to safeguard the interests of different religious groups and communities, allowing them to "live and let live."[85] This secular society was based on the ideology of "equal treatment of all religions" and therefore regarded religion as a private matter not to be dealt with in public. However, this attempt to safeguard religious communities by political means could work only if all the political parties were "neutral" in their policy-making. But as "religious nationalism" entered Indian politics, the motivating factors of political parties became deeply religious and Hindus, particularly the Parivar, pushed hard to protect the rights of their community and promote Hindutva ideology, and left little room for religious toleration. Ironically, in treating Christian conversion as a socio-political issue concerned with the protection of Hindu society, they used Hindu notions of tolerance to suppress the freedom of individuals, who were pressured to conform to society and Hindu ideology. When Christians experienced Hindu "toleration" in the context of violent attack, it was not only Christian communities that were in trouble but also the Hindu virtue of tolerance that was at risk. The making of the Constitution based on a secular ideology and its preservation through the political and social turmoil of post-Independence India has been a remarkable achievement. However, it is clear that, as well as the political and legal protection given it, Indian religious tolerance needs to be drawn from religious sources.

This is also the conclusion of Ashis Nandy, who raised the question of religious tolerance in the Indian politics of secularism in the context of communal violence, particularly between Hindus and Muslims. In his vigorous attack on secular ideology, he put forward the importance of "religion as faith" over against "religion as ideology" and claimed that the Indian secular-state had failed to acknowledge the importance of the former since it was easier to deal with the latter. Furthermore, he found that, by regarding communal clashes as the result of socio-economic problems, the supporters of secularism had failed to realize the deeper problem of "conflicting interests and a philosophical encounter between two metaphysics." He insisted that because Indian secular politics suppressed the public role of religious faith, it was not able to meet the needs of a people "to whom religion is what it is precisely because it

---

[85] *Lok Sabha Debates* 2/9 (December 2, 1955), 1113.

provides an overall theory of life, including public life, and because life is not worth living without a theory, however imperfect, of transcendence."[86] While Nandy's critics accused him of naïvety about post-colonial India and political leaders (including Gandhi), and of an over-reactionary attitude to secular politics,[87] he nevertheless drew attention to the impossibility of marginalizing religion from society in India. He suggested that the solution ought to include exploration not only of "tolerance of religions but also tolerance that is religious."[88] Christians are challenged to play their part in searching for a religious solution to communal problems in India and this will involve formulating a theology of conversion. In doing so, Christian theologians need not only to express their theology in ways appropriate to the culture and socio-political context of India, but also to see their attempts through the eyes of people of other faiths.[89] A Christian theology of conversion for India needs to be open to the scrutiny of those who do not profess Christianity. It is therefore important that Christians respond to Nandy's suggestion and consider what "tolerance that is religious" means in Christian terms, and even whether tolerance could provide the alternative foundation for conversion that Christians seek.

Conclusion

While Hindus attempt to make Freedom of Religion Acts to cover the whole of India, Christians campaign against such attempts or to repeal the existing Acts. As I have argued in the previous sections, while the intention of the Acts is to "protect" the vulnerable sections of society from aggressive conversion activities, this is not an appropriate measure to deal with the issue for the following reasons. First,

---

[86] Ashis Nandy, "The Politics of Secularism and the Recovery of Religious Tolerance," *Alternatives* 13, no. 2 (April 1988): 177-194.

[87] See Rajeev Bhargava, ed., *Secularism and Its Critics* (Delhi: Oxford University Press, 1998), especially the article by Rajeev Bhargava, "What Is Secularism For?" 486-542.

[88] Nandy, "The Politics of Secularism," 192.

[89] Joseph Mattam and Sebastian Kim, "Introduction" in *Mission and Conversion: A Reappraisal*, eds. Joseph Mattam and Sebastian Kim (Mumbai: St Pauls, 1996), 8.

it is impractical because it is extremely difficult to "prove," in legal terms, for "force," "fraud," "inducement," or "allurement" in the process of conversion, since it has to rely on the personal testimony of the convert or the person who conducted the conversion ceremony (e.g. baptism). The fact that, since the enactment of the Orissa Act, no one has actually been convicted under the Acts, demonstrates the difficulty of establishing the case. Second, the Acts are open to misuse of state authority over faith matters of an individual or a community because the terms applied in the legislation are not clearly defined. For example, mentioning heaven or any kind of spiritual blessings could be interpreted by account as "grant of any benefit, either pecuniary or otherwise," or "misrepresentation or any other fraudulent contrivance." In filling in the form required by the legislation, the converts have to be very cautious, otherwise some "wrong" phrase may end up causing their conviction. This leads to the third problem that what the Acts effectively achieve is to create an atmosphere in which any form of conversion (out of Hinduism) is regarded undesirable or even unacceptable, because it is "anti-social" or "exploiting the innocent people belonging to depressed classes" (Tamil Nadu Act). In particular, the Orissa Act specifically mentions its rejection of conversion itself: "conversion in its very process involves an act of undermining another faith."

In fact, the Acts serve the purpose of deterrence of any conversion in those states, which in itself, without anyone being convicted, plays a vital role in preventing the problem of conversion for Hindus. However, this in turn creates the problem of a secular state exercising its legislative power on the basis of a Hindu understanding of "freedom of religion" and ignoring that of the Christian community's understanding. Furthermore, the Acts "effectively" violate the fundamental rights of the Indian Constitution and the international laws on human rights. Yes, the clause of the fundamental right to "propagate" in the Indian Constitution was rightly interpreted by the Supreme Court to mean that there is "no fundamental right to convert others," but individuals still have fundamental rights to preach and evangelize others, which may lead to the conversion of others. The key issue, in my view, is to do with ethics of the evangelism which leads to conversion, by both Christians and Hindus, as both parties agree that unethical means for conversion are unacceptable, not only because of the Indian multicultural context, but also due to the teachings of their respective religious traditions. Having rich traditions, both religions should be able to draw out some solutions from their own religious resources, as Ashis Nandy points out.[90]

In order to address the problem of conversion, there has been a recent attempt to produce a "code of conduct" for conversion in Christian mission. The World Council of Churches, the Pontifical Council for Inter-religious Dialogue and World Evangelical Alliance have recently produced a document called "Christian Witness in a Multi-Religious World: Recommendations for Conduct."[91] In its section on "principles," it states that "Religious freedom" includes "the right to publicly profess, practice, propagate and change one's religion" and that it "flows from the very dignity of the human person which is grounded in the creation of all human beings in the image and likeness of God." It also calls for Christians "in mutual respect" to promote together "justice, peace and the common good." In its section on the "basis of Christian witness," it affirms that while it is a Christian responsibility to witness to Christ, conversion is ultimately the work of the Holy Spirit. Although this is a very encouraging initiative on behalf of Christian churches which could challenge those of other faiths, I would like to see the Christian community acknowledge the importance of religious freedom as the right to protect, preserve or maintain one's own faith commitment in the document.

Although the Acts may have provided a certain "protection" of existing religious communities, the use of legislation is far from satisfactory. One of the key signs of a healthy society is its ability to maintain open public debate as far as possible on any issue, however difficult it may be, and not to shy away from controversy, and certainly not to be monopolised by any particular ideology, religion, political party, or group. Indian secularism has maintained its strengths as a state giving equal treatment to all religious

---

[90] Nandy, "The Politics of Secularism," 177-94.

[91] "Christian Witness in a Multi-religious World: Recommendations for Conduct," accessed August 2, 2017, http://www.worldevangelicals.org/pdf/1106Christian_Witness_in_a_Multi-Religious_World.pdf.

traditions[92]; it is vital also to respect the different perspectives on conversion of the Hindu and Christian communities. Perhaps, as a way forward, there should be a series of consultations on conversion, including scholarly examination of the meaning of "freedom of religion" and biblical concepts of conversion. At the practical level, the ethics of Hindu and Christian activities, and the suggested "code of conduct," could be applied through a Hindu-Christian forum. This could also advocate against some of the violence (both physical and verbal) and misconduct in conversion activities taking place in contemporary India. It seems the road to a consensus on conversion between Hindus and Christians is long and hard, but it is worth the journey and is preferable to attempting to solve the problem by legislation. As I see it, legislation will not achieve the intended purpose, since it is based on a particular interpretation of conversion, and furthermore it is a hindrance to healthy and open Hindu-Christian relations.

---

[92] See Donald E. Smith, *India as a Secular State*.

Rights, Responsibilities and Rebirth: Balanced Biblical Christianity and Extremism[1]

Christopher D. Hancock[2]

INTRODUCTION

This book addresses a theme of immense contemporary importance in India—and, indeed, in many parts of the world. "Religious freedom" in name and reality is in crisis worldwide. It is abused as often as it is honoured (by those who want to manipulate politics and promote religious agendas). It is misused as often as it is misunderstood (by co-religionists and cool humanists as simply another name for "human rights"). If we are to exercise the prophetic ministry Swiss theologian Karl Barth (1886–1968) envisaged for true theologians, our task is first to stand back from the frontline (to consider principles and strategy), and then to speak out with godly confidence and clarity (to call our churches and society to account). It isn't easy. Being a theologian never is: true, evangelical theology is always joy-filled reflection on painful matters and pain-filled meditation on divine truth and human triumph. So off we go; mindful of the unique socio-political pressures and ancient cultural assumptions of India, a land with which my family had links for generations.

The trauma and trials of postmodern Europe have—perhaps unsurprisingly—re-kindled existentialist themes in theology and popular literature and culture; truth found through doubt, hope through tragedy, meaning through confusion, authentic life

---

[1] I approached writing this paper with considerable nervousness. The situation for Christians in India is fluid and intensely complex for resident insiders—let alone, this international outsider!

[2] Dr. Christopher Hancock is Director of Oxford House, an academic initiative to provide high-level advice on culture, faith and contemporary geo-politics. He is a former professor of theology, Vicar of Holy Trinity, Cambridge, Dean of Bradford Cathedral and Director of the Centre for the Study of Christianity in China at King's College, London.

through real death. There is much here for us to grasp and work with. To see no possibilities for revelation or discovery in the Indian church's present situation is faithless and hopeless. The Christian existentialist impulse should drive us here, too, to our knees, to take us back to the cross, and to encourage us to speak into *and out of the lived experience* of our struggling—and, of course, our succeeding—Indian neighbours. So let me plead with you, first, *not to play at theology* (but to work to revitalize the mind, heart and hands of the church) and *not to be dilettante socialists*, as if the "kingdom of heaven" depends on your effort. No, to recall Barth once more, a true theologian of the Word begins and ends his work in love for the crucified. Our work and witness are to his glory and for the extension of his kingdom here in India.

Two Fears

Monitoring (happily once-removed from modern discussions—as an academic and Track II diplomat, I find "religious freedom" issues *intensely complicated*!) fierce, contemporary "religious freedom" debate in Europe and elsewhere has led me to *fear two things* more than I used to.

First, that Christians—and, perhaps especially, evangelical Christians—will be blithely co-opted by less worthy causes and individuals into a kind of *religious exceptionalism*. That is, that they (for a host of often rather self-important reasons) *deserve to be treated differently*, exceptionally. They have particular spiritual priorities that need to be honoured. They have special ceremonies that must not be disturbed. They have a distinctive culture that must be protected. If we are not careful, a once robust faith comes to see itself and to be seen by others as *expecting to be pampered*. And so, my preferences turn to petulance, and *my* needs are more pressing than those of my neighbour and my society. It is an egotistical, Adamic temptation to want to be treated *exceptionally*—and a dangerous one at that. A moment's biblical reflection will surely remind us that a primary duty of a disciple is *not* to expect special treatment, but to put God and neighbour always and everywhere first. Beware of *Christian exceptionalism*: it is a nasty, effete, unworthy thing. The Indian church is worthy of something far better.

Second—and cousin to this temptation—is the danger of *cultural elitism*. Christian history tells a sorry tale of the church's predisposition to be—and, even more troublingly, to appear to be—*self-righteously better than others*. We confess sin at the altar and then profess superiority on the street. It is a not uncommon (but essentially tribal) inclination. We are proud of being different. We believe we are right. We have the truth, and God loves us for it. Let me be clear, godly Christian confidence[3] is an apostolic principle and a biblical virtue; Christian *overconfidence* and condescending *cultural elitism* are not. If we are not careful in the act of claiming truth, we lose a creedal principle; that is, that God, "the Father Almighty, the maker of heaven and earth," holds *the whole world*—and every tribe, culture and language in it—in his loving hands. The particularity of our claim to Christ and the gospel's uniqueness should never be made at the expense of the universality of God's love for all. If I am always telling myself "He loves *me*" and "I am *right*," I may forget he loves *you, too*—oh, and that I, too, am a miserable sinner! If *religious exceptionalism* breeds cuddly spiritual bunnies, this kind of *cultural elitism* births what Chinese call "little prince-lings"; that is (because of its one child policy), only children who are nauseatingly demanding and incorrigibly opinionated. What else should we expect? However we view globalization, it is a God-given reminder that we—be we Indian, English, Christian, Muslim or Sikh—are not alone in this world. We all belong here. God has many children. Christian humility never goes amiss and further than imagined—especially amid talk of "religious freedom." *Cultural elitism* has no scriptural sanction and should not find a home in our churches.

---

[3] Greek *parrēsia, parrēsiadzomai*, lit. openness, frankness, plainness of speech (in public), courage, confidence, boldness, fearlessness, joyousness of heart (for instance, see Mark 8:32; John 7:4, 13, 26, 10:24, 11:14, 54, 16:25, 18:20; Acts 2:29, 4:13, 29, 31, 6:10, 14:19, 28:31; 2 Cor. 3:12, 7:4; Eph. 6:19; 1 Thess. 2:2; 1 Tim. 3:13; Heb. 4:16, 10:35; 1 John 3:21, 5:14, and so on.).

MY THEME AND WHY

And so to my theme, in light of these dangers, *"Rights, Responsibilities and Rebirth: Balanced Biblical Christianity and Extremism."* It will come, perhaps, as no surprise to hear me say that the "religious freedom" debate is too often cast, to my mind, in terms of *my* or *our "rights."* "Rights" language risks pandering to my desire to be treated *exceptionally*: it can too easily feed my habitual and sinful need to *be best and first*. Christian history and classical Christian theology speak often of "divine rights," and then move quickly to impress on the faithful their "responsibilities" to heaven and earth as citizens, spouses, parents and children, workers, disciples and friends. But you know all that!

So I want to consider these well-known themes rather differently, to review thinking about "rights" and "responsibilities" in light of the biblical theme of "rebirth." Here, I suggest, is a profound spiritual and existential truth that speaks into society's crying need for help and authenticity, and also into the church's need for a gospel message that causes us to stand tall, to speak and live well. There is another reason I am drawn to look at religious freedom through the lens of the very Indian and biblical theme of *rebirth*. The language of *rebirth* awakens a Hindu sense of reincarnation and the divine empowerment of a chosen few. It also offers a biblical Christian a vision of Christian identity that is more profound, more radical, more demanding, and more compelling than any of the more superficial or particular claims we might make about or for our "rights," our culture and even, perhaps, our very social and Christian "responsibilities"; as the apostle Peter writes in his first epistle,

> Praise be to the God and Father of our Lord Jesus Christ! In his great mercy he has given us new birth into a living hope through the resurrection of Jesus Christ from the dead, and into an inheritance that can never perish, spoil or fade - kept in heaven for you. (1 Pet. 1:3, 4).[4]

Personally, I do not find appeals to religious freedom as compelling, exciting, or radical as that! So we look closely at what the Bible

---

[4] Biblical quotations are taken from the New International Version (Grand Rapids, MI: Zondervan, 1996).

says of *rebirth* in the context of ancient and modern India. Here is a theme to turn Indian culture towards Christian hope, and an Indian image into a Christian message.

Rebirth in the Bible and Beyond

To begin with, then, a few general points about *rebirth in the Bible and beyond*. I stick to scripture to keep things simple and clear: I feel safer holding this hand-rail than launching out here unsupported.

First, *the image of rebirth was well-known to the Jews and Greeks of Jesus' day*, as it is to a Hindu today. In Judaism, it was a *rebirth* the proselyte experienced when he became a Jew. When Jesus raised the issue of *rebirth* with the Pharisee Nicodemus in John 3, it wasn't that Nicodemus would never have thought about *rebirth*: he simply wouldn't have defined it as comprehensively as Jesus did. To a Jew *rebirth* was a change of name and religion: to Jesus it was a change of heart, a new, true experience of "life" (John 10:10). To first-century Greeks, *rebirth* was linked in mystery religions with fertility cults and the annual resurrection of the dying gods Isis and Osiris. Ritual and worship transmitted what happened to gods onto the souls and bodies of devotees. The fact, though, that *rebirth* was well-known to the Jews and Greeks of Jesus' day shouldn't lead us to see New Testament usage as somehow artificial or syncretistic. On the contrary, it represents a proven evangelistic practice (use of a popular image; hence its use in this paper in India) to convey a profound evangelical truth (new life as a gift to faith in Jesus Christ; not spiritual reincarnation or the empowerment of chosen few, but a completely *new* life); as the apostle John writes in the "Prologue" to his Gospel:

> Yet to all who received him, to those who believed in his name, he gave the right to become children of God - children born not of natural descent, nor of human decision or a husband's will, but born of God. (John 1:12)

Rebirth: it takes us back to basics and to a distinctive Christian principle. In light of this, my "rights" and "freedoms" are always to be seen as *secondary* to the transformative event of *spiritual rebirth*.

Second, in the New Testament *the image of rebirth has clear, corporate connotations*. In the apostle Paul's epistles, *rebirth* is an objective act performed by God in the lives of all believers. They are *all* reborn, adopted, saved and raised to new life. This comprehensive act of redeeming grace and gift of new life is *the shared privilege and experience of Christians*. It is what defines their shared identity. It makes them a new, spiritual community. This is not for a few special *sadhu*s. The external acts of circumcision and ritual conformity do not reach into the core of a person's identity in the way this shared act of spiritual *rebirth* does. In Indian culinary terms, *rebirth* to a Christian isn't like the *smell* of *masala*, it's the taste of it, too! As we have seen, the apostle Peter connects *rebirth* with the creation of a new people who share "a living hope" and experience of "resurrection" through faith in Jesus Christ. They know the taste of new life. In other words, at the heart of a Christian's identity and ethnicity is a shared spiritual experience, the experience of *rebirth*. This is hugely important. It means who I am, and how I see myself, are transformed—or, better perhaps, radically transfigured, as Jesus was (Matt. 17:2; Mark 9:2ff)—by the radiant truth of an objective act of God's redeeming grace. However I used to see myself, wherever I was born, and whatever language I spoke, I share with you now a common identity and glorious inheritance as a "born again" Christian. Why would I ever want to risk requiring social accreditation or suggesting legal pre-conditions before you or I are somebody, when this definition of our true identity is so substantial and so glorious? We have feasted on truth together. This is our new, spiritual, ethnic identity.

Third, in the New Testament *the image of rebirth is more than an image*. As we have begun to see, it is associated with a profound *ontological change* and with the creation of a *new spiritual identity*; as St. Paul writes, "if anyone is in Christ, he (or she) is a new creation; the old has gone, the new has come!" (2 Cor. 5:17). The objective act of God's justifying work through Jesus Christ's death on the cross redefines the believer's relationship to God and reconfigures their being: *they are not what they were*. Of course, an ongoing process of sanctification accompanies this gracious, divine act of justification, but "the new" has been created. *I am not what I was before*. It is not only that I have a new relationship to you, my Christian brother or sister, I have a new relationship to God as Father and to myself as his child. I have access into the Father's presence through the torn flesh of Jesus, the crucified, and I have new knowledge of myself by God's revelation of my sin, my salvation, my belonging and my vocation. It is so easy in a visual world and superficial culture to be seduced by appearance and to be preoccupied with the surface, when God always goes deeper. It is so easy in situations sensitized to the language of "rights" and to "difference" to forget the deeper truth and security of being "in Christ" as saviour and belonging "to God" as Father. If we need the Bible to teach us what a person is—that they are more than the atoms of biology, or a state's subject, or an object of legal rights, as one created "in the image of God"—we need the Bible to induct us also into the mysterious truth and reality of "new birth" through faith in Jesus Christ. But that is what *rebirth* means to a believer. The old has gone, I am *"a new creation."* In a world of many faiths vying for supremacy and claiming legitimacy, the Christian should not dishonour their integrity and disown their identity in doubting or denying what God has done in them. Too often, I fear, shrill Christian appeals to "rights'" are borne of thin Christian confidence in God's work. It should not be thus.

So three general points about *rebirth in the Bible and beyond*: it is an image *well-known to the Jews and Greeks of Jesus' day* as it is to Hindus today (that takes us back to basics); it has *clear, corporate connotations* (which force us to face commonalities and communities we might choose to forget); and it is *more than an image* (speaking of a profound *ontological change* and a *new spiritual identity*). In other words, it is an image and a truth which should condition the way we think about all sorts of things as believers: in this instance we choose to remember to apply it to our thinking about "religious freedom" in the context and complexity of modern secular, Hindutva-ized India.

Rebirth, Rights and Responsibilities: Three Specific Risks the Biblical Christian Should Remember

In the second part of this paper, I want to address what seem to me to be *three particular risks* the New Testament describes that we should remember and so avoid.

The first risk the New Testament reveals is, I suggest, *the materialism of Nicodemus*. The dialogue between Jesus and Nicodemus in John 3:1-21 (at the start of John's evolving narrative about this clearly rather remarkable man; see also John 7:50-52; 19:38ff) shows Nicodemus to be a brave, honourable, highly-placed, extremely well-connected, Jewish leader. But his so-called "world view" and spirituality are (predictably) pre-conditioned by Jewish law, tradition, culture, ethnicity and propriety. When Jesus says, "No one can see the kingdom of God unless he is born again" (John 3:3), Nicodemus misunderstands him. Why? Not because Nicodemus, the educated Jew, did not know the language of *rebirth*, but because he applied different categories to its meaning and interpretation; just as a Hindu might hear *reincarnation* in Christian talk of *rebirth*. Nicodemus' response here makes this clear: "How can a man be born when he is old? Surely he cannot enter a second time into his mother's womb to be born!" (John 3:4) Nicodemus' categories are literal, material, physical and biological. They are not the terms in which Jesus defines *rebirth*. Jesus invokes the water of baptism and the wind of the Spirit.

> I tell you the truth, no one can enter the kingdom of God unless he is born of water and the Spirit. Flesh gives birth to flesh, but the Spirit gives birth to spirit. You should not be surprised at my saying, "You must be born again." (John 3:5-6)

As we have seen above, the *rebirth* a Christian names and experiences is *spiritual, not material*: it is the fruit of divinely-appointed ritual water *and* dynamically-empowered spiritual wind. Despite this, *the risk of materialism haunts the church*. We see our life with God, our identity as believers, and our work and witness in society, in predominantly *material* terms. So "church" comes to mean building, "worship" is singing, "growth" is defined numerically, and in some traditions, "conversion" or "faith" is equated with Sunday attendance or baptismal regeneration.

If we are not careful, like Nicodemus, inherited Christian laws, traditions, cultures, rituals, ethnicities, or a general sense of propriety, condition what we hear from God and read in the Bible. He says one thing: we hear another. He says we are "free from our sins by Christ's blood" (Rom. 6:18; Rev. 1:5); he speaks of, "the glorious freedom of the children of God" (Rom. 8:21); he proclaims, "Where the Spirit of the Lord is, there is freedom" (1 Cor. 3:17); he exhorts us not to use our freedom "to indulge the flesh" (Gal. 5:13), or to "cover-up for evil" (1 Pet. 2:16); he assures us, "the truth will set you free" (John 8:32). And what do we hear? Like Nicodemus, *we hear material categories when he means spiritual ones*. We simply—sometimes, wilfully—mis-hear. If we need to explain *rebirth* carefully to a Hindu, we need to explain Christian freedom carefully in our work. For, I suggest if we are not very careful, we define religious freedom not in the New Testament's primarily spiritual categories but in the material terms of *our* laws and *our* justice, *our* rights and *our* expected privileges. How wrong and sad. My point is not to deny for one moment Jesus' earthly ministry and heavenly mandate (shared with believers) to "set prisoners free" (Ps. 146:7; Luke 4:18) from whatever bondage grips them (a message caste-ridden India constantly needs to hear): it is, however, to reckon with the *spiritual priority* Jesus' meeting with Nicodemus teaches. Yes, God redeems the physical and the material in the incarnate Christ; yes, he renews the physical and heals the temporal; but he also reveals the ephemeral and rejects the sinful. For, our God is a discriminating God, who wants his children to be like him. Not every appeal to "religious freedom" is wisely, truthfully, carefully or biblically cast. Darkness lurks in its distortion: God's reputation and ours are both at risk from this.

The second risk the New Testament reveals is *the pessimism of the Diaspora*. Many scholars have pointed to the terms in which St. Peter reminds the scattered pockets of Christian believers in "Pontus, Galatia, Cappadocia, Asia and Bithynia" (1 Pet. 1:1)—that is much of modern day central and northern Turkey—of their identity and inheritance in Jesus Christ. They are "God's elect" though "strangers in the world" (1 Pet. 1:1); they are "chosen according to the foreknowledge of God the Father, through the sanctifying work of the Spirit, for obedience to Jesus Christ and sprinkling by his blood" (1 Pet. 1:2); they are, we find in 1 Peter 2:9, "a chosen people, a royal priesthood, a holy nation, a people belonging to God"; they have been given, as we saw earlier, "new birth into a living hope through the resurrection of Jesus Christ from the dead" and into "an inheritance that can never perish, spoil or fade—[that is]

kept in heaven for you" (1 Pet. 1:3-4). It is a remarkable reminder of God's gracious and providential work as their saviour, Lord, Father, guardian and guide in the face of what St. Peter describes generally as "suffering" and "grief in all kinds of trials" (1 Pet. 1:6). In this, the silent, suffering, unjustly-treated Jesus, who trusted in God's deliverance and vindication, is to be their inspiration and example (1 Pet. 2:21-23; 3:13ff; 4:1). Hence, in 1 Peter 4 the apostle writes,

> Dear friends, do not be surprised at the painful trial you are suffering, as though something strange were happening to you. But rejoice that you participate in the sufferings of Christ, so that you may be overjoyed when his glory is revealed. (1 Pet. 4:12ff)

It is clear—and not surprising—that these new believers are struggling. Their faith is stretched, their trust in God severely strained, their morality compromised.

Peter's pastoral appeal to the believers in the *Diaspora*—caused, of course, by the persecution of the Jerusalem church after Stephen's martyrdom (Acts 7:8-15, 54-60)—is enlightening. Into the cloud of pessimism that we sense hangs over them, Peter speaks a dispelling, authoritative word of exhortation: "Be clear-minded," "alert" and "self-controlled" (1 Pet. 4:7; 5:8; 1:13); "Be holy" (1 Pet. 1:16) and "abstain from sinful desires" (1 Pet. 2:11); rejoice (1 Pet. 1:6) and believe (1 Pet. 1:8) trials will prove the "genuineness" of your faith as of "greater worth than gold" (1 Pet. 1:7); "Submit [...] to every authority instituted among men" (1 Pet. 2:13ff) and always "be prepared to give an answer to everyone who asks you to give the reason for the hope that you have" (1 Pet. 3:15). And he pleads, be armed with a Christ-like "attitude" of self-denial and silent suffering (1 Pet. 4:1f), "cast all your anxiety on him because he cares for you" (1 Pet. 5:7), be filled with "inexpressible and glorious joy" as you gain "the goal of your faith, the salvation of your souls" (1 Pet. 1:9).

So what is Peter's answer to the threat pessimism posed to the heart, mind and behaviour of the new, little churches of the Asian *Diaspora*? His response is theological not legal, it is pastoral not logistical, it is intimate not intellectual. He doesn't propose a path out of, or around suffering, but *a Christ-like way through* suffering and trials of "all kinds" (1 Pet. 1:6); a phrase that captures so well the life and experience of many Indian Christians at the present time. The problem with pessimism is that it can incline us *either* to renounce faith *per se* or to reject this Christ-like response. I say it hesitantly, but in much European discussion of "religious freedom," talk of a *human right* to worship freely is, I fear, more prominent than a *Christian responsibility* to suffer silently. I wonder what Peter would say. It is vital we listen and not mis-hear what he says. His first epistle certainly doesn't teach naïve triumphalism or even hungry masochism in the face of persecution. Nor is it defensively legalistic or piously optimistic about the inevitable trials a believer will face. Life is hard; discipleship more so. If pessimism tempts with pre-emptive apostasy, it also works to twist truth advantageously. Neither is right. Peter reminds his readers, "You have been born again, not of perishable seed, but of imperishable, through the living and enduring word of God" (1 Pet. 1:23). Trusting God's word, balanced biblical Christianity—my deliberate focus in this paper—gives weight to Peter's apostolic wisdom. It prays "deliver us from evil" *and* follows Christ's faith-filled example.

The third risk the New Testament reveals is *the individualism and chauvinism of Corinth*. Come back to 2 Corinthians 5 and the language of "new creation" Paul employs there. It is of a piece with what Jesus says in John of *rebirth* (by water and the Spirit) and Peter writes of *imitation* (of Jesus' silent suffering and trust). When writing to the young church in Rome that he didn't know and hadn't founded, Paul reminded them that as Christians they had "received the Spirit of sonship," that "testifies with our spirit that we are God's children" and so "heirs of God and co-heirs with Christ" (Rom. 8:15, 16, 17). In this, as the following chapter makes clear, the Spirit is effecting in them what circumcision, the law and the promises of God had done to Israel under the old Levitical code (Rom. 9:4). In his epistle to the Galatians, Paul again links the work of Christ and the gift of the Spirit to the believer's new identity as a "son" or "child" of God.

> Because you are sons, God sent the Spirit of his Son into our hearts, the Spirit who calls out "Abba", Father. So you are no longer a slave, but a son; and since you are a son, God has made you also an heir. (Gal. 4:6, 7)

In 2 Corinthians 5 this fundamental change is connected to the reconciling work of Christ. It leads Paul to say that he views others "no longer from a worldly point of view" (2 Cor. 5:16), but as those who are recipients of the message, work and divine mandate and ministry of reconciliation (2 Cor. 5:18-20). Chapter 6 then begins, "As God's fellow-workers we urge you not to receive God's grace in vain." Appealing to them "as to my children," Paul pleads "open wide your hearts," as he has opened his heart to them (2 Cor. 6:11,13). Hence, in a range of ways, and through inter-related images, Paul defines Christian identity as the result of a common act of divine grace in Christ and the shared experience of the gift of the Spirit for renewal and empowerment. This is a work done in *all God's children*: it is the work Paul longs to nurture in *all his spiritual children*. The church in cosmopolitan Corinth was famously arrogant, dissolute and fractious. At the heart of Paul's ministry and message to them is their shared indebtedness to God's grace and common reception of his Spirit. Though "many" they are "one" by adoption, grace and the gift of the Spirit. It is this supreme miracle he reminds them of constantly. It is this message that offers them a way out of their habitual conflict and corruption.

How does this relate to our theme? It represents a primary New Testament resource to counter the mindset that says *either* "Christian identity is defined by subscription to prevailing Church priorities" *or* "Christian individuality is elevated above community in the New Testament." No, surely, to both! But the fact is *cultural individualism and ideological chauvinism are rampant in our churches*. The problems Paul faced in Corinth are *our* problems. As a consequence, "religious freedom" debates are harder because some Christians claim, "No debate is needed. The church is persecuted. Those who deny this are wrong." Likewise, discussions of "religious freedom" are hobbled by ideologues who want "religious freedom" *to uphold a particular cause or advance a particular agenda*. As ever with ideology, its perspective is perfect and its power over critics absolute! It can get very messy. Paul's appeal to believers to acknowledge their shared spiritual identity (and thence unity) in Christ and his remarkable generosity of spirit are invaluable wisdom and essential aids for biblical Christians today. Balanced biblical Christianity will never incline to seek scriptural sources to justify human agendas, nor will it require human approval of gospel priorities. We must beware: Christian freedom is often more at risk from theological or ecclesiastical prejudice than from social or political antipathy. Paul knew this; hence, his appeal in Galatians, "It was for freedom Christ set us free" (Gal. 5:1) and reminder in 2 Corinthians, "The Lord is the Spirit, and where the Spirit of the Lord is there is freedom" (2 Cor. 3:17).

So, *three specific risks* the biblical Christian in India, or wherever, should remember: the *materialism of Nicodemus*, the *pessimism of the Diaspora*, and the *individualism and chauvinism of Corinth*. We have begun to see how these relate to the theme of "religious freedom." In the final part of this paper, I want to look at *four key lessons or practical applications* of what we have seen already.

RIGHTS, RESPONSIBILITIES AND REBIRTH: LESSONS AND APPLICATIONS

First, in light of what has been said of *rebirth*, it should be clear that to a biblical Christian his or her *primary "right"* is to be and to be called a "child of God"; as John 1:13 states, "...to all who received him, to those who believed in his name, he gave *the right* (Gk. *exousia*; lit. authority, right, power) to become children of God."[5] The privilege and miracle this represents should never be vouchsafed. Christian distinctiveness is defined in these relational and spiritual terms. What's more, balanced biblical Christianity will, surely, recognize that this *primary "right"* to become a child of God goes deeper than a *human right* to be a child of man: the latter is an inevitable biological state while the former is a gracious divine gift. God's creation ordinance of man "made in God's image" is transfigured by his redemptive gift of new life in Christ. Indeed, it is dangerous—if not idolatrous—for a Christian to allow their *birthright as a believer* to be displaced by their *birthright as a human*. As Nicodemus learned, the spiritual has pre-eminence over the material. But, as we saw at the start, to claim that this spiritual birthright warrants *exceptional* treatment, or makes Christians *first*

---

[5] The word translated "right" here is the Greek word *exousia*, meaning lit. (acc. Arndt and Gingrich) freedom of choice, right to act or to decide, ability, control, warrant, authority and the exercise of official power.

and better, misses the point: for, to a biblical Christian "rights" *per se* are redefined by recognizing God affords the *primary "right"* to be born again as a child of his. In the end, theology trumps law and biology. The contingent nature of this spiritual "right" ensures the believer is indebted to God for every aspect of life: gratitude and humility should mark their every move. Law is important and a relationship with God more so: it is the ground of our being and ultimate hope for our life in this world and the next.

Second, as a consequence of this, the believer has a *primary "responsibility,"* as a re-born child of God, to seek to "please" his or her Father; as St. Paul writes again in 2 Corinthians 5, "we make it our aim to please (Gk. *euarestein*; lit. be well-pleasing) him" (v. 9). This recurrent theme in the New Testament expresses the core trajectory of Christian endeavour. It is all *to please him*; as is said of Enoch in Hebrews, "For before he was taken, he was commended as one who pleased God," adding "without faith it is impossible to please God...." (Heb. 11:5, 6). Likewise, Paul warns, "Those controlled by the sinful nature cannot please God" (Rom. 8:8). To "the strong" he points out, we ought not "to please ourselves [...] but to please our neighbour for his good to build him up," (Rom. 15:1) again adding "for even Christ did not please himself but, as it is written, 'The insults of those who insult you have fallen on me'" (Rom. 15:2, 3). In whatever context, then, a re-born Christian finds that her *primary "responsibility"* is to seek to *please God*. This *primary "responsibility"* conditions what is thought or said or done about "religious freedom." The issue is *not* what do *I* want, but what does *God* want? His will and command to love my neighbour "as myself" means God's honour and my neighbour's well-being and freedom precede my concern to uphold *my rights* or advance *my particular agenda*. It is not surprising faith is said to be necessary to please God in the New Testament: for, if faith engenders our desire to please God, it also helps us discern the mind of God and to serve my neighbour's needs and "rights" as I should. And let's not be surprised if we find we too say, "The insults of those who insult you have fallen on me."

Third, it is clear from the New Testament that an important *secondary "duty"* the Christian has is to "honour the king" and to "submit to" and to "pray for those who are in authority" (1 Pet.

2:17; 1 Tim. 2:2; Heb. 13:17). In this, the disciple follows his master's command to "render to Caesar the things that are Caesar's" (Matt. 22:21). For, as in the Old Testament, the New Testament teaches that temporal power comes from and is answerable to God. How does this relate to our theme, "Rights, Responsibilities and Rebirth"? Quite simply, the fact or experience of *spiritual rebirth* should never be used to justify political or social behaviour which is politically disrespectful or socially irresponsible. Our identity in Christ maps directly onto our civic identity and social responsibility as earthly citizens, subjects, workers and leaders. It is significant that Peter's first epistle, which addresses the *Diaspora* churches' persecution and pessimism, also exhorts its readers to "Show proper respect for everyone: Love the brotherhood, fear God, honour the king" (1 Pet. 2:17). To Peter, Paul and the early church, the hope-filled security of a Christian's new identity and their promised inheritance as a "born again" citizen of heaven could and should be reflected in the godly "confidence" with which they engaged humbly, prayerfully, actively and constructively in national politics and other programmes in society; never to sanction human power uncritically, nor to undermine that power wantonly. But balanced biblical Christianity will also stress, I believe, that political and social activity is never an end in itself: it is an authentic means to serve God and neighbour, and it is a God-appointed mechanism to enact God's reign of justice, freedom and peace. This *secondary "duty"* gives flesh and form to our *primary "responsibility"* to please God. We "please him" in the way we live our faith in the "public square."

Fourthly, and finally, a *secondary "right"* of the "born again" child of God is the priestly ministry of "access" to the Father, to pray for the world, to ask God's blessing and forgiveness, and to intercede for the needy.[6] This freedom of access to God should undergird the church's work to safe-guard freedom in society. It should also be at the heart of the church's discernment of when and how to address the complex issue of "religious freedom" in the public square and in the life of the church. As we see in Galatians and Ephesians, membership of a nation, state and church will demand of disciples a decision to "stand" *and* a readiness to "pray" (v.

[6] See the classic statement of the Christian's "confident" priestly access to God in Hebrews 10:19-22.

1). For the freedom of a Christian is constantly under threat from inside and outside the church. Hence, the Apostle Paul's appeal to the Galatian Christians at risk from legalistic Judaizers,

> It is for freedom Christ has set us free. Stand firm, then, and do not let yourselves be burdened again by a yoke of slavery [...] You, my brothers [and sisters], were called to be free. But do not use your freedom to indulge the sinful nature; rather, serve one another in love [...] Let us not become weary in doing good, for at the proper time we will reap a harvest if we do not give up. Therefore, as we have opportunity, let us do good to all people, especially to those who belong to the family of believers. (Gal. 5:1, 13)

Likewise, in Ephesians the call to spiritual warfare ends, "...and after you have done everything, to stand...And pray in the Spirit on all occasions with all kinds of prayers and requests" (Eph. 6: 13, 18). The believer's *secondary* "*right*" of access that derives from their *rebirth* is the secret source of their strength, wisdom, peace and power. We should never underestimate its place in addressing the complex question of "religious freedom" we face as Christian believers in the world today. God knows every aspect of any problem we ever face, and is best able to help us interpret and address it.

Conclusion

In this paper, keeping a very close eye on what the Bible says, we have looked at the allurement of *Christian exceptionalism* and danger of *cultural elitism*. We have considered *three general characteristics* of the biblical theme of *rebirth* (viz. as known to Jews and Greeks—and, of course, our Hindu neighbours—as having clear corporate connotations, and as more than an image) and we have looked at *three risks* contemporary discussion of "religious freedom" faces in the church (viz. the materialism of Nicodemus, the pessimism of the *Diaspora*, and the individualism and chauvinism of Corinth). In the last part I have tried to draw out *four practical applications* of this in relation to a Christian's primary and secondary "rights" and "responsibilities." But the quest for balanced biblical Christianity does not end there. Our task as evangelical theologians is that of a sailor more than an engine driver. We do not set a theological course along pre-set rails to known ends. We tack and trim our sails constantly, to ensure the boat is upright and responsive to new issues in a rapidly changing world, and an ever more complex India. It isn't easy, but with the wind of the Spirit in our face and word of God in our hand, it is invigorating.

Is Secularism Compatible with Hinduism?

Aruthuckal Varughese John[1]

INTRODUCTION

Where severely contested beliefs are held within pluralistic societies, they ought to be governed by principles that provide a framework for those pluralities to be practised unhindered, if not help flourish. Secularism has functioned as a vehicle to enable societies that are plural to navigate through stark differences in a civic manner.

However, given that secularism itself has doctrines that are presupposed, which specific parties/voices within society may or may not agree with, conflicts remain not only despite secularism but also because of it. Several current discussions have drawn attention to this pivotal question. For instance, Arvind Sharma raises objection to the notion of religious freedom articulated in the Universal Declaration of Human Rights,[2] which has also been adopted by most secular democracies, because they are specifically derived from within a Judeo-Christian framework.[3]

---

[1] Dr. Aruthuckal Varughese John is RZIM Chair of Apologetics and Professor of Theology at SAIACS, India. He is currently a Post-doctoral Research Fellow with Langham, UK. He is the author of *Truth and Subjectivity, Faith and History* (OR: Pickwick, 2012).

[2] Arvind Sharma, *Problematizing Religious Freedom* (New York/ London: Springer Dordrecht, 2011).

[3] Some Hindu thinkers have argued that the Indian Constitution is loaded with Judeo-Christian religious assumptions rather than Hindu religious assumptions. Thereby freedom of religion defined by the Indian Constitution follows from a Judeo-Christian religious doctrine rather than from the Hindu religious doctrine. Underlying this argument is the assumption that the conception of religious freedom functions as a subset of religious doctrine. This entails a conflict, where, the conception of freedom of religion in India via constitutional law conflicts with the Hindu concept of religion, wherein such a freedom of religion is not part of the religious doctrine. Hindu commentators therefore, see the Judeo-Christian assumptions within the Constitution of India as a point of conflict from the perspective of the Hindu religious laws. Hence, the repeated calls to re-write the Constitution.

Sharma's objection is one that demands engagement for any discussion on *Religious Freedom and Conversion in India*. Similarly the question, "what sorts of comprehensive doctrine within societies nurture a secular framework?" demands our consideration. Both these questions require a meta-level engagement and are part of a project I have undertaken elsewhere. This paper, however, addresses the specific question of whether or not Hinduism is compatible with secularism.

Clarification of Terms

Given the fluidity of meanings associated with both the terms – "secular"[4] and "Hinduism" – it is important to clarify what these terms mean.

Hinduism: Given the wide range of meanings associated with the term, some clarification is in order. As Gavin Flood writes, the question "'what is Hinduism?' is a complex question, the response to which ranges from claiming that Hinduism is a unified, coherent field of doctrine and practice to claiming that it is a fiction, a colonial construction based on the miscategorization of indigenous cultural forms."[5]

Definitions can have a circular relation to their purposiveness and the question of compatibility is one such, which lends itself to selective descriptions. Accordingly, some tend to define Hinduism as "a unified field of belief, practice, and history, intimately linked to nationhood and the historical struggle of a people against its colonizers. On this view, Hinduism has an essence manifested in multiple forms."[6] On the other hand, in contrast to "religion(s) with clearly defined boundaries... (like) Christianity or Islam," Hinduism is defined as "a group of traditions united by certain common features, such as shared ritual patterns, a shared revelation,

---

[4] What exactly is secularism is hard to define, And understandably so, because the meaning of secularity/laïcité [Laïcité root = laïkós, meaning "of the people/layman", as opposed to the clergy] is not static but is constantly evolving.

[5] Gavin Flood, "Introduction: Establishing the Boundaries," in *The Blackwell Companion to Hinduism* (Oxford: Blackwell Publishing, 2003), 2.

[6] Flood, "Introduction," 2.

a belief in reincarnation (samsara), liberation (moksa), and a particular form of endogamous social organization or caste."[7] More clearly, Hinduism is seen as better characterized by its accent on the practice of tradition rather than belief in a creed.

Secularism: Secularism is understood as a mechanism by which *politics is separated from religion.* "The core idea of secularism," says Bhargava, is the "separation of religion and state for the sake of civic peace, religious liberty and equality of free citizenship."[8] While different shades of secularism are practised in different countries, argues Bhargava, there are broadly speaking, two kinds. The first one (generally identified with the West) marks the "separation with exclusion." In the West, the separation of the secular and sacred was initially an internal demarcation within the ecclesial framework, which eventually became an external divide. With the increased secularization of societies, the secular gradually acquired the polemical connotation of *being against* religion and in some cases attained the sense of *anti-religion.* As Bhargava argues, "This anti-religiosity may be interventionist or non-interventionist. In its interventionist form the state actively discourages religion. In its non-interventionist incarnation, it typifies a hysterical brahminical attitude: Religion is untouchable, so any contact with it contaminates secularist purity."[9]

The initial impetus for the separation of Church and state in the United States was for the state to function from a position of neutrality towards various competing Christian denominations. The neutrality of the state in this scenario meant that it could not support one denomination over another. However, with increased secularization of Western societies, the divide became more

---

[7] Flood, "Introduction," 2.

[8] Rajeev Bhargava, "What is Indian Secularism and What is it For?," *India Review* 1, no. 1 (January 2002): 10.

[9] Rajeev Bhargava, "What is Secularism for?" in *Secularism and its Critics*, ed. Rajeev Bhargava (New Delhi: Oxford University Press, 1998), 493. Understandably, much of the angst within the religious community in the West is caused by the shift from how the "secular" functioned as a subset within the larger ecclesial setting to how it now has become the overarching framework within which the faith community scrambles for space. This indicates that there is a sense of nostalgia associated with the changes in the condition of belief, in the West.

prominent, so much so that secularism as a political system is now increasingly seen as standing against religion.[10]

The second type, which is identified with India, seeks "to mark distance or boundaries"[11] between the two. As Bhargava argues, "The second view on separation does not demand total exclusion. Some contact is possible but also some distance. In fact, the relation between religion and politics requires neither fusion nor complete disengagement but what can be called principled distance."[12] Giving a nuanced meaning to the second type, Bhargava elaborates,

> Principled distance itself takes two forms. I believe the first entails a commitment to some version of political neutrality. Only when religion has been distanced from politics can the state do one's best to help or to hinder different sorts of believers and unbelievers in an equal degree. The second form of principled distance requires that the boundaries between religion and politics be respected. Religion and politics form distinct spheres with their own respective areas of jurisdiction. Each is valuable in its own right. Religion and politics respect each other as well as their own limits. The world of worship and congregation, of prayer and conscience must not be intruded upon by politicians and bureaucrats. Likewise, deeply religious people, in particular, leaders of religious communities must not tread on the toes of politicians.[13]

While Bhargava is right on the broad categorization of different forms of secularism and the forms of principled distance, it ought

---

[10] This separation of state and religion has played out differently in different Western cultures. As Taylor articulates, the question of religious expressions in public spaces like the wearing of Hijab, illustrates the difference. The French approached it by imposing a wholesale ban on wearing any conspicuous religious symbols such as Hijab in government operated public spaces. The German response to this has been that positions of authority should not be marked by religious symbols, thus preventing offices such as that of teachers and those in authority from wearing religious symbols, while allowing students to wear them. Notwithstanding the differing shades, the separation intends for the secular state to protect individuals from religion. Thus the legal law equally applies to everyone, irrespective of religion.

[11] Bhargava, "What is Secularism For?," 493.

[12] Bhargava, "What is Secularism For?," 493.

[13] Bhargava, "What is Secularism For?," 493-494.

to be noted that the distinctions themselves do not point to two (or more) distinct ontologies of the secular. It could be legitimately argued that the modern notion of the secular clearly emanates from within the church-state dialectic in the West. While this does not endorse a static view of the term, nor entail an essentialist view of the concept, it nonetheless resists the idea that the term can take any meaning or shape depending on the circumstance.

Partha Chatterjee is right on target in being cautious about any quick separation of the Western and Indian forms of secularism. He argues that in the "current usage" of the term "in India, with apparently well-defined 'Indian' referents, the loud and often acrimonious Indian debate on secularism is never entirely innocent of its Western genealogies . . . (and) the resort to 'new meanings' is . . . a mark of the failure of this attempt."[14] What Chatterjee argues is pivotal in locating the ontology of the secular. He writes,

> [I]f one is to consider the 'new' meaning acquired by the word 'secularism' in India, it is not as though the plea of the advocates of secularism that the concept bears application to modern Indian state and society has won general acceptance, and that the concept has thereby taken on a new meaning. If that had been the case, the 'original' meaning of the word as understood in its standard sense in the West would have remained unmutilated; it would only have widened its range of referents by including within it the specific circumstances of the Indian situation. The reason why arguments have to be made about 'secularism' having a new *meaning* in India is because there are serious difficulties in applying the standard meaning of the word to the Indian circumstances. The 'original' concept, in other words, will not easily admit the Indian case within its range of referents.[15]

Further, the idea of distinct forms of secularism also tends to overlook historical necessities and contingencies—akin to reasoning that there are two kinds of yoga, Indian and Western, which would not hold entirely true even if the West practised yoga for the next hundred years. It obliterates the distinction between the historical

---

[14] Partha Chatterjee, "Secularism and Tolerance" in *Secularism and its Critics*, ed. Rajeev Bhargava (New Delhi: Oxford University Press, 1998), 349-351.
[15] Chatterjee, "Secularism and Tolerance," 349-350.

necessity in the organic birthing of an idea within a cultural and theological setting and the historical contingencies of even the intentional adoption of it into an alien culture propelled by pragmatism. One may legitimately argue that the secular is a child of Christianity—a prodigal child, so to speak—which, when it wandered into distant lands, became an adopted child of the diverse traditions of the Indian sub-continent, via historical contingencies.[16]

This helps us account for the relative natural reception and legitimacy of an organically birthed concept in the West, in contrast to the abrupt introduction of an artificial concept for a people to suddenly live by. On the view that the secular is an adopted child in the Indian sub-continent, we may anticipate the problems associated with an arbitrary adoption, especially when the ideals of the secular constitution conflicts with traditional beliefs and practices. This legitimizes the question at hand: is secularism compatible with Hinduism?

The Shape of Secularism in India

Having stated this, we may safely begin to describe the meaning of the term secular in the context of the Indian state, by highlighting some of its unique features. First, the Indian separation of church and state is instanced in the fact that India identifies herself as a secular state instead of a Hindu state. This is especially crucial, given that Pakistan was carved out from the Indian sub-continent on the basis of religious identity, with the Pakistani Constitution, which declared Islam as its state religion.[17] Consequently, India had sufficient motivation to declare herself a Hindu state in contradistinction to Pakistan, but it did not. So, unlike a state (whether

---

[16] For further discussion on locating an ontology for the secular, see Aruthuckal Varughese John, "Tayloring Indian Secularity: What has Changed Because of Secularism?" in *Re-Imagining the Idea of Nation*, ed. Jeremiah Duomai (New Delhi: TRACI publication, forthcoming).

[17] One of the consequences of the State of Pakistan functioning as an "Islamic Republic" and the adoption of Islam as the state religion is, as the Constitution defines, "All existing laws shall be brought in conformity with the injunctions of Islam as laid down in the Quran and Sunnah and no law shall be enacted which is repugnant to such injunctions." See, Article 227(1)-227(3) in Part IX: Islamic Provisions of the Constitution of Pakistan.

a republic or a monarchy) where religious laws effectively dictate state laws, India chose to remain secular and religious laws were circumscribed by liberal secular laws, most of which were adopted from within an enlightenment framework.

Second, the separation also ensures that the state does not favour one dominant religion(s) over others, either by way of privilege or by affording special protections. Unlike Malaysia and Pakistan, which, despite their celebrated democracy, afford special protections to one religious community, India treats all religions equally. For this reason, although Malaysia and Pakistan remain technically democratic in that they are a form of rule by the majority, the state functions contrary to the modern-Western notion of democracy.

Third, in India, the separation of Church and State is understood as the state not only taking a position of neutrality between religions, but also allowing them to flourish separately without disregarding special interests that are unique to each religion. To ensure this, separate personal laws govern religious adherents according to their distinct religious convictions. Therefore, personal laws that apply to religious adherents dictate laws concerning marriage, divorce, adoption, inheritance of property etc., as circumscribed by religious sanctions, which are codified. Unlike the West, where religious beliefs are circumscribed within a common civil code in the form of individual rights, Indian secular commitment allows for a plurality of social practices to co-exist. This then is the uniqueness of Indian secularism.

The above description of Indian secularism lays out the intent in adopting a secular Constitution, even though the term secular was inserted only later, as one of the descriptors of the Constitution.[18] However, the Indian adoption of secularism as the operating principle has not been without contestations. The inherent contest can be surmised from the presence of two broad, yet dominant views about the secular.

The first view is that secularism is fundamentally opposed to and is *against* the Hindu tradition. On this view, which is also held by the Hindutva ideologues, secularism is understood as an

---

[18] The Preamble of the Constitution, which initially read "sovereign democratic republic" was amended to read "sovereign socialist secular democratic republic" in the 42nd Amendment of 1976 and was enacted in 1977.

instrument to dismantle the Hindu tradition. Defenders of secularism, therefore, are aggressors from the outside who engineer the destruction of Hindu orthodox tradition. Some are overwhelmingly convinced of a Western (Christian) plot to de-stabilize India.[19] With focus on alleged Western intentions, such a prognosis leads to resistance and adoption of counter measures[20] against secularism and the secularization process. In short, on this view, regardless of assigned intentionality, secularism is seen as being *against* the Indian tradition.

The second construal of the secular sees it as a historical (therefore, accidental) corollary to the British rule, which is followed by the process of globalization. Even though it may be accompanied by a sense of loss of tradition, the secular is seen as a positive development—a condition to usher in a state of equal opportunity, liberty, and humanistic values within the society. More often than not, such preference of the secular over the sacred is for pragmatic reasons rather than because of any deliberate acceptance of the secular doctrine or rejection of Hindu metaphysics. The secular ethos, the democratic process, and the Constitution are merely of instrumental value within this pragmatic calculus.

On this view, secularity is embraced to mediate the peaceful co-existence of multiple interest groups represented by different ethnicities, religions, and cultures. Given the conflict of interest within such diverse groups of the society, secularism is a *necessary* condition for the toleration of conflicting viewpoints, although it may not a *sufficient* condition. Tolerance of diversity within the society can provide a measurable index for the possibility of peaceful *co-existence* as opposed to coercive *integration*, where dominant groups control the nature and scope of diversity.

---

[19] This could take various shapes and sizes. From foreign governments to religions such as Christianity or Islam, diverse groups are seen as agents who seek to destroy Hinduism. Among its ranks would be those of the likes of Rajiv Malhotra and Aravindan Neelakandan who co-authored, *Breaking India: Western Interventions in Dravidian and Dalit Faultlines* (Princeton: Amaryllis, 2011).

[20] Very often such a background understanding also leads to persecution of minorities as they are seen as Western agents who are working against Hindu tradition.

Religious Doctrine and the Shape of Secularism

While the secular state profits from theological doctrines that are commensurate with a broad secular outlook, the secular state cannot by any stretch of imagination create those theological foundations within a culture. The Western separation of Church and State may at least minimally be seen as flowing out of a theology that gives to Caesar and to God what belongs to them respectively. The Islamic theology with its integrated view that conjoins political and religious goals, makes such a separation harder. India, given that Hindu theology has no specific prescription for a separation or integration of Church and State, has for pragmatic reasons adopted the institutional mechanisms of the modern state.

Although Orthodox Hindu beliefs do not impose any specific mode of separation of Church and State, the shape of secularism seems to depend on the nature of the background culture and its comprehensive doctrine. In short, the majority religion provides an overarching doctrine for shaping the nature of secularism. I shall first look at D. E. Smith's commentary on two specific doctrines—the Hindu view of history and the Hindu attitude toward other religions—both of which are pivotal for this discussion.

> First, the view of history taken by a religion, that is, whether human history is regarded as real and important, is a vital point. A religion that views history as unreal, or if real, ultimately unimportant, may be assumed to be unconcerned with securing or maintaining temporal power. This should be favourable to the secular state. On the other hand, a religion that views the proper course of history as crucial and central to its task in the world, is more likely to rely upon political power in order to influence history. The challenge to the secular state would be correspondingly greater.
>
> Second, we must consider the attitude of a religion toward other religions. Since the peaceful co-existence of diverse faiths is basic to the secular state, the degree of tolerance shown by the majority religion to other religions will obviously be important. Widespread intolerance would make the secular principle practically impossible to realize.[21]

[21] D. E. Smith, "India as a Secular State," in *Secularism and its Critics*, ed.

Let us look at both the doctrines suggested by Smith. First, according to Smith, the theory of history operating within a culture makes it favourable or unfavourable to a secular state. Accordingly, Hinduism provides a favourable background for secularism to flourish because within the Hindu culture "history is metaphysically at a lower level of reality, and is ultimately not significant."[22] That is, cultures where the sense of time is aligned toward myths rather than history may be expected to be indifferent to history, because it is unlikely that history is viewed as a vehicle to realize some specific eschaton. There would then be no theological motivation to be concerned "with securing or maintaining temporal power."[23]

While I am sympathetic to Smith's argument that there is a general lack of Hindu religious motivation to secure temporal power, I find his pronouncement that Hinduism is "favourable to the secular state" a bit farfetched. Smith's conclusion based on sense of history alone, that Hindu doctrines are compatible with secularism, seems to ignore other more important variables in the equation. For instance, theological indifference to social action and change also simultaneously rules out religious motivation to seek any change, whether positive or negative. Smith's conclusion also seems to ignore how some other theological doctrines may impede the possibility of a secular ethos. For instance, the theological endorsement of hierarchical social structures would seriously hamper *social equality* and *absolute value of the individual*, both of which are presupposed in the envisioning of a modern state and secularism. Similarly, the doctrine of *karma* could inhibit one's self-view as an agent of change and thus lead to a general sense of hopelessness in the culture.

So while Hindu indifference to history may be favourable to the separation of Church and State per se, theological foundations for social civility that are an equally important precondition for a secular state would find challenges in the Hindu context. The conclusion that Hinduism is favourable to secularism is thus based on a weak, *via negativa* argument, which hinges solely on the Hindu theological disinterest toward socio-political engagement. Rather,

Rajeev Bhargava (New Delhi: Oxford University Press, 1998), 186.

[22] Smith, "India as a Secular State," 187.

[23] Smith, "India as a Secular State," 186.

it may be the case that theological interest (or disinterest) need not necessarily be favourable or unfavourable to secularism unless analyzed against specific variables.

The second doctrine that Smith rightly mentions is the attitude of tolerance toward other religions. Undoubtedly, any mature democracy that is pluralistic will need a discursive space and a *public reason* that allows competing voices to robustly contest with each other. This democratic plurality is by its very definition a comprehensive one, in that the beliefs and justifications behind those voices seek to share the same public space while conflicting with each other. The pluralistic character of the Indian context would rightly anticipate conflicting opinions that could often be an irritant to the parties involved. Central to defining the shape of public reason would be the recognition that people function from beliefs that are fundamental to them—be it religious, non-religious or cultural.[24]

However, here again, Smith is too quick to pronounce that Hinduism is "*extremely tolerant* philosophically, and generally so in practice"[25] without providing any empirical basis for it. Understandably, writing in 1963, this would have been a common conclusion to arrive at. However, this was a time long before right-wing Hindu fundamentalism gained the traction that it has today.[26] It

---

[24] That is, even the liberal secularists who may not appeal to any specific religious doctrine retain an epistemic justification for their beliefs that is religious in its form. In this sense, atheistic naturalists would be just as religious as theistic supernaturalists or Advaitic monists, in that their fundamental beliefs function as presuppositions—a position argued from rather than a position argued to.

[25] Smith, "India as a Secular State," 187.

[26] Since the election of the BJP government in 2014, the level of intolerance has significantly increased. As I have recorded elsewhere, "Dr. M. M. Kalburgi, the former vice-chancellor of Hampi University was killed on August 30th [2015]. In February 2015, CPI leader Govind Pansare was gunned down by two assailants as a reaction to his biography on Shivaji titled *Shivaji Kon Hota*. Likewise, in August 2013 the founder-president of *Andhashraddha Nirmoolan Samiti* (an organization that works to eradicate superstitions), Narendra Dhabholkar, was murdered." Also for a discussion on how laws are enacted in Indian States affecting freedom to convert, see my article, "Anti-Conversion Laws in India: Circumscribing Freedom of Conscience within Dharmic Assumptions" in *Mending the World: Possibilities and Obstacles for Religion, Church and Theology*, eds. Niclas Blåder and Kristina Helgesson Kjellin (OR: Pickwick, 2017), 182. More recently, the total impunity with which *Gau*

was also still a period that was governed by the general perception that polytheistic cultures were inherently tolerant. This assumption to which we now turn, however, is a myth.[27]

The Myth of Polytheistic Tolerance

There exists a strong myth—quite hard to shake off—that polytheism is inherently tolerant. Polytheistic religions are construed as more tolerant because of their theological/doctrinal inclusiveness, unlike monotheistic religions, which are characterized by doctrinal exclusiveness. This however, is clearly something that needs re-examination. For too long, liberals have associated monotheism with bigotry and polytheism with generous inclusivity. Edward Gibbon, a pioneer in this misrepresentation, writes,

> The devout polytheist, though fondly attached to his national rites, admitted with implicit faith the different religions of the earth .... Every virtue, and even vice, acquired its divine representative; .... A republic of gods of such opposite tempers and interests required, in every system, the moderating hand of a supreme magistrate .... Such was the mild spirit of antiquity, that the nations were

---

rakshaks (cow protectors) have mercilessly beaten and killed those transporting cattle, the government imposed beef-ban, the anti-conversion laws that have been passed in several state assemblies, the anti-Romeo squads that intimidate and terrorize young people—all in the name of preserving culture—illustrate another kind of story that is anything but tolerant.

[27] Writing before the turn of a new millennium, Partha Chatterjee argues, "it is unlikely that a conception of the 'Hindu Rashtra' will be seriously propagated which will include, for instance, a principle that the laws of the state be in conformity with this or that *samhita* or even with the general spirit of the *Dharmasastra*" Chatterjee, "Secularism and Tolerance," 346. One may consider that a quasi-theocratic imagination has gained more traction two decades since then. However, Chatterjee is right on target when he argues that "the comparison with fascism in Europe points to the very real possibility of a Hindu Right locating itself quite firmly within the domain of the modernizing state, and using all of the ideological resources of that state to lead the charge against people who do not conform to its version of the 'national culture'. From this position, the Hindu Right can not only deflect accusations of being anti-secular, but can even use the arguments for interventionist secularization to promote intolerance and violence against minorities." Chatterjee, "Secularism and Tolerance," 346.

less attentive to the difference than to the resemblance of their religious worship. The Greek, the Roman, and the Barbarian, as they met before their respective altars, easily persuaded themselves, that under various names, and with various ceremonies, they adored the same deities.[28]

This faulty presupposition perpetuates an attitude, which often dismisses or underestimates religious persecutions in polytheistic contexts. This association has become so strong within the liberal thinking, that it has become counterintuitive to think otherwise.

The confusion seems to be in the default perception that monotheistic exclusivism is, for that reason, inherently intolerant, unlike polytheistic inclusivism, which embraces a plurality of gods and theologies. However, let us examine this assumption. First, because polytheism is inclined toward inclusiveness as regards the concept of God, where it just about embraces any idea of God, it makes it harder for it to be counted as true toleration. After all, tolerance, in the true sense of the term, would first require the object of toleration to be something that one disagrees with. Otherwise, what is there to tolerate? Further, there are no virtue points in practising tolerance toward something that one is favourably predisposed to. Second, that polytheism allows plurality at the conceptual level (holding the view that different conceptions of God are equally valid) need not translate as acceptance of plurality at the practical level. In fact, it may be the case that for greater social cohesion, the elasticity in thinking about God at the conceptual level, precisely for that reason, could impose rigidity in religio-social expressions at the practical level. Polytheism, by its very nature, cares little about what is believed but cares a great deal about what is practised.

Further, historical confirmations are that polytheistic cultures are anything but inherently tolerant. As David Bentley Hart observes,

> The very notion that polytheism is inherently more tolerant of religious differences than is 'monotheism' is, as a historical claim, utterly incredible. Proof to the contrary, in fact, is so plentiful that any selection of particular examples is necessarily somewhat arbitrary. Even if one confines

---

[28] Edward Gibbon, *The History of the Decline and Fall of the Roman Empire*, Vol. 1 (Paris: Baudry's European Library, 1840), 27-28.

oneself, just for the sake of convenience, to the ancient societies from and within which Christianity arose, one suffers an embarrassment of riches.[29]

As regards polytheistic acceptance of divergent beliefs, it may be noticed that the acceptance really is only of those beliefs that are similar to itself—polytheistic beliefs. Hart summarizes it well:

> [T]he larger Indo-European and Near Eastern pagan world was often quite welcoming, within reason, of new gods—one could never really have too many—but only so long as those gods were recognizably inhabitants of a familiar mythic and religious universe, who could be integrated into a variegated and ramifying network of licit devotions without any turmoil. In this sense, and in this sense only, was the greater Roman world religiously 'tolerant': it was tolerant of creeds that were, in consequence, easily absorbed. It was tolerant, that is to say, of what it found tolerable. When, however, it encountered beliefs and practices contrary to its own pieties, alien to its own religious sensibilities, or apparently subversive of its own sacral premises, it could respond with extravagant violence.[30]

It seems reasonable that we consume the often-repeated notion that Hinduism, because of its polytheistic nature, is intrinsically tolerant of other beliefs with a pinch of salt. It also helps locate the confusion about the idea of tolerance vis-à-vis religions that practise exclusive doctrine.

Is Secularism Compatible with Hinduism?

In this section, I shall pursue the question: is Hinduism compatible with secularism or not? This I shall pursue by examining scholars and thinkers who have argued differently on this issue.

---

[29] David Bentley Hart, *Atheist Delusions: The Christian Revolution and its Fashionable Enemies* (New Haven, CT: Yale University Press, 2010), 119.
[30] Hart, *Atheist Delusions*, 118-119.

Non-compatibilist View

Essential to the non-compatibilist view is the idea that the secular vision of the nation the Indian Constitution seeks to espouse and protect, did not evolve from within the Dharmic tradition. Instead (although not every non-compatibilist view necessarily articulates it), it is generally agreed that secularism has a strong connection with protestant Christianity and its offspring—enlightenment and modern science. Consequently, Hinduism and the Constitution have fundamentally different visions of life and the adoption of secularism has led to the rupture and erosion of Hindu beliefs and practices. On this view, the Hindu orthodoxy/tradition and secularism are and will continue to be in conflict.

Even without necessarily correlating them with political overtones, one could hold a non-compatibilist view by merely contrasting the moral visions of the Indian Constitution and Hinduism. Robert Baird argues, "By highlighting the concepts of justice, liberty, equality, and fraternity, the Constitution of India reads like a document with roots in Enlightenment thought."[31] Baird's reasoning is not as much a comment on whether secularism can survive in India or not, but rather that the secular framework is rooted fundamentally in an ethos alien to Hinduism. Similarly, highlighting the deep chasm between Hinduism and secularism, Markham writes, "the Indian Constitution, while advocating neutrality ostensibly, is, in fact, deeply partisan: the Constitution is opposed to traditional forms of Hinduism. This contradiction is in part responsible for the continuing religious and cultural instability in India."[32]

Along similar lines, Subrahmanian locates at least two areas where the secular Constitution disturbed the Indian religio-cultural fabric. First, Western education caused a "spiritual confusion in the sense that an education based on Western values involving ideas of democracy, the freedom of the individual, sacredness of personality etc., violently conflicted with caste and all that it implied." The second was "English jurisprudence especially the Penal Code, the

---

[31] Robert D. Baird, "Expansion and Construction of Religion: The Paradox of the Indian Secular State," in *Religious Conscience, the State, and the Law*, eds. J. McLaren and H. Coward (New York: SUNY Press, 1990), 191.

[32] Ian S. Markham *A Theology of Engagement* (Oxford: Blackwell, 2003), 123.

Criminal Procedure Code, and the Evidence Act jointly treating all subjects of the government as equal under law. British jurisprudence is a far cry from the *Dharma Sastras* which prescribed different penal codes for different ranks."[33] M. N. Srinivas likewise argues that apart from bringing in a host of new technologies, "modern knowledge, the ideal of the equity of human beings before the law, democracy, and human dignity were a few of the new ideas"[34] that the British brought into the Hindu civilization.

In all of the above categorizations, the idea of secularism is traced to non-Indic, Western origins. Despite understanding it as having deeply ruptured the Indian religio-cultural matrix, the above voices readily acknowledge its pragmatic value for the Indian subcontinent and thus embrace the idea of the secular. The pragmatic reception of the secular tends to embrace an instrumental use of the secular ideology towards a certain *telos*, such as social progress, rather than viewing it as a doctrine that demands ideological commitment. On this view, one may identify a certain cross-pressure between *pragmatic affinity* towards secularism and a *doctrinal alienation* from it. That is, even though there is a sense of incongruity as regards secularism as a doctrine, it is nonetheless embraced as an instrument of progress and development.

Within the non-compatibilist view, we may also locate the idea that the goal of secularism is unattainable in the Indian context. Whatever the reason for incompatibility, this view identifies a *telos* for secularism. Accordingly, the survival of secularism is not indicative of the cultural embrace of such a *telos*. For instance, T N Madan argues, "in the prevailing circumstances secularism in South Asia as a generally shared credo of life is impossible, as a basis for state action impracticable, and as a blueprint for the foreseeable future impotent."[35]

Madan provides reasons for the hurdles listed, each of which, in my opinion, falls back to the foundational statement that

---

[33] N. Subrahmanian, *Hinduism at the Crossroads of History* (Delhi: Kanishka Publishing House, 1993), 233.

[34] M. N. Srinivas, "An Obituary on Caste as a System,' *Economic and Political Weekly* 38, no. 5 (February 1-7, 2003): 457.

[35] T. N. Madan, "Secularism in its Place," in *Secularism and Its Critics*, ed. Rajeev Bhargava (New Delhi: Oxford University Press, 1998), 298.

secularism as the "credo of life is impossible." Madan writes, "It is impossible as a credo of life because the great majority of the people of South Asia are in their own eyes active adherents of some religious faith."[36] Central to Madan's argument is the fact that the genesis of secularism lies in a unique historical framework of "the dialectic of modern science and Protestantism" and not as it is sometimes erroneously assumed, "a simple repudiation of religion and the rise of rationalism."[37]

Adoption of secularism into such societies where the definition of good life and cultural/anthropological *telos* do not correspond with that of secularism leaves traditional societies with a sense of loss and nostalgia. Madan writes, "[T]ransfer of secularism to… traditional or tradition-haunted societies…can only mean conversion and the loss of one's culture, and, if you like, the loss of one's soul."[38] Given these reasons, he argues, "secularism as an alien cultural ideology which, lacks the strong support of the state, has failed to make desired headway in India."[39]

Although the focus in the above reasoning is upon the creed of life, Madan seems to hint that the same argument could be the reason why secularism is also "impossible." He further argues that in the South Asian context, "people do not know whether it is desirable to privatize religion, and if it is, how this may be done, unless they be Protestant Christians but not if they are Buddhists, Hindus, Muslims, or Sikhs."[40]

Contrary to those who accept secularism for the purpose of civility in a plural context despite viewing it as incompatible with Hinduism, there are other non-compatibilists who reject secularism because it is incompatible with Hinduism. Jaideep Prabhu argues that religious liberty as imagined within the Nehruvian secular framework of the Indian Constitution a) neither originates from the Dharmic faiths nor is compatible with it, and b) does not provide

---

[36] Madan, "Secularism in its Place," 298.

[37] Madan, "Secularism in its Place," 308.

[38] Madan, "Secularism in its Place," 308. For further discussion on how "secularity" as a condition has led to a sense of loss and nostalgia, see my essay, "Tayloring Indian Secularity."

[39] Madan, "Secularism in its Place," 313.

[40] Madan, "Secularism in its Place," 298.

a level playing ground for Dharmic systems vis-à-vis Abrahamic faiths. Given these, Prabhu argues for "a complete ban on proselytism and religious conversion in India."[41] Along with Prabhu, there are a host of voices within the Rashtriya Swayamsevak Sangh (RSS)[42] and other right-wing organizations, which reject the liberal secular Constitution on account of it being incompatible with the Hindu *dharma*. This has led to repeated calls to re-write the Constitution by the exponents of the Hindutva ideology.[43]

Whether secularism is viewed hospitably as a welcome change to the Hindu traditions and beliefs or is viewed as hostile—an intrusion into the Hindu way of life—the above view sees secularism and Hinduism as incompatible, leading to some unavoidable conflicts fundamentally because of the vast difference in the purposive visions of both.

---

[41] Jaideep Prabhu, "Is Religious Conversion Really a Fundamental Right, or Can we Ban it?" *Firstpost,* September 8, 2014, accessed on October 9, 2014. See, http://www.firstpost.com/india/religious-conversion-really-fundamental-right-can-ban-1701877.html Interestingly, Jaideep Prabhu is the Jawaharlal Nehru Professor of Business and Enterprise at the Judge Business School at the University of Cambridge, England. Also see my response titled, "Can we Ban Religious Conversions: A Response to Jaideep Prabhu" at https://varughesejohnblog.wordpress.com/2014/10/10/can-we-ban-religious-conversions-a-response-to-jaideep-prabhu/

[42] Rashtriya Swayamsevak Sangh (RSS, means National Voluntary Organization) is the rightwing nationalistic body that is considered the parent organization of the ruling right-wing political party, the Bharatiya Janata Party (BJP).

[43] As Pavan Kulkarni argues, "The campaign of the RSS to implement the *Manusmriti* instead of the constitution continued well into the following year, even after the constitution was officially adopted by the country. In an editorial titled, 'Manu Rules Our Hearts,' the RSS asserted in a tone of defiance: 'Even though Dr. Ambedkar is reported to have recently stated in Bombay that the days of Manu have ended it is nevertheless a fact that the daily lives of Hindus are even at present day affected by the principles and injunctions contained in the Manusmriti and other Smritis. Even an unorthodox Hindu feels himself bound at least in some matters by the rules contained in the Smritis and he feels powerless to give up altogether his adherence to them.'" In "History Shows How Patriotic the RSS Really Is," *Wire,* April 17, 2017, accessed on April 18, 2017, https://thewire.in/124685/rss-hindutva-nationalism/.

The compatibilist view

Let me now turn to those who espouse the compatibilist view. Unlike the above voices, Amartya Sen in his *Argumentative Indian* espouses a compatibilist view by seeing a connection between secular democracy and "public argument" in India. He complains that it "is often missed, through the temptation to attribute the Indian commitment to democracy simply to the impact of British influence (despite the fact that such an influence should have worked similarly for a hundred other countries that emerged from an empire on which the sun used not to set)."[44]

Although Sen's focus is on democracy, it nevertheless overlaps enough with the question of secularism that his view may be categorized as a compatibilist view. For Sen, the grounding for the compatibilist view is the survival of democracy in India, which is not instanced in several other cases where secular democracy does not automatically follow as a post-empire phenomenon. In other words, if the British presence were the sole causal antecedent to Indian democracy, then it should be instanced in every such situation where secular democracy succeeds the British rule.

Sen does not carry the argument forward to show what features other than the British presence could have aided the possibility of a secular democracy. For instance, do monolithic cultures behave differently in their post-British empire avatar? These sorts of questions help unearth whether secular democracy has succeeded for pragmatic reasons or whether there is some essential democratic quality within the Indian sub-continent that was fanned to flame by the British presence. That would provide additional variables necessary to answer the question of whether there is a natural, underlying democratic affinity among Indians as a people that can be credited with for the present democracy that is, to a large extent, functional. Sen's view cannot be uncritically adopted, especially given that Ambedkar resoundingly stated, "Constitutional morality is not a natural sentiment. It has to be cultivated. We must realize

---

[44] Amartya Sen, *The Argumentative Indian* (New Delhi: Penguin Books, 2005), 12.

that our people have yet to learn it. Democracy in India is only a top dressing on an Indian soil which is essentially undemocratic."[45]

Yet, it may be noted that the presence of democracy is a slightly different question and we cannot draw a straight line between democracy and toleration, where the latter may be marked as a more fundamental quality of secularism in the Indian context. Claims about the presence of democracy in India exist as early as 6th century BCE. They occur in the writings of Megasthenes, which, although in limited detail, are later recorded in the works of Diodorus Siculus, according to which, several generations after the reign of Dionysus, "the cities received a democratic form of government."[46]

For Sen, this suggests there is something inherent in the Indian ethos that makes democracy possible. He argues, "Democracy is intimately connected with public discussion and interactive reasoning. Traditions of public discussion exist across the world, not just in the West. And to the extent that such a tradition can be drawn on, democracy becomes easier to institute and also to preserve."[47] Accordingly, for Sen, if there were an antecedent tradition of public argument for a culture to draw from, then the immediate cause of the British Empire would function more as a rekindling of an existing fire.

Similarly, Romila Thapar explores how they can be compatible.[48] About the relationship between secularism and religion, Thapar records, "There are two popularly held approaches in India: one argues that secularism confronts religion and this leads to a rupture; the other defines secularism as the co-existence of, or, the equal respect for, all religions."[49] But Thapar regrets that

---

[45] M. V. Pylee, *Constitutional Government in India*, 8th ed. (New Delhi: S. Chand & Company Ltd., 2012), 6.

[46] See Diodorus Siculus, *Library of History*, Book II, (35-60, especially 38).

[47] Sen, *The Argumentative Indian*, 13. The correlation between public discourse and toleration requires further deliberation, especially in terms of whether the presence of public discourse can be construed as promoting toleration within the society.

[48] Romila Thapar, "Is Secularism Alien to Indian Civilization" in *The Future of Secularism*, ed. T. N. Srinivas (New Delhi: Oxford University Press, 2007).

[49] Thapar, "Is Secularism Alien to Indian Civilization," 89.

"discussions of secularism are frequently limited to seeing it superficially as antithetical to any and every traditional or contemporary religious articulation."[50] She clarifies that "when secularism is posited as opposed to religion in India, the discussion is generally limited to only a segment of Hinduism, namely Vedic Brahmanism and some aspects of Puranic Hinduism, and the more extensive articulation of religion in India is not included."[51] Therefore in bringing about a corrective to this understanding, Thapar extends "the meaning of Indian religion to include the religious identity of not just the few but of the larger population that would be involved in the secularizing of Indian society."[52]

Thapar's compatibilist view does not deny that dominant Hindu tradition and secularism are opposed to each other in their essential visions, but she argues that there are other Indian traditions, perhaps in the periphery, that can be seen as compatible with secularism. Accordingly, Buddhism, Jainism and other heterodox schools, which "tended to give greater weight to social ethics rather than to prescriptive texts regulating religious observances"[53] are better seen as useful "antecedents to secular concerns in pre-modern India," rather than "Vedic Brahmanism and Puranic Hinduism."[54]

If we were to scout beyond the dominant "Vedic Brahmanism and Puranic Hinduism," and search "other religious expressions—both within and outside what is called the Hindu tradition"[55] that Thapar talks about, what would we find? Both Thapar and Sen draw from the rich Buddhist tradition. Further, among those who ruled India, they draw from Ashoka and Akbar, who encouraged robust discussions and pursued public reason.

However, what Thapar fails to establish is whether accounting for parallel traditions sufficiently establishes the practice of toleration of multiple background cultures within the society. Where there are dominant traditions, which inherently disallow space to parallel traditions, it is bound to create problems. If Buddhist and

[50] Thapar, "Is Secularism Alien to Indian Civilization," 84.
[51] Thapar, "Is Secularism Alien to Indian Civilization," 83.
[52] Thapar, "Is Secularism Alien to Indian Civilization," 83.
[53] Thapar, "Is Secularism Alien to Indian Civilization," 92.
[54] Thapar, "Is Secularism Alien to Indian Civilization," 93.
[55] Thapar, "Is Secularism Alien to Indian Civilization," 84.

other parallel traditions were to truly find space within the dominant Hindu culture, then their decline and disappearance from the land of their origin need an explanation. Historians like S. R. Goyal have "attributed the decline and disappearance of Buddhism from India to the hostility of the Brahmanas,"[56] which challenges the notion that polytheistic beliefs are inherently tolerant. Similarly, in *The Early History of India*, Vincent Smith "gives a long list of Brahmin persecution of the Buddhists."[57] Thapar's argument remains debatable, given how the dominant Hindu traditions have almost eliminated the very traditions she credits as being compatible with a social ethic that corresponds with secularism. This then is a question of whether secularism is compatible with the dominant tradition of the land rather than finding any tradition where some compatibility can be noticed.

Similarly, while a case can be made for the presence of public interactive reasoning in the earlier Indian traditions as Sen argues, it would be important to examine who the parties invited for these interactive reasonings were. In short, it is crucial to establish that the parties were not merely the various voices within the dominant/upper caste traditions. Besides, even if public reasoning as an essential feature of democracy existed in whatever form described by Sen, could a liberal democratic society result merely from these public discourses?

Conclusion

In short, it is hard to find a strong case that draws a straight line from early Indian traditions to secular democracy. But, to their credit, both Thapar and Sen have attributed "the development and survival of democracy in India"[58] to the strength of the ancient heterodox Indian traditions. But what needs further examination can follow from Sen's acknowledgement that "While democracy must also demand *much else*, public reasoning, which is central to

[56] Shenali Waduge, "Why Buddhism Prospered in Asia but Died in India," *Asian Tribune*, June 10, 2012.
[57] Paulos Mar Gregorios, "Speaking of Tolerance and Intolerance," in *India International Centre Quarterly* 22, no. 1 (Spring 1995): 23.
[58] Sen, *The Argumentative Indian*, 16.

participatory governance, is an important part of a bigger picture."⁵⁹ A discussion on what the *much else* is, that is needed for secular democracy, would helpfully shape our discussion.⁶⁰

Both Thapar (who appeals to Indian peripheral traditions) and Sen (who appeals to traces of public reasoning in early traditions) do not provide sufficient grounding to establish that Indian traditions are sufficient antecedents to the embracing of secular democracy. Their argument becomes more problematic if we invoke a political system that upholds liberty, justice, and a strong sense of human rights. Those virtues seem to be alien to the Hindu religio-cultural imaginations, as we have noted earlier.

This opens itself to the question: Why has secular democracy survived in India for over 60 years, given the overwhelming understanding that the Hindu ethos is innately undemocratic? That the secular Constitution presupposes an idea of self that is fundamentally different from not only the Brahminic and Vedic Hindu traditions but also the heterodox traditions, seems to suggest that secular democracy has survived in India more for pragmatic reasons rather than ideological reasons. Further, even if heterodox traditions do exhibit some features essential for democracy, can they assume such prominence to influence the social thinking of a nation-state? Perhaps any claim in this regard should remain extremely modest. Pavan Varma discerningly writes,

> The truth then is that democracy has survived in India not because Indians are democratic, but because democracy has proved to be the most effective instrument for the cherished pursuit of power. A people stifling in the pressure cooker of a hierarchically sealed society embraced the *machinery of democratic politics* for the promise it held of upward mobility within the inherited framework of an undemocratic society.⁶¹

The above discussions give us a clue as to why actualizing the spirit of the Constitution still remains a challenge, despite embracing a

---

⁵⁹ Sen, *The Argumentative Indian*, 16. Emphasis added.
⁶⁰ The antecedent factors that led to the framing of the Indian Constitution, such as the philosophical basis that the Constituent Assembly appealed to for founding a secular, democratic nation, would also be equally important.
⁶¹ Pavan K. Varma, *Being Indian* (New Delhi: Viking, 2004), 54.

functional secular democracy. Cultivating constitutional morality has been a challenge precisely because it is based in an ethos that is inaccessible within the background culture. Where the predominant background culture conflicts with egalitarian ethos, it makes the democratic functioning all the more challenging. Understandably, where the popular religious and cultural doctrines promote inequality and disparity, the state's task becomes an arduous one, in that it has to uphold ideals that are contrary to the popular beliefs of its people. Given this reality, the case of Indian secular democracy needs a sympathetic evaluation. The law cannot deliver beyond what it can! It is pointless to demand of a people a behaviour fitting to the spirit of the Constitution, without shaping what Alexis de Tocqueville calls, "the habits of the heart."[62]

---

[62] Alexis de Tocqueville, *Democracy in America* (New York: Madison Park, 2010).

Freedom of Religion in India: Violated in Practice, Questioned in Principle

Tehmina Arora[1]

>...'absorption' in the sense of cultural or religious or any other absorption is something against which it is necessary for us to guard... the strength of this land will be based upon the strength of the individual members of the different communities. And they will not achieve their full strength unless they base themselves on convictions and ideals which are their very own. Cultural autonomy for which I am pleading and which has been promised as far as it is not inconsistent with national strength, even though it may appear in some sense as opposed to national unity, is still consistent with it.[2]

India has a longstanding tradition of communal tolerance and diversity. Home to many religious traditions, customs and beliefs such as Hinduism, Islam, Christianity, Buddhism, Jainism, Sikhism, Zoroastrian, and numerous other tribal and animists traditions, India is also known as the birthplace of several religions.

The framers of modern India, the drafters of the Constitution of India, recognized the need to preserve pluralism in India and took special efforts to protect the rights of religious and linguistic minorities.[3] The Constitution of India recognizes the fundamental

---

[1] Tehmina Arora is an advocate practising in Delhi. The present paper is a revised version of an article by the same author which appeared in *International Institute of Religious Freedom Report* 1, no. 2 (2012): 1-16.

[2] Jerome D'Souza, "Constituent Assembly Debates," III, 296.

[3] See Articles 25, 26, 29.1, 30.1 of the Constitution of India. Not only does each individual have the freedom to profess, practice and propagate his religion (Article 25), every religious group or denomination has the right to establish and maintain institutions for religious and charitable purposes, to manage its own affairs in matters of religion, to own and acquire movable and immovable property and to administer such property in accordance with law (Article 26). Further, any section of citizens of India that has a distinct language, script or culture has the right to conserve the same (Article 29.1). All minorities, whether based on religion or language, have the right to establish and administer educational institutions of their choice (Article 30.1).

rights of religious and linguistic minorities; placing them in two broad categories—the common domain and a separate or special domain. The rights which fall in the common domain are those which are applicable to all the citizens of India. The rights which fall in the separate domain are those which are applicable to minorities only and these are reserved to protect their identity. These safeguards in the light of partition of the country, were aimed at creating a society where citizens shared a strong sense of national identity despite cultural, ethnic and religious diversity and where historically disadvantaged groups were protected.

However, as B. R. Ambedkar stated during the Constituent Assembly debates, "Constitutional morality is not a natural sentiment. It has to be cultivated. We must realise that our people have yet to learn it. Democracy in India is only a top dressing on an Indian soil which is essentially undemocratic."[4]

All across India, individuals and religious communities are subjected to discrimination, abuse, perpetrated and sanctioned violence for exercising their faith or for identifying with a certain religion. In *365 Days Democracy and Secularism Under The Modi Regime—A Report*,[5] Dayal and Hashmi noted several cases of targeted violence, many times leading to death, against Muslims and Christians. The Minister of State for Home Affairs, Kiren Rijiju told the Rajya Sabha,[6] that a total of 113 communal incidents took place in various parts of the country during May-June in which 15 people were killed and 318 others were injured.

Reports by faith-based rights agencies recorded[7] over 147 incidents where Christians were targeted, with many more going

---

[4] Parliament of India, "Constituent Assembly of India - Volume VII," accessed on May 3, 2017. http://parliamentofindia.nic.in/ls/debates/vol7p1b.htm *[editorial note: when last checked on August 15, 2017, the web-link was inactive]*

[5] John Dayal and Shabnam Hashmi, eds., *365 Days Democracy and Secularism Under The Modi Regime: A Report* (Delhi: ANHAD, 2015). (available at https://archive.org/details/365DaysReport). *[editorial note: when last checked on August 15, 2017, the web-link was inactive]*

[6] Press Trust of India, "113 Communal Incidents in May-June, 15 killed," *Hindustan Times*, 16 July 2014, accessed on August 15, 2017, http://www.hindustantimes.com/india-news/113-communal-incidents-in-may-june-15-killed/article1-1241014.aspx.

[7] *Hate and Targeted Violence against Christians in India - Report 2014* (Delhi:

unrecorded in 2014. The states of Karnataka, Madhya Pradesh and Chhattisgarh have recorded the most number of attacks in the past two years. Most of the incidents include threats, intimidations and violence against members of the community. In some cases, churches, places of worship, and burial grounds were targeted and desecrated. Another very common phenomenon is the social boycott being experienced by Christians in several parts of the country; local panchayats are also known to have imposed fines on Christians for practising their faith. Social exclusions are also common tactics to victimize minorities by denying basic human rights that are common to every citizen. These exclusion orders make Christians vulnerable to excessive violence and denial of social privileges like access to water, electricity and work.

Subsequent to an aggressive campaign[8] by the Vishwa Hindu Parishad (VHP), three villages in the central Indian state of Chhattisgarh banned the entry of and propaganda by non-Hindu missionaries, especially Christians, by way of a village council resolution.[9] According to media reports,[10] 50 villages have since imposed the ban. According to reports available on the website Speak Out Against Hate,[11] members of the Christian minority community have been targeted in over 68 incidents across the country in the period of January-April 2015. In the light of these attacks and incidents of Ghar Wapsi (homecoming) conducted by

Evangelical Fellowship of India and Alliance Defending Freedom India, 2014), accessed on September 1, 2015, http://us8.campaign-archive1.com/?u=d8567 1af78bbf54876608a2de&id=e95d57b851.

[8] Varghese K. George, "BJP, Parivar outfits to intensify campaign against 'love jihad'," *The Hindu*, August 8, 2014.

[9] The translated text of the order passed by the special Gram Sabha organized by the Sirisguda Gram Panchayat in the Tokapal block of Bastar Chhattisgarh on May 10, 2014 states that: "i. It was decided to maintain and preserve the traditional cultural unity of the village. ii. To prohibit the Religious preachers other than those of Hindu religion to preach or profess other religions. They are totally debarred from holding prayers meet and deliver discourses. iii. To prohibit construction of any religious place without prior permission of Village Panchayat...."

[10] Pavan Dahat, "In Bastar, 50 villages ban non-Hindu missionaries," *The Hindu*, July 5, 2014, accessed on August 15, 2017, http://www.thehindu.com/news/national/in-bastar-50-villages-ban-nonhindu-missionaries/article6180825.ece

[11] http://speakoutagainsthate.org/

various groups affiliated to the Sangh Parivar,[12] there are also shrill voices calling for India to have a national law[13] regulating religious conversions in line with laws already in place in several states across India, commonly known as anti-conversions laws.

The demand to regulate religious conversion however is not new. The precursor to the present day Freedom of Religion Acts were first introduced in the 1930s in the princely states. The Raigarh State Conversion Act 1936, the Patna Freedom of Religion Act of 1942, the Sarguja State Apostasy Act 1945 and the Udaipur State Anti-Conversion Act 1946 are some examples of these laws.[14]

Post-independence, the Indian parliament took up for consideration a legislative enactment regulating religious conversion known as Indian Conversion (Regulation and Registration) Bill of 1954, and later the Backward Communities (Religious Protection) Bill of 1960, and then the Freedom of Religion Bill of 1978 introduced by Member of Parliament OP Tyagi, who was a member of a Hindu nationalist party.[15] Since then, at least 10 private members' Bills have been introduced in both the lower and upper house of parliament, where they have met with little success and were dropped for lack of majority support.[16]

However, things have been different at the state or provincial level. The first state in independent India to enact the Freedom of Religion Act was Odisha in 1967 during the rule of the then Swatantra Party, known for its Right leanings. The Madhya Pradesh

---

[12] Goldie Osuri, "Foreign Swadeshi," *The Frontline*, January 9, 2015, accessed on August 15, 2017, http://www.frontline.in/the-nation/foreign-swadeshi/article6715524.ece. TNN, "Sangh Parivar plans Ghar Wapsi in Udupi," *Times of India*, 24 December 2014, accessed on August 15, 2017, http://timesofindia.indiatimes.com/city/bengaluru/Sangh-Parivar-plans-ghar-wapsi-in-Udupi/articleshow/45621692.cms.

[13] Anita Joshua, "Rajnath pitches for anti-conversion law," *Hindu*, April 18, 2015, accessed on August 15, 2017, http://www.thehindu.com/news/national/states-should-act-against-communal-incidents-rajnath/article7150757.ece.

[14] Arpita Anant, "Anti-conversion laws," *Hindu*, December 17, 2002, accessed on August 15, 2017, http://www.thehindu.com/thehindu/op/2002/12/17/stories/2002121700110200.htm.

[15] Anant, "Anti-conversion laws."

[16] Arcot Krishnaswami, *Study of Discrimination In The Matter Of Religious Rights and Practices by Special Rapporteur of the Sub-Commission on Prevention of Discrimination and Protection of Minorities* (New York: United Nations, 1960), 9.

Freedom of Religion Act was enacted in 1968 and when Chhattisgarh was carved out of Madhya Pradesh in November 2000, it inherited the anti-conversion law from the latter.

The Congress Party enacted the Freedom of Indigenous Faith Act in Arunachal Pradesh in 1978 to preserve indigenous faiths. However, until today the law has not been implemented as the Rules governing the Act are yet to be framed. In 2002, the Tamil Nadu state assembly ruled by a regional party passed the Prohibition of Forcible Conversion of Religion Bill. But, after the defeat of the BJP-led coalition in the 2004 general elections, the state government repealed the law. A year later, the BJP government in Gujarat passed the Freedom of Religion Act, in March 2003.

In April 2006, the BJP-led government in Rajasthan passed a similar Freedom of Religion Bill. However, assent of the President of India is still awaited after the Bill was forwarded to the President by the then Governor of Rajasthan, Pratibha Patil. The BJP in Madhya Pradesh and Chhattisgarh also unsuccessfully sought to tighten the existing laws the same year, even as the Congress Party government in Himachal Pradesh passed the Freedom of Religion Act or political consideration months before state assembly elections.

Basic Features of the Acts

Preamble

The Freedom of Religion Acts claim to prohibit conversions by force, fraud and inducement or allurement. The Acts state that no person shall convert or attempt to convert, either directly or otherwise, any person from one religious faith to another by the use of force or by inducement or by any fraudulent means, nor shall any person abet any such conversion.

Definitions

The Acts in Orissa, Madhya Pradesh and Himachal Pradesh define conversion as "renouncing one religion and adopting another."

The Arunachal Pradesh Law differs slightly, as it defines it as "renouncing an indigenous faith and adopting another faith or religion."[17] The Gujarat Law states that conversion means "to make one person to renounce one religion and adopt another religion."[18]

All the Acts define "force" as "a threat of injury of any kind, including the threat of divine displeasure or social ex-communication," and "fraud" or "fraudulent means" as "misrepresentation or any other fraudulent contrivance." The term "inducement" has been defined in some of the Acts[19] as "the offer of any gift or gratification either in cash or in kind, including the grant of any benefit, either pecuniary or otherwise," while other Acts[20] use the term "allurement" and define it as offer of any temptation in the form of any gift or gratification either in cash or kind, and grant of any material benefit, either momentary or otherwise.

Contravention

The Acts carry penal provisions and punishments generally ranging from upto one year of imprisonment and a fine of upto 5,000 Indian rupees, to upto three years of imprisonment and a fine of upto 25,000 Indian rupees.

The punishment is more stringent if there is evidence of conversion by force, fraud or inducement among women, minors and Dalits (formerly "untouchables" as per India's caste system) or Tribals (aborigines). Apart from penal action, the Himachal Pradesh Law states that if any person has been converted by force, fraud or coercion, she or he shall be deemed as not converted.[21]

Failure to send notice to or seek permission from the district magistrate before converting or participating in a conversion ceremony is liable for a fine under the Acts.

---

[17] Section 2 (b), Arunachal Pradesh Freedom of Religion Act, 1978.

[18] Section 2 (b), Gujarat Freedom of Religion Act, 2003.

[19] Section 2 (d) the Orissa Pradesh Freedom of Religion Act, 1967 and the Himachal Pradesh Freedom of Religion Act, 2006.

[20] Section 2 (a) the Madhya Pradesh Freedom of Religion Act, 1968 and the Gujarat Freedom of Religion Act, 2003.

[21] Section 3, proviso of the Himachal Pradesh Freedom of Religion Act, 2006.

EFFECT OF THE LEGISLATION

The primary factor behind the reason for the enactment for such Acts has allegedly been that such laws would act as a deterrent against fraudulent conversions and would also ensure that there would not be any law and order problems due to grievances in the community due to such fraudulent practices. However, reports from the various minority communities and human rights agencies reveal that these laws foster hostility against minority communities.

In several states, prosecutions have been launched under the Freedom of Religion Acts against members of the minority Christian community. There have also been frequent attacks against the community by members of right-wing Hindu groups on the pretext of "forcible" conversions. However, in spite of the existence of these acts, in some states for over forty-five years, there have been very few convictions, though cases are registered under the Acts almost every month. For example, in the year 2010, at least eighteen arrests were reported under the anti-conversion and other restrictive laws in Chhattisgarh and Madhya Pradesh alone.[22]

Taking note of this trend, in its 2011 report, the United States Commission on International Religious Freedom (USCIRF) noted that: "the harassment and violence against religious minorities appears to be more pronounced in states that have adopted 'Freedom of Religion' Acts or are considering such laws...."[23]

The report further stated that,

> These laws have led to few arrests and reportedly no convictions. According to the U.S. State Department between June 2009 and December 2010 approximately twenty-seven arrests were made in Madhya Pradesh and Chhattisgarh, but resulted in no convictions. Compass Direct reported that in March 2011, police arrested twelve Tribals in Orissa's Mayurbhanj district for violating the

---

[22] United States Department of State, "International Religious Freedom Report – 2010," accessed on September 1, 2015, http://www.state.gov/g/drl/rls/irf/2010/148792.htm. *[editorial note: when last checked on August 15, 2017, the web-link was inactive]*

[23] United States Commission on International Religious Freedom, "USCIRF Annual Report 2011–The Commission's Watch List: India," April 28, 2011, accessed on August 15, 2017, http://www.refworld.org/docid/4dbe90bac.html.

Orissa 'Freedom of Religion Act' by converting to Christianity without a permit issued by the authorities.[24]

Asma Jahangir, the Special Rapporteur on Freedom of Religion or Belief, also noted in her report after a visit to India that,

> Even in the Indian states which have adopted laws on religious conversion there seem to be only few–if any–convictions for conversion by the use of force, inducement or fraudulent means. In Orissa, for example, not a single infringement over the past ten years of the Orissa Freedom of Religion Act 1967 could be cited or adduced by district officials and senior officials in the State Secretariat....[25]

However, such laws or even draft legislations have had adverse consequences for religious minorities and have fostered mob violence against them.

> The report goes on to state that, ...there is a risk that Freedom of Religion Acts may become a tool in the hands of those who wish to use religion for vested interests or to persecute individuals on the grounds of their religion or belief. While persecution, violence or discrimination based on religion or belief need to be sanctioned by law, the Special Rapporteur would like to caution against excessive or vague legislation on religious issues which could create tensions and problems instead of solving them.[26]

A fact-finding team of the National Commission for Minorities in India in a report after a visit to the states of Madhya Pradesh and Chhattisgarh between June 13 and 18, 2007, noted that Hindu extremists frequently invoked the anti-conversion law in Madhya Pradesh as a means of inciting mobs against Christians or having them arrested without evidence. They noted in their

---

[24] "USCIRF Annual Report 2011."

[25] United Nations General Assembly, "Promotion and Protection Of All Human Rights, Civil, Political, Economic, Social And Cultural Rights, Including The Right To Development: Report Of The Special Rapporteur On Freedom Of Religion Or Belief," A/HRC/10/8/Add, 3, January 26, 2009, http://daccess-ods.un.org/TMP/5744267.70210266.html. *[editorial note: when last checked on August 15, 2017, the web-link was inactive]*

[26] United Nations General Assembly, "Promotion and Protection Of All Human Rights."

report: "Obviously, the life of Christians has become miserable at the hands of miscreants in connivance with the police. There are allegations that when atrocities were committed on Christians by the miscreants, police remained mere spectators and in certain cases they did not even register FIRs [First Information Reports]."[27]

CRITIQUE OF THE ACTS

Vague and overly broad definitions

The primary critique of the Acts due to their vague and overtly broad definitions has come from several jurists. The United Nations Special Rapporteur on Freedom for Religion or Belief in her report on India[28] noted that while these laws appear to protect religious adherents only from attempts to induce conversion by improper means, they have been criticized on the ground that the failure to clearly define what makes a conversion improper bestows on the authorities unfettered discretion to accept or reject the legitimacy of religious conversions. All of these laws include in the definition of use of force any "threat of divine displeasure or social excommunication."

Moreover, the terms "inducement" or "allurement" are defined to include the offer of any gift or gratification, either in cash or in kind, as well as the grant of any benefit, either pecuniary or otherwise. These broad and vague terms might be interpreted to cover the expression of many religious beliefs.

In March 2007, the National Commission for Minorities noted the enactment of the Himachal Pradesh Freedom of Religion Act with concern, especially "the terminology used in the [Himachal Pradesh Freedom of Religion] Act and the methodology prescribed for implementing it." The Commission also expressed its "profound concern" over the "attempt of the Act, and reportedly by similar pieces of legislation contemplated in some other States, to interfere

---

[27] "State In India Tightens Controls On Conversions," *Compass News Direct*, July 25, 2006.
[28] United Nations General Assembly, "Promotion and Protection of All Human Rights."

with the basic right of freedom of religion that is the birth right of every Indian."[29]

Laws should give a person of ordinary intelligence a reasonable opportunity to know what is prohibited, so that he may act accordingly. Vague laws may trap the innocent by not providing fair warning. Such a law impermissibly delegates basic policy matters to policemen and also judges for resolution on an ad hoc and subjective basis, with the attendant dangers of arbitrary and discriminatory application. More so uncertain and undefined words used inevitably lead citizens to "steer far wider of the unlawful zone... than if the boundaries of the forbidden areas were clearly marked."[30]

Conversion

The definition of "conversion" in these Acts overlooks the fact that conversion is primarily a thought process which may span several days, weeks or even years. And the definition in the Gujarat Act in particular suggests that conversion requires an external agency almost without the will of the prospective convert.[31]

On the contrary, the Supreme Court of India has held in several judgments that mere declaration of conversion cannot be taken as evidence of conversion; "but a bonafide intention to be converted in the Hindu faith, accompanied by conduct unequivocally expressing the intention may be sufficient evidence for conversion. No formal ceremony for purification or expiation is necessary to effectuate conversion."[32]

---

[29] National Commission for Minorities Press Release, "The Himachal Pradesh Freedom of Religion Act," May 4, 2007, NCM website, accessed on August 15, 2017, http://ncm.nic.in/The-Himachal-Pradesh-Freedom-of-Religion-Act.html.

[30] SCC refers to Supreme Court Cases. But here it refers to a particular volume where these cases are recorded. SCC (3), 569 (1994).

[31] Sec. 2 (b) of the Gujarat Freedom of Religion Act, 2003.

[32] SCR refers to Supreme Court Reporter. But here it refers to a particular volume where these cases are recorded. SCR (1), 49 (1971).

Force

The definition of the term "force" as "threat of divine displeasure" unjustifiably impinges on possible interactions between potential converts and those seeking to propagate their faith. It restricts the latter from informing the former about non-adherence, for example, as that may involve teachings on hell or God's wrath. And without being informed, a potential convert cannot meaningfully exercise his or her freedom to change religion.

Proponents of these laws often quote the Orissa High Court ruling in Yulitha Hyde vs. State of Orissa,[33] which held, "Threat of divine displeasure numbs the mental faculty; more so of an undeveloped mind and the actions of such a person thereafter, are not free and according to conscience."

The courts in India have also reasoned that threatening anyone with divine displeasure puts great pressure on the threatened person and deprives them of the capacity of exercising their rational judgment. Repeatedly the courts have held that a suggestion of divine displeasure deprives a person of their abilities to make a choice.

> However, this argument overlooks the fact that inherent in the propagation of a faith or religious belief is the articulation of the effects of failure to comply with the said beliefs. Commenting on this, noted social commentator, Pratap Bhanu Mehta says: In some ways this argument is bizarre. The intent of the statute seems to be to exclude certain kinds of religious appeals. There might be good reasons for excluding such appeals. The principal one might be the Hobbesian [of political theorist Hobbes] insight that in order to discharge our obligations to the state faithfully, we have to be relieved of all those sources of authority that induce even more fear in us than the state might. Or one might argue, on Rawlsian [of theorist John Rawls] grounds, that as a mark of reciprocity, one ought not to appeal to one's own comprehensive conception of the good in making public arguments…
>
> …In Yulitha Hyde vs. State of Orissa, the court wrote: "Threat of divine displeasure numbs the mental faculty; more so of an undeveloped mind and the actions of such a person thereafter, are not free and according to

---

[33] All India Reporter, Ori 116 (1973).

conscience." In cases involving the Representation of People's Act (RPA) the same assumption is made throughout.

If this analysis is correct, we can see a fairly stable set of assumptions about citizens that underlie two different domains that require abridging religious speech, whether it is attempts at conversion and the exclusion of religious appeal from elections. The court assumes throughout that citizens are, when it comes to receiving religious speech, or speech about religion, incapable of managing the impressions they receive – to use an old stoic concept.

If the insult is to one's religion, or an exhortation is made in the name of religion, we are incapable of receiving the expression on our own terms; incapable of managing our own responses, condemned to receiving these expressions unfreely and helplessly, incapable as it were of self-discipline. We can manage our impressions, exercise our religious choices and practice judgment, only when left alone. Hence the court's emphasis that the right to freedom of religion just means the right to freedom from other people's religion. Our choices are impaired, or faculties numbed, more so because we have undeveloped minds. This is the "secret" rationale behind both anti-conversion legislation and the RPA.[34]

Article 19 (1) (a) of the Indian Constitution states that all citizens shall have the right to freedom of speech and expression. This fundamental right is curtailed by limiting what aspects of one's faith can be shared. Members of the Constitution Drafting Committee noted that freedom of speech covers the right to propagate one's faith:

> ...Under the freedom of speech which the Constitution guarantees it will be open to any religious community to persuade other people to join their faith. So long as religion is religion, conversion by free exercise of conscience has to be recognized. The word "propagate" in this clause is nothing very much out of the way as some people think, nor is it fraught with dangerous consequences.[35]

[34] Pratap Bhanu Mehta, "Passion and Constraint," *India Seminar*, January 2003, accessed on June 12, 2017, http://www.india-seminar.com/2003/521/521%20pratap%20bhanu%20mehta.htm.

[35] Constitution Assembly Debates, Official Report, Vol. 7, no. 4 (November

Fraud

The definition of the word "fraudulent" as "misrepresentation or any other fraudulent contrivance" also opens the door for potential misuse. In spiritual matters, could a statement like, "Prayers will heal you," or "God will grant you material blessings," be construed as employing fraudulent means? There is no answer.[36]

The state cannot sit in authority to test the veracity of the claims of religion. For people often believe what cannot be proved. They cannot be put to the proof of their religious doctrines or beliefs. Religious experiences which are as real as life to some may be incomprehensible to others.

Inducement/allurement

A problem in defining the term "inducement" or "allurement" as "offer of any temptation in the form of any gift or gratification either in cash or kind or grant of any material benefit either monetary or otherwise" was noted by the Orissa High Court in Yulitha Hyde vs. State of Orissa.[37] The court held that the vague nature and wide scope of the term would impinge on various legitimate methods of proselytizing.

Noted advocate Prashant Bhushan commenting on the provision is quoted as saying, "Anything can be called allurement. In many Christian institutions, education for Christians is free, so if somebody changes his or her religion, even education can be defined as allurement."[38]

While the Supreme Court subsequently overruled the Orissa High court's decision in Rev. Stanislaus vs. Madhya Pradesh,[39] a landmark judgement which upheld the constitutionality of the

---

1948 to 8 January 1949), Reprinted by Lok Sabha Secretariat, New Delhi, Third Reprint, 1999, 437-438.

[36] "AIFOFDR Report, 1999" in *The Politics Behind Anti Christian Violence*, ed. Ram Puniyani (Delhi: Media House, 2006), 410.

[37] All India Reporter, Ori 116 (1973).

[38] Avinash Dutt, "Raipur's One-Way Conversion Street," *Tehelka*, September 2, 2006.

[39] SCC (1), 677 (1977).

MP and Odisha Freedom of Religion Acts, the court chose not to comment on the definitions provided under the Acts.

Requirement of notice/prior permission

The laws give district authorities wide and sweeping powers to inquire into both the reasons behind a religious conversion and the procedure adopted for the same. The Acts require the person converting to give details of his or her conversion to the district magistrate, either prior to the conversion ceremony or subsequent to it.

The Gujarat Law states that the person seeking to be converted must obtain prior permission from the concerned district magistrate before any conversion ceremony is performed. Section 5 of the Gujarat Act makes it obligatory for a person to intimate the District Magistrate about his or her intention to convert. The rules also require that any person participating in a conversion ceremony or conducting a ceremony must seek prior permission from the district authorities.

The rule states that "On receipt of an application made under sub-rule (1) of rule 3, the District Magistrate shall, after making such inquiry as he thinks necessary, either grant the permission or refuse to grant permission, within a period of one month from the date of the receipt of the application."[40]

The Acts therefore greatly impinge on the freedom of conscience of a prospective convert and also on their right to privacy. The person is rendered incapable of taking the final decision with regards to his or her faith and instead requires the seal of approval of the local district authority. This is a gross violation of the right to freedom of association, the right to privacy and the freedom of conscience. The Acts cast an onerous burden on the part of the convertee and the persons seeking to propagate their faith without providing the required checks and balances to ensure protection against misuse of authority.

Article 18 of the Universal Declaration of Human Rights distinguishes the freedom of thought, conscience, religion or belief from the freedom to manifest religion or belief. It does not permit

---

[40] Rule 4 (1) of the Gujarat Freedom of Religion Rules, 2008.

any limitations whatsoever on the freedom of thought and conscience or on the freedom to have or adopt a religion or belief of one's choice. These freedoms are protected unconditionally, as is the right of everyone to hold opinions without interference in Article 19.1. In accordance with Articles 18.2 and 17, no one can be compelled to reveal his thoughts or adherence to a religion or belief.[41]

The United Nations Special Rapporteur on Freedom of Religion or Belief, Asma Jahangir, in her report noted that:

> The requirement of advance notice or prior permission seems to be unduly onerous for the individual who intends to convert. Any state inquiry into the substantive beliefs and motivation for conversion is highly problematic since it may lead to interference with the internal and private realm of the individual's belief (forum internum). This approach is aggravated if such a Freedom of Religion Act awards specific protection to the state government and its officers against prosecution or legal proceedings with regard to "anything done in good faith or intended to be done under the Act or any rule made thereunder." Moreover, it seems unclear who may bring an action for, or lodge an appeal against, decisions with regard to the permissibility of a religious conversion.[42]

She also noted that: "Any concern raised with regard to certain conversions or how they might be accomplished should primarily be raised by the alleged victim."[43]

The provisions of the Acts fail to provide any safety mechanisms for those on whom they are casting a burden to disclose sensitive information. Besides, the mandatory declaration sought by the Acts violates Article 19 (1) (b) and (c) which give every citizen the right to assemble peaceably without the interference of

---

[41] United Nations, CCPR General Comment No. 22: Article 18 (Freedom of Thought, Conscience or Religion) Adopted at the Forty-eighth Session of the Human Rights Committee, on July 30, 1993, CCPR/C/21/Rev.1/Add. 4, General Comment No. 22. (General Comments), accessed on August 15, 2017, http://www.refworld.org/docid/453883fb22.html.

[42] United Nations General Assembly, "Promotion and Protection Of All Human Rights."

[43] United Nations General Assembly, "Promotion and Protection Of All Human Rights."

the State. Besides, the provision for public enquiry into conversions and the mandatory intimation violate the right to privacy, which the Supreme Court of India has repeatedly held to be implicit in the right to life in Article 21.

In September 2012, the High Court of Himachal Pradesh struck down Section 4 of the Himachal Pradesh Freedom of Religion Act, which made it obligatory for a person to give a 30-day prior notice to the district magistrate about his or her intention to convert. The Court held that the procedure is oppressive and struck it down as violative of the Indian Constitution. The court held that:

> A person not only has a right of conscience, the right of belief, the right to change his belief, but also has the right to keep his beliefs secret. No doubt, the right to privacy is, like any other right, subject to public order, morality and the larger interest of the State. When rights of individuals clash with the larger public good, then the individual's right must give way to what is in the larger public interest. However, this does not mean that the majority interest is the larger public interest. Larger public interest would mean the integrity, unity and sovereignty of the country, the maintenance of public law and order. Merely because the majority view is different does not mean that the minority view must be silenced... the State must have material before it to show what are the very compelling reasons which will justify its action of invading the right to privacy of an individual. A man's home is his castle and no invasion into his home is permissible unless justified on constitutional grounds. A man's mind is the impregnable fortress in which he thinks and there can be no invasion of his right of thought unless the person is expressing or propagating his thoughts in such a manner that it will cause public disorder or affect the unity or sovereignty of the country.
>
> Why should any human being be asked to disclose what is his religion? Why should a human being be asked to inform the authorities that he is changing his belief? What right does the State have to direct the convertee to give notice in advance to the District Magistrate about changing his rebellious thought?[44]

---

[44] Writ Petition No. 438 of 2011 in the matter of Evangelical Fellowship of India and Anr. vs. State of Himachal Pradesh.

Similarly, the Bombay High Court in the case of Ranjeet Mohite and Ors Vs. UOI and Ors held that :

> No authority which is a State within the meaning of Article 12 of the Constitution of India or any of its agency or instrumentality can infringe the fundamental right to freedom of conscience. Any individual in exercise of right of freedom of conscience is entitled to carry an opinion and express an opinion that he does not follow any religion or any religious tenet. He has right to say that he does not believe in any religion. Therefore, if he is called upon by any agency or instrumentality of the State to disclose his religion, he can always state that he does not practice any religion or he does not belong to any religion. He cannot to be compelled to state that he professes a particular religion.[45]

Discriminatory provisions: exemption of re-conversion

In addition, certain provisions are discriminatory in giving preferential treatment to re-conversions, for example by stipulating that returning to the forefathers' original religion or to one's own original religion shall not be construed as conversion. The exclusion of "re-conversions" in some of these laws violates the right to equality before law as promised under Article 14 of the Constitution of India, which states: "The State shall not deny to any person equality before the law or the equal protection of the laws within the territory of India."

The proviso to Section 4 of the Himachal Pradesh Act, states that "no notice will be required if a person reverts back to his original religion." This is an unreasonable classification and the legislature has failed to distinguish why a special provision is required for non-notification in the event of re-conversion to "original religion."[46]

---

[45] Supreme Court Cases Online, Bom. 1121 (2014).
[46] Proviso to Section 4 Himachal Pradesh Freedom of Religion Act, 2006, section 2 (f) of the Arunachal Pradesh Freedom of Religion Act, 1978. See also proposed Rajasthan Dharma Swatantrya (Freedom Of Religion) Bill, 2008, which was passed by the Legislative Assembly and is pending with the President of India.

Similarly, the law in Arunachal Pradesh defines the term "conversion" as "renouncing an indigenous faith and adopting another faith or religion," and further defines the term "indigenous" to mean "such religions, beliefs and practices including rites, rituals, festivals, observances, performances, abstinence, customs as have been found sanctioned, approved, performed by the indigenous communities of Arunachal Pradesh...."[47]

> The Acts seek to differentiate between "indigenous faiths" and other religions and yet they fail to provide a rationale as to why "indigenous" faiths require special protection under the law.... "Original religion" has not been defined in the Himachal Act. According to Dr. Subramanian Swamy, the original religion is Hindu religion alone. We cannot accept this submission of his. The general consensus of opinion used was that the original religion would be the religion of the convertee by birth, i.e the religion he was born into.
>
> We fail to understand the rationale why if a person is to revert back to his original religion, no notice is required. It was urged before us that since he was born in his religion and knows his religion well, therefore, it was thought that while reverting back to his original religion, no notice be issued. This argument does not satisfy the parameters of Article 14 of the Constitution of India. Supposing a person born in religion A converts to religion B at the age of 20 and wants to convert back to religion A at the age of 50, he has spent many more years, that too mature years, being a follower of religion B. Why should he not be required to give notice?
>
> Another question which is troubling us is if a person born in religion A, converts to religion B, then converts to religion C and then to religion D. If he converts back to religion B or C, he is required to give notice, but if he converts back to religion A, then no notice is required. This also, according to us, is totally irrational and violative of Article 14 of the Constitution of India.[48]

---

[47] Section 2 (c), Arunachal Pradesh Freedom of Religion Act, 1978.

[48] Writ Petition No. 438 of 2011 in the matter of Evangelical Fellowship of India and Anr. vs. State of Himachal Pradesh.

Freedom of religion cannot be restricted via threat of violence

The restrictions under the various anti-conversion laws fall foul of the principle laid by the Supreme Court of India that constitutional rights cannot be denied simply because of hostility to their association.

The fear of mob violence due to conversions by "force," "fraud" and "allurement" cannot be a criterion to restrict religious freedoms. It is the duty of the state to control or contain non-state actors rather than impose restrictions on the fundamental rights of others. The test or standard is that of a reasonable man.

The Statement of Objects and Reasons in the HP Freedom of Religion Act, 2006 refers to "rise in conversions based on allurement generally" and to "a persistent demand from across the different strata of the society, urging the State Government to curb it" as, otherwise it may "erode the confidence and mutual trust between the different religious and ethnic groups in the State."[49]

Similarly, the statement of objects and reasons of the Law in Gujarat states that,

> ...conversions from one religion to another are made by use of force or allurement or by fraudulent means. Bringing in a legislation to prohibit such conversions will act as deterrent against anti-social and vested interest groups exploiting the innocent people belonging to depressed classes and will enable people to practice their own religion freely. It will also be useful to maintain public order and to nip in the bud the attempts by certain subversive forces to create social tension.[50]

The anti-conversion laws have been enacted on the basis that conversions by force, fraud or inducement disrupt public order.

Besides, the Indian Penal Code has several provisions to deal with coercion and threats. Hamid Ansari, the former Vice President of India and the former chairperson of the National Minorities was quoted in *Tehelka* as saying, "If somebody has carried out a conversion by use of force or cheating, then there are enough provisions in the Indian Penal Code to bring him or her to book." He added,

---

[49] Himachal Pradesh Freedom of Religion Act, 2006.
[50] Gujarat Freedom of Religion Act, 2003.

"Also, there is no data to establish that cases of conversion derived through coercion or cheating were sufficient to deserve special laws. It is sheer absurdity."[51]

Conclusion

A detailed analysis of the Acts reveals that far from promoting or protecting religious freedom, they have served to undermine the religious freedom guarantees under Article 14, 19, 21, 25 and 26 of the Constitution of India and various international laws and treaties to which India is signatory.

Primarily motivated by a religious ideology, the anti-conversions laws fail to achieve the very purpose for which they have been enacted. On the contrary, they provide an opportunity to divisive forces within the country to target the constitutionally protected rights of minority groups and pose a serious threat to the free practice and propagation of religious beliefs.

The presence of religious freedom in a country mathematically correlates with the presence of other fundamental, responsible freedoms (including civil and political liberty, press freedom, and economic freedom) and with the longevity of democracy. Studies[52] have found that religious freedom fosters better health outcomes, higher levels of earned income, fewer incidents of armed conflict and better educational opportunities for women.

India's civil society, judiciary, legislature and executive, as well as the international community, need to work towards the repealing or striking down of these laws as they threaten not only the Indian ethos of tolerance and communal harmony but also undermine India's overall economic and social development.

---

[51] Dutt, "Raipur's One-Way Conversion Street," 37.

[52] Brian J. Grim and Clark, Greg and Snyder, Robert Edward, "Is Religious Freedom Good for Business?: A Conceptual and Empirical Analysis" *Interdisciplinary Journal of Research on Religion* 10, no. 4 (2014). See also Amartya Sen, *Development as Freedom,* 2nd ed. (Oxford, New York: Oxford University Press, 2001).

Contours of Democracy, Freedom, and Faith in the Indian Context: A Brechtian Approach to "Seeing" the Complexities Involved

A. S. Dasan[1] and Nalini Xavier[2]

Today, we live in an era of globalization, moving cultures, and ever-expanding knowledge-societies. Migration, cross-cultural communication, and crisscrossing of cultural identities which may be viewed as ripple effects caused by the era, have widened the prospects for broader understanding of democracy, freedom, faith, and human development mediated through cross-cultural influence and interdependence. Globalization as such has facilitated the emergence of global elitism that has altered power-relations and has created polarization "between the mobility of capital (global) and the immobility of labour (local)."[3] It ardently supports a variety of consumerist ethos and lifestyles that tend to glorify opulence and criminalize poverty which are, in fact, its own by-products. The "human consequences,"[4] to use the phrase of Zygmunt Bauman, wrought in by this era, are so mixed and complex that life in general, especially for the common man, becomes a struggle for "so many freedoms,"[5] to use a phrase of Mulk Raj Anand (1905-2004), the author of *Apology for Heroism* (1945). Living together in a multicultural ambience in the midst of differences, conflicts and tensions, and the midst of pursuits of so many freedoms, has become a perennial challenge. A "complex seeing,"[6] to borrow the

---

[1] Dr. A. S. Dasan has been the Professor of English at the University of Mysore (UoM). He is currently the Director of Shukrodaya's Academy for HRD (Human Resource Development), Mysore. He is co-editor of *India: A People Betrayed* (Goodwill Fellowship Academy, 1993).

[2] Mrs. Nalini Xavier is the Associate Professor of English at Teresian College, Mysore.

[3] Zygmunt Bauman, *Globalization: The Human Consequences* (New York: Columbia University Press, 1998), 7.

[4] Also the subtitle of Bauman's book.

[5] Mulk Raj Anand, *Apology for Heroism* (1945; repr. New Delhi: Arnold-Heinemann Publishers, 1975), 39.

[6] Bertolt Brecht, *Brecht on Theatre: The Development of an Aesthetic*, trans. John

phrase of Bertolt Brecht (1898-1956), an outstanding German poet and playwright of the 20th century, is required to capture the ingredients, complexities, and implications of the human consequences and the challenges faced, and to look for answers to the problems endured.

Furthermore, quite a number of problematizations vis-à-vis human consequences have already been documented by various thinkers and writers. "The clash of civilizations,"[7] interrogation and deconstruction of monosyllabic arrogation of power (Derrida, Foucault, and others), challenging of all forms of cultural hegemony, exploitation, and oppression, questioning of ex-cathedra dogmas and teachings, and above all, critiquing of "the globalization of indifference,"[8] to use the phrase of David B. Couturier, to the plight of the poor, marginalized further by the processes of globalization, may be mentioned here as areas/arenas documented. Huntington's *The Clash of Civilizations and the Remaking of World Order* (1996), Zygmunt Bauman's *Globalization: The Human Consequences* (1998), Thomas Nail's *The Figure of the Migrant* (2015) and *Civilizational Dialogue and World Order* (2009), edited by M.S. Michael and Fabio Petito—these writings are eminently readable reflections based on the musings/works from philosophers, historians, sociologists, thinkers with the background of cultural anthropology and political economy, theoreticians, and theologians, taking a hard look at history, ethics, and economic and social consequences of globalization. A reading of the these books could enlighten us further on the mappings of how cultures and new knowledge societies across civilizations have been on the move, negotiating the human consequences globalization and migration have wrought in, dismantling cultural hegemonies and colonial and neo-colonial impacts, and redefining identities with a perennial plea for reciprocal recognition of one another's worldviews, existential concerns, and

Willett, ed. Steve Giles (New York: Hill and Wang, 1964), 44.

[7] Samuel P. Huntington, *The Clash of Civilizations and the Remaking of World Order* (New York: Simon and Schuster, 1996).

[8] David B. Couturier, "The Globalization of Indifference and the Franciscan Imagination," St. Bonaventure University, accessed on August 15, 2017, https://www.academia.edu/8839118/The_Globalization_of_Indifference_and_the_Franciscan_Imagination.

hopes and aspirations. These readings substantiated by learnings and insights across disciplines, which divergently comment on the developments and impacts happening in the era of globalization, would convince us why we need to appreciate the fact that we also live in an age of civilizational dialogue and why we need to sustain dialogue, accommodativeness, and inclusivity as paramount values in any human living context across civilizations.

Vis-à-vis the theme of the Consultation proposed and organized by SAIACS, it is relevant to note that this era has also contributed to, as Augustine Kanjamala notes, "an unprecedented sprouting of unbelievers and practical atheists" in the midst of "increase in the number of faith seekers."[9] As this era has amplified the contours of democracy, freedom, and faith as concomitant values, it is important that the thematic focus of the Consultation, namely Religious Freedom and Conversion, is deliberated upon in the light of and against the backdrop of the human consequences endured by humans everywhere. It is important to note that, with traditional religion and ritualistic spirituality on the decline, particularly in the developed West, which makes its denting impact upon developing countries by way of extension of globalization and moving cultures, conventional exclusivist approaches to the proclamation of the Word, evangelizing missions bordering on adding numbers to a particular religious fold as if salvation were possible only through that particular religion, has been another area problematized in varied circles. As Kanjamala comments further, "multiple conflicts, contradictions, and dichotomies of life" have propelled humans to search for the ultimate meaning of life.[10] It is towards this search that religions continue to play strategic roles "in creating sacred cosmos for protecting humanity against the nightmare of chaos."[11] In the course of negotiating and defining individual, social, cultural, and collective identities, humans are also aware of the fact that "man does not live by bread alone," and he needs to tap other intangible resources required to face the human

---

[9] Augustine Kanjamala, *The Future of Christian Mission in India: Toward a New Paradigm for the Third Millennium* (Mumbai: St. Paul's Publications, 2014), 292
[10] Kanjamala, *Future of Christian Mission*, 293
[11] Kanjamala, *Future of Christian Mission*, 315

consequences, required for cultivating collective responsibility to promote social harmony and human solidarity and for expanding and enhancing the opportunities for upholding the principles of personal freedom, self-dignity, social equality, economic security, and distributive justice beneficial to all.

Against this backdrop, it is important that, we, as Christians in the public square, cultivate and nurture a glocalized/holistic perspective of the era we live in. Such a perspective arrived at by using complex seeing as a device for critical analysis calls for a number of paradigm shifts in the way we think, communicate, interrelate, negotiate, and formulate our worldviews and organize our mission stations and perform public ministries. It calls for, as Snyder insists, "witnessing to Kingdom values rather than building Churches" in terms of numbers added on to the Christian fold.[12] In the light of such a perspective, democracy and freedom, not totalitarianism, monarchy, dictatorship, or army-regime, are viewed as the best means to realize the above-mentioned objectives and to strive to achieve the goals set. Democracy and freedom are two well-known intangible resources which could serve as valuable means towards achieving the goals which could facilitate building a civil society capable of safeguarding, enhancing, and ennobling the dignity of all without discrimination or exploitation. Democracy and freedom have also contributed to the contours of religious freedom and faith, ushering in the blossoms and fragrances of inter-religiosity as part of multicultural living. Vice versa, religious freedom and diversity of faiths have also enriched the traditions of democracy and freedom, widening the discourses on human rights and enhancing the scope for affirming human solidarity. Research done with reference to political histories of select nations also points out that it is the religious freedom that serves as the source of strengthening all other freedoms and facilitating the longevity of democracy.

There is a perception that when migration is inevitable and when inter-cultural communication has its own conflicts and tensions, it is religion—religion as an agency of questing for transcendence, for God, or for self-realization—that stands as a leveller, as a pillar of hope for resolving crises arising out of ethnic clashes, class tangles, communal tensions, and intolerance towards

[12] H. Snyder, *Liberating the Church* (Illinois: Inter-Varsity Press, 1983), 373

heterodox orthodoxies. Religious freedom is a matter of individual conviction and choice. There are also legal, socio-cultural, and theological implications. The Apex Court of India has intervened on the question of religious freedom as a fundamental right, and on the question of conversion by the use of force or by inducement or by any fraudulent means. Against the backdrop of exclusivist models of Church activities pursuing conversion to the Christian fold, the documents of the Catholic Church, especially reflections from the Second Vatican Council, Redemptoris Missio, Dialogue and Proclamation, Statements of Indian Theological Association, and the writings of Christian thinkers like Raymond Panikkar, D. S. Amalorpavadas, Bede Griffiths, M. Amaladoss, H. Snyder, M. M. Thomas, K. C. Abraham, A. J. Appasamy, Chenchiah, Kaj Baggo, J.R.Chandran, S. J. Samartha, Monica Cooney and others who proposed and supported different modes of conversion (models of inclusive mission, meaning redemption wrought by Jesus Christ is an inclusive one), other than physical conversion/proselytization, as tenable alternatives/options in the age of civilizational/inter-religious/cross-cultural dialogues, is useful. The point of concern is when religious freedom is extended to convert people coercively, especially the people at the grassroots, through baits and inducements, when the marginalized or voiceless poor yield to the gratis granted and get converted under the compulsions of poverty and ignorance without any kind of personal enlightenment, conversions become problematic, all the more when violence intrudes with hatred in the name of defending faiths, forcing the State to enact laws against coerced conversions. This is a reality in India today, in the land that has been the birthplace and cradle of four major world religions, namely Hinduism, Jainism, Buddhism and Sikhism; the land that has centuries-old legacies for a tolerant and understanding culture rather than abstraction culture; the land that has consciously promoted compassionate aesthetics manifesting concern for the Other with a fine spirit of accommodativeness.

Questions such the ones mentioned here below have been raised in various fora: Can religious freedom mean absolute fundamental right to convert? What is the meaning of conversion? Is not conversion from one faith to another an act that is against the very nature of religion? If all religions lead to God, why should there be conversion? Is Christianity superior to other religions? Should Christianity be the only pathway to salvation as some evangelist-missionaries believe, argue, and propagate when they indulge in conversion activities? Is dialogue relevant? Is Christian mission one of expansion of churches? Is not witnessing to gospel values more meaningful than mission construed as expansion? Is mass conversion tenable in a democracy where it counts in terms of demography and vote banks? When India has sufficient number of religions, where is the necessity for conversion? When conversion causes cultural alienation, and ruptures and conflicts in society, and when it has alarming political consequences, should it be encouraged? Is it okay when conversion is exercised as an act of social protest against caste oppression/discrimination?

In the light of these introductory observations and reflections, this paper posits that although India's success story of democracy, freedom, and faith co-existing amidst diverse and ethnically heterogeneous social groups with politicized caste and class divisions is a significant phenomenon, India is a paradoxically complex entity. Complex Seeing, the Brechtian critical canon, is a discursive way of reading the contrapuntal relationality of an issue or a subject matter in question or a problem in hand. Brecht used this canon as a way of "evoking critical response from the audience so as to transform society."[13] We bring in this canon here in order to stress on and highlight the complex co-relationality India evokes when we think of the contours of faith, freedom, and democracy. Complex Seeing, in the words of Brecht, is a critical exercise in "thinking above the stream rather than thinking within the stream."[14] It opens critical possibilities from the point of the audience, expert-detachment perspective of the spectator. Commenting on the idea of Brecht, Raymond Williams states that Complex Seeing is also capable of projecting a double edged-vision, both within and above as well, that could usher in a contrapuntal, diachronic-synchronic perspective. Using the Brechtian critical canon for reading the contrapuntal relationality of the issues related to the theme of the Consultation, this paper, a joint-venture (co-authorship), draws its argumentative strength from the foundational value-matrices

[13] Brecht, *Brecht on Theatre*, 47
[14] Brecht, *Brecht on Theatre*. 49

stated in the introductory part of the paper and views India's intriguing but tainted democracy as a paradoxical-metaphorical site for multiperspectival Complex Seeing. Complex Seeing facilitates making sense of the present out of the existential angst and turmoil endured. It accommodates a glocal and dialogic way of looking at ground realities. In the course of self-reflexive and discursive musings, this paper connotes that an applause to religious freedom and conversion is tenable when they are practised in an ambience of enlightened dialogue, wherein shared wisdom prevails without discrediting other faiths, and more importantly, when they are geared towards realizing the principles stated above. Conversion happening in such an ambience will seldom be faulted.

To elaborate, religious freedom today is a hot and sensitive topic in the midst of the clash of civilizations, to quote Huntington again. Those who are familiar with his above mentioned book could see how Huntington, through his seminal mapping of paradigm shifts, examines "the struggle between democracy and communism based on ideological differences giving way to cultural patterns in the context of a post-Cold War New World Order, and how he posits that cohesion could be found within cultural boundaries."[15] Our point is that within these new cultural patterns which foreground dialogic paradigms, there is little space for cultural hegemony as a monolithic force, say the hegemony of the West for instance; little space for triumphalist expansionism in the name of crusades, discrediting other religions and faiths, to which the Christian-proselytization-effort has contributed its share with or without qualms of culpability, or desecrating temples, or churches, or mosques, or gurudwaras indulged in by radical fundamentalist-groups which tend to promote chauvinism and religious fanaticism with violence as a strategy; and little space for hidden agendas of varied shades and intents sustained with an eye on demography and vote bank politics, or for certain other mundane reasons.

India is a fine metaphorical site for such a Complex Seeing. India's complex cultural politics makes it inevitable that not only the correlation between faith, freedom, and democracy is strong, evolving, interstitial and complex, but also the democratic option to practise one's faith, or to opt for, or facilitate others to opt for another

[15] Huntington, *Clash of Civilizations*, 6

faith, which is often construed as conversion, is often constricted by a number of extraneous factors coming in the form of imbibed belief-systems and attitudes, ideological differences, contested secular ethos, interventionist or interferential politics, cultural chauvinism, religious orthodoxies, fundamentalist importuning, traditional and conservative hermeneutics, and political hypocrisy and misgovernance aggravated by systemic deficiencies. This is one of the paradoxes with which we live in India today.

The Complex Seeing, as we see vis-à-vis the focus of this paper, is twofold: On the one hand, the challenges Hindutva's chauvinistic-discourse poses today with averments such as "the nation is Hindi, Hindu, and Hindustan," strike at the core of the founding vision of India, ingrained in the Constitution of India; incites and perpetuates the politics of hatred; and causes disunity among citizenry; and on the other, the minoritarian triumphalist approach to evangelical mission, often espoused in the name of narrow interpretations of Jer.10:8-10, Is. 44:9-20, Ps. 115:4-8, Mark 15:16, Acts 4:12, 1Pet. 2:9, Exod. 19:5, and Rom. 10:9, and fanned by mission-aid agencies, proclaiming as if "Christianity were the only hope for salvation," batter the fate of the converted poor to a realm of passive receptivity besides irritating Hindutva's fringe elements who see all missionary activities with a suspicious mind. Readers may be aware of the mission history of churches and of evangelical missionaries like street preachers, exclusive salvation-sellers, Bible peddlers, charismatic miracle workers, and missionaries of apocalyptic eschatology fanning positions such as the one taken by Hendrik Kraemer (1880-1965), the Dutch theologian who was a missionary in Java, Indonesia, against the backdrop of the International Missionary Conference in Jerusalem in 1928 and later in Tambaram, Chennai, in 1938, and who, influenced by the neo-orthodoxy of Karl Barth, restated that "non-Christian religions are human achievement," meaning that "there is a radical discontinuity between non-Christian religions and the revelation of Jesus Christ, and the Ultimate Reality can be known only by God's gratuitous revelation."[16] In this context, it may be relevant to remember what S. Radhakrishnan, one of the finest exponents of Indian philosophy states: "All truth about God has its source in God. The conception

---

[16] Kanjamala, *The Future of Christian Mission*, 290

of a unique revelation of a chosen people is contrary to the love and justice of God," and he adds, "In the new world order such a view of spiritual monopolies has no place."[17]

Critical considerations point out that Hindutva's nationalism is an antithesis to democracy, to the religious pluralism of India, and to the multi-perspectival and multi-dimensional view of secularism tenable within the framework of the Constitution of India. As per the Constitution of India, India is "a secular State" (Preamble), and religious freedom—"freedom to believe in, practise, and promote one's religion peacefully"—is a guaranteed fundamental right (Articles 15 and 25) available to every citizen of the country. From this point of view, the modern Statehood of India is built, as Rajni Kothari comments, "on the foundations of a civilisation that is fundamentally non-religious."[18] But the ground reality is that in the course of balancing ideas such as modernity, liberalism, secularism, and democratic citizenship, Indian polity has been having an uphill task in maintaining a safe distance between religion and State. As Deepa Das Acevedo points out in an article titled, "Secularism in the Indian Context," "the desire to separate religion and State" may be an integral part of the Constitutional framework but "in reality India is never meant to be secular."[19] Here lies the ambivalence, ambiguity, and dilemma that fans the majoritarian and minoritarian discourses, often ending up with social conflicts and tensions.

It is unfortunate, shallow and communal that the political wing of RSS/VHP-prompted Hindutva today speaks of instilling cultural nationalist consciousness in the minds of minorities as if minorities were outsiders and anti-national. The subtlety with which saffronized agendas are forced into the psyche of the citizenry of India under the tutelage of the RSS that has a say in the Modi-fied version of Indian polity, smacks of the extent of the ideological addiction to which the promoters of RSS/VHP agendas are expected to adhere, causing enormous damage to the cause of

---

[17] Sarvepalli Radhakrishnan, *Religion in a Changing World* (New York: Humanities, 1967), 59

[18] Rajini Kothari, *State and Nation-Building* (Bombay: Allied, 1976), 26

[19] Deepa Das Acevedo, "Secularism in the Indian Context," *Law & Social Inquiry* 38, no. 1 (Winter 2013): 138-167.

religious pluralism that the Indian Constitution subscribes to and to the appreciation and assimilation of polymorphic constants in the course of arriving at truth, a process with which we Indians, in general, are fine with. Hindutva's subtle attempts to saffronize education in India based on Hindu *dharma* enunciated by V.D.Savarkar (1883-1966) and the ideology of the RSS formulated by Kesav Baliram Hedgewar (1889-1940), the founder of the RSS, and modified and restructured by M. S. Golwalkar (1906-1973), the successor of Hedgewar, and the recent ruptured attempt to ban the Ambedkar Periyar Study Circle (APSC), a student-association at IIT, Chennai, for having criticized Modi, the government's Hindutva agenda, and the Brahminical caste-hegemony at the IIT, may be cited here as instances. In parenthesis, it is significant to note, as Shreya Roy reports, quoting Shehla Rashid Shora, Vice-President of Jawaharlal Nehru University Students' Union (JNUSU), that JNUSU has "consistently raised its voice against the blatant attempts by the Modi government at backdoor appointments of RSS members to key institutions, against Hindutva myths being passed off as 'ancient science', against introduction of regressive content in textbooks and against the homogenisation of culture in the name of vegetarianism, and linguistic uniformity."[20]

Diversity, inclusivity and accommodative-ness are principles ingrained in the assimilation of the Indian cultural polymorphic constants. Hindutva affiliates, "more than fifty in number" as per Kundukulam, fabricate theories and arguments to deny these principles "through their strategy of syncretism."[21] As Ambrose Pinto critiques, "the Sangh Parivar is anti-national and unconstitutional group. They have not been part of our freedom struggle. They are uncomfortable with the Constitution of India,"[22] and they have a hidden agenda of rewriting the Constitution of India to redefine

[20] Shreya Roy Chowdhury, "Subramanian Swamy as JNU VC: Students Threaten Protests," *Times of India*, September 24, 2015, accessed on August 15, 2017, http://timesofindia.indiatimes.com/home/education/news/Subramanian-Swamy-as-JNU-VC-Students-threaten-protests/articleshow/49091157.cms.

[21] Vincent Kundukulam, "Conversion in the Hindutva Context," June 23, 2012, accessed on August 15, 2017, https://nelsonmcbs.wordpress.com/2012/06/23/conversion-in-the-hindutva-context/.

[22] Ambrose Pinto, "The Challenges of Hindutva to Minorities, Christians, and Dalits," *Vidyajyoti Journal of Theological Reflection* 79, no. 5 (May 2015): 339.

the notion of building a secular India on their terms, which are inimical and detrimental to the spirit of religious freedom guaranteed in the Constitution. If any breed or brand of evangelical Hinduism thrives on negating these ingredients, it is doing a disservice to the tradition of Indic thought. The "new-age gurus" and "ammas," with their huge following from across continents and huge funds generated, may sustain their new-age evangelism for some more time. But that does not prevent us from seeing their negation of the polymorphic constants as a subtle way of amputating the Indian constitutional provision that guarantees co-existence of various religions and diverse beliefs and provides scope for religious freedom and conversions, without belittling other faiths.

In this context, a sticky point for the strain in majority-minority relations and for religious and communal tensions, must be addressed. It is a known and repeated allegation that religious conversion to Christianity is "a deliberate and organised campaign to undermine Hinduism," and this strain boils down, as Rudolf C. Heredia points out, periodically "into riots and pogroms against defenceless Christians."[23] This allegation, as Heredia adds, is "part of the Hindutva's political ideology," a long-time strategy "to instil cultural and Hindu religious nationalism" that "seeks to gain popular religious legitimacy for a partisan, chauvinistic politics."[24] Hindutva's agenda "to identify India as Hindu, or Muslims as aliens, negates a millennium-old tradition of Indo-Islamic culture, besides the numerous other cultural streams that have flowed into and vitalized the rivers of Indian civilization."[25] Sufficient documentation is available to argue that Hindutva's fears are unfounded. In this regard, we wish to draw the attention of the audience to an essay titled, "Why Christianity Failed in India," published in *Outlook*, dated April 13, 2015. Tony Joseph, former editor of Business World (though he bears a Christian name, he considers himself an atheist with a liking for the original teachings of the Buddha), critically comments on one of the known Hindutva right-wing narratives,

---

[23] C. Rudolf Heredia, "Hindu Rashtra and Religious Minorities," *Vidyajyoti Journal of Theological Reflection* 79, no. 5 (May 2015): 348.
[24] Heredia, "Hindu Rashtra," 351.
[25] Heredia, "Hindu Rashtra," 351.

namely "Christianity is a serious threat to Hinduism."[26] He notes that right-wingers hold onto this argument all the more if they are aware of a book like the one (1876) written by James Vaughan, a missionary who spent 19 years in Kolkatta and who made a prediction then about "a great turnabout in the fortunes of Christianity in India," 150 years hence, say by 2026.[27] He states that they press this panic button also when they see certain evangelists/charismatic pastors of different denominations (these may not be affiliated to mainstream churches) doing conversion activities openly in poverty-stricken areas with some material benefits added, or when they come to know of faith-healing meetings bordering on quackery.[28] But in the course of his critical and precise comments, he debunks and demolishes, with convincing data-based evidence, the myth / misinformed assertion that Christianity is a threat to Hinduism.[29] The comparative statistics he gives in the essay are crystal clear in pointing out where Christianity stands in India today vis-à-vis demography (just around 3% even after its presence in India for more than eighteen centuries).[30]

Coming back to the twofold focus of Complex Seeing, minoritarian triumphalism can also be a dangerous phenomenon as it subtly tends to deny the prospect of soteriological pluralism, implying that there is no redemption outside the Christian fold/faith. Its targeting the poor who are not part of the mainstream, is viewed as suspect. It is high time that mission-aid agencies and evangelical pastors realize that salvation is possible outside the churches as the Holy Spirit blows wherever it wills, even outside the churches, and therefore, inter-religious dialogues and witnessing to gospel values are more important and relevant than adding numbers to the Christian fold. Mere material support received from abroad or from sources within the country cannot be the basis for ghetto-evangelical missions or conversion ventures. With more and

---

[26] Tony Joseph, "Why Christianity Failed in India," *Outlook*, April 13, 2015, accessed on August 15, 2017, http://www.outlookindia.com/article/why-christianity-failed-in-india/293895.

[27] Joseph, "Why Christianity Failed in India."

[28] Joseph, "Why Christianity Failed in India."

[29] Joseph, "Why Christianity Failed in India."

[30] Joseph, "Why Christianity Failed in India."

more Christians moving away from dogmatic-influence-wielding churches because the issues and problems they grapple with in the contemporary postmodern age—such as contraception, abortion, cohabitation, gay marriages, absence of effective women-leadership within churches, and failure to capture the angst of the youth—are so heavy and hot that churches across continents are failing to address them efficaciously and therapeutically because they lack adequate moral and spiritual resources to tackle these, and with more and more churches being converted into shopping malls/business centres by virtue of the alarming decline among church-goers, evangelical missions in aid-receiving countries are likely to face hard times in terms of material support, and ministering pastors will have to cope with survival problems.

As noted earlier, there are warning bells rung and heard from varied emerging trends and forces in the name of cultural nationalism and religious fundamentalism to indicate that conversions will be problematized, challenged, and countered by violence or by re-conversion processes, which gentle and peace-loving missionaries may find difficult to match or compete with. Hindutva's Ghar Wapsi programme is one instance of countering. The comfort levels these forces enjoy when parties sympathetic to their moves are in power are far reaching and have some disturbing consequences. The "filial endorsement RSS tends to give to Modi government" and "individual ministers of Modi government encouraged to meet with Sangh-Parivar-affiliate organisations on issues concerning their ministries" may be cited here as an instance of such "cozy arrangements."[31] It is a known fact that such outside interferences in the governance of the country are not taken to kindly by minorities. Muslim and Christian communities feel the heat but are helpless as they are often at the receiving end. Less said the better about minority-conscious fringe elements opting for bomb-culture or such other violent means.

Unless the majoritarian and the minoritarian discourses give up their muscular approach towards religion and to leadership; unless the ghetto-nationalist gimmickry of RSS agenda and the triumphalist ecclesiastical or evangelical authoritarianism get

---

[31] Nistula Hebbar, "A New Cozy Arrangement," *Hindu* (Bangalore), September 12, 2015.

deconstructed; and unless all the stakeholders are in a position to adapt to the changes happening and evolve and ensure certain paradigm shifts towards dialogicity and temporality (proclamation of the word / the mission as a dialogic temporal agency towards realizing certain common social goals) which would focus on cleansing politics, reducing, if not eliminating corruption, distributive social justice and aesthetics of harmonious living, people—believers in religion. The faithful are likely to move away from organized forms of religion. Their faith affinities are likely to be more liberal and flippant. Religious freedom and conversion will not be viewed as a better option. Conflicts will remain unresolved. Nihilistic relativism is likely to assert its presence, fanning existential angsts and contradictions. True freedom and democracy for all and development for all will take a backseat. Tainted MPs and MLAs will be on the rise. Leaders, like leeches, sucking India dry of her riches, will roam free. Fault lines will continue on caste and corrupt practices. "Remembering and deifying Ambedkar as an iconic leader," for instance, will have, as Sandipan Sharma notes, "many advantages," to political power-mongers in terms of vote banks.[32] In fact, in parenthesis, this is an affront against Ambedkar, whose analyses against casteism are seminal and whose vision for the conscientization of the oppressed classes is of paramount and enduring significance. His own conversion to Buddhism was a conscious option against the upper-caste hegemony. It is sad to note that even after decades, Ambedkar's dream of annihilating caste has not been achieved. Many of our politicians, afflicted with hubris, have no qualms in being self-incriminating when they say casteism and inequality are still there in India. Unless and until these issues are tackled, religious freedom and conversion will have little relevance to the marginalized poor whom zealous evangelical missions are particular to convert. As long as these issues remain as part of the maladies afflicting democracy in India, not only will freedom be an elusive goal but religious freedom will also be futile deadwood.

[32] Sandipan Sharma, "Bye, Bye Nehru, Hello Ambedkar: Here's What Rahul was Doing in Mhow," accessed on June 3, 2015, http://www.firstpost.com/politics/congress-new-avatar-more-of-dalits-and-ambedkar-less-of-nehru-gandhi-dynasty-2275598.html. *[editorial note: when last checked on August 15, 2017, the web-link was inactive]*

Another issue that should haunt the conscience of believers and preachers of majoritarian and minoritarian discourses is their affinity with the economically and politically powerful elite. It reminds us of the ethics that tended to promote the perception that salvation is more easily available to those who are economically fit. This can be noticed in the mentality of a number of churches, in spite of their tall claims and extraordinary proclamations on servant/self-emptying leadership with Jesus as the supreme role model. The poor among Christians, especially the poor converted from poverty-stricken backgrounds, feel let down by their pastors when they see their pastors hobnobbing with the rich and the powerful. The agony of true Christian believers—believers in various faith expressions/experiences—is that a this-worldly tendency prevails in spite of the affirmation of the incarnational presence of the Son of God, proclaiming the gospel of liberation of the marginalized poor, and in spite of the salvific value wrought in by Jesus's death on the cross with a preferential option for the poor. The hypocrisy behind such assertions, a sign of the chasm between proclamations and practice, is a perennial pinprick in our effort to witness to gospel values. It dents our credibility and makes religious freedom—as an option to move to Christianity— a mockery. It is time that we, as one community of believers in risen Christ, are collective and effective enough to solve this crisis of credibility, by a lifestyle of concrete witnessing to gospel values that include a conscious option for the education and development of the poor. It is only on the basis of our credible lifestyle that religious freedom can make many more positive impacts upon the moral and spiritual psyche of the people, believers in other faiths, to favourably consider the option for Christianity if they were to convert from one faith to another. Otherwise, we, as Christian believers in the risen Christ, have the risk of being branded as "ordinary people with extraordinary claims."

In the light of these observations and comments, this Consultation may be viewed as an occasion for self-reflexivity and redefining priorities for future ministries by churches. It would be good and illumining:

- to critically examine why and how a triumphalist approach to faith and conversion, just like Hindutva's nationalist approach to saffronization of education in India and to its Ghar Wapsi programmes, is doomed to be a risky failure in a country like ours where the very context of living is multicultural in terms of language, religion, faith, ideologies, attitudes, and practices, and where the clash of majority vs minority is an enduring phenomenon;

- to sensitize ourselves, whichever may be the denomination we belong to, in the art of de-learning and re-learning, re-learning to appreciate the fact that the Gospel of Jesus Christ and the Kingdom values Jesus preached are broad and wide enough to embrace all great humanistic traditions which cherish and promote "humanity that is plural." The Bible is quite articulate about the oneness and diversity of humanity. We, as Christians, are not alien to assimilating shared wisdom that accommodates differences and diversity. The shared wisdom that gospel values promote, cannot afford to ask: "am I the keeper of my brother?" Freedom to propagate one's religion, and freedom to convert, is not an absolute right to be upheld at the cost of disrespect to other religious traditions. Let us not ignore the prospect that salvation is possible outside the Church;

- to appreciate the fact that in today's plurality of cultures and contexts, new critical idioms for hermeneutics are indispensable and that we are all active partners / participants in the ongoing civilizational dialogue and that the new cultural patterns emerging from varied civilizations and continents promote dialogue, inclusivity, reciprocal recognition, and interdependence rather than hegemony, arrogation of power, and self-interest at the cost of the Other. Dialogue is not a naïve and idealistic notion. It is a way of listening to one another without mistrust, prejudice, and arrogation. Through dialogue, existential angsts can be addressed, turmoil and tensions can be reduced, and misunderstandings can be erased. Dialogue is a common platform where people meet together for common causes and priorities such as conscientizing education and critical literacy, that would ensure that people/masses believing in varied faiths and religious traditions come together for the cause of comprehensive human development, without discrimination based on religion, faith, class, caste, or community. Christians as a collective force, as one ecumenical community believing in one risen Christ, can play a leading role in this, in spite of their minority status in India;

- to encourage ways of journeying together as we are all part of the entirety of humanity and cannot afford to hold onto isolated/

islanded consciousness, as we are bound by varied cultures and faiths capable of intermingling cross-culturally, interlacing differences and foregrounding the importance and relevance of multi-perspectival dialoguing, lest conflicts and tensions should overpower humanity. Enculturation/inculturation that foregrounds and celebrates the contours of many-ness could be a fine strategy. It is a prerequisite for harmonious living that promotes inter-religious dialogue, mutual listening, shared wisdom, and understanding culture rather than abstraction culture. In fact, this strategy is in tune with the cosmopolitan tradition of Indic thought that accommodates hybridity and compassionate aesthetics. Indic civilization has been a significant contributor to sustaining the richness of the plurality of the human race;

- to read the signs of contemporary times wherein postmodernist ethos tries to ensure that relativity prevails, that religion and faith as universal categories with fixity of meaning and interpretations are problematized, that religion and faith become more or less a private affair or individual concern than a community celebration, that conversion from one religion to another, or from one faith to another, be viewed just as an act of convenience, and people, especially the youth, are fine with agnosticism, if not atheism, and to respond to the challenges involved in addressing the issues associated with such signs and trends;

- to subscribe to the view that true conversion in the sense of metanoia is seldom. This is why Jesus, by implication, maintained, as L. Legrand, one of the finest internationally acclaimed and ecumenically esteemed Biblical scholars, used to emphasize at in the course of his teaching and interaction with students, that "witnessing is always by a few". What should matter to us, just as to Jesus, is not the number but quality. Whether true religion and true faith can survive in the midst of institutionalization of religions, hierarchical paraphernalia, pharisaic lifestyles of preachers, majority-minority conflict-induced fear-psychosis, and helplessness of believers who are just fine with Sunday obligations and popular devotions, is a moot point. What would really count in terms of attracting more people to believe in Jesus is our own lifestyle that could serve as "the fifth gospel exhibiting the values and fruits of the Spirit,"[33] inspired and strengthened by the four Gospels of the New Testament. In the words of Snyder, those who live a lifestyle witness to gospel values are known as "Kingdom

---

[33] Madathikandam, "Conversion in the Hindutva Context," 2

people" different from "church people."³⁴ He states: "Kingdom people seek first the Kingdom of God and its justice; church people often put church work above concerns of justice, mercy and truth."³⁵ Church people think about how to get people into the church; Kingdom people think about how to get the Church into the world.³⁶ Church people worry that the world might change the Church; Kingdom people work to see the Church change the world,"³⁷ and by doing so,

- to acknowledge the fact that the life of Jesus of Nazareth is the finest story of unconditional and embracing love ever told and exemplified on earth with the cross as an oxymoronic metaphor for "the violence of love." Oscar A. Romero, the author of *The Violence of Love*, draws attention to "the violence that nailed Jesus to the Cross, the violence of brotherhood that inspires and propels us to overcome our selfishness and cruel inequalities among us."³⁸ Romero's own martyrdom in the El Salvadorian context of poverty and social injustices and his book are reminders that the gentle-shepherd-leadership approach Jesus promoted by his lifestyle is in sharp contrast to the muscular leadership practised by politicians of varied hues and ideologies and also by some of our bishops and pastors.

To conclude, India's saga is one of oxymoronic complex paradoxes vis-à-vis democracy, freedom, and faith. In this saga, many things co-exist in the midst of miracles and misdeeds, strengths and weaknesses, and greatness and deficiencies. Policy changes and policy paralysis and religious and social attitudes have travelled together in making India what she is today. Though we, the people of India, are in a democracy—democracy of the people, by the people, and for the people—ours is a tainted democracy mainly because it is based on corrupt vote bank politics, where votes of the most of the common people, especially the poor and the marginalized, have often, if not always, been up for grabs. This is so even today, even after almost seven decades of India's Independence. In the midst

---

[34] Snyder, *Liberating*, 376
[35] Synder, *Liberating*, 376
[36] Synder, *Liberating*, 376
[37] Snyder, *Liberating*, 378.
[38] A. Oscar Romero, *The Violence of Love* (Chicago: Orbis Books, 1988).

of such a state of affairs, our perception of religious freedom and conversion cannot be a simple phenomenon.

Ideally, from the perspective of true freedom, democracy as a form of governance should challenge all forms of discrimination based on caste, class, religion, and faith. It should uphold a system of openness based on equal rights of citizenship. It should provide opportunities for the people to exercise their choices in a free and fair manner. In a multi-cultural and multi-religious country like ours, democracy should encourage freedom of conscience to every citizen, promote religious tolerance and inter-religious dialogue, and ensure that conversion does not become a reason for social ostracism or exclusion. The problem in India is that the taint of democracy makes sure that democracy is the enemy of the liberty of the people to exercise free choices. Democratic vote bank politics is so corrupt that politicians with tainted mindsets get elected by popular support, forcing thinking minds to ask whether India's democracy revolves around the formula, thus-the-leaders-so-the-governance or thus-the-people-so-the-governance. Let us not forget that even Adolf Hitler was democratically elected. The point is that when democracy is tainted to this extent, governance becomes a subtle form of denying people freedom as an opportunity. The point is that corruption smothers India's prospects for development for all, and it is political and moral corruption that pervades all spectrum of life in India. In other words, the idea of a truly democratic India is still a mirage. Despite efforts among India's elite in politics, the media, the academia and think tanks to re-define issues and recast the political debate, people are subjugated to underdevelopment that may not be viewed anymore as starvation and hunger but poverty endured in terms of classes and disparities. Let us, as Christians, be sensitized more towards these ground realities so that our focus, social activism, and witnessing ministries are geared towards changing/creating a new society of true democracy and true freedom meaningful to all, rather than just adding numbers to our own respective Christian folds.

The role and importance of religion and faith in world politics cannot be ignored in the midst of pursuing economic development goals. Religion, with its renewed vigour and vitality, can serve as a refuge against all kinds of onslaughts upon human freedom, inspiring people to ensure that right values are cherished and practised. As Huntington comments, religion as "a major social factor in shaping identity, giving stability to community, and providing certain moral precepts with a sense of meaning and purpose," has always been impactful and significant throughout history across civilizations.[39] As India is in the throb of globalization, as the country is a land of many cultures and religions, and as we are all participants in one way or the other in the process of civilizational dialogue, let us learn to appreciate the fact that cultures are on the move, role and relevance of religions are undergoing metamorphoses, and identities are crisscrossing. Let this appreciation caution us against hegemony, cultural chauvinism, or evangelical triumphalism, or religious fundamentalism, all of which takes us nowhere, definitely not to God-consciousness. Dialogue is the way forward to human progress, equality, fellowship, social harmony, happiness, and peace. Let religious freedom revolve around dialogue and let us leave the task of conversion to God and the person concerned. Then, *metanoia* will happen, ushering in social, cultural, and spiritual transformation.

It is time that we, Christians, fine with valuing religious freedom and the consequent right to convert, are sensitized with deeper critical literacy on these ground realities, which can make us realize that the right to convert is not an absolute one and it is tamed by, mediated through, and is subject to public order, social harmony, and peace. Let churches focus more and more on becoming instruments of transforming structures that sustain corrupt politics, tainted democracy, and dehumanizing poverty, lest they should be seen as agents of conversion. It is time that ex-cathedra/dogmatic/magisterial approach in the name of being the official holders of truth gives way to dialogic reasoning, lest hegemonic and monological base and superstructures should prevail. Monocratic, muscular-leadership oriented, and exclusivist evangelical churches could give way to servant-leadership churches with more and more people-centric, justice-and fellowship-focused concrete action plans, so that churches could be better equipped to demand similar paradigm shifts in the secular polity and bureaucracy of the nation, in a much more credible and convincing manner.

[39] Huntington, *Clash of Civilizations*.

Let us be more sensitive to and be concerned about witnessing to gospel values, and act and behave in such a way that our trust in faith in the true Christian sense of the term does not remain as a constant deficit. It is time that Christian mainstream churches, particularly evangelical/missionary sects and charismatic groups, realize this fact so that they guide their community of believers in the right direction. The more and more they subscribe to di-achronic-synchronic civilizational dialogue, the better equipped they are in their mission of proclaiming and witnessing to the gospel values practised by Jesus Christ. Urging the Indian citizenry to move in the direction of de-communalising politics and fellowships of religious faith so that politics and faith could find their genuine democratic or human character, M. M. Thomas, an ecumenical theologian of repute, commends, in his cogently argued and lucidly written book, *The Church's Mission and Postmodern Humanism* (1996), that the effort of the main churches must be "to adapt to a secular mode as herald of the Kingdom and servant of the world in a pluralist society like India."[40] He calls for more and more "Open Churches," prepared, ready, and willing to be "in dialectical and dialogical relationship with religions and ideologies and cultures and in solidarity with peoples' movements for justice."[41] It is worth reading the book even today.

A Christian way of appreciating religious freedom has to emerge from and evolve within this experience of "gentle-shepherd-leadership."[42] Gentle-shepherd-leadership is capable of "becoming incarnate among the poor, becoming science for those who have no science, becoming the clear voice of those who have no voice," to use the words of Rev. Jon Sobrino, a Jesuit theologian.[43] Such leadership is part of "a pilgrim church, subject to misunderstanding, to persecution, but a church that walks serene, because it bears the force of love" as Romero insists.[44] Such leadership is

---

[40] M. M. Thomas, *The Church's Mission and Postmodern Humanism* (Tiruvalla and New Delhi: CSS and ISPCK, 1996).

[41] Thomas, *The Church's Mission.*

[42] Jon Sobrino, *Jesus the Liberator: A Historical-Theological View* (New York: Orbis Books, 2003).

[43] Sobrino, *Jesus the Liberator.*

[44] Romero, *Violence of Love.*

capable of seeing and critiquing the complexities associated with a polarized India that tends to "fragment into narrow domestic walls" and is prophetic enough to caution the flock never to "bend their knees before the insolent might," to refer to the musings of Rabindranath Tagore.[45] Such leadership witnesses to gospel values with the audacity of hope in action. This leadership knows that the gospel is a gift but it is also aware of the risks involved in witnessing to it, especially in secular/civil/social contexts, in the course becoming "the salt of the earth and the light of the world" (Matt. 5:13-16; Isa. 42:6). Such leadership would be a therapeutic way of dialoguing with the people of varied faiths and mental and spiritual dispositions, besides facilitating the people to find a surer way of genuflecting ultimately before the altar of "truth" that will makes all of us "free" (John 8:31-32). That altar is a yonder vision, a sign of hope for all, a venue for the carnivalesque/celebration of many cultures, identities, and shared values, which would be in resonance with many other religious/faith traditions, in the presence of God who is particular to save every one of us without discrimination or exclusion.

Let us permit ourselves to be led into that heaven of freedom, which is inclusive, humane, and Christian at the same time. Let all our resources, both tangible and intangible, flow towards this end that could usher in a common fellowship, *koinonia* (κοινωνία) wherein all could take part transcending/sublimating all our religious and cultural particularities into a unification of aesthetics and sensibilities, godly and earthly at the same time, which could reflect and manifest the glory of existence against all forms of brutality in the name of religion. Let us ensure that all our theological pedagogies and methodologies have, as K.C. Abraham suggests, "paradigm-shifts towards a new transforming vision" like the one envisaged in this paper.[46] As Christians, let us be open to God's intervention in our lives, move ahead with prayer and with capacity to be born again of the Spirit. Let us outreach to the world with hope in action through dialogue. It is in such openness and

---

[45] Rabindranath Tagore, *Gitanjali* (Song Offerings) (London: Macmillan, 1913).

[46] K. C. Abraham, *Transforming Vision: Theological-Methodological Paradigm Shifts* (Tiruvalla: Christava Sahitya Samithi, 2006), 281

dialogue that, as Francis Gonsalves reminds us, "the challenges and immense possibilities of Churches in India" lie today.[47] Let our revised Christology acknowledge "One Christ and many Religions," as Samartha says.[48] Let us not forget that the Spirit of God "blows wherever it pleases" (John 3:8), and that should guide us towards dialogue with other religions, keeping in mind certain common goals for the cause of humanity. In the light of such openness and conviction, let us learn to recite the *shanthi mantra* (prayer of peace) taken from Brihadaranyaka Upanishads (1.3.28):

Asato mā sadgamaya
(From ignorance, lead me to truth)

Tamasomā jyotir gamaya
(From darkness, lead me to light)

Mrityormāamritam gamaya
(From death, lead me to immortality).

---

[47] Francis Gonsalves, "The Challenges and Possibilities of Indian Church Today" *Religion and Society* 55, no. 4 (December 2010): 74
[48] S. J. Samartha, *One Christ, Many Religions: Towards a Revised Christology* (Bangalore: SATHRI, 1992).

Reconstructing Early Christian Posture in Lucan Historical Writing from a Postcolonial Perspective

Roji T George[1]

Introduction

This paper seeks to view the *Acts of the Apostles* as a postcolonial literature articulating an ambivalent response of the Christian minority community constantly in consent-conflict with the dominant cultural-political forces in power. The issue of freedom to practise one's own religion and to propagate, accept, or reject, any religion has been a bone of contention transculturally through the centuries. Even Luke, the author of Acts of the Apostles, appears to narrate the story of the "Freedom of Religion and Conversion" of the early Christians in his Jewish and Greco-Roman context. Through the centuries, the Lucan scholarship has consistently maintained that Luke's primary intention was to narrate the origin, growth, and expansion of Christianity from Jerusalem, the capital of a defeated nation (Judea), to Rome, the imperial capital.[2] However, what is often forgotten in such a reconstruction of the Lucan intent is to consider Acts as a discursive literary response of the early Christian subjugated community towards "the Powers that Be" in the context of threat to the rights of the colonized subjects to preach, teach, and practise "the Truth."

---

[1] Dr. Roji T. George is Professor of New Testament at SAIACS, Bangalore. He has authored *Paul's Identity in Galatians: A Postcolonial Appraisal* (New Delhi: CWI, 2016). He has recently published an edited volume under the title *The Holy Spirit and Christian Mission in a Pluralistic Context* (Bangalore: SAIACS Press, 2017).

[2] For instance, Brian S. Rosner, "The Progress of the Word," in *Witness to the Gospel: The Theology of Acts*, eds. I. Howard Marshall and David Peterson (Grand Rapids, Michigan/Cambridge: Eerdmans, 1998), 215-233; E. E. Ellis, "'The End of the Earth' (Acts 1:8)," *BBR* 1 (1991): 123-132; Daniel R. Schwartz, "To The End of the *Gē* (Acts 1:8): Beginning or End of the Christian Vision?" *JBL* 105, no. 4 (1986): 669-676.

So, the study seeks to analyze and reconstruct the Lucan representation of the first century Christians, without claiming to be exhaustive in nature, as to their ambivalent political posture in a hostile imperial context with an aim to both assert their right to the "freedom of religion" as well as to avoid strict imperial censures. In the remainder, at first, we shall seek to interface Luke's purpose in writing the *Acts of the Apostles* with postcolonialism.[3] Then, an attempt shall be made to draw a socio-rhetorical context of the Lucan discourse within the larger (post)colonial discursive world in relation to the issue under study. This will set the stage ready for us, finally, to articulate Luke's representation of the early Christian mission and conversion from a postcolonial perspective. It is purported that the present study will yield relevant insights for the Christians in India, with regard to practising the freedom of religion and conversion while living under the new political dispensation of the National Democratic Alliance (NDA) led by the Bharatiya Janata Party (BJP), the political arm of the Hindu cultural nationalist group, the Rashtriya Swayamsevak Sangh (RSS).

INTERFACING THE PURPOSE OF ACTS AND POSTCOLONIALISM

Luke, a missionary companion of Paul, was a citizen of the eastern Mediterranean region and a Greek by culture. This implies his colonized subject status within the Roman imperial order. Apparently later, Luke became a member of an emerging radical social group called "the Christians" that disrupted every "static" ethnic difference which reified hierarchical relations in the hybrid context created by the empire. Thus, the Lucan writings testify to the formation of a transcultural hybrid community, called the *ekklēsia*, that was "in

---

[3] Postcolonialism as a tool in textual praxis seeks to interrogate (biblical) texts in order to exhume, expose, and expunge their colonial entanglements. It does so with a firm realization that through the centuries these texts have either regularly played a significant role as catalysts in promoting, establishing, and naturalizing the colonial rule or were/are co-opted by dominant powers to strengthen their rule. According to Musa Dube, "a post-colonial approach is best understood as a complex myriad of methods and theories which study a wide range of texts and their participation in the making or subversion of imperialism." Musa Dube, "Towards a Post-Colonial Feminist Interpretation of the Bible," *Semeia* 78 (1997): 14.

Christ" beyond every socio-cultural and religio-political bipolar, and negotiating power in dialectic terms without claiming superiority, to articulate the vision of the community ambivalently. In Bhabha's words, as a hybrid community located at the liminal space of cultures, "[i]t is a contaminated yet connective tissue between cultures—at once the impossibility of culture's containedness and the boundary between. It is indeed something like culture's 'in-between', bafflingly both alike and different."[4] In this interstitial space, the early Christians proclaimed their undeterred loyalty ("faith in Him") and allegiance to the new (universal) "Messiah"/"King," by risking the Roman repressive measures for their "illegal" missionary activities while appearing to be ideal citizens of Rome, simultaneously. It is their story of preaching, converting, and expanding of the community, that Luke narrates in the *Acts of the Apostles*.

It must be borne in mind that Luke wrote his two-volume treatise between 70-85 CE with an apologetic purpose. Some like Richard J. Cassidy have rejected a political/ecclesial apologetic purpose of Luke, arguing that the author neither presents Christians as law-abiding citizens of Rome, nor as fully cooperative with Roman officials. In fact, it is argued that the readers of Luke will find Christianity as anti-Roman in character. Similarly, to them, Luke neither puts the Roman imperial administration in positive light, nor does he appear to present the early Christians as fully submissive to the Roman authorities.[5] However, Cassidy's outright rejection of an overarching apologetic motive in favour of an "allegiance-witness theory"[6] is untenable, especially if the Lucan writings are viewed from a postcolonial perspective as an ambivalent twin-forked response to the authoritarian Roman domination and Jewish oppositional discourse in consensual-conflictual, assimilative-abrogative terms.[7] In a hybrid context, it is inherent to

---

[4] Homi K. Bhabha, "Culture's In-Between," in *Questions of Cultural Identity*, eds. Stuart Hall and Paul du Gay (London: Sage Publications, 1996), 54.

[5] Richard J. Cassidy, *Society and Politics in the Acts of the Apostles* (Maryknoll, New York: Orbis Books, 1987), 145-157.

[6] Cassidy, *Society and Politics*, 159.

[7] In postcolonial discussions, such contradictory terms are put in hyphenated relationship in order to represent the complex, ambivalent relationship that exists between the colonizer and colonized within a (post)colonial hybrid

a postcolonial intellectual to oscillate between the polar opposite, *pro-* and *anti-*imperial, political postures in order to articulate one's affiliative-disruptive response while camouflaging identity as a tacit survival technique. According to Bhabha, it is "not a harmonization of repression of difference, but a form of resemblance, that differs from or defends presence by displaying it in part, metonymically."[8]

Scholars like Dunn, Witherington III, and others, have supported Luke's apologetic motive, stating that "the overarching objective includes an apologetic strand in relation to the power of Rome."[9] For Witherington III, the repetition of Paul's trial thrice, like the conversion narrative of Cornelius and the turning of face to the non-Jews by Paul thrice, proves that

> Luke has a concern to show that the Roman Empire was not basically antagonistic towards, nor should it oppose, the Christian church, just because it had become a separate entity from synagogue-based Judaism. ...The state, then, should not be concerned that these Gentiles will not sacrifice to the emperor. They are good citizens, as indeed especially Paul shows on his voyage when he helps the centurion, and earlier when he refuses to escape from jail when he could. The missionary to the Gentiles is a Roman citizen, and he makes good use of this, as does God, for as Luke wishes to show, God is using even the Roman state to spread his gospel. Therefore it should not oppose it as Herod did.[10]

---

context. They standing in hyphenated relationship imply the contradictory responses that are evoked, at the same time, without differentiation both from the colonial margins and centre.

[8] Homi K. Bhabha, "Of Mimicry and Man," in *The Location of Culture* (London and New York: Routledge, 1994), 128.

[9] James D.G. Dunn, introduction to *The Acts of the Apostles* (Peterborough: Epworth Press, 1996), xiii.

[10] Ben Witherington III, *The Acts of the Apostles: A Socio-Rhetorical Commentary* (Grand Rapids, Michigan/Cambridge: Eerdmans/ Carlisle: The Paternoster Press, 1998), 73. Cf. I. Howard Marshall, *The Acts of the Apostles: An Introduction and Commentary*, TNTC (Leicester, England: Inter-Varsity Press/ Grand Rapids, Michigan: Eerdmans, 1980), 21. Marshall treats the apologetic purpose as "a subordinate aim as compared with the main theme of the presentation of the historical basis for Christian faith."

Such a view on Luke's purpose of writing a two-volume treatise narrating the origin, development, and expansion of Christianity, assumes a hostile and unfavourable environment of its writing. Witherington III maintains that "[p]erhaps Luke was also writing at a time when the church faced some opposition from (local?) Roman authorities as well as Jewish ones."[11] If so, we ask: Why were the Christians persecuted by (local?) Roman or Jewish authorities? Was the hostility they faced across the empire directly or indirectly related to their act of proselytization? How would the Romans have perceived the early Christian missionary activities?

SOCIO-RHETORICAL CONTEXT OF ACTS: FREEDOM OF RELIGION AND CONVERSION IN ROMAN ANTIQUITY

The task of reconstructing the socio-rhetorical context of Acts is complex, especially in relation to the question of "freedom of religion" and religious conversion in Roman antiquity. As a general rule, religious pluralism was generally accepted within the empire,[12] though the imperial cult flourished rapidly, at times becoming the "magic plate" of the "Alibaba and the Forty Thieves" in *Arabian Nights*, to test the loyalty of the colonized subjects towards the emperor.[13] Several circumstantial and literary evidences point to a grim picture of religious freedom, especially concerning any conversion to fringe religious movements within the empire.

First, what was the attitude of Romans towards Christians? E. A. Judge's conclusion regarding the Roman origin of the term "Christians" (Acts 11:26) used for the early members of the *ekklēsia* in Syrian Antioch may hold a clue to it. He says that the term could "hardly be invented by orthodox Jews, since it concedes the messiahship of Jesus. Its suffix implies the word was coined by speakers

---

[11] Witherington III, *The Acts Of the Apostles*, 73.

[12] Bruce W. Winter, "Dangers and Difficulties for the Pauline Missions," in *The Gospel to the Nations: Perspectives on Paul's Mission*, eds. Peter Bolt and Mark Thompson (Leicester, England: Apollos/ Downers Grove, IL: IVP, 2000), 289-290.

[13] The loyalty of the Jews was doubted because of their refusal to participate in the imperial cult. See, James McLaren, "Jews and the Imperial Cult: From Augustus to Domitian," *JSNT* 27, no. 3 (2005): 257-278.

of Latin.... The suffix–*ianus* constitutes a political comment. It is not used of the followers of a god. It classifies people as partisans of a political or military leader, and is mildly contemptuous."[14] Though it is unclear as to why such a military term was used to define the identity of the early followers of "the Way," it is clear that for certain reason(s) unknown to us (presumably, the reason was the crucified identity of Jesus and the undeterred allegiance of Christians to him), Christians were viewed differently from other religious associations to certain degree and must have been under the suspicious eyes of "the Eagle" (locally?).

By the ninth decade of the first century, the process of the "parting of the ways" between Judaism and Christianity was already peaking, though it appears to have culminated a little later.[15] Thus, the hostile attitude of the Jewish elites towards Christians in Acts is explainable. Nevertheless, the attitude of the Romans towards Christians was ambivalent. While we notice no law was uniformly promulgated against the "freedom of religion" across the Empire in the first century, we find several instances of curbing the religious freedom of the subjects, including Christians. For example, on several occasions prohibitory orders were issued against new religious cults for reasons like threatening Pax Romana or the imperial interests, and so on. Undoubtedly, the Empire guarded her interests with an iron hand and kept strict vigil over the activities of various associations (*ekklēsiai*). Romans prohibited associations, except for the Jews, from gathering more than once in a month, which points to the reluctance of the Empire concerning their free activities. If so, the weekly gathering of the early Christians in the Greco-Roman cities in the name of a crucified messiah, could have made Romans not just curious about them but extremely suspicious too.[16]

Further, the initial Jewishness of early Christianity is assumed to argue for the immunity of Christians from Roman persecution

---

[14] E.A. Judge, "Judaism and the Rise of Christianity: A Roman Perspective," *TynB* 45, no. 2 (1994): 363.

[15] Roji T. George, "The Early Christian Ambivalent Posture in the Context of Jewish Internal Colonization," *New Life Theological Journal* 3, no. 1 (2013): 56-57.

[16] O.F. Robinson, *The Criminal Law of Ancient Rome* (London: Duckworth, 1995), 80, cited by Winter, "Dangers and Difficulties," 289-290.

and for the liberty to practise religion.[17] Although it may be historically true, yet this was not a universal and permanent reality. Brigitte Kahl argues that the religious privileges accorded to Judaism, a privilege that seemingly the early Christians too enjoyed freely by disguising their separate identity for some time, was not permanent. It was a "flexible and relatively reliable mode of accommodation and inclusion" based on the compromise made between Jews and Romans. It exempted the former from direct participation in imperial sacrifices and celebrations, yet they were subjected to mandatory offering of (twice) daily sacrifices on behalf of the emperor in the Jerusalem temple.[18] Sherwin-White states that the general laxity of the Julio-Claudian dynasty towards foreign cults was not permanent; instead an "ill-enforced ban" was repeatedly invoked when the activities of any association, including Jewish, transcended the permitted boundaries under the imperial system.[19]

If so, how was Jewish proselytism perceived by non-Jews, especially Romans? Initially, it does not appear to have been problematic for Rome, as evidences prove that several Romans even from the high class became Jews.[20] However, Brian Rapske argues that the issue of proselytism with the Roman Empire is different from the privileges granted to Judaism as an ancestral religion.[21] The reason is that when a Roman espoused Judaism (similarly Christianity), it required a substantial drift away from Roman customs and culture. For example, imperial cult, including the social rituals and practices,

---

[17] From the time of Julius Caesar, Jews were free to practise their religion under the charter of religious liberty. See, E. Mary Smallwood, *The Jews Under Roman Rule: From Pompey to Diocletian: A Study in Political Relations* (Boston/Leiden: Brill Academic Publishers, 2001), 124.

[18] Brigitte Kahl, *Galatians Re-Imagined: Reading with the Eyes of the Vanquished* (Minneapolis: Fortress Press, 2010), 216.

[19] A.N. Sherwin-White, *Roman Society and Roman Law in the New Testament* (Oxford: The Clarendon Press, 1963), 79.

[20] Sherwin-White, *Roman Society and Roman Law*, 81.

[21] In recent studies, "(il)licit religion" categories are mostly rejected with a simple acknowledgement that Romans dealt with religions/cults on *ad hoc* basis. They did accord privileges to religions of ancient origin i.e., ancestral tradition/religions. Philip Francis Esler, *Community and Gospel in Luke-Acts: The Social and Political Motivations of Lucan Theology*, SNTSMS 57 (Cambridge: Cambridge University Press, 1987), 211-215.

was the fastest growing religion in the Roman world, but Roman conversion to Judaism (thereby, later Christianity) prohibited the person from participating in it any more. Proselytism "threatened effectively to destroy the web of conventions which represented the Roman cultural order and social relations and the Roman religion which preserved and sanctified them."[22] Thus, Roman conversion to such religions was a criminal offence, which probably the Philippian Roman slave-owners knew pretty well (cf. Acts 16:20-21).[23]

Moreover, the Jewish identity marker, circumcision, had political significance in Roman imperial discourse, especially as it depicted Jewish identity and, thereby, inscribed their defeated political status against the victorious Roman identity. Further, Kahl maintains that in the Galatian context, circumcision was viewed as "a kind of *shorthand for conversion* to Judaism," implying a proselyte's "*separation* from the community at large." It was "*more offensive in proselytes*, who actively decided to make a transition from *us* to *them*" as it "signified of Jewish godlessness, *nonpatriotism*, and neglect of patriarchal and family ties" and of Roman piety, loyalty, etc.[24] It seems a convert was hated for the socio-cultural, religio-political uprooting that followed conversion. How does this relate to Christians within the Roman empire? It must have been relevant in two ways: (a) The early Christian movement with a large number of Jewish Christians and similar theology would have probably forced Romans to view them as a Jewish variant/sect.[25] Thereby, to a certain extent, both the derision felt towards Jews and the legal

---

[22] Brian Rapske, *Paul in Roman Custody*, in *The Book of Acts in its First Century Setting*, vol. 3 (Grand Rapids, Michigan: Eerdmans/Carlisle: Paternoster Press, 1994), 118.

[23] Rapske, *Paul in Roman Custody*, 118-119.

[24] Kahl, *Galatians Re-Imagined*, 213 (Emphases added, except for "us" and "them").

[25] It is unclear how the early Christians were identified separately from Jews but the process had at least begun by 64 CE. Cf. Marcus Borg, "A New Context for Romans XIII," *NTS* 19 (1973): 208; Leon Morris, *The Epistle to the Romans* (Grand Rapids, Michigan: Eerdmans/ Leicester: IVP, 1988), 458; James C. Walter, *Ethnic Issues in Paul's Letter to the Romans: Changing Self-Definitions in Earliest Roman Christianity* (Valley Forge, Pennsylvania: Trinity Press International, 1993), 38, 62; Smallwood, *The Jews Under Roman Rule*, 217.

protection provided to them under the law were parts of the early Christian experience. (b) Like in Judaism, the early Christians too prohibited converts from participating in imperial religion, rituals, and celebrations. In the eyes of the Roman (local?) officials, it would have been a subversive centrifugal move ("us to them") towards a *koinonia* in the postcolonial peripheries, particularly when these Christians were uncircumcised "look-like Jews" blurring colonial stereotypes, especially in Galatia.

It is in this context that Luke's presentation of the Christian mission and aggressive conversion must be studied. How does Luke represent the early Christian mission within the Roman imperial context? What, according to Luke, defines the nature and scope of the Christian "freedom" to practise and propagate Christian faith within a hostile context?

Mapping the Early Christian Practice of Religious Freedom and Conversion

The theme of "conversion" is central to Lucan historiography, probably quite intentionally so, in order to defend it before religious and political opponents while teaching his community members its essential contours of meanings. While Charles H. Talbert considers conversion as "a central focus of Acts, may be *the* central focus,"[26] Thomas M. Finn treats it as "the major theme in Luke's second volume."[27] Gerald L. Stevens argues that Luke's conscious use of *epistrepho* in Luke-Acts in a technical sense implies that he "consciously has worked his thematic presentation of the gospel story using the terminology of conversion as a literary motif."[28] So, Luke preserved several conversion accounts in varied degrees of detail in the book,[29]

---

[26] Charles H. Talbert, *Reading Luke-Acts in its Mediterranean Milieu*, SupNovT 107 (Leiden/Boston: Brill, 2003), 135.

[27] Thomas M. Finn, *From Death to Rebirth: Ritual and Conversion in Antiquity* (New York: Paulist Press, 1997), 27.

[28] Gerald L. Stevens, "Conversion in Luke-Acts: Literary Observations on Epistrepho," *The Theological Educator* 42 (1990): 122. For an in-depth study on conversion in Acts, see Babu Immanuel, *Repent and Turn to God: Recounting Acts* (Perth: HIM international Ministries Inc., 2004).

[29] Finn argues that there are twenty-one conversion accounts in total but Talbert is bit orthodox in his enumeration to locate only ten conversion

which are important for us to understand the complex theme from a postcolonial perspective. In the remainder, an attempt shall be made to analyze a dominant Lucan motif from a postcolonial perspective, unravelling its ambivalent cultural-political nature, its subversive tone through self-assertion of religious freedom, and the liberative thrust through accepting citizenship in the postcolonial interstitial space in Christ within the Roman imperial context.

Religious Conversion: An Inevitable Threat to the *Pax Romana*?

Traditionally, Luke's understanding of conversion is studied in *a*political terms. The language of repentance is thought to be foundational to the Lucan idea of conversion, which is a process of unravelling step-by-step the forgiveness of sins, the reposing of faith in Jesus, discipleship, baptism, and the gift of the Holy Spirit, throughout the Acts of the Apostles.[30] What is often missed in such a perception of Luke's understanding, is the communal/political implication of conversion. It is treated in a very individualistic manner. However, Schwartz maintains that during the Greco-Roman times, religious conversion in the eastern Mediterranean political sphere was undertaken to form friendly political alliances, apart from through marriage and fictive kinship, between fragile polities at the fringes of the empire.[31] If so, one must not be oblivious of the truth that while Luke emphasizes the theme "conversion" amidst the twin-forked conflict of Christians with Jews and Romans, it was also undertaken by the early Christians with an explicit desire of forming a transcultural fictive kinship in Christ at the postcolonial margins, at the same time. In Horsley's

---

narratives plus other passing references to similar phenomena in Acts. See, Finn, *From Death to Rebirth*, 27; Talbert, *Reading Luke-Acts*, 135.

[30] Finn, *From Death to Rebirth*, 27-29. See also, Immanuel, *Repent and Turn to God*, 29-42; Stevens, "Conversion in Luke-Acts," 113-116. Stevens also adds, as an important condition preceding repentance, one's unpreparedness to the coming of the Lord, leading to conversion.

[31] Seth Schwartz, "Conversion to Judaism in the Second Temple Period: A Functionalist Approach," in *Studies in Josephus and the Varieties of Ancient Judaism: Louis H. Feldman Jubilee Volume*, eds. Shaye J. D. Cohen and Joshua J. Schwartz (Leiden/Boston: Brill, 2007), 223-236.

words, Paul too recognized the *ekklēsia* "as an alternative assembly set sharply over against the established *ekklēsia* of Corinth."[32] If so, the local *ekklēsial* communities formed "beyond" ethnic, cultural, and political binaries through aggressive proselytization could have evoked political meanings.

Thus, in Acts, the conversion events are more than mere private/individualistic affairs. They produced constant ripples in the public sphere. Though they happened in different geo-cultural contexts, they were potent enough to evoke violent religio-political responses from others. In other words, the aggressive missionary activities of the early apostles had, at times, disturbed socio-political harmony for varied reasons. Luke, on different occasions, mentions a large number of conversions, of both Jews and non-Jews, as repeated instances of political/civil unrests like in Jerusalem (Acts 5:14, 17-18), Iconium (Acts 14:1-2), Philippi (Acts 16:20-21), Thessalonica (Acts 17:4-5), Corinth (Acts 18:8-13), and Ephesus (Acts 19:26). These, undoubtedly, prove that "religious" conversions in the first century pluralistic context were neither intentionally overlooked by the non-Christian population, nor were allowed to be practised unconditionally. Luke with his apologetic motive seeks to gloss over such seeming self-defeating materials in his own writing by mentioning: (i) Paul's innocence during his defence before Agrippa (Acts 26:20-21), (ii) the unethical motives of certain Jews and Roman officials like Felix (Acts 24:26-27) in arresting and imprisoning Paul, and (iii) a happy ending of Paul's trial in Rome and the failed "smear" campaign by rival Jews (Acts 28:30-31). But Luke obviously fails to deny that conversion did disturb the social dynamic and, as a result, civil peace.

Does this imply that the Christians in the Roman Empire were at fault for disturbing peace in the society? From Luke's testimony, at least three (political) reasons may be stated for the regular civil unrest caused due to conversion in Acts. However, none appear to be concrete evidences against Christians. The reasons are: (i) the "jealousy" of Jews over large conversions (Acts 5:17), (ii) Christians

---

[32] Richard A. Horsley, "Rhetoric and Empire – and the 1 Corinthians," in *Paul and Politics: Ekklesia, Israel, Imperium, Interpretation: Essays in Honor of Krister Stendahl*, ed. Richard A. Horsley (Harrisburg, Pennsylvania: Trinity Press International, 2000), 91.

perceived as threatening established cultural-political traditions, customs, and social norms (Acts 16:20-21; 18:13), and (iii) Christian subversion of selfish exploitative economic/business interests of the dominant class in the name of religion (Acts 16:19; 19:25). Luke defends the innocence of the Christian missionary activity by pointing out that in every instance of conflict due to conversion, the Christian apostles as members of the vulnerable community, received immediate assistance to freedom or protection by God or the Roman officials, from the hands of their powerful opponents.

Thus, for Luke, Christian conversion activities have been a contentious issue in the socio-political life of the Greco-Roman cities during the time of apostles but often they have been caused due to legally untenable reasons by those with illegitimate reasons. For Luke, Christians at their best do not involve in anti-imperial or anti-national activities. Although conversion is primarily one's return to God in repentance, it evokes strong reactions from varied socio-political corners founded on baseless accusations, misinterpretations of reality, or motivated behaviours. If so, how should one understand the early Christian articulation of "the gospel of Jesus Christ" in lofty Romanized vocabulary? Does the Christian message of the Kingdom of God exclude the human sphere of authority?

Religious Conversion for Citizenship in the 'Third Space' of Self-Emancipation

In a postcolonial transcultural hybrid context, the (post)colonial discourses criss-cross discursively both from the imperial centre and the margins. In this context, "the gospel of Jesus Christ" preached in hybrid terms by the early Christians mimics and mocks the Roman imperial gospel, simultaneously. Such display of hybridity evokes terror in the authority with its ruse of identification (mimicry-mockery) breaking "down the symmetry and duality of self/other, inside/outside."[33] In this sense, their "religious" preaching was politically subversive because while Jesus, the Jewish messiah, suffered a criminal's death on the colonial cross, he offered, unlike the Roman Caesar, the true "salvation," "peace," and "unlimited

---

[33] Homi K. Bhabha, "Sign Taken for Wonder," in *The Location of Culture*, 165.

freedom" to all, without terror and violence. Allen Brent contends that because the circle of Theophilus took the imperial propaganda seriously, Luke seeks to present Christianity as the fulfillment of Judaism in parallel to the Roman anticipation of the divine *Pax* in both nature and society. He demonstrates that the new found religion of Theophilus is far better in achieving the purpose of the imperial cult, i.e., Caesar's "peace" and "salvation" offer, in and through the life and mission of Jesus.[34] Thus, by mimicking high imperial titles to Jesus, Luke implies that Jesus alone is truly the Lord, Christ, Saviour, bringer of Divine Peace, and so on.

If so, in contrast to Caesar's rule, God's sovereignty above all other powers (human and spiritual), including the Roman Empire, is maintained in multiple ways in Acts: (i) The book of Acts begins with a strong apocalyptic expectation among disciples of Jesus, the Messiah, that now the resurrected Jesus is about to establish His Kingdom (Acts 1:6 i.e., the "Kingdom of Israel"), which occupied the central role in the later apostolic preachings (Acts 8:12; 19:8; 20:25; 28:23, 31). Although the evasive reply of Jesus in Acts 1:7 reduces its immediate political significance, his ascension into the heavens subverts the claim of Augustus' special status as the "son of god" *via* the apotheosis of Caesar Julius.[35] For Luke, Jesus is the real God who ascended into heaven and the "Son of God" (8:37). (ii) Jesus, the man, is the King (i.e., "the Christ," Acts 5:42; 17:3; 18:5, 28) and the "Lord of all" who brings true peace (Acts 10:36). His rule is truly universal, unlike the claim of universal lordship by the Roman Caesar. (iii) Further, he is the transcosmic apocalyptic figure, the "Son of Man" (Acts 7:56 = Dan. 7:13-14), who stands beyond every human authority including the Roman Empire. It is into this transcosmic Kingdom of Jesus, the Messiah, that the

---

[34] Allen Brent, "Luke-Acts and the Imperial Cult in Asia Minor," *JTS* 48 (1997): 111-138.

[35] See, Gary Gilbert, "Roman Propaganda and Christian Identity in the Worldview of Luke-Acts," in *Contextualizing Acts: Lukan Narrative and Greco-Roman Discourse*, eds. Todd Penner and Caroline Vander Stichele, SBLSympS 20 (Atlanta: Society of Biblical Literature, 2003): 242-247; Drew J. Strait, "Proclaiming Another King Named Jesus? The Acts of the Apostles and the Roman Imperial Cult(s)," in *Jesus is Lord, Caesar is Not: Evaluating Empire in New Testament Studies*, eds. Scot McKnight and Joseph B. Modica (Downer Grove, Illinois: IVP Academic, 2013), 134-136.

apostles invited *all* the (post)colonial Roman subjects to enter by "faith" alone through "many tribulations" (Acts 14:22). In other words, by their "loyalty" (*pistis* in Greek or *fide* in Latin) towards Jesus Christ, people from every *ethnos* become citizens of Jesus' kingdom (cf. Phil. 1:27). Interestingly, the subversive significance of the gospel did not go unnoticed but was recognized by the Thessalonian Jews in Acts 17:7 ("they all act contrary to the decrees of Caesar, saying that there is another king, Jesus").

Are these two kingdoms mutually exclusive? Does it mean that, in the Lucan vision, through conversion, the early Christians ceased to be Roman subjects? Does conversion to Christianity entail treason because they choose to join the "rival" messianic kingdom? The answer cannot be given in unilateral terms. They share an exclusive-inclusive complex relationship. On the one hand, as Vernon K. Robbins maintains, the evidences within Acts prove that "Christianity functions in the domain of the Roman Empire, and this Empire is good because it works symbiotically with Christianity. Roman law, correctly applied, grants Christians the right to pursue the project started by Jesus, and the goals of Christianity, rightly understood, work congruently with the goals of the Roman Empire."[36] On the other hand, in Acts, the Jesus event as the decisive divine intervention into human history is the ultimate expression of God's mighty act of reversing the human course of history, even through death. Although the immediate audiences of Peter on the day of Pentecost were Jews, to whom his subversive political rhetoric was aimed, its larger meaning must have been clearly audible to all colonized Roman subjects (Acts 2:23-24 "you…put Him to death, but God raised Him up again"). Similarly, in Caesarea, everyone in the house of Philip, the evangelist, submitted to "the *will* of the Lord" (Acts 21:14, emphasis added) knowing well that the political fallout of Paul's gentile mission was waiting for him in Jerusalem because the early Christians believed in God's sovereignty over every human authority—not excluding the Roman Caesar—even when they seemingly act against God. Such instances are when God vetoes against the opposing human powers.

---

[36] Vernon K. Robbins, "Luke-Acts: A Mixed Population Seeks a Home in the Roman Empire," in *Images of Empire*, ed. Loveday Alexander (Sheffield: Sheffield Academic Press, 1991), 202.

In postcolonial terms, such an exclusive-inclusive space of the two kingdoms, the *ekklēsia*, creates an interstitial space, the "Third Space"[37] of self-actualization. It is in this liberative space, the *ekklēsia*, that a colonized Christian subject operates subversively towards the oppressive, hegemonic, and exploitative elements. They affiliate-disrupt, at the same time, the colonial discourse(s) to effect liberation. In Acts, Luke repeatedly seeks to project Christians as law-abiding Roman subjects (Acts 19:37; 26:31-32) who refuse to submit to human authority whenever it contradicts the divine plan/command. The apostles dared to question the Sanhedrin, the religio-political body of pro-imperial Jewish elite, when they were commanded not to speak in the name of Jesus because they chose to obey God than human powers (Acts 4:19; cf. 5:29; 26:19). Their witness to Jesus is unconditioned by human influences, though it does not threaten to overthrow the Roman Empire. For example, in Ephesus, Paul's mission resulted in burning of native literature in colonial fashion or was viewed by native subjects as threatening to annihilate the Cult of Artemis/Diana, yet it does not overthrow the Roman imperial establishment itself.[38]

It is their "partial" presence as "loyal citizens of the empire but not quite the same" that menaces the imperial religio-cultural dominant discourse(s). Within the postcolonial "Third Space," the early Christian appeared to be (dis)loyal Roman subjects but they stood "innocent" before the Roman law. They defied essentialist imperial discourse that valorizes identities, enforces slavish subordination, and overrules freedom of the colonized subjects. If so, is the early Christian mission a celebration of the freedom of religion?

Ambivalent Christian Mission: Practising the Ultimate Freedom of Religion

The origin, matrix, and development of the early Christian mission have been contentious for long. While for some, similar to the Lucan depiction of the universal Christian mission based on

---

[37] Homi K. Bhabha, "The Commitment to Theory," in *The Location of Culture*, 54; Dunn, introduction to *The Location of Culture*, 2.

[38] Roji T. George, "Luke's Portrayal of Paul's Ephesian Ministry in Acts 19:11-41: A Postcolonial Reflection," *DTJ* 10, no. 1 (2013): 24-28.

the divine commission (Acts 1:8), the early Christians inherited intentional proselytizing missionary spirit from the Jews,[39] several others based on varied historical-documentary evidences argue for a contrary position.[40] Martin Goodman maintains that the Christian proselytization, at best, from the earliest time was practised by some Christians who viewed Christianity and non-Christian religions in polar opposite terms.[41] Thus, these Christians considered themselves responsible to convert others and consciously adopted an oppositional stance towards other religions, which others like Celsus noticed and condemned.[42] Whatever may be the case, Luke as the author of Acts appears to be one of such early Christians who considered proselytization as central to the practice of his religion.

Luke represents the early Christian Spirit-empowered mission relative to the geography of Jerusalem, modelled after the universal Roman imperial mission. The early Christian self-consciousness, as the centre of divine universal mission in the eschatological times, was coloured by the first century Jewish discourse that rested Jerusalem at the centre of the universe. Especially in Jewish eschatological thought, Jerusalem is the place of gathering for both Jews

---

[39] See for instance, Louis H. Feldmann, *Jews and Gentiles in the Ancient World: Attitudes and Interactions from Alexander to Justinian* (Princeton, New Jersey: Princeton University Press, 1993); J. Jeremias, *Jesus' Promise to the Nations*, 2nd ed., SBT 24 (London: SCM Press, 1967), 11; D. Georgi, *The Opponents of Paul in Second Corinthians* (Edinburgh: T&T Clark, 1987), 83-228; D. Georgi, "The Early Church: Internal Jewish Migration or New Religion?" *HTR* 88 (1995): 35-68.

[40] E.g., Rainer Riesner, "A Pre-Christian Jewish Mission?" in *The Mission of the Early Church to Jews and Gentiles*, eds. Jostein Adna and Hans Kvalbein, WUNT 124 (Tubingen: Mohr Siebeck, 2000), 211-250; Martin Goodman, *Mission and Conversion: Proselytizing in the Religious History of the Roman Empire* (Oxford: Clarendon Press, 1994); Martin Goodman, "Jewish Proselytizing in the First Century," in *Judaism in the Roman World: Collected Essays* (Leiden/Boston: Brill, 2007), 91-116; S. McKnight, *A Light Among the Gentiles: Jewish Missionary Activity in the Second Temple Period* (Minneapolis: Fortress Press, 1991); P. Fredriksen, "Judaism, the Circumcision of Gentiles, and Apocalyptic Hope: Another Look at Galatians 1 and 2," in *The Galatians Debate: Contemporary Issues in Rhetorical and Historical Interpretation*, ed. Mark D. Nanos (Peabody, Massachusetts: Hendrickson Publishers, Inc., 2002), 235-260.

[41] Goodman, *Mission and Conversion*, 96-97.

[42] Goodman, *Mission and Conversion*, 97-99.

and Gentiles from the four corners of the world to "participate in the messianic salvation."[43] By imitating it, Luke fashions the early Christian mission in Acts as beginning in Jerusalem and radiating out in "concentric circles 'to the end of the earth,'"[44] as a fitting response to the Roman universal mission of conquest beginning at Rome. However, unlike the Roman conquest mission of subjugation, exploitation, and silencing of the defeated races, the Jerusalem-centred Spirit-impelled Christian mission was neither ethnocentric nor exclusivistic but empowering and inclusivistic towards the "other." So, it is the narrative of the subaltern, the believers in Christ practising the freedom to religion boldly even under threat.

Further, in Acts 4, we see the apostles arrested for their fearless proclamation of the prohibited gospel of salvation in the name of Jesus. They, as postcolonial subjects inspired by the Holy Spirit, appear to exercise their freedom to practise religion in a complete sense. According to Luke, "they (Ruler and elder) observed the confidence (*parrasian*) of Peter and John" (Acts 4:13, parenthesis added). It is "a reflection of the freedom of speech akin to the free and powerful subjects of the empire"[45] because in the classical Greek literature, as mentioned by Fitzmyer, it was a characteristic of a free citizen which later came to be related to the important Cynic concept of freedom (*eleutheria*). In Greek understanding, it marked a person who was "morally free and able to resist public attention or opposition."[46] Luke depicts their capability to practise religion irrespective of their subaltern status, by mentioning that the Jewish leaders had "nothing to say in reply" (Acts 4:14). Similarly, even before Stephen, a man saturated with "the wisdom and the Spirit," his interlocutors failed to argue (Acts 6:10).

[43] Richard Bauckham, "James and the Jerusalem Church," in *The Book of Acts in its Palestinian Setting*, in *The Book of Acts in the First Century Setting*, vol. 4, ed. Richard Bauckham (Grand Rapids, Michigan: Eerdmans/Carlisle: Paternoster Press, 1995), 425.

[44] James M. Scott, "Acts 2:9-11 as an Anticipation of the Mission to the Nations," in *The Mission of the Early Church to Jews and Gentiles*, eds. Jostein Adna and Hans Kvalbein, 100.

[45] George, "The Early Christian Ambivalent Posture," 66.

[46] Joseph A. Fitzmyer, *The Acts of the Apostles: A New Translation with Introduction and Commentary*, vol. 31 (New York: Doubleday, 1998), 302.

Notably, this is despite their essentialist posture in denying availability of salvation, except in the name of Jesus (Acts 4:12), from any other source, including Caesar, the *soter*. They refused to compromise, in practice, their freedom of conscience/belief. Such an essentialist posture of the apostles is their decision to practise both, in the words of Vonck, "conscientious disobedience"[47] and, to use Spivak's words, a "strategic essentialism."[48] While "conscientious disobedience" is a colonized/subordinate subject's resistance to submit to the colonizer/authority's commands slavishly by contradicting one's own conscience, "strategic essentialism" is a deliberate essentialist posture adopted temporarily by a postcolonial subject as a survival tactic and to affirm one's own (political) space without resorting to a valorization of relationship. In other words, although the Christian mission claims are essentialist and progresses undeterred despite the opposition in Acts, it does not seek to establish vertical relationship based on ethnocentric, cultural, or political binaries.

Interestingly, the Spirit-impelled speech is not limited to the apostles in Acts. It is common even to the unnamed preachers in Acts 11:19-21, who too are the agents of practising religious freedom, even after being driven from their homeland due to persecution. According to Luke, their missionary zeal in turning people "to the Lord" (Acts 11:21) is the way to be constantly allied with the Lord, which Barnabas encouraged them to continue to do (Acts 11:23). More importantly, the Lucan conversion account of Paul, the prime model of true conversion in Acts, implies the conversion itself as a call to practise the "ultimate expression of freedom of religion" at all cost. According to Luke, at his conversion, he was commissioned to wait in Damascus to receive further instruction (Acts 9:6), which through prophet Ananias comes to be as his appointment "to bear My name before the Gentiles and kings and sons of Israel" (Acts 9:15). Although such a detail is typical to Paul's

---

[47] P. Vonck, "'All Authority Comes from God' Romans 13:1-7 – A Tricky Text about Obedience to Political Power," *AFER* 26 (1984): 343.

[48] Gayatri Chakravorty Spivak, "Subaltern Studies: Deconstructing Historiography," in *The Spivak Reader: Selected Works of Gayatri Chakravorty Spivak*, eds. Donna Landry and Gerald Maclean (New York and London: Routledge, 1996), 214.

conversion account, there is no hint throughout Acts that limits it to some like Paul. The impression created, in general, by Luke is that every convert was to practise his "right" to freedom of religion absolutely. Thus, Paul fulfils it blamelessly (cf. Acts 26:19). The moral courage these early Christians gained was from their absolute conviction, as the "soldiers of Christus" (*Christian[o]i*),[49] ultimately their obedience is to God and not human beings, which worked as an ideology for them to practise strategic essentialism, at times in a postcolonial transcultural hybrid context.

Conclusion

In conclusion, a postcolonial reading of Acts proves that Luke considered Christian mission and proselytization as central to Christian witness. Luke, as a postcolonial subject, responds ambivalently towards the imperial suspicion and potential censure. While he presents the early Christians and their religious activities as law abiding, their theology lying behind the act of proselytization is quite subversive. According to the Lucan testimony, despite the conversion events having sporadically caused social-political unrest in different Greco-Roman cities, bearing Christian witness and proselytizing was an irreconcilable religious activity that was never found, by the Roman officials, to be involved in illegal acts. However, it is subversive in nature because conversion decentres Rome by inviting the Roman subjects of all races to move into the transcultural hybrid location in Christ, i.e. the *ekklesia* of Christ, to experience liberation and the ultimate freedom in the power of the Holy Spirit. In this interstitial cultural-political discursive space, Jesus the Messiah is represented, unlike the Roman Caesar, as the transcosmic Sovereign King/Lord who is the true bringer of "Salvation," "Peace," and "Freedom," without unleashing terror and violence. As a result, Christians appear to stand simultaneously in an exclusive-inclusive complex relationship with human authorities, while confessing their irreconcilable submission to the "will of the Lord" (Acts 21:14), by actively being involved in Spirit-impelled mission. At this juncture, the role of the Holy Spirit as the

---

[49] A. F. Walls, "Christian," in *New Bible Dictionary*, 2nd ed., 1st Indian ed. (Leicester, England: IVP/ London and Bombay: Pillar Projects, 1990), 186.

true enabler of "free speech" (e.g., Acts 4:13) was the celebration of "freedom of religion," even under imperial threat in-and-through the Christian mission. It helps to articulate the Lucan representation of the Spirit-impelled Christian mission in strategic essentialist terms as a temporal essentialist posture, both as a survival tactic of a colonized subject community and its quest for self-actualization, without reifying inter-ethnic, inter-racial and inter-cultural relationships in bipolar terms.

Reading John's Gospel as a Jewish-Christian Conflict Narrative: A Paradigm for Contemporary India

Johnson Thomaskutty[1]

Introduction

This paper attempts to investigate how the narrator of the Fourth Gospel captures the socio-religious realities of the first century through his narrative. The rhetoric of John is a reflection of reality. In that sense it is a *mimesis*.[2] In a context in which emerging Christian communities were denied religious freedom and were widely persecuted, the Johannine community members realized that their very existence was at risk. The community was undergoing persecution at the hands of both the Jewish religio-political authorities as well as the Empire of Rome.[3] Johannine community's antilanguage and antisocial outlook placed it well over against Jewish and Roman power structures.[4] While the narrator employs dualism as a major

---

[1] Dr. Johnson Thomaskutty is Head of the Department of NT Studies at Union Biblical Seminary, Pune, India. He is the author of *Dialogue in the Book of Signs: A Polyvalent Analysis of John 1:19-12:50* (Biblical Interpretation Series 136; Leiden/Boston: E.J. Brill, 2015) and *Saint Thomas the Apostle: New Testament, Apocrypha, and Historical Traditions* (Jewish and Christian Texts Series 25; London/New York: Bloomsbury T&T Clark, 2017). His forthcoming monograph is entitled *Saint Bartholomew the Apostle: New Testament, Apocrypha, and Historical Traditions* (Minneapolis: Fortress Press).

[2] It is the Greek word for imitation, a central term in aesthetic and literary theory since Aristotle. Baldick describes it as follows: "A literary work that is understood to be reproducing an external reality or any aspect of it is described as mimetic, while mimetic criticism is the kind of criticism that assumes or insists that literary works reflect reality." See C. Baldick. *The Concise Oxford Dictionary of Literary Terms* (Oxford/New York: Oxford University Press, 1990), 137.

[3] In this paper, we will look at the conflict between the Jews and the Christians and related aspects.

[4] Malina and Rohrbaugh state, "Antilanguage derives from an antisociety that is set up within another society as a conscious alternative to it." They further say, "An antisociety, along with its antilanguage, is an alternate society rooted in a

narrative means to decipher the realities, the *from above* ideology of Jesus is in constant conflict with the *from below* ideology of the Jews. In this way, two ideologies are brought into a sharp contrast.[5] The narrator's usage of conflict and characterization as a major narrative device, adds vigour and flavour to the narrative, turning it into a dramatic masterpiece.[6] This situation persuades the reader to pose the following questions: How does the narrator of John's Gospel exemplify religious freedom and persecution both in explicit and implicit terms? How does the narrator convert the message from the *Sitz im Leben Jesu* to the *Sitz im Leben Kirche*?[7] How does the narrator employ the narrative techniques of *mimesis* and *diegesis*?[8] How can the Johannine community realities be used as a paradigm in the contemporary Indian context where religious freedom and conversion remain as prime factors?[9] The task of the paper is threefold: first, identify the Johannine tenets of narration to decipher the socio-religious realities; second, investigate how religious freedom and persecution are used as elements that propel the narrator to foreground contextual realities; and third, understand the relevance

---

form of social conflict carried on by dissociated persons living in a hollowed-out social sphere within the dominant social order." See B. J. Malina and R. L. Rohrbaugh, *Social-Science Commentary on the Gospel of John* (Minneapolis: Fortress Press, 1998), 46.

[5] See N.R. Petersen, *The Gospel of John and the Sociology of Light: Language and Characterization in the Fourth Gospel* (Eugene, Oregon: Wipf & Stock, 1993).

[6] For more details about conflict and characterization, see J. H. Neyrey, *The Gospel of John in Cultural and Rhetorical Perspective* (Grand Rapids, Michigan: William B. Eerdmans Publishing Company, 2009), xi-xii; Baldick, *The Concise Oxford Dictionary of Literary Terms*, 61-62; S. Chatman, *Story and Discourse: Narrative Structure in Fiction and Film* (Ithaca: Cornell University Press, 1978).

[7] These expressions mean: The life situation of Jesus and the life situation/s of the early Christian community/ies. See W. Marxen, *Der Evangelist Markus* (Eng. Tr. *Mark the Evangelist*, 1959/1969).

[8] Baldick says *diegesis* is "an analytic term used in modern narratology to designate the narrated events or story (French, *histoire*) as a 'level' distinct from that of the narration." See Baldick, *The Concise Oxford Dictionary of Literary Terms*, 57. Also see A.J. Greimas and J. Courtés, *Semiotics and Language: An Analytical Dictionary* (Bloomington: Indiana University Press, 1979), 79.

[9] For more understanding about conversion from the NT point of view, see R.V. Peace, *Conversion in the New Testament: Paul and the Twelve* (Grand Rapids/Cambridge: Eerdmans, 1999).

of the topic in the present day Indian context where Ghar Wapsi and other anti-conversion activities are widely practised.

SOCIAL MILIEU OF THE JOHANNINE COMMUNITY

In a patron-client social context in which one's honour/shame was determined on the basis of several factors, people had to strive hard to usurp superiority status over prevailing inferiorities.[10] It was in such a context that the Christian communities, especially the Johannine community as an emerging group, had to undergo constant existential struggles.[11] As a newly emerged community, without having canonized scriptures and a highly organized ecclesiastical set up, it had to suffer persecution both from the conservative religious Jews and from the imperial authorities. The attitudinal trends of the religious Jews described in the Gospel of John provide ample and explicit details pertinent to: How did Judaism of the day tolerate minority faith/religious communities? How were the minority communities affected due to religious intolerance? How were the Johannine sectarians persecuted extensively?[12] The very existence of the Johannine community was in danger as it was a minority community without power and influence.[13] The bossy attitude

---

[10] See D.A. deSilva, "Patronage," *Dictionary of NT Background*, eds. C.A. Evans and S.E. Porter (Downers Grove: Inter-Varsity Press, 2000), 766-771.

[11] Keener defines the patron-client relationship as follows: Patrons are "the social superior in the Roman patron-client relationship, who granted favours to and acted as political sponsor for his clients, or social dependants. The obligations in the relationship were to grant the patron honor as their benefactors." See C.S. Keener, *The IVP Bible Background Commentary: New Testament* (Downers Grove: Inter-Varsity Press, 1993), 827; cf. deSilva, "Patronage," *DNTB*, 766-771. For Keener, a 'client' is "a person socially dependent on a patron in Roman society." See Keener, *IVP Bible Background Commentary*, 824.

[12] Köstenberger says that, "John acknowledges that 'salvation comes from the Jews' (4:22), yet he portrays Israel as part of the unbelieving world that rejects Jesus. Jesus' 'own' (the 'Jews') did not receive him (1:11). In their place, the Twelve, who are now 'his own,' become the recipients of his love (13:1; cf. chap. 17). The Jewish leaders, on the other hand, are said not even to belong to Jesus' flock (10:26)." See A.J. Köstenberger, *John*, BECNT (Grand Rapids: Baker Academic Press, 2004), 15.

[13] The members of the community would have been people like fisherfolk, Samaritans, Galilean peasants, and the healed ones (i.e., invalids, blind, and

of the Jewish religious authorities toward the emerging Christian community/ies led the situation to violent and traumatizing ends. John the narrator captures *the story of Jesus* as the protagonist in order to re-tell and re-interpret that with greater efficacy. In *the story of Jesus,* his mission initiatives were extended to Cana (2:1-11; 4:46-51), Capernaum (4:46-51; 6:22-59), Sychar (4:1-42), Bethany (11:1-42), and other Israelite provinces.[14] In that sense, Jesus' mission flourished from the southern provinces to the northern parts of the country. The engagement of Jesus as an agent of God resulted in the establishment of several faith communities across the Israelite context. A good number of communities that emerged during the time of Jesus, later on accepted John the beloved disciple as their leader. In that sense, the Johannine church was not merely a Jerusalem-centric congregation in its beginning stages but rather a confederation of several churches.[15] The community/ies had to bear with and overcome growing opposition from part of the Jerusalem and temple-centric religious authorities. While Jesus' ministry is mostly concentrated in the Jerusalemite context in John, later on the community of the beloved disciple grew from its Jerusalem-rootedness to the Ephesus-centric Gentile context.[16] The narrator adds further ingredients to *the story of Jesus* (i.e., *Sitz im Leben Jesu*) in order to re-create and re-tell it according to the new demands of his situation (i.e., *Sitz im Leben Kirche*; see Figure 1).[17]

---

poor). Also see Köstenberger, *John*, 15-16.

[14] And also to some Greeks (cf. 12:20-25).

[15] The North and South riddles of the Gospel clearly bring this aspect to the fore.

[16] In that sense, the Johannine community had several stages of development. See also J. L. Martyn, *History and Theology in the Fourth Gospel* (Nashville: Abington, 1968); R. E. Brown, *The Community of the Beloved Disciple* (New York: Paulist, 1979). The community would have changed its headquarters from Jerusalem to Ephesus due to constant persecutions from the Jews. Cf. A.J. Köstenberger, *The Mission of Jesus and the Disciples: According to the Fourth Gospel* (Grand Rapids: Eerdmans, 1998).

[17] One has to understand that the Johannine church had roots in both the Israelite and the Gentile contexts. See also Marxsen, *Der Evangelist Markus.*

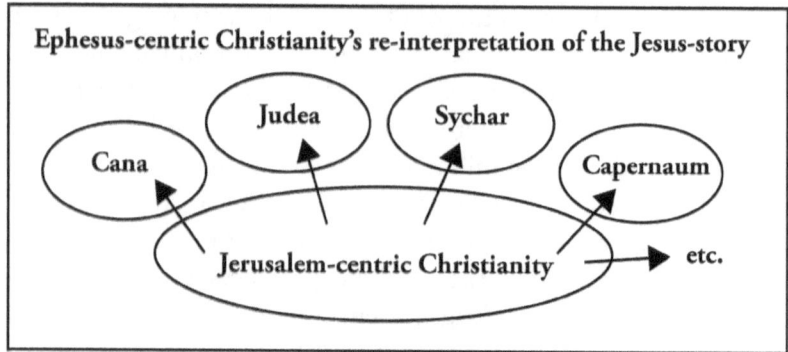

Figure 1: Sitz-im-leben Jesu to Sitz-im-leben Kirche

Toward the end of the first century CE, John's community started to flourish around the beloved disciple. As Martyn explains, the story of Jesus was used as a paradigm to understand the Johannine situation where the community had to undergo persecution at the hands of the Jews and the Empire of Rome.[18] The Ephesus-centric Johannine community focused on the person and work of Jesus, his life situation, and his *ethos-pathos-logos* as kernels to develop their ideological and epistemological framework. The community's theology emerged out of their ideological conflicts and contextual beckoning in its developmental stages. Keener is of the view that, "The Johannine Christians had been made unwelcome by local synagogue authorities, treated as if their very Jewishness was held in question because they believed in Jesus as the Messiah and kingdom-bringer. The Roman authorities were also suspicious of people who did not worship the emperor but were not Jewish."[19] As the Johannine narrator merges the *Sitz im Leben Jesu* with the *Sitz im Leben Kirche*, the conflicting situation of Jesus in the thirties was familiarized in relation to the Johannine community struggles in

---

[18] See Martyn, *History and Theology in the Fourth Gospel*.
[19] See Keener, *IVP Bible Background Commentary*, 261. Köstenberger states that, "If Thomas' confession of Jesus as 'my Lord and my God' is intended to evoke associations of emperor worship under Domitian (81-96 CE), a date after 81 CE would appear most likely." See Köstenberger, *John*, 8; cf. Brown, *The Gospel According to John (i-xii)*, The Anchor Bible, vol. 1 (Garden City: Doubleday, 1966), lxx-lxxv; J. H. Neyrey, *The Gospel of John*, The New Cambridge Bible Commentary (Cambridge: Cambridge University Press, 2007), 30-31.

the latter half of the century (see Figure 1).[20] The Jews are presented in the Gospel as those hostile to Jesus and all those who confess that he is the Christ (John 9:22; 12:42; 16:2). Their antagonistic trends are widespread in the narrative framework of the Fourth Gospel (John 11:45-53; 18:28-19:16; 19:17-22; 20:19).[21] Moloney says that, "The conflicts between Jesus and the Jews are more the reflection of a Christological debate at the end of the first century than a record of encounters between Jesus and his fellow Israelites in the thirties of that century."[22] Thus John's typical vantage point enables him to realign *the story of Jesus* within the narrative framework of *the story of the Johannine community*.[23]

The geographical/topographical details and the eye-witness statements of the Fourth Gospel provide ample evidences concerning the attachment of the beloved disciple in the mission initiatives of Jesus.[24] The narrator portrays Jesus as the incarnated Word, the agent of God, the Saviour of the world, and the glorious Son of Man.[25]

---

[20] Moloney says, "Frequently during the Johannine story of Jesus the opponents of Jesus are bluntly called 'the Jews.' After initial hints that all is not well between Jesus and 'the Jews' (cf. 1:19; 2:13-22) they gradually enter into public conflict (5:16-18), and a decision is made that Jesus must be slain (5:18)." See F. J. Moloney, *The Gospel of John*, Sacra Pagina Series, ed. D. J. Harrington (Collegeville: The Liturgical Press, 1989/1998), 9. See also C. L. Blomberg, *The Historical Reliability of John's Gospel: Issues and Commentary* (Leicester: Apollos, 2001); Marxsen, *Der Evangelist Markus*.

[21] See Moloney, *The Gospel of John*, 9-11; C. Bennema, "A Comparative Approach to Understanding Character in the Gospel of John," in *Character and Characterization in the Gospel of John*, ed. C. W. Skinner (London/New York: Bloomsbury, 2012/2013), 44.

[22] See Moloney, *The Gospel of John*, 10. Beasley-Murray states that, "The Evangelist and his community were not so isolated . . . and their view of Jesus does not betray a beleaguered sectarian group reacting negatively to the society in which it is set." See G.R. Beasley-Murray, *John*, Word Biblical Commentary, vol. 36 (Waco, Texas: Word Books Publisher, 1987), xliv; also see Brown, *The Gospel According to John*, vol. 1, lxx-lxxv.

[23] See D. Tovey, *Jesus, Story of God: John's Story of Jesus* (Adelaide: ATF Press, 2007).

[24] Cf. J. C. S. Redman, "Eyewitness Testimony and the Characters in the Fourth Gospel," *Character and Characterization in the Gospel of John*, ed. C.W. Skinner (London/New York: Bloomsbury, 2012/2013), 59-78.

[25] See M. W. G. Stibbe, *John, Readings: A New Biblical Commentary* (Sheffield: Sheffield Academic Press, 1993), 16-17.

This portrait of Jesus introduces a conflicting situation between traditional Judaism and the newly emerged Christian community.[26] John's two-level drama brings to the reader in rhetorical and performative means, the conflicting situation of the Johannine church. While the Qumran community adopted a *rhetoric of distance*, the Johannine community maintained a *rhetoric of difference*.[27] The Johannine community was a resistance movement that emphasized an ideological conflict between *from above* and *from below* rather than a conflict between *this aeon* and *coming aeon*.[28] Thus Johannine eschatology is more convincingly realized and existential. The Christology of John coupled with his eschatology derives its roots from the existential struggles of the people. Brown says, "John emphatically insists that Jesus is the Messiah, the very claim that the Jews rejected. John uses the Greek form of this title (*Christos*) more frequently than does any other Gospel and is the only Gospel to use the transliterated form *messias* (1:41; 4:25)."[29] The emphasis on

---

[26] See A. J. Kelly and F. J. Moloney, *Experiencing God in the Gospel of John* (New York/Mahwah: Paulist Press, 2003), 44-48.

[27] Though we outline a lot of similarities between Qumran and Johannine communities, this difference is one of the striking areas to be seriously considered in the process of interpretation.

[28] The *vertical eschatology* of John develops steadily within the framework of the "from above" and "from below" conflict. But in the Synoptics, a *horizontal eschatology* is at focus as "this aeon" is in conflict with "coming aeon." See also J. Thomaskutty, "Glo[b/c]alization and Mission[s]: Reading John's Gospel," *New Life Theological Journal* 5, no. 1 (January-June 2015/4): 57.

[29] See Brown, *The Gospel according to John*, lxx; also see Köstenberger, *John*, 13-16; D. Guthrie, *New Testament Introduction*, rev. ed. (Leicester: Apollos/Downers Grove: Inter-Varsity Press, 1961/1990), 251-252. Tasker states that, "That Jesus is *the Christ* is a major theme of all the Gospels. Had He not claimed Messiahship, most of the controversies with the Pharisees would never have arisen, and He would never have been crucified. The fourth evangelist stresses as fully as his predecessors that many Old Testament prophesies about the work the Messiah would accomplish find their fulfilment in Jesus." See R.V.G. Tasker, *The Gospel according to St. John: An Introduction and Commentary* (Leicester: Inter-Varsity Press/Grand Rapids: Eerdmans, 1960/1988), 28; See also B. Milne, *The Message of John*. The Bible Speaks Today (Downers Grove: Inter-Varsity Press, 1993), 25-27; Stibbe, *John*, 19; Namita, *A New Paradigm for Evangelization in the Third Millennium: In the Light of Mission in the Gospel according to St. John and Early Upanishads* (Bangalore: St. Peter's Pontifical Institute Publications, 2000), 21-22.

Jesus' messiahship enabled the community to develop their own idiom in performative linguistic pattern.[30] Borchert says, "The Johannine community, which probably developed within the context of a Jewish cradle, was . . . unable to continue within the protected status of Judaism as a *religio licita* (a licensed religion) in the Roman world."[31] Thus the narrative master plan of John draws the attention of the reader toward the social realities of the first century. This was actualized by merging the story of Jesus with the story of the Johannine community, and with the help of the techniques of *showing* and *telling*.

SYNAGOGUE-AND-CHURCH CONFLICT WITHIN THE STORY OF JOHN

The narrator of the story uses the *ipsissima vox* of Jesus (very *voice* of Jesus) rather than *ipsissima verba Jesu* (very own *words* of Jesus).[32] This

---

[30] Huie-Jolly says, "Johannine Christology makes a division between those who honour Jesus, the 'Son,' as the equal of God, and those who refuse to accept these claims. It associates 'the Jews' with resistance to Jesus' claims to sonship." Quast states that, "Throughout the Gospel, statements about 'the Jews' are directed specifically against certain religious leaders who rejected Christ and his followers. In other words, more so than other Christian groups, the Johannine community forged its identity in reaction to critics in the synagogue community." See M. Huie-Jolly, "Maori 'Jews' and a Resistant Reading of John 5:10-47," in *John and Postcolonialism: Travel, Space and Power*, eds. M.W. Dube and J.L. Staley (London/New York: Sheffield Academic Press, 2002), 94; K. Quast, *Reading the Gospel of John: An Introduction* (New York/Mahwah: Paulist Press, 1991/1996), 5.

[31] Borchert says, "Christianity plainly developed in a context of crisis and hostility especially in terms of its Jewish setting. Also evident is an undercurrent of deep feeling that resulted from the rejection of Jesus (who was born of a Jew) and his early Jewish followers by 'the Jews.'" Blomberg points out that, "John's sharp polemic against Judaism seems more understandable if it is addressed to Christians, some of whom come from Jewish backgrounds, trying to reassure them and others who may wonder about such intense Jewish opposition that they have made the right choice." See G.L. Borchert, *John 1-11*, The New American Commentary (Nashville: B&H Publishing Group, 1996), 72-73; L. Morris, *The Gospel According to John*, Revised Edition (Grand Rapids: Eerdmans, 1995), 35-42; Blomberg, *The Historical Reliability of John's Gospel*, 62; Quast, *Reading the Gospel of John*, 4-5.

[32] *Ipsissima Vox* is a Latin expression meaning "the very voice," and describes the view that the NT Gospel-accounts capture the concepts that Jesus expressed, but not exact words. *Ipsissima Vox* is contrasted with *Ipsissima Verba*, meaning

narrative style enabled him to delineate the synagogue-and-church conflict with the help of dialogue at the intradiegetic (i.e., among the characters within the story) and metadiegetic (i.e., between the narrator and the reader) levels.[33] The narrator of the story convinces the reader of the underlying disputation through the narratorial phenomenon called conflict and characterization. The agent of God schema where Jesus comes to the world as *one from above* over against the prevailing schema of *the world from below* brings out a conflict of its own.[34] In the story of the blind man who was healed (John 9:1-41), the synagogue-and-church conflict emerges convincingly. One of the conspicuous factors is the progression of the man through his apprehension about the person of Christ: first, "the man called Jesus" (John 9:11); second, "He is a prophet" (John 9:17); third, he talks about fearing God and being obedient to his will (John 9:30-33); fourth, he calls him "Lord" and tells him "I believe" (John 9:38); and fifth, he "worshipped him" (John 9:38).[35] As a member of the local synagogue he makes all these assertions and comprehensions; but the religious authorities categorically reject them all.[36] This situation introduces a conflicting situation within the synagogue.[37] In order to convince the reader, the narrator

---

"the very words."

[33] Culpepper quoted in the "Foreword" of J. Thomaskutty, *Dialogue in the Book of Signs: A Polyvalent Analysis of John 1:19-12:50* (Biblical Interpretation Series 136; Leiden/Boston: E.J. Brill, 2015), x. These terms were introduced by G. Genette, *Narrative Discourse: An Essay in Method* (Ithaca: Cornell University, 1980), 228-234.

[34] See, for instance, Martyn, *History and Theology in the Fourth Gospel*, 24-36; J.G. Van der Watt, *An Introduction to the Johannine Gospel and Letters* (T&T Clark Approaches to Biblical Studies; New York: T&T Clark, 2007), 112-114.

[35] See Thomaskutty, *Dialogue in the Book of Signs*, 349-350; Köstenberger, *John*, 277-296; R.A. Culpepper, *Anatomy of the Fourth Gospel: A Study in Literary Design* (Philadelphia: Fortress Press, 1983), 140.

[36] See Martyn, *History and Theology in the Fourth Gospel*, 24-36.

[37] Moloney says, "This group ['the Jews'] casts out the man born blind from the synagogue (9:22, 34); some of its members are afraid to confess that Jesus is the Christ lest they too be cast out of the synagogue (12:42); and Jesus warns his disciples that they will be thrown out of the synagogue and even slain by people who regard their actions as rendering praise to God." See Moloney, *The Gospel of John*, 10; also see Brown, *The Gospel according to John*, vol. 1, lxxiii-lxxv; Martyn, *History and Theology in the Fourth Gospel*, 37-62.

adds more material to the story of Jesus from within the existential struggles of the community.[38] Petersen says, "John's community is an *anti-society* because it understands itself as other to the dominant society that has made it other. The very identity of his people is dependent upon their being other, and this is evident in their special use of the everyday language of the society that has rejected them."[39] Thus the Johannine polyvalence is exemplified through its layered treatment of contexts and issues.

Just as *the story of Jesus* developed in the Israelite context, initially *the story of the Johannine community* developed in the surroundings of the temple at Jerusalem. Later on, the community flourished in the North Israelite (i.e., Galilee and Samaria) and in the Gentile (most possibly Ephesus) contexts. The shift of the community's headquarters from Jerusalem to Ephesus can be inferred from the geographical/topographical details and narrative asides that include the transliteration of Hebrew terms in the text.[40] While the Northern and Southern Israelite contexts introduce a riddling situation at the local level, the Israelite and Gentile contexts introduce a wider riddling situation within the narratorial framework of the Gospel. Moloney notes, "The community began as a small group of Jerusalem Christians and its members developed an increasingly unique understanding of Jesus as they responded to a variety of experiences, both religious and social."[41] In the Gospel,

---

[38] See also Brown, *The Community of the Beloved Disciple*, 1979.

[39] Petersen further says that, "The sociology of Light begins with the conflict between the disciples of Moses and the disciples of Jesus, and it ends with the sociology of language, in which John's special language proves to be the anti-language of the anti-society comprised of Johannine disciples of Jesus." See Petersen, *The Gospel of John and the Sociology of Light*, 89, 108.

[40] The narratorial techniques used in the Gospel are with an aim to describe the story of Jesus with a larger intent. Hence, the narrator describes the geographical/topographical details, Hebrew/Aramaic terms, concepts and chronological aspects.

[41] Moloney further says that, "People foreign, and even hostile to the traditions of Israel were admitted to the community (cf. 4:1-42), and this led to a stage when the members of the Johannine community could no longer be accepted by their fellow Jews." See Moloney, *The Gospel of John*, 12; also see R. Kysar, "The Whence and Whither of the Johannine Community," *Life in Abundance: Studies of John's Gospel in Tribute to Raymond E. Brown*, ed. J.R. Donahue (Collegeville: Liturgical Press, 2005), 65-81.

Jesus is introduced as an agent of transformation in the existing socio-political and religio-cultural phenomena. He invites people toward a new experience under the power of God. Believing in Jesus is suggested as the foundational step in order to experience life in its abundance.[42] People without a repenting heart and an experience of *metanoia* cannot enter into such a situation. This messianic axiom divides *the world from below* into two groups, those who follow the light-logos-life (*licht-liebe-leben*; i.e., converted) and those who follow the way of the world and hence under darkness (i.e., non-converted).[43] This religious scenario introduces a conflict situation within the socio-political and religious context. From all these details it is evident for the reader that the Johannine community underwent opposition and persecution at the hand of Jewish religious authorities within the Palestinian and Gentile contexts.

The motif of newness in the deeds and discourses of Jesus and its further propagation by the Johannine community usher a conflicting situation between the old hierarchical system of Judaism and the newly advancing group of John.[44] The introduction of the new Genesis (1:1-18), new wine (2:1-11), new temple (2:19-22), new birth (3:3), new water (4:13-14; 7:37-38), new life (4:46-54; 11:1-54), new exodus (6:16-21), new manna (6:22-59), new Moses (6:22-59),[45] new bread (6:22-59), new light (8:12; 9:5), and the like were severe attacks on the existence and sustenance of the age-old Jewish hierarchical system.[46] Köstenberger says,

> Like his portrait of Jesus, John's presentation of the new messianic community follows a salvation-historical pattern. In keeping with OT typology, believers are

---

[42] See Stibbe, *John*, 9-19.

[43] See G. Voigt, *Licht-Lieve-Leben: Das Evangelicum nach Johannes* (Gottingen: Vandenhoeck & Ruprecht, 1991).

[44] See J. Thomaskutty, "Reading John's Gospel to the Nepali Context," *Nepali Theological Journal* (South Korea: ACTS College, 2015/3), 63-82.

[45] Petersen also explains the True Moses motif of the text. See Petersen, *The Gospel of John and the Sociology of Light*, 104-109.

[46] Keener says that, "John's controversy narratives often utilize argumentation similar to that of the rabbis and similarly employ the opponents as a foil to the protagonist's case. But John's accounts are much longer than rabbinic, Synoptic, or other stereotypical accounts." See C. S. Keener, *The Gospel of John: A Commentary*, vol. 1 (Peabody: Hendrickson, 2003), 68.

described as a flock (chapter 10) and as branches of the vine (chapter 15). John, however, does not teach that the church replaces Israel. Rather, he identifies Jesus as Israel's replacement: He is God's vine taking the place of God's OT vineyard, Israel (Isa. 5).[47]

Thus, the incarnation of logos as the fulfiller of the Messianic hopes and as the harbinger of a new covenantal relationship was against the axioms of the Jewish religious authorities. The presentation of Jesus as the "first utterance" and the "wisdom of God" facilitated the idea that Jesus supersedes everything.[48] John as a genre mosaic vibrantly enthuses the reader to get involved in the story-world. The focalization of the story develops as the voices of the protagonist (i.e., Jesus) and the narrator merge together and persuasively influence the implied/historical/contemporary reader(s) of the text. This facilitates the gnomic (rather than the descriptive) significance of the Johannine story.[49]

In Jesus' arguments with the Jews, as Brown states, "There is an attack... against the religious position of Judaism—Jesus is the Messiah, and in his presence and face to face with that he has done, Judaism has lost its pre-eminence."[50] Moreover, Martyn elaborates, there were debates within the synagogue and the introduction of the curse of the heretics or deviants in Judaism (*Birkat ha-Minim*).[51]

---

[47] See Köstenberger, *John*, 15. Also see W.F. Howard, *The Gospel according to St. John*, The Interpreter's Bible, Vol. 8 (New York/Nashville: Abingdon Cokesbury Press, 1952), 449-450; Morris, *The Gospel according to John*, 55.

[48] See Kelly and Moloney, *Experiencing God in the Gospel of John*, 43-48.

[49] See J. Thomaskutty, "Biblical Interpretation in the Global-Indian Context," *Fuller Magazine: Reading Scripture Globally* 8 (2017): 64-68.

[50] Refer further, Brown, *The Gospel According to John*, vol. 1, lxx-lxxv. Bennema says, "John draws a great deal of attention on the themes of conflict, opposition and persecution. He essentially describes the clash between the world 'from above,' represented by Jesus, and the world 'from below,' represented by 'the Jews.'" Bennema further says, "In the coming of Jesus into the world, heaven has penetrated the earth, the divine has entered into human history, and God's kingdom has broken into a dark world. This causes conflict, opposition and persecution." See Bennema, "A Comparative Approach," 14; Also see, Thomaskutty, "Glo[b/c]alization and Mission[s]," 64; C. H. Dodd, *The Interpretation of the Fourth Gospel* (Cambridge: The University Press, 1960), 289-443.

[51] See Martyn, *History and Theology in the Fourth Gospel*, 92, 131. Borchert says, "Martyn has understood that the stories involving the healing and

Martyn's thesis certainly has attracted a great deal of attention that involves exclusion from the synagogue and the relationship of this exclusion to the conflict texts in John.[52] Manns says, "The benediction of the *Minim* no longer allowed members of the two communities to pray together. Discussions on the person of Jesus were at the origin of the 'benediction' of the *Minim*. John attaches great importance to these discussions (7:26-28; 7:40-43; 12:34)."[53] The emerging opposition in Jerusalem (chap. 5), in Galilee (chap. 6), the domination of the Pharisees (chaps. 7-10), the domination of the chief priests (chap. 11), and Jesus' trial and death (chaps. 18-19) are the local manifestations of the plot of this world against Jesus.[54]

The *sending out of the synagogue* (*aposunagogē*) and the struggle of the newly emerged Johannine community are vividly portrayed by the narrator in both explicit and implicit terms.[55] Painter says, "In the *diaspora* the Johannine Christians were excommunicated

---

excommunication of the blind man (9:1-41), and other texts such as confrontation with the Jews when Jesus called God his Father (5:18-24), reflected the painful experience of the community at that subsequent time." See Borchert, *John 1-11*, 46; Also see F. Manns, *John and Jamnia: How the Break Occurred between Jews and Christians c. 80-100 CE* (Jerusalem: Franciscan Printing Press, 1988).

[52] Bennema says that, "'The Jews' consist of those Jews who are hostile and opposed to Jesus, especially from among the religious leaders in Jerusalem (e.g., 1:19; 5:16-18; 6:41, 52; 7:1; 8:31-59; 9:13-34; 10:31-39)." See Bennema, "A Comparative Approach," 13; cf. Borchert, *John 1-11*, 47.

[53] See Manns, *John and Jamnia*, 32. Bennema says, "Besides persecuting Jesus . . . Jewish rulers also instigated religious persecution against fellow Jews who confessed Jesus as Messiah, as the expression 'the fear of the Jews' indicates (7:13; 9:22; 12:42; 19:38; 20:19)." Bennema further explains, "This persecution seems primarily to have been the threat of excommunication from the synagogue, and hence of becoming a social outcast (9:22, 34; 12:42), but even murder was in view (16:2). In John, 'the Jews' are characterized as murderers, liars and belonging to the devil (8:44)." See C. Bennema, *Excavating John's Gospel: A Commentary for Today* (Delhi: ISPCK, 2005), 13-14; Quast, *Reading the Gospel of John*, 5.

[54] Van der Watt sees a contrast between the family of God and the children of devil within John's narrative framework. See Van der Watt, *An Introduction to the Johannine Gospel and the Letters*, 30-77; also see Thomaskutty, "Glo[b/c]alization and Mission[s]," 64; Neyrey, *The Gospel of John*, 5-9.

[55] See Martyn, *History and Theology in the Fourth Gospel*, 37-62; Brown, *The Community of the Beloved Disciple*; Tovey, *Jesus, Story of God*, 148-152.

from the synagogue. The threat of excommunication was a fearful weapon as is evidenced by John 9:22; 12:42. At some stage it was the purpose of the Johannine tradition to encourage secret believers to confess their faith and to face excommunication."[56] The dualistic contrast and the performative linguistic phenomenon of the Johannine text dramatically foreground the community conflict in the first century context. The contrast between the "believing" and "unbelieving," "sons of light" and "sons of darkness," and "world from above" and "world from below" rhetorically introduce the Jewish-Christian conflict with the use of figurative language and the help of socio-political and religio-cultural phenomena.[57] Thompson says, "The plot of the Gospel cannot be determined unless the readers comprehend the dialectical structure. In John's Gospel, God incarnate in Jesus has a controversy with the world, the Jewish leaders who epitomize the world in its opposition to the Gospel (John 5:16, 18; 6:41; 7:1; 10:31; 11:8)."[58] This reality is at the heart of John's Gospel. A paradigmatic reader of John's Gospel can understand the larger picture only by grasping the narratorial dynamism which elucidates the synagogue-and-church conflict and the subsequent minority assaults in the first century context/s.

DIALOGUE AT THE CENTRE OF THE JOHANNINE NARRATIVE

The narrator of the Johannine story develops his rhetoric by placing a Jewish-Christian dialogue at the centre. The narrator aligns the characterization of *the story of Jesus* within *the story of the Johannine community* context, i.e., as one between the protagonists (the followers of Jesus/the community of John) and the antagonists (the

---

[56] See J.P. Painter, *The Quest for the Messiah: The History, Literature and Theology of the Johannine Community* (Nashville: Abingdon, 1993), 128; also see Quast, *Reading the Gospel of John*, 59-77.

[57] See Moloney, *Gospel of John*, 11; Borchert, *John 1-11*, 47-9; Howard, *The Gospel According to St. John*, 449-450.

[58] Thomaskutty says that, "The Gospel is framed in a fashion in which the dialectical role of belief and unbelief moves antithetically. Mostly the discourse sections are fashioned by strategically inserting the 'belief-unbelief conflict.' This hidden agenda of the story is the pavement of the Gospel's dialogic structure." See J. Thomaskutty, "Dialogical Nature of John's Prologue," *Union Biblical Seminary Journal* 8, no. 2 to 9, no. 1 (September 2013-March 2015): 13.

religious Jews within the community context). This narrative style helps the reader to understand the macro-structure of the Gospel through the medium of the micro- and meso-structures. Keener is of the view, "Most of Jesus' discourses in John 3-12 are conflicts with the Jewish authorities and thus bear some resemblances to the briefer rabbinic accounts of arguments with opponents."[59] John's Gospel is structured as a multi-layered drama at the *exchange, episode,* and *narrative* levels.[60] The Jewish-Christian conflict is narrated in a concentrated form in chapters 7-9, and 11-12. The narrator uses dialogic trends at the intradiegetic and metadiegetic levels.[61] The elements of dialogue and drama within the story of John make it a persuasive artistry. The narrator as a riddler draws the reader's attention toward the underlying conflict and the resultant characterization through the means of the two-level story.[62]

Some of the prominent dialogues between Jesus and the Jewish leaders occur in the following settings: Jesus and the religious leaders in Jerusalem in John 5:16-47 and John 7:14-8:59; with the crowd and the Jewish leaders in John 6:25-59; with the Greeks and the Jerusalem crowd in John 12:20-36; with the high priest and the guard in John 18:19-24; and with Pilate in John 18:28-19:16.[63] These dialogues develop in antonymous terms as the religious ideologies of the Jews are in conflict with the ideologies of Jesus. In chapter 5, a dramatic protagonist-and-antagonist conflict begins to develop and the protagonist takes full control by turning the dialogue into a monologue.[64] Johannine dialogues are reproductions of constant interactions, encounters, conflicts, and accommodation and disruption tendencies developed within the Johannine community

---

[59] See Keener, *The IVP Bible Background Commentary*, 262.

[60] See Thomaskutty, *Dialogue in the Book of Signs*.

[61] *Intradiegetic* means "dialogue among the characters within the story," and *metadiegetic* means "dialogue between the author/narrator and the reader of the story."

[62] See Martyn, *History and Theology in the Fourth Gospel;* P. N. Anderson, *The Riddles of the Fourth Gospel: An Introduction to John* (Minneapolis: Fortress Press, 2011).

[63] See, for instance, Anderson, *The Riddles of the Fourth Gospel*, 13-14.

[64] While vv. 1-18 develop in the form of dialogues, vv. 19-47 develop most as a monologue. Also see, Quast, *Reading the Gospel of John*, 59-77.

context. The Johannine community was a marginal group expelled from the synagogue (John 16:2) and had to deal with the issues of: first, their relationship to Judaism; second, questions of self-identity; third, minority status; and fourth, oppression.[65] The narratives play a vital role at the intervals of utterance-units, as in chapter 6, they add dramatic setting to the story. The "murmuring" scene in v. 41, "arguing" scene in v. 52, and "grumbling" scene in vv. 60-61 are implicitly introduced as "community dialogues."[66] The Johannine community's concerns over the other majority cultures are reflected through the dialogic interactions of the characters.[67] In order to sharpen the conflicts, plot features such as *reversal, recognition* and *suffering* are integrally embedded within the dramatic narrative.[68] In chapters 7 and 8, the responses and actions of the Jews against Jesus are mostly without evidence, shallow in description, emotional in attitude, verbally abusive, unknowing and misunderstanding in sense, and violence-ridden.[69] In chapter 9, "The Jews are viewed as 'unbelieving' and antagonistic characters, who misunderstood the words of Jesus, and revile and drive out the 'believing.'"[70] In John's dialogue, Jesus, the protagonist, is in constant dialogue with his interlocutors in order to reveal his messiahship and to lead them toward eternal life perspectives. On several occasions, the narrator employs the *question-and-answer, request-rebuke-response,* and *challenge-and-riposte* methods to maintain the dialectical nature of the dialogues.[71] Thus, Judaism as a religion is majorly portrayed as antagonistic and a great threat to the faith and practices of the newly emerged Johannine community.

---

[65] For more details, refer to J. Thomaskutty, *Proefschrift: The Nature and Function of Dialogue in the Book of Signs* (Nijmegen: Radboud Universiteit Nijmegen, 2014).

[66] See Culpepper, *Anatomy of the Fourth Gospel*, 127.

[67] See Thomaskutty, *Proefschrift*, 289.

[68] See Thomaskutty, *Proefschrift*, 289; Dodd, *The Interpretation of the Fourth Gospel*, 297-389.

[69] Refer to Thomaskutty, *Dialogue in the Book of Signs*, 308; Dodd, *The Interpretation of the Fourth Gospel*, 297-389; Quast, *Reading the Gospel of John*, 59-77.

[70] Refer to Thomaskutty, *Dialogue in the Book of Signs*, 349; Quast, *Reading the Gospel of John*, 59-77.

[71] See Thomaskutty, *Dialogue in the Book of Signs*, 446; Baldick, *Concise Oxford Dictionary of Literary Terms*, 56.

Dialogues at the micro-level are flavoured and supplemented with several literary devices. Dialogue forms such as *double meaning-misunderstanding-clarification* (see John 8:12-20, 21-30; 9:39-41; 11:7-16, 17-27; 12:12-36a),[72] *question-and-counter question* (John 6:60-66), *community type* (John 7:37-44; 9:8-12), *religious-theological* (John 7:14-36; 8:31-59), *controversial* (John 5:1-13; 6:22-59; 7:14-36; 8:31-59; 9:1-41; 11:7-16, 17-27; 12:12-36a), *forensic* (John 7:45-52; 8:31-59; 9:8-12, 13-17, 18-23, 24-34, 39-41; 10:22-39) and others appear at the exchange level.[73] At the meso-level, the following episodes delineate the conflicting ideologies of the protagonist and his interlocutors in detail.[74] At the macro-level, especially in the Book of Signs, all the dialogues are dynamically interlocked within the narrative framework (John 1:19-12:50; see Figure 2).[75]

Episode #	Texts	Episode Title (at the Meso-level)
1	2:13-22	A Challenge and Riposte Dialogue
2	5:1-47	A Sign and a Controversy Dialogue Leading to a Monologue
3	6:1-71	From Sign-centric Dialogues to Question-and-Answer Dialogues
4	7:1-52; 8:12-59	A Religious-Theological Dialogue Formed in a Series of Challenge and Riposte
5	9:1-10:21	A Dramatic Dialogue Leading to a Monologue and a Community Dialogue
6	10:22-42	A Forensic Dialogue Develops from-Antithetical-to-Synonymous Mode
7	11:1-53	A Glory-focused Revelatory Dialogue
8	11:54-12:50	A Conflict-centric Dialogue as a Conclusion

Figure 2: Some of the Jesus-and-Jews conflicts in the Book of Signs (i.e., dialogues at the episode level)

The animosity-centered and dualistic pattern of the Book of Signs provide insights concerning the hate language of the Jews

---

[72] See, Neyrey, *The Gospel of John*, 12-13, 78, 90-91, 195-196.

[73] See Thomaskutty, *Dialogue in the Book of Signs*, 435-436; also see J.D. Hernando, "Episodes of Personal Encounter: Inquiry into John's Christology," in *But These are Written . . . Essays on Johannine Literature in Honor of Professor Benny C. Aker*, eds. C.S. Keener, J.S. Crenshaw, and J. Daniel May (Eugene: Pickwick Publications, 2014), 80-90.

[74] See Dodd, *The Interpretation of the Fourth Gospel*, 297-389.

[75] See Quast, *Reading the Gospel of John*, 59-77. The table is taken from Thomaskutty, *Dialogue in the Book of Signs*, 438.

against Jesus the protagonist, his speeches, and his mission initiatives (see Figure 2). Their hate language is evident in their branding him as a "deceiver" (7:12), "demonic" (7:20; 8:48, 52; 10:20-21), "Samaritan" (8:48), and "Son of Joseph" (6:42).[76] Other aspects of hate language such as *diminution* and *reduction* are also obvious in the language of the Jews (6:42, 52).[77] The narrator's memory of the actual speeches and events concerning Jesus is reproduced in the light of the ongoing struggles of the community.[78] The violent actions of Jesus' interlocutors are beyond the pattern of the dialogue.[79] The antagonistic and exclusivistic attitudes of the Jews toward those who do not partake of their religious ideologies are obvious in the ongoing vocal exchanges within John's narrative.[80] This is portrayed vividly through their actions: i.e., "attempting to kill Jesus" on several occasions (5:18; 7:19-20, 25; 11:45-53), "driving" the healed man out of the synagogue (9:34b), and "plotting to kill Lazarus" (12:9-11).[81] John's dialogue has polyvalent connections within the narratorial framework as it works well with the *sign language* and the "I AM" sayings. The signs and dialogues are integrally connected in John and together they help the protagonist to reveal himself.[82] Moreover, Jesus' revelatory aspects are potentially reflected through his "I AM" sayings (see 6:35, 48; 8:12; 9:5; 10:7, 9, 11; 11:25; 14:6; 15:1, 5).[83] Through all these the narrator foregrounds the undercurrent struggles and conflicts of the Johannine community. Furthermore, dialogue development is significant in chapters 18 and 19. The passion discourse includes the verbal interactions

---

[76] Roy explains four language structures: naming, diminutives, reduction, and metaphors. See J. M. Roy, *Love to Hate: America's Obsession with Hatred and Violence* (New York: Colombia University Press, 2002), 25-42.

[77] See Roy, *Love to Hate*, 32.

[78] Refer to Thomaskutty, *Dialogue in the Book of Signs*, 466-467; Dodd, *Interpretation of the Fourth Gospel*, 297-389; Martyn, *History and Theology in the Fourth Gospel*, 24-151.

[79] See Martyn, *History and Theology in the Fourth Gospel*, 24-151.

[80] Refer to Thomaskutty, *Dialogue in the Book of Signs*, 468; Quast, *Reading the Gospel of John*, 59-77.

[81] See Neyrey, *The Gospel of John*, 210-211.

[82] See Thomaskutty, *Dialogue in the Book of Signs*, 447.

[83] Refer to Thomaskutty, *Dialogue in the Book of Signs*, 450; Dodd, *Interpretation of the Fourth Gospel*, 297-389.

during Jesus' betrayal and arrest (18:1-11), Jesus' conversation with Pilate and the Jews (18:28-19:15), post-crucifixion events (19:16-24), and Jesus' words from the cross (19:25-30) in dialogue-centric and dramatic fashion.[84] Thus, the conflict stories are fashioned with the help of dialogues, the controversies are discussed from the point of view of eternal life, and the characterization is portrayed in dualistic terms and themes.

To show the undercurrents and the conflicts between the Jewish and Johannine communities, the narrator uses socially intertwined linguistic phenomena. Brant sees *episodic* structure and *transitions* as key elements in the organization of the Johannine plot. She identifies *peripeteia*,[85] *anagnōrisis*, and *pathos* as the significant plot elements.[86] Within the dramatic plot structure the narrator adds significant elements that propel the story.[87] The narrator of the story uses several other literary and linguistic aspects in order to the interlock the reader with the text. Brant says, "The exchanges of insults that occur in the Fourth Gospel may not simply be pieces of reciprocal verbal abuse. Such interactions in Greek tragedy belong to a literary type of scene and category of dramatic dialogue known as 'flyting.'"[88] The usage of flyting helps the narrator to show the conflicting nature of the story.[89] The Sabbath conflicts in chapters

---

[84] See Thomaskutty, *Dialogue in the Book of Signs*, 482; D.A. Carson, *The Gospel According to John* (Leicester: IVP/Michigan: Eerdmans, 1991); Quast, *Reading the Gospel of John*, 59-77.

[85] Brant says that, "The idea of peripeteia as a single event or as a simple reversal of fortune belies the complexity of how reversals are handled in Greek tragedies." J.A. Brant, *Dialogue and Drama: Elements of Greek Tragedy in the Fourth Gospel* (Peabody: Hendrickson Publishers, 2004), 26-32, 42-63.

[86] Brant describes: "When Aristotle asks what sort of action is appropriate to drama, he identifies three means of moving the soul to pity and fear (the emotions that drama ought to arouse): reversal (*peripeteia*), recognition (*anagnōrisis*), and suffering (*pathos*)." See Brant, *Dialogue and Drama*, 42-43; also see Stibbe, *John*, 13-14.

[87] See T. L. Brodie, *The Gospel according to John: A Literary and Theological Commentary* (New York/Oxford: Oxford University Press, 1993); G.L. Parsenios, *Rhetoric and Drama in the Johannine Lawsuit Motif*, WUNT 258 (Tübingen, Germany: Mohr Siebeck, 2010).

[88] See Brant, *Dialogue and Drama*, 123-124.

[89] Also refer J. A. Brant, *John*, Paideia Commentaries on the New Testament (Grand Rapids, Michigan: Baker Academic, 2011); Stibbe, *John*, 13-14.

5 and 9 maximally bring out this conflict.⁹⁰ The author includes several group encounters (other than the individual encounters) in 6:41-59; 7:11-24; 8:13-47; 9:40-10:18; 10:22-39; 11:3-16; and 12:27-36.⁹¹ The above discussion gives us ample evidences to prove the fact that the dialogue that developed between Jesus and the Jews was not synonymous but antithetical in every sense. Through these dialogues the narrator points out the following things: first, the Johannine community didn't enjoy religious freedom as the Jewish authorities never allowed them to do so; second, as a community comprised of Jewish converts (and also others), the Jews always considered them as anti-religious and anti-social; and third, the narratorial framework, antithetical dialogue, dualistic language, and the literary dynamism of the Gospel facilitate a protagonist-and-antagonist duel both at the ideological and contextual levels.

RELIGIOUS FREEDOM AND CONVERSION IN TODAY'S CONTEXT

How can the Johannine phenomenon of religious freedom and conversion be understood in relation to the existent struggles of the Christian communities in India? While the Indian Constitution provides freedom to express and propagate one's religion, the Hindu fundamentalist groups go against the very rights of the minority religions. In several ways, the struggles of the Christian communities in India are equivalent to the struggles of the Johannine community. In a multi-religious Indian context, politicization of religion and communal tendencies are on the rise and the minority

---

⁹⁰ Smith says, "That the Johannine Jews are primarily concerned to oppose Jesus' claims concerning himself is also somewhat at odds with the synoptic portrayal, as well as Paul." See D.M. Smith, *John*, Abingdon New Testament Commentary (Nashville: Abingdon Press, 1999), 35.

⁹¹ Painter sees the following Jewish purposes behind the composition of the FG: *first*, to win the Palestinian Jews to faith; *second*, to appeal to Jews of the *diaspora*; *third*, to appeal to secret believers within the synagogue; *fourth*, opposition to and condemnation of the Jews; and *fifth*, to encourage the Johannine believers. See Painter, *The Quest for the Messiah*, 125; Quast, *Reading the Gospel of John*, 7. Hernando says, "...outstanding feature of John's gospel is the attention the author gives to personal encounters. This is evidenced by the numerous personal interviews or exchanges that he records." See Hernando, "Episodes of Personal Encounter," 81, 88-90.

rights are not protected. These contextual realities invite the attention of the reader to look at things from a *gnomic* perspective rather than *descriptive* perspectives. In the contemporary context, John's Gospel can be better understood by aligning the *Sitz im Leben Jesu* and the *Sitz im Leben Kirche* within the *Sitz-im-leben India*.[92] While Martyn perceives the Gospel of John as a two-level drama, an Indian reader who looks at the Gospel from her/his existential struggles can better understand it as a tri-level drama (see Figure 3).[93]

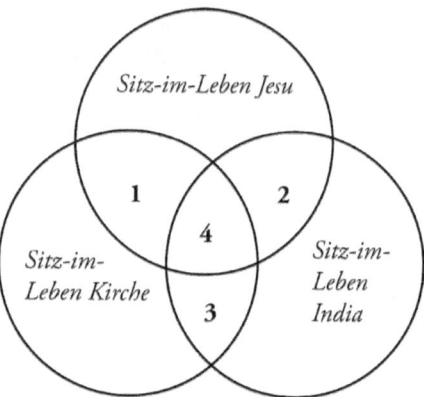

Figure 3: Sitz-im-Leben Jesu, Sitz-im-Leben Kirche, Siz-im-Leben India interaction: space #1 is the Sitz-im-Leben Jesu and Sitz-im-Leben Kirche meeting point; space #2 is the Sitz-im-Leben Jesu and Sitz-im-Leben India meeting point; space #3 is the Sitz-im-Leben Kirche and Sitz-im-Leben India meeting point; and space #4 is the common meeting point of all

The BJP-led Indian Government under Narendra Modi does not protect minority rights. Christian communities are persecuted throughout the country by way of aggressive *Ghar Wapsi* campaign and other anti-conversion means.[94] These issues and others at the local and national levels have called into question the very nature of

---

[92] Marxsen distinguished between three *Sitz-im-Leben*: "The first is the *Sitz-im-leben* in the life of Jesus himself and has to do with the relationship between written records and actual events. The second has to do with the *Sitz-im-Leben* of the early church and its illuminated by form-critical attempts to differentiate community theology from the words and acts of Jesus. The third has to do with the authors and strives to delineate the theology of the evangelists as distinguished from the community theology." See Marxsen, *Der Evangelist Markus*, quoted in Guthrie, *New Testament Introduction*, 237-238.

[93] See Martyn, *History and Theology in the Fourth Gospel*.

[94] See S.M. Michael, *Challenges to Christian Mission: Problems and Prospects* (Pune: Ishvani Kendra, 2014), 30.

religious freedom and conversion. This situation invites the reader of the Gospel of John to merge *the story of the Indian context* with that of *the story of the Johannine community*. John's accommodative power encompasses the feelings and existential struggles of the Indian masses. In this way the Gospel functions as a persuasive and performative artistry. John provides us with ample evidences to cross-pollinate our contextual struggles with that of the story world of the Fourth Gospel. In the Gospel of John, "freedom" (*eleutheria*, John 8:31-47) is understood as freedom from the bondage of sin. It is emphasized to be the inner spiritual aspect of a believer. Inner spiritual aspect of freedom is not just an end in itself, but the cause to further freedom in the personal and collective experience of eternal life in the world. This holistic aspect must be emphasized if freedom is to be understood and experienced in its complete sense.[95] In that sense, in John, experiencing freedom is not only individualistic but also relational. One who experiences freedom is obligated to invite others to have the same experience. Therein comes the role of evangelism and missions that further leads to religious conversion. This aspect of the Johannine ideology is at odd with the Jewish and Hindu ideologies. Hence there are conflicts within the *Sitz im Leben Kirche* and in the *Sitz im Leben India*. Wingate says, "The Christian encounter with India produces particular issues, because it has been, in the religious area, primarily an encounter with Hinduism."[96] An extreme view expressed by the Rashtriya Swayam Sevak (RSS) can be stated below:

> The non-Hindu people in Hindustan must adopt Hindu culture and language, must learn to respect and hold in reverence to Hindu religion, must entertain no idea but those of the glorification of the Hindu race and culture… They must cease to be foreigners or may stay in the country completely subordinate to the Hindu nation, claiming, deserving no privileges or any preferential treatment, not even citizens' rights.[97]

---

[95] See Martyn, *History and Theology in the Fourth Gospel*; Brown, *Community of the Beloved Disciple*.

[96] See A. Wingate, *The Church and Conversion: A Study of Recent Conversions to and from Christianity in the Tamil Area of South India* (Delhi: ISPCK, 1997/1999), 232.

[97] Quoted in Wingate, *The Church and Conversion*, 234; R. Robinson and S.

The above statement is by all means anti-nationalistic in its essence. In spite of freedom of religion being guaranteed as a fundamental right, several attempts have been made in state and central assemblies or in committees to overthrow the essence of Article 25 of the Indian Constitution.[98] This is the situation in which the Johannine community feelings and struggles are to be reinterpreted. Moreover, the rhetorical and dramatic configuration of the Johannine story enables the Indian readers to understand its efficacy in their existential struggles here and now. The *gnomic* rather than *descriptive* linguistic phenomenon of the Gospel makes it a paradigm for the Christian communities in India to reinterpret their contextual struggles.[99]

Concluding Remarks

The genre components such as content, form, and function of the Fourth Gospel incorporate the existent struggles of the Johannine community. The church-and-synagogue conflict lies at the heart of the narrative which in turn provides both explicit and implicit clues pertinent to the Johannine social dynamics. The narrator's attempt to merge the story of Jesus with the story of the community persuades the reader to consider the Gospel as a paradigm in the contemporary Indian context. The story of the Indian church, which delineates the existent struggles of the Christian community within the extended socio-religious milieu, has to be merged with

---

Clarke, eds., *Religious Conversion in India: Modes, Motivations, and Meanings* (New Delhi: Oxford University Press, 2003).

[98] Thavare says that, "Conversion from one religion to another has always been an issue of friction in a pluralistic situation, where the process of change affects one's religion, society, and culture. Conversion has become a controversial issue in India and has led to serious communal conflicts and tensions, and has resulted in law and order problems in some places." See B. Tavare, "Trends in Theology of Conversion in India," in *Conversion in a Pluralistic Context: Perspectives and Perceptions*, eds. K. C. Marak and P.S. Jacob (Pune/Delhi: CMS/ISPCK, 2000), 47.

[99] While *descriptive linguistive phenomena* guide the reader to the *there and then* aspects, *gnomic linguistic phenomena* guide the reader to the *everywhere and ever* perspective. See Thomaskutty, "Biblical Interpretation in the Global-Indian Context," 64-68.

the Johannine story in order to recreate the Indian realities with efficacy. As in the case of the Johannine community, the Indian church suffers from minority-and-majority issues. In the Johannine narrative framework, Jesus' dialogue with his interlocutors foregrounds the antonymous trends, verbal duel, and the violent attitudes of the religious leaders. Similar bossy and dehumanizing tendencies of the Hindu fundamentalists are categorically manifested in the contemporary Indian context. In an at-risk environment for freedom of expression and freedom of belief, the Johannine narrator persuades the reading community to develop a rhetoric of difference rather than a rhetoric of distance. The Johannine narrator develops his discourse through the means of a protagonist-and-antagonist dialogue that further impacts the implied/historical/contemporary reader/s to take side with Jesus. In today's context, the church should take advantage of the ongoing antagonism of the Hindu fundamentalists by placing Jesus at the centre of the Christian discourse. The Johannine narrator does not background the person and work of Jesus even in the face of growing opposition. He foregrounded the messiahship of Jesus in dramatic and rhetorical terms in order to stabilize the kernel of his story. The Indian church should adopt the same (i.e., a Christ-centred missiology and ecclesiology) irrespective of the growing antagonism against its missions and ministry. Thus the Gospel of John can be considered as a tri-level drama in order to encompass the struggles and aspirations of the Christian communities in the Indian context.

An Indian Pentecostal Reading On Conversion

Wessly Lukose[1]

The issue of religious freedom and conversion is not new in the Indian milieu. However, in the recent years, it has become a complex issue, and with the coming of the current BJP government into power, the issue has drawn serious attention of global community. The Hindu militant groups have been vociferously raising their voice for a debate on conversion. Very recently while inaugurating the tenth Annual Conference of State Minorities Commissions, Rajnath Singh, the Union Home Minister of India, called for a national debate on the issue of conversion and the need for an anti-conversion law.[2]

Although Charismatic-Pentecostal Christianity is making significant progress in several parts of India, very little research is done on their theology.[3] The current paper aims to make a Pentecostal contribution towards the study of religious conversion in the Indian context. It is expected that this study will enrich the discussion, to take the debate forward.

As Anderson observed, it is an enormous task to define "Pentecostal" as the term refers to various movements, including indigenous movements in the Majority World "that have adapted to their cultural and religious contexts."[4] The present study adopts a more

---

[1] Dr. Wessly Lukose is the Senior Minister of Birmingham Pentecostal Fellowship Ministries in England. He is also a Lecturer at Birmingham Christian College. His dissertation was published under the title, *Contextual Missiology of the Spirit: Pentecostalism in Rajasthan, India* (Oxford: Regnum, 2013).

[2] Bharti Jain, "Rajnath Calls for a National Debate on Anti-Conversion Law," *The Times of India*, March 23, 2015, accessed on August 15, 2017, http://timesofindia.indiatimes.com/india/Rajnath-calls-for-a-national-debate-on-anti-conversion-law/articleshow/46666362.cms.

[3] Significant researches include Geomon K George, *Religious Pluralism: Challenges for Pentecostalism in India* (Bangalore: CFCC, 2006); Abraham Shaibu, "Ordinary Indian Pentecostal Christology," (PhD diss., University of Birmingham, 2011); Lukose, *Contextual Missiology of the Spirit*.

[4] Allan Anderson, "Introduction: World Pentecostalism at a Crossroads," in *Pentecostals After a Century: Global Perspectives on a Movement in Transition*, JPTS 15 eds. Allan H. Anderson and Walter J. Hollenweger (Sheffield: SAP,

inclusive definition, following Walter Hollenweger,[5] Anderson[6] and Amos Yong.[7] Such a definition embraces Classical Pentecostals, Charismatics, Neo-Pentecostals and others, who share a common emphasis on the experience of the Holy Spirit. Pentecostalism has become a leading force in global Christianity today.[8] Pentecostal Christianity is growing rapidly in India, just as in many parts of the world. Stanley Burgess observes that Indian Pentecostalism is the fifth largest sector of Global Charismatic Christianity.[9] Although this study is from the perspective of Pentecostals in general, most reflections are drawn from North India. Pentecostal impact in the North is significant and tribal Christianity, which is mostly first generation, is predominantly Pentecostal.

There is a popular notion in India that Christianity is an imported religion from the West. In many parts of the nation, Christianity is generally identified with colonization.[10] Such a misrepresentation will cause others to view Christians as foreigners, and places them in a potentially vulnerable situation, which may lead to faith conflicts. Although all Christians are exposed to attack from Hindu militant groups, Pentecostals seem to be a particular target as they have been labelled as a proselytizing group even by

---

1999), 19-20.

[5] Walter J. Hollenweger, *Pentecostalism: Origins and Developments Worldwide* (Peabody: Hendrickson, 1997), 1.

[6] See Allan Heath Anderson, *An Introduction to Pentecostalism: Global Charismatic Christianity*, 2nd ed. (Cambridge: Cambridge University Press, 2014), 1-15. He calls them "spiritual gifts" movements (14).

[7] Amos Yong, *The Spirit Poured Out on All Flesh: Pentecostalism and the Possibility of Global Theology* (Grand Rapids, MI: Baker Academic, 2005), 18–19. He aligns himself with *The New International Dictionary of Pentecostal and Charismatic Movements* (Grand Rapids, MI: Zondervan, 2002), xviii–xxi. In *Discerning the Spirit (s): A Pentecostal-Charismatic Contribution to Christian Theology of Religions* (Sheffield: SAP, 2000), 21, though he initially adopts a more exclusive definition, later he calls for a more inclusive approach.

[8] In the present study, the terms "Pentecostal" and "Charismatic" are used interchangeably with the same meaning unless otherwise stated.

[9] Stanley M. Burgess, "Pentecostalism in India: An Overview," *AJPS* 4, no.1 (2001): 85.

[10] For a detailed discussion, see Paul M. Collins, *Christian Inculturation in India* (Aldershot, Hampshire: Ashgate, 2007), 18-22.

many other Christians.¹¹ There have been occasions where mainline Christianity distanced themselves from Pentecostals when it came to conversion issues.

Pentecostalism offers a mission theology, which gives more insights into the Spirit dimension, which is neglected by others, including Bosch.¹² Although missiologists like Jan Jongeneel and Hwa Yung recognize the significance of the Spirit element in missiology, they have failed to see its distinctive dimension.¹³ While discussing Evangelical and Pentecostal theologies in Asia, Hwa Yung anticipates that "in the future the church worldwide will have to give the gifts of the Spirit...a greater role in its mission and theology."¹⁴

Pentecostal Missiology reveals the potential of the Spirit dimension in conversion. It tries to introduce a conversion missiology from the perspective of the Spirit. This missiology attempts to keep a balance between the changing situations of the community as well as their Spirit experiences, as both have their own influence in shaping the theology of Pentecostals. This conversion missiology can serve as a viable alternative in the discussion of conversion. It is not to argue that all other models should be discarded, but rather to propose this as another potential alternative alongside other proposals. This model seems to be more flexible as it is sensitive to the particular cultural or local situations on the one hand, and at the same time it takes the experiences of the Spirit seriously. This paper focuses on conversion from an Indian Pentecostal Perspective. This does not mean that Pentecostals see the role of the Holy Spirit only

---

[11] For a better understanding of this claim, see Chad M. Bauman, *Pentecostals, Proselytization, and Anti-Christian Violence in Contemporary India* (Oxford: Oxford University Press, 2015).

[12] See K. Kim's critique on Bosch's missiology, Kirsteen Kim, *Mission in the Spirit: The Holy Spirit in Indian Christian Theologies* (New Delhi: ISPCK, 2003), 172-174. Although he recognizes the importance of the Holy Spirit in mission, his treatment of the role of the Spirit in contextual missiology is limited.

[13] Hwa Yung, *Mangoes or Bananas? Quest for an Authentic Asian Christian Theology* (Oxford: Regnum, 1997), 57-58.

[14] Hwa Yung, "Mission and Evangelism: Evangelical and Pentecostal Theologies in Asia," in *Christian Theology in Asia*, ed. Sebastian C.H. Kim (Cambridge: Cambridge University Press, 2008), 266.

in conversion; on the contrary, the Holy Spirit has a role in various aspects including social, political, environmental, medical, educational and economic aspects of community.[15]

Although the present study is a missiological study, it endeavours to integrate research from various fields in order to provide a comprehensive perspective on a complex issue. Many contemporary missiologists have explored the interdisciplinary nature of missiology. The Catholic missiologist, Francis Anekwe Oborji, argues, "Mission is an *intersubjective* reality in which missiologists, missionaries and the people among whom they labour are all partners."[16] According to Samuel Escobar, "*missiology* is an interdisciplinary approach to understanding missionary action. Missiology examines missionary facts from the perspectives of the biblical sciences, theology, history and social sciences."[17] Intercultural theology also recognizes the importance of a "multi-disciplinary approach."[18]

The complex dynamics of Pentecostalism requires an interdisciplinary approach. As Anderson observes, Pentecostal theology is "more than written and academic theology," but is "found in the preaching, rituals and practices of churches." He refers to the "enacted theology" (theology in practice) seen in Pentecostalism.[19] While discussing the problems of Pentecostal traditioning, Simon Chan points out that the "strength of Pentecostal traditioning lies in its powerful narratives," but its "weakness lies in its inability to explain itself."[20]

The voice of Louis Malieckal regarding the role of a theologian is significant here while developing a missiology:

---

[15] For more details, see Lukose, *Contextual Missiology of the Spirit*.

[16] Francis Anekwe Oborji, *Concepts of Mission: The Evolution of Contemporary Missiology* (Maryknoll, NY: Orbis, 2006), 54.

[17] Samuel Escobar, *The New Global Mission: The Gospel from Everywhere to Everyone* (Illinois: IVP, 2003), 21.

[18] Werner Ustorf, "The Cultural Origins of "Intercultural Theology,"" *Mission Studies* 25, no. 2 (2008): 244.

[19] Allan Anderson, "The Contextual Pentecostal Theology of David Yonggi Cho," *AJPS* 7, no. 1 (1999): 102.

[20] Simon Chan, *Pentecostal Theology and the Christian Spiritual Tradition*, JPTS Series 21 (Sheffield: SAP, 2000), 20.

> ...theology today is seen as a living search arising out of commitment to the people. The starting point is praxis and the subject is people themselves in their life-struggle. They do the initial articulation, which will be in the form of a search for ultimate meaning of this struggle. The role of the professional theologian is to ponder, interpret and highlight this meaning, while participating in it as a member of this struggling community, and thus enable them to discover it more fully.[21]

Encountering Conversion in India

In this volume, Sebastian Kim argues that the conflicting views on conversion by Hindus and Christians are crucial while discussing the issue of religious freedom and conversion. It seems that the issue of conversion has been chiefly viewed in India through socio-economic and socio-political spectacles. Sometimes, these dynamics have been overemphasized, neglecting other aspects in conversion. As Kim notes elsewhere, Hindus link conversion "with colonial power, ecclesiastical expansion, political manipulation" and "social disturbance."[22] Consequently, they are suspicious of everything including the awarding of the Nobel Prize. Ashok Singhal commented on the award of the 1998 Nobel Prize to Amartya Sen, an Indian economist, for his work on welfare economics, that this was a "western conspiracy to promote literacy in developing societies in order to bring them within the ultimate pale of a global Christian order and thus 'wipe out Hinduism from this country'."[23] On the other hand, Christians think that it is the plan of the upper caste Hindu nationalists to oppose conversion, as Christians link conversion with "social uplift, caste mobility, and the search for

---

[21] Louis Malieckal, "Realising an Indian Theology of Mission," in *A Missiology for Third Millennium: A Contextualized Mission Theology*, ed. Thomas Aykara (Bangalore: Dharmaram Publications, 1997), 128.

[22] Sebastian C.H. Kim, *In Search of Identity: Debates on Religious Conversion in India* (New Delhi: Oxford University Press, 2003), 188.

[23] Gauri Viswanathan, "Literacy and Conversion in the Discourse of Hindu Nationalism," in *The Crisis of Secularism in India*, eds. Anuradha Dingwaney and Rajeswari Sunder Rajan (Durham/London: Duke University Press, 2007), 133-134.

justice."[24] Christians argue that the supremacy and dominion of these nationalists will be affected as the Dalits and tribal communities will be educated and their identity strengthened, and that is why the social work done by the Christians is opposed by militant Hindus.

History has witnessed a number of counter-devices used by Hindu extremists to check conversion by Muslims and Christians. The early approach to protecting Hindus from religious conversion was the implementation of Hindu personal laws against those who were converted to other religions from Hinduism.[25] The converts were expelled from the Hindu community, and various benefits and privileges of converts from a Scheduled Caste and Tribe background were withdrawn. Another approach was the criticism of untouchability.[26] Following many socio-religious reformers, V. D. Savarkar criticized the practice of untouchabiltiy, as he believed that favours for untouchables were necessary to counter the conversion attempts. However, Lise McKean's research reveals that others reacted against Savarkar's policy to please untouchables.[27] There are untouchables who argue against Hindutva ideology.[28]

One of the most effective tools has been the Hindu counter-conversion movement called Ghar Wapsi (homecoming) launched by the Sangh Parivar. They started their own schools and other social activities in the tribal areas, that function under Hindutva ideology. Dharm Jagran Samanway Samtiti (DJSS), an RSS affiliate, made a resolution in August 2015 to stop conversion

---

[24] Kim, *In Search of Identity*, 188.

[25] Kim, *In Search of Identity*, 140.

[26] There was a social practice among the Hindus in pre-independent India to consider people of lower castes as well as outcastes as impure, and so the people of higher castes were not willing to have contact with them. For more details of the practice, see Valerian Rodrigues, ed., *The Essential Writings of B.R. Ambedkar* (New Delhi: Oxford University Press, 2002), 95-98, 114-118, 321-406.

[27] For more details of the discussion, see Lise McKean, *Divine Enterprise: Gurus and the Hindu Nationalist Movement* (Chicago/London: The University of Chicago Press, 1996), 84-87.

[28] For example, see Kancha Ilaiah, *Why I am not a Hindu: A Sudra Critique of Hindutva Philosophy, Culture and Political Economy*, 2nd ed. (Calcutta, India: Samya, 2005).

by 2020 and continue Ghar Wapsi so that the Hindu population increases by the next census in 2021.[29] VHP leader Pravin Togadia re-emphasized the issue of Ghar Wapsi, asking the government to either ban religious conversions or allow Hindu militants to go ahead with Ghar Wapsi. He said that, "Hindus can no longer be silent on conversions which resulted in the dwindling of their population."[30] However, this counter conversion programme was practised by the Arya Samaj, and the practice was called *shuddhi* (purification). McKean observes that in spite of the opposition from "conservative upper castes," Savarkar promoted *shuddhi*, and subsequently many "untouchables, Christians, and Muslims publicly embraced Hinduism."[31]

Conversion is likely to be the purpose behind the origin of the VHP. The words of Chinmayananda, the founder of the organization, reveals the same:

> When your pope came to India [Paul VI in December 1964], he said he was going to convert 125 people to Christianity. Public opinion made him withdraw his plan but I was in Bombay and announced that I would convert 200 people to Hinduism and I did. Then I had the idea to start a group to work for conversions. I didn't have enough people of my own so I asked the RSS for their help. Guruji [RSS head, Golwalkar] liked the idea and had thousands of workers everywhere. ... After I started the VHP, I returned to my own mission as spiritual teacher of Vedanta.[32]

It is strange that the issue of conversion is treated differently with regard to diverse religious communities. When people embrace Christian faith, it is called conversion and is regarded as a threat to social order. However, when people are forced or enticed to become

---

[29] Shyamlal Yadav, "No More Conversion by 2020: Affiliate Sets Target Under Ghar Wapsi," *Indian Express*, August 17, 2015, accessed on August 15, 2017, http://indianexpress.com/article/india/india-others/no-more-conversion-by-2020-affiliate-sets-target/

[30] Vinod Khanal, "India Pass Anti-Conversion Law to Stop Ghar Wapsi: VHP," *The Times of India*, January 18, 2015, accessed on August 15, 2017, http://timesofindia.indiatimes.com/india/Pass-anti-conversion-law-to-stop-ghar-wapsi-VHP/articleshow/45926620.cms

[31] McKean, *Divine Enterprise*, 85.

[32] McKean, *Divine Enterprise*, 102.

Hindus, it is referred to as *suddhi* or Ghar Wapsi. As Tehmina Arora has rightly commented in her paper, even the so-called "Freedom of Religion Bill" introduced in many states has "discriminatory provisions" for they give "preferential treatment to re-conversion."[33]

Another approach by Hindu militants to check conversion has been written Hindu criticism of Christian exclusive truth claims, dogmas, and their conversion activities.[34] Kim notes the work of both Ram Swarup and Sita Ram Goel, and concludes that "through their extensive research and reading of Muslim and Christian material, they provided important sources for Hindus in their opposition to Islam and Christianity in general and conversion in particular."[35] According to L. Stanislaus, the summary of most literature and documents that oppose Christianity is that missionaries are involved in "mass conversions by incentives, deceit, allurement" and "coercion."[36]

The most alarming approach is the use of physical violence to oppose conversion. Both the converted and the converter are attacked, and in many cases, Christians are assaulted without any clear evidence of conversion. Hundreds of cheaply available books, booklets, pamphlets, documents, and CDs containing material against Christians are distributed everywhere to "create an atmosphere of hatred and abhorrence towards Christians ...."[37] The speeches of many Hindu militant leaders including Members of Parliament have intensified the tension, and caused trouble.[38] Although persecution is not new in India, many parts of the nation have witnessed an intensified attack against Christians since the latter part of the last millennium. Many sociologists as well

---

[33] Tehmina Arora, "Freedom of Religion in India: Violated in Practice, Questioned in Principle," in this volume.

[34] For example, see Arun Shourie, *Missionaries in India: Continuities, Changes and Dilemmas* (New Delhi: Rupa, 2004). For more details on such Hindu literature, see Kim, *In Search of Identity*, 140–42; L. Stanislaus, "A Christian Response to Hindutva," in *Nationalism and Hindutva*, 198-99.

[35] Kim, *In Search of Identity*, 141.

[36] Stanislaus, "Christian Response to Hindutva," 198-99.

[37] Stanislaus, "Christian Response to Hindutva," 199.

[38] For details, see S. Soban Kumar Daniel, "The Challenges of the Hindutva Movement and Christian Responses in India," (MPhil thesis, University of Birmingham, 2004), 50, 60-61.

as Christian writers conclude that the accelerated phase of assault on Christians began in 1998, when the BJP came into power to head the Central Government.[39] This view became stronger as the violence against Christians deepened when the current BJP government came to power.

The next means to curtail conversion is the law banning religious conversion that has been introduced in several states of India as another measure to counter conversion.[40] Although such law is called the Freedom of Religion Bill, Christians see that the chief purpose has been to make conversion illegal and this has created more religious tension. A careful observation of this law creates doubt about its purpose. Christians see it as part of a hidden agenda of the Hindutva advocates as this law has been introduced mostly under the BJP rule. There are ambiguities in the law. The papers of both Kim and Tehmina succinctly explain this issue in detail.

As Kim argues, the militant Hindus have little room for religious tolerance as they use "political power to deal with conversion. By regarding Christian conversion as a socio-political issue and also by imposing the Hindutva ideology on the people regardless of their beliefs and practices, the Sangh Parivar suppresses the freedom of individuals," and thus fails to safeguard the Constitution.[41]

---

[39] Pradeep Mandav, *Communalism in India: A Paradigm Shift to Indian Politics* (Delhi, India: Authors Press, 2000), 191-194; Michael, "Hindu Nationalism," 475-476; Bengt G. Karlsson, "Entering into the Christian Dharma: Contemporary 'Tribal' Conversion in India," in *Christians and Missionaries in India: Cross-Cultural Communication since 1500*, ed. Robert Eric Frykenberg (Grand Rapids: Eerdmans, 2003), 133-134.

[40] Although the Indian Constitution advocates religious freedom, a number of states in India, including Arunachal Pradesh, Madhya Pradesh, Himachal Pradesh, Orissa, Gujarat, Chattisgarh and Rajasthan, have passed anti-conversion laws. Interestingly, the laws are introduced as "Freedom of Religion Bill." However, they are generally known in India as "Anti-conversion Bill" as these laws are to "provide for the prohibition of conversion from one religion to another."

[41] S. Kim, "Hindutva, Secular India and the Report of the Christian Missionary Activities Enquiry Committee: 1954-57," in *Nationalism and Hindutva: A Christian Response*, ed. Mark T. B. Laing (Delhi/Pune, India: ISPCK/CMS, 2005), 141.

Engaging Conversion: A Pentecostal Reading

As Kim suggests, more than a "socio-political" interpretation, a "spiritual" dimension of conversion is required to deal with the problem. Hindus object to conversions mainly because it seems to them to be a "purely human enterprise and not a spiritual transformation," and so despite the complex Indian socio-political situation, Hindus look for "genuine" or "spiritual" conversions, a clear demonstration of spirituality in Christian conversion.[42] Elsewhere he states: "we may need a 'recovery of the spirituality' of conversion. Whatever it might be, one thing is sure: neither holding on to the 'traditional' approach to conversion nor dismissing the importance of conversion in Christian theology is the way forward."[43] It is significant to investigate various aspects involved in conversion: anthropological, psychological and spiritual elements. Pentecostalism provides a conversion missiology, which focuses on the spiritual dynamics of conversion. It seems that the contemporary Indian context of conversion indicates the significance of the Spirit dimension in the development of a conversion mission theology. WCC's Shared Code of Conduct also underlines this need, for it says, "conversion is not our prerogative; it is the work of the Holy Spirit in the heart of the individual."[44]

Although there is unprecedented growth in the movement, Pentecostal missiology is still developing. It seems that "Pentecostal missiological literature has not kept pace" with Pentecostal growth.[45] However, it seems that what has developed thusfar shows that a Pentecostal missiology should be pneumatocentric. In order to make a Pentecostal Missiology of Conversion, "the

---

[42] S. Kim, *In Search of Identity*, 197–200.
[43] Sebastian C. H. Kim, "Indian Christian Mission Ecclesiology: Models for Engagement with Hinduism- with Special Reference to Conversion," in *The Indian Church in Context: Her Emergence, Growth and Mission*, ed. Mark T. B. Laing (Pune/Delhi: CMS/ISPCK, 2002), 183.
[44] "Christian Witness in a Multi-Religious World," accessed on August 15, 2017, http://www.worldevangelicals.org/WCC_WEA_Vat_Code_Draft.pdf.
[45] M.A. Dempster, B.D. Klaus, and D. Petersen, "Editor's Introduction," in *Called and Empowered: Global Mission in Pentecostal Perspective*, ed. M.A. Dempster, B. D. Klaus, and D. Petersen (Peabody, MA: Hendrickson, 1991), xv.

Spirit-Text-Community," the triad of sources as proposed by Pentecostal scholars Kenneth Archer and John Thomas while developing a Pentecostal Hermeneutics, is used.[46] For Pentecostals, the voice of the Spirit, the voice of the scripture and the voice of the faith community, the Church, are important in forming their theology. As Cartledge observes, all these "three sources are expected to work together in order to generate theological reflection and inform ecclesial decisions in relation to missiological praxis."[47]

Textual Reflection

Many missiologists like David Bosch argue that a viable theology of mission should not only be concerned with context but also with the Bible.[48] Bevans argues that in order to do theology contextually, two issues, the "faith experience of the past that is recorded in the scriptures" and "the experience of the present, the context," must be taken into account.[49] Biblical grounding is important to Christians in general, and so also for Pentecostals. The emphasis on biblical authority for mission theology and practice by Pentecostals prompted Pomerville to refer to them as "People of the Book."[50]

Pentecostals always explore the life of the early Christian community in the book of Acts to discover their continuity with them.

---

[46] See Kenneth J. Archer, *A Pentecostal Hermeneutic for the Twenty-First Century: Spirit, Scripture and Community* (London: T & T Clark International, 2004), 156-196.

[47] Mark J. Cartledge, "Pentecostal Theological Method and Intercultural Theology," *Transformation* 25, no. 2-3 (April & July 2008): 94.

[48] For details, see M.R. Spindler, "The Biblical Grounding and Orientation of Mission," in *Missiology: An Ecumenical Introduction: Texts and Contexts of Global Christianity*, eds. F.J. Verstraelen and others (Grand Rapids, MI: Eerdmans, 1995), 143.

[49] Stephen B. Bevans, *Models of Contextual Theology*, rev. ed. (Maryknoll, New York: Orbis Books, 2002), 3-5. By "experience of the past" he means experiences that are "recorded in scriptures and kept alive, preserved, defended- and perhaps even neglected or suppressed- in tradition," and "experience of the present" means "individual and contemporary-collective experience."

[50] For further details, see Grant McClung, "Truth on Fire: Pentecostals and an Urgent Missiology," in *Azusa Street and Beyond: Pentecostal Missions and Church Growth in the Twentieth Century*, ed. Grant McClung (Gainesville, FL: Bridge-Logos, 2006), 79-80.

They believe that the Acts community was following the teachings of Jesus Christ. His teachings included two significant aspects connecting the Holy Spirit and conversion. First, the role of the Spirit is crucial in the actual conversion of a person, for He convicts a person of sin, of righteousness and of judgment (John 16:8–11). Second is the role of the Spirit in motivating a person for mission, for the Spirit empowers disciples to witness Christ (Acts 1:8). There are several stories in Acts showing that the Spirit empowered the messenger to witness Christ, and also convicted the hearer of sin, and turned the person to follow Jesus. These examples reveal that the Spirit experiences of the early Christians played a significant role in the reality of conversion. There are other examples of how the Spirit empowers the disciples to witness more, even when they wanted to withdraw. Spirit experiences like dreams, visions and audible voices played a significant role in formulating and reformulating both the mission theology and practice of early Christianity. The following discussion is a reflection from Acts to explain the role of the Holy Spirit in witnessing as well as conversion.

There are examples which indicate that the Spirit took initiative in guiding the missionary to a particular person, family or group. The best example is the mission of Peter to Cornelius' household. Peter was asked by the Spirit to go to the house of the Gentile centurion Cornelius (Act. 10:19-20). He had the "direct instruction of the Holy Spirit" and a "complementary vision."[51] It is important to note that Cornelius, a man from outside the Christian community, also received a voice to send men for Peter. The Spirit initiated two simultaneous events, in the lives of both Cornelius and Peter, which resulted in the transformation of both. As Roland Allen has observed, Peter "realized that his action was liable to be called in question, but he acted under the impulse of the Spirit."[52] While he was preaching, the Spirit fell upon the people and they started speaking in tongues, and this changed Peter's theology. He asked, who could forbid the *Spirit-filled, tongues-speaking Gentiles*

---

[51] Roger Stronstad, *The Prophethood of All Believers: A Study in Luke's Charismatic Theology*, JPTS Series 16 (Sheffield: SAP, 1999), 109.

[52] Roland Allen, "The Spirit the Source and Test of New Forms of Missionary Activity," in *The Holy Spirit and Mission Dynamics*, ed. McDonnell C. Douglas (Pasadena, CA: William Carey Library, 1997), 100.

from being baptized? This shows that he, like many other Jewish Christian leaders of the time, believed that the Spirit would work only among certain groups of people, and so baptism was only for them. Now these Gentiles had received the Holy Spirit before they were baptized in water.

On another occasion, Philip was told by the Spirit to go to the desert between Jerusalem and Gaza (Acts 8:26-39). Apart from being a man "full of the Holy Spirit and wisdom," Roger Stronstad saw two other Spirit experiences of Philip in this context. He was "led by the Spirit to the Ethiopian Court official" (Acts 8:29), and "he was supernaturally transported by the Spirit after he had baptized the Ethiopian" (Acts 8:39).[53] While there was severe persecution in Jerusalem and all were scattered to diverse places, Ananias had a dream telling him to go to the house of Judas to heal Saul (Acts 9:10-12). It is significant that all Christians in Jerusalem knew that Saul was a leading persecutor and they were afraid of him (Acts 9:26). However, in response to the dream, Ananias went to meet Saul, and as a result he was healed, filled with the Holy Spirit and became a disciple. Later he became one of the leading voices of the early Christian community.

In all these cases, conversion is to be seen as the end result of an initiation by the Holy Spirit. The missionary responded to the Spirit's initiation and the subsequent result was the conversion of people.

There are examples of the Spirit's intervention when there were threats to early Christians from the religio-political sphere of society. Diverse responses by the Holy Spirit are reported in Acts. First, there are examples when the Spirit enabled the Christians to continue to speak in the same location without fear. For example, Peter and John, the disciples of Jesus, were taken into custody by the local authorities, who told them "not to speak at all nor teach in the name of Jesus" (Acts 4:18). On their release they reported all that happened to the other disciples. When they prayed, the Spirit came upon them, and they spoke the Word with more boldness (Acts 4:31). On another occasion, Stephen, a man "full of the Holy Spirit," was empowered in his preaching in the midst of persecution

---

[53] Roger Stronstad, "Affirming Diversity: God's People as a Community of Prophets," *Pneuma* 17, no. 2 (Fall, 1995): 153.

(Acts 7:54-56). This incident can be seen as an example of "supernatural Spirit-inspired defence" in midst of persecution.[54] The Spirit empowered the persecuted believers to witness Christ even in prison (Acts 16:24-34). When Paul was opposed by the Jews in Corinth, he wanted to withdraw from his mission. However, he heard the voice through a vision in the night, saying, "do not be afraid, but speak, and do not keep silent; for I am with you, and no one will attack you to hurt you; for I have many people in this city" (Acts 18:9,10). As a result, he continued his ministry in the same city for another one and a half years.

In certain cases the Spirit told people to move from their existing locations after facing challenges. While Paul was preaching to the crowd in Jerusalem, he said that he moved from Jerusalem because he was asked to do so. During a prayer in the temple in Jerusalem he heard a voice in a trance, which said, "make haste and get out of Jerusalem quickly, for they will not receive your testimony concerning Me" (Acts 22:18). Consequently, he shifted his focus from Jews to Gentiles and moved out of Jerusalem.

In conclusion, the early Christians realized the role of the Holy Spirit in conversion. The early community responded to the Spirit, and Spirit experiences had a crucial place in their mission theology and practice. In complex situations, the Spirit intervened and enabled His people to come through the crisis, and He played a significant role in directing the mission. The voice of Newbigin, a missionary in India for several years, is significant here:

> It [church] is not in control of mission. Another is in control, and his [Spirit's] fresh works will repeatedly surprise the church, compelling it to stop talking and to listen. Because the Spirit himself is sovereign over the mission, the church can only be the attentive servant.... The church's witness is secondary and derivative. The church is witness insofar as it follows obediently where the Spirit leads.[55]

---

[54] Stronstad, *Prophethood of All Believers*, 90.
[55] Lesslie Newbigin, *The Open Secret: An Introduction to the Theology of Mission*, rev. ed. (Grand Rapids: Eerdmans, 1995), 61.

Reflection from Pentecostal Community

More than any other reason, Pentecostals see a spiritual dynamic in conversion. They prefer the term transformation to conversion, for they believe in the total transformation of a person by the power of the Spirit of God. They claim that a genuine conversion experience is the work of the Spirit. The Holy Spirit is the initiator, inspirer and igniter in a true conversion. He guides both the agency, the church or the missionary, as well as the recipient. A reflection from the Pentecostal Community in North India shows that although they may not necessarily aim at the conversion of people, their lives and works may ultimately bring transformation in the lives of people.

This study of conversion reveals that there are two types of Pentecostal engagements. The first one is the intentional engagement of Pentecostals in conversion. Pentecostals intentionally engage in evangelistic activities with the aim of turning others to follow Jesus. They believe that the Spirit empowerment is primarily for evangelism. As Anderson notes, "the power of the Spirit in Pentecostal thinking is always linked to the command to preach the gospel to all nations."[56] That is why even in the midst of severe oppositions, the growth of the movement has not been arrested. Although old methods of evangelism, such as literature distribution, street preaching and the like have been avoided, "Spirit experiences" like healing, exorcism, and other manifestations, have brought growth to Pentecostal churches. Ordinary believers are encouraged to be empowered by the Spirit and exercise their spiritual gifts for community building and growth. The responsibility for evangelism has been shifted from the clergy to ordinary believers, and consequently traditional evangelistic methods have been replaced by charismatic experiences like healing and exorcism.

The story of the beginning of the FFCI church in Jawar village in Rajasthan illustrates that exorcism and healing help the planting and growth of churches. Pannalal[57] came from a non-Christian tribal background, and practised witchcraft and magic. He was tormented by evil spirits, his wife was seriously ill, and finally he

---

[56] Allan Anderson, *Spreading Fires: The Missionary Nature of Early Pentecostalism* (London: SCM, 2007), 212.

[57] Pseudonym.

decided to commit a family suicide. However, he says that he was guided by some inner voice to visit his neighbour, where he found a Pentecostal pastor who was on an accidental visit to the village. The pastor prayed for Pannalal and his family, and as a result, he was delivered from the evil spirits and his wife was healed. Soon he started witnessing Christ and praying for the sick, and he gradually formed a congregation, till today he oversees four growing congregations in the Girva Tehsil.[58] Another story, the experiences of Kantilal[59] and his family, shows the way ordinary women are involved in the healing mission. Kantilal too came from a non-Christian family, and his wife had been seriously ill for more than two months. Mrs. Laxmi,[60] a Pentecostal believer went and prayed for Kantilal's wife and she was healed. Soon the whole family came to Christian faith, and later Kantilal became a full-time Pentecostal minister.[61] Therefore, as Paul Mathews has suggested, most Pentecostal churches in north Indian villages should be regarded as "healing communities."[62]

The increase in the number of sick people and the lack of medical privileges in remote villages in North India is explained as one of the reasons for Pentecostal emphasis on healing. In almost all their meetings, there is a separate time for praying for the sick. People bring bottles of water and oil when they come for meetings, and they expect pastors to pray over these bottles. These are used as means for the healing of their sick people and even cattle.

The second one is the unintentional engagement of Pentecostals in conversion. There are numerous incidents where conversion happens as a result of action without evangelistic intention. Pentecostals unintentionally engage in the life crises of people and the end result is conversion of individuals and families. The growth of

---

[58] For more details of the story, see Reji Chacko, "Sharing the Living Manna," *Cross and Crown* 37, no. 2 (November-December 2007): 24.

[59] Pseudonym.

[60] Pseudonym.

[61] For more details of the story, see C&C Correspondent, "They Believed and They Saw the Glory of God," *Cross and Crown* 37, no. 5 (May-June 2008): 9.

[62] Paul Mathews, interview by author, Udaipur, Rajasthan, August 27, 2014. He is the National President of FFCI, one of the largest Pentecostal organizations in North India and also the senior pastor of the largest Pentecostal congregation in Rajasthan.

the movement in several rural areas in North India is the outcome of various activities of Spirit-guided Pentecostals, without aiming at the conversion of others.

> Even today there are villages in North India where there are no medical facilities and means of transport. People have to carry their sick for several miles to get them into a vehicle. Their particular situations prompt ordinary believers to pray for their needy friends or neighbours. There are numerous stories in such tribal villages where conversion happened as the result of an answer to prayer to Jesus by a neighbour during the most difficult and helpless situations in the lives of others. The story of a convert from a remote village in Rajasthan to Pentecostal faith explains that the love and care of Spirit-guided people for their neighbours also produces conversion: My daughter was seriously ill. We took her to a nearby clinic, but there was no relief. We did not have money to take her to far away private hospitals. We came back home hopeless. Meanwhile one of our neighbours talked to us about going to *girija ghar* (prayer house) and praying to Jesus for the healing. We were not interested in the beginning, but one late night my daughter became seriously ill. There was no transport to take her to any hospital. We began to cry thinking that our daughter will die. She began to throw her tongue out, open her eyes wildly, and move the body violently. Then we called our neighbour, and as soon as they saw the girl, they began to pray to Jesus to heal our daughter. To our surprise, she began to be normal. Then she sat on the cot and asked for water. The next Sunday we went to the *girija ghar* along with our neighbour. From then onwards we began to go to church every Sunday. The Holy Spirit is our helper in every situation. He began to bless us in every aspect of our life. Then why can't we worship Jesus? We do not have proper transport in our village, proper medical facilities; we do not have money to go to private hospitals in the far away cities. Jesus is healing us freely, then how can you say that we cannot turn to Jesus.[63]

---

[63] Kanakam Bai (pseudonym), interview by author, Udaipur, Rajasthan, May 23, 2006.

The story of Mr Prasad[64] and family best explains that conversion can happen as the result of the fruit of the Spirit exhibited by Spirit-led people. Mr Prasad comes from a high caste orthodox Hindu family. He was formerly serving as the Vice President at Binani Industries Limited. His youngest daughter Pooja is an otherly abled person, and so she needs special care. She had a Pentecostal friend Amy in her school. Being guided by the Spirit, Amy began to demonstrate Christian love to Pooja and she used to take time to help her. Moved by Amy's behaviour and service, Prasad's family began to search for the reason. When they found that Jesus was the reason, they were so curious and passionate to find a purposeful life. That is how they started coming to Amy's house and finally embraced the new life in Jesus as a family, and started publically inviting others to follow the Lord.

The story of Leela[65] and her family, who became followers of Christ as a result of the friendship and hospitality of Praveen[66] and family, shows the importance of the "theology of hospitality" as proposed by the Pentecostal scholar Amos Yong.[67] Praveen and family shared cooking skills and expertise with Leela's family, who was running a restaurant. They often visited each other's houses and had meals together. Gradually, Leela's family developed an interest in prayers, and they asked Praveen's family to pray for their business to flourish, and this happened. Consequently Leela and her family became Christians. Praveen said that they neither aimed at the conversion of the other famliy nor called them for prayer, but "it is the work of the Holy Spirit, and we became an instrument for Him to bless this family."[68]

Pentecostals' unintentional engagement with others, particularly in their life crises, motivates them to use their spiritual gifts to help their neighbours in need. They engage with people of other

---

[64] Pseudonym. Email message to author, September 8, 2015.

[65] Pseudonym.

[66] Praveen (pseudonym) and family became Pentecostal from a non-Christian background.

[67] Amos Yong, *Hospitality and the Other: Pentecost, Christian Practices, and the Neighbour* (Maryknoll, New York: Orbis, 2008).

[68] Praveen (pseudonym), interview by author, Udaipur, Rajasthan, May 5, 2006.

faiths, not necessarily with the intention of conversion but on a compassionate dimension of the Spirit, although such engagement may sometimes bring conversion. Therefore, the result of this charismatic engagement,[69] whether healing or exorcism, conversion is to be understood as the work of the Holy Spirit, not as human achievement.

Conclusion

The above discussion shows that the Pentecostal conversion missiology can be understood as a missiology of engagement. Whether intentional or unintentional, they engage with people irrespective of race or religion. Conversion is understood as the result of such engagements. Although conversion may involve various dynamics such as social, political, and anthropological, it is to be primarily understood as spiritual reality. The spiritual dynamics in conversion cannot be ignored. The Spirit experiences of people also should be taken seriously in the discussion on conversion. A rediscovery of the theological dimension in conversion is needed in the present Indian context. A shift from anthropological to theological can also contribute in our inter-religious engagements. Such a shift from human to divine can be a genuine contribution in the discussion on conversion.

The history of Pentecostalism shows that such a shift is significant. It is argued that the Holy Spirit factor was the chief reason for the outstanding growth of Pentecostalism in the first half of 20th century CE. A study of the impact of both Edinburgh 1910[70] and Pentecostalism will make this fact more clear. The major thrust of the Edinburgh Conference was "an invitation to Christians around the globe to join in the task of evangelizing the entire world."[71] At the same time, the newly formed movement Pentecostalism also

---

[69] Here the phrase "Charismatic engagement" is used to mean the use of various charismatic gifts.

[70] The World Missionary Conference that met in Edinburgh, Scotland, in 1910 is a significant event in the history of the Protestant missionary movement.

[71] M. Thomas Thangaraj, *The Common Task: A Theology of Christian Mission* (Nashville: Abingdon Press, 1999), 11.

had the same goal—of world evangelization—and was involved extensively in evangelistic work of the non-Christian world. Although the Conference had hardly any influence on Pentecostalism, it soon became a global missionary movement.

As Thangaraj observes, "confidence and optimism" was the ethos of the Conference and "the evangelization of the world in our own generation" echoed its mood.[72] Bosch saw that "more than in any preceding period, Christians of this era believed that the future of the world and of God's cause depended on *them*."[73] The closing address of John Mott, one of the leaders of the Conference, shows this spirit. He said, "we go out with a larger acquaintanceship...and that is a rich talent which makes possible wonderful achievements. Our best days are ahead of us because of a larger body of experience now happily placed at the disposal of Christendom...."[74]

One of the major reasons for such optimism is the self-confidence in the Human. Although it was acknowledged that the task of making "Christ known to all men is a superhuman work,"[75] it is clear from the report of the Conference that there was a firm belief that the goal of world evangelization could be achieved through human agencies, resources and strategies. The report says:

> Its [Western church's] resources are more than adequate. There are tens of millions of communicant members. The money power in the hands of believing Christians of our generation is enormous. There are many strong missionary societies and boards in Europe, America, Australasia and South Africa, and they have accumulated a vast fund of experience, and have developed a variety of helpful methods and facilities through generations of activity throughout the world. Surely they possess directive energy amply sufficient to conceive, plan and execute a campaign literally worldwide in its scope. The extent, character and promise

[72] Thangaraj, *Common Task*, 16-17.
[73] David J Bosch, *Transforming Mission: Paradigm Shifts in Theology of Mission* (Maryknoll, New York: Orbis Books, 1994), 334-338.
[74] World Missionary Conference, 1910, *The History and Records of the Conference Together with Addresses Delivered at the Evening Meetings* (Edinburgh/London: Oliphant, Anderson and Ferrier, n.d.), 347-348.
[75] World Missionary Conference 1910, *The Church in the Mission Field* (Edinburgh/London: Oliphant, Anderson and Ferrier, n.d.), 361.

of the Christian Church make it by no means an inefficient part of the Body of Christ.[76]

Although the Edinburgh delegates left the Conference with enormous enthusiasm, the optimistic confidence for evangelizing the whole world in a generation has been gradually toned down. The confidence in the efforts of missionaries to evangelize the whole world was eroded after the World Wars, and the events and changes that have taken place since 1910 had a radical effect on Christian mission theology and practice.[77]

It is significant to note that when the optimistic confidence of Evangelical Christians for world evangelization was in decline in the post-Edinburgh period, Pentecostal missionaries were found to be evangelizing several parts of the globe. Anderson's *Spreading Fires* provides a clear picture of Pentecostal expansion during this period. According to him, the Edinburgh Conference and its emphasis had little influence on Pentecostal missions, as Pentecostals had not been invited to participate.[78] His study reveals that Pentecostal missionaries were sent out from Azusa Street and other centres to places as far as "China, India, Japan, Argentina, Brazil, all over Europe, Palestine, Egypt, Somaliland, Liberia, Angola and South Africa," within two years of the beginning of the Azusa Street revival. Anderson claims that this achievement is "arguably the most significant global expansion of a Christian movement in the entire history of Christianity."[79] Most early Pentecostal missionaries were "poor, untrained and unprepared for what awaited them," and they went out "by faith without any income," but with "very little

[76] World Missionary Conference 1910, *Carrying the Gospel to All the Non-Christian World* (Edinburgh/London: Oliphant, Anderson and Ferrier, n.d.), 10.

[77] See Brian Stanley, *The World Missionary Conference, Edinburgh 1910*, Studies in the History of Christian Missions, ed. R. E. Frykenberg, Brian Stanley (Grand Rapids/Cambridge: Eerdmans, 2009), 16; Thangaraj, *Common Task*, 18-26.

[78] Anderson, *Spreading Fires*, 211. Also see Allan Heath Anderson, "The Emergence of a Multidimensional Global Missionary Movement: A Historical Review," in *Pentecostal Mission and Global Christianity*, eds. Wonsuk Ma, Veli-Matti Karkkainen and J. Kwabena Asamoah-Gyadu, Regnum Edinburgh Centenary Series, vol. 20 (Oxford: Regnum, 2014), 10-25.

[79] Anderson, *Spreading Fires*, 68.

and trusting God to supply the necessary finances usually through home contacts and periodical support."[80] However, it is significant to understand that in 100 years after Edinburgh Conference, Pentecostalism has become a leading force in global Christianity today. It is the second largest segment of Christianity after Roman Catholicism. Analyzing the phenomenal growth of Pentecostalism, Philip Jenkins comments that it is "perhaps the most successful social movement of the past century."[81]

It is a fact that the centre of gravity of global Christianity has shifted indisputably from north to south and from west to east. The rapid expansion of the Pentecostal movement is argued to be a major reason for the unprecedented growth of Christianity in the south and east.[82] Brian Stanley's observation in his study on the Edinburgh Conference is noteworthy:

> The measure of missionary success enjoyed by Christianity in the century that followed arguably owed rather little to the priorities set and the objectives enunciated at Edinburgh. The Christian faith was indeed to be transfigured over the next century, but not in the way or through the mechanisms that they imagined. The most effective instrument of that transfiguration would not be western mission agencies or institutions of any kind, but rather a great and sometimes unorthodox miscellany of indigenous pastors, prophets, catechists, and evangelists, men and women... they professed instead to rely on the simple transforming power of the Spirit and the Word.[83]

The growth of Pentecostalism in the post-Edinburgh period shows that there has been a clear theological shift in mission. As discussed above, the call of Edinburgh failed in achieving the goal of world evangelization by the most able and intellectual people having sufficient human resources. On the other hand, the ordinary, poor and not highly educated Pentecostal missionaries accomplished things far greater in terms of evangelization. Thus they established the fact

---

[80] Anderson, *Spreading Fires*, 54-55.
[81] Philip Jenkins, *The Next Christendom: The Coming of Global Christianity* (Oxford: Oxford University Press, 2002), 8.
[82] Jenkins, *The Next Christendom*, 6-8.
[83] Stanley, *World Missionary Conference*, 17.

that mission is beyond a human enterprise. The Edinburgh Conference emphasized the anthropocentric dimension of mission, and so they had the optimistic confidence in human resources, as discussed above. However, Pentecostals believed that although they are just ordinary people, they could be empowered by the extraordinary power of the Spirit of God, and with that power they could achieve global mission. Therefore they asked their missionaries to be filled with the Holy Spirit, and so it was the most essential qualification, and in some cases the only qualification, to be a Pentecostal missionary. Pentecostals believed that they were empowered to reach the end of the world with the Gospel message. Being filled with the Spirit and being motivated by the Spirit, they took the challenge of global mission. That is why the Spirit-filled Pentecostal missionaries went to every part of the globe. This is not to argue that they were successful in all cases. However, we see the shift from anthropocentrism to theocentricism, particularly pneumatocentricism in mission. This theological shift is one of the greatest contributions of Pentecostalism to theology of mission.

Emerging Challenges

Employing contextual discernment

It is important that Pentecostals should be sensitive to issues that arise out of particular Indian situations. As the issue of the foreignness of Christianity in India, a product of colonialism, is a serious concern, Pentecostals should be cautious about applying western charismatic ideologies and practices in local contexts. Any attempt to do this without proper regard to local sensitivities may have far reaching consequences, which in turn may affect the growth as well as the image of Christianity in general and the movement in particular. For example, economic improvement is an important concern in the poor tribal context of North India. However, overemphasizing and importing prosperity theology from the West may create problems. Therefore, a contextual discernment is very important. Imitation of western, especially North American, Pentecostalism is to be avoided.

Every effort must be made to alleviate unnecessary tensions within and without the movement. Popularizing conversion stories must be discouraged.[84] Schism and competition should be avoided. Speaking and doing anything useless in the name of the Spirit should not be encouraged. People entering full-time, especially pastoral ministry, should be encouraged to undergo theological education. These concerns can serve as cautions in the formation and development of a Pentecostal missiology of conversion.

Empowering the ordinary in their engagements

As ordinary people are engaged with people of other faiths, it is very important to train and equip ordinary people within the movement. As more local people join the movement, it is high time to train and equip tribal people into the leadership of the movement, especially in North India. Individual organizations and churches have to make concrete efforts to encourage and empower ordinary believers in their engagements with people of other faiths.

Exploring the spiritual dimension of conversion

As the socio-political or socio-economic interpretation of conversion does not do much benefit in the Indian context, a spiritual dimension of conversion is to be emphasized. It is significant that Indian Pentecostals see spiritual dynamics in conversion, an outcome of their public mission like healing and exorcism. Therefore, the role of charismatic dimension in conversion is to be researched. For example, the stories of deliverance and healing among the poor and weak tribal communities, and the resultant formation and growth of most Pentecostal churches in Rajasthan, are to be unearthed. There are numerous stories of conversion of individuals and families as the result of healing, exorcism and other miracles. Such stories need to be recorded and the spiritual dimension of conversion is to be investigated.

---

[84] There is a tendency to popularize conversion stories through literature, internet, and other media. Sometimes overemphasizing conversion statistics causes religious tension.

A Theology of Religious Freedom: An Engagement with the Odisha Freedom of Religion Act, 1967

Nimai Charan Suna[1]

"If we do not have peace, it is because we have forgotten that we belong to each other." Mother Teresa.

Introduction

India, an ancient civilization, is the mother of many religions. However, invasions, migrations, subjugations, and consequent social/religious sediments constitute the DNA of her long history. In this conflicting pool of sediments, of ancient and modern values, India has witnessed uncounted incidents of violence against the weak and exploitation of the minority. Interestingly during these dark Indian nights of violence and exploitations Gautama Buddha, Mahatma Gandhi and Mother Teresa have appeared as luminous meteors of non-violence and peace. In fact, Mahatma Gandhi, the father of the nation, made non-violence the cornerstone of India's independence struggle and succeeded against the colonial British empire. What do we make of such great success through non-violence? Unfortunately, with the rise of Hindutva in recent times, the cocktail of aggressive religion and controlling politics, is striving for a nationalism, a whole scale religious and political awakening—a high breed Hindu identity.[2] Religious intolerance and persecution of the minorities have been the highlight of India's 21st century record. How does the Bible respond to such violence in independent India today?

To address this vital question, let us first define the meaning and dynamics of communal violence. Theology is the lens through

---

[1] Dr. Nimai Charan Suna is the Founder Principal of Life Theological Seminary, Bhubaneswar, Odisha.

[2] Varghese V. Appileyil, "Violence Against Christians of India in the First Decade of the Twenty-First Century." DMin thesis, Brite Divinity School, 2009, 27.

which a religious community interprets the created world and the destiny of humanity. Moreover, a community's theology determines the value of human life and their responsibilities towards creation. Although religions are repressive at times, they are necessary allies and champions of global human rights as well. Unfortunately, Odisha has recently witnessed unprecedented religious violence. What is religious persecution? Persecution is a "violent rejection." Persecution of Christians is the violence against Christians in rejection of Jesus Christ and His gospel. But why is this rejection so violent? Persecution often involves at least two irreconcilable positions. First, the righteously indignant majority, who are "offended" and have come to the end of their patience. Second, the minority, a remnant, who are being persecuted because "they have the truth." The majority position is determined to preserve the tradition while the minority position is dedicated to reform the system. One wonders, then, what is freedom of religion—to continue in one's tradition freely or to question a tradition and embrace the truth freely? If religions exist for human well-being through the promotion of peace, justice and kindness, what justification is there for persecuting the weak and the minority of a plural community?

What is the methodological high ground to define religious freedom in this 21st Century Word War between Majority Worldview and Minority Worldview? Life and reality are much too large to be captured through the lens of "rights" and "issues" for a comprehensive vision. Visions of life and reality from the prisms of "rights" and "issues" are bound to be narrow and shallow, legal and local. How can we then understand an issue so important to the two contrasting Worldviews of India? First, it is necessary that our methodology be broad based. It will avoid drilling an interpretive well deeper in the parched land of Indian Constitution that has no signs of water until now. Second, an exercise of this nature must be done with common theological fibers that generally weave the majority and minority worldviews. We, therefore, turn our eyes beyond constitutional rights, to the very nature of man. Man is not a mere biological product of chance. Man is the special creation of God. This paper assumes theistic creationism. Third, our argument is based on the claim that man is a moral/spiritual being, whose religious rights and rites are rooted in the image of God. Singh Deo concurs, "Fundamental rights are something which are fundamental and natural and are permanent. Fundamental rights are nothing else but the natural rights, the primordial rights of human being."[3] Finally, the paper will interact with contemporary thinkers, Indians as well as non-Indians, with their research on religious freedom and its need in today's India.

Keeping these methodological boundaries intact, this paper furnishes the biblical foundations of religious freedom to lay the theological underpinning of our argument—religious freedom is a fundamental human right, the first of human rights. Having this issue settled, this paper engages with the Freedom of Religion Act, which was introduced in the Legislative Assembly of Odisha in 1967 and was implemented in 1999, which eventually became the sting of the Kandhamal persecution of August 2008.

Biblical Foundation for Religious Freedom

Image of God: The seed of religious freedom

The creation of man in the image of God is the divine initiative of human religious freedom. It is difficult to read the creation narrative (Gen.1-2) and miss the prominence God has bestowed on mankind in His entire creation. We can observe man's eminence structurally as well as verbally. Genesis 1 presents Adam, the crown of creation, as the climax of God's six-day creative act. Then in Genesis 2, man is presented as the center of the sixth day creation narrative. Moses' choice of words here to make this point obvious, is fascinating. Genesis 1 sets apart man in three ways. First, man is said to be created in the image of God. Second, he is given dominion over the created order of earth. Third, the special word "created" is used three times, ensuring that the readers take note of the unique creation of man.

> This word is used at only three points in the creation narrative: first, when God created matter from nothing (v.1); second, when God created conscious life (v.21); and third,

---

[3] R. N. Singh Deo, "Speech at Rotary Club, Baripada, 1971," (Nayapalli, Bhubaneswar: Randing Print), 166.

when God created man (v.27). This is a progression, from the body (matter) to soul (personality) to spirit (life with God-consciousness).[4]

The extended length given to the narrative of man's creation (Gen. 1:24-31) is to highlight the importance of human "creation," that man is created "in the image of God." James M. Boice rightly sees this image in terms of personal, moral and spiritual capabilities. He affirms that some creatures have personality to certain degrees like man has personality.[5] But man's moral likeness to God is the point of departure from brute creation. However, moral likeness is both "freedom and responsibility." Freedom and responsibility are two sides of the same coin. Responsibility is the just requirement of freedom and freedom is the just reward of responsibility. Even before the fall, freedom was never "absolute." Adam and Eve "were not autonomous." Eve acknowledges it in her conversation with the serpent (Gen. 3:3). Despite the fall, man continues to enjoy "freedom with responsibility" to some degree. The possibility and call for "sanctification of the believer" is grounded on this moral likeness (Col. 3:10; Rom. 8:29). "[I]t is the moral righteousness of the individual that is most in view, though of course this may also refer to the perfection of personality in ways we do not as yet understand fully."[6] The moral likeness is special but the spiritual likeness is eminent. This spiritual likeness has seminal importance with regard to religious freedom. Why is it so important? It is because, in the spiritual likeness with God, the worth and uniqueness of man's creation must be seen. God is spirit and through this spiritual likeness, man enjoys his unique capacity to communicate with God in the spirit. Hence, men and women are "God's unique and valued companions."[7] This precious endowment is the outflow of divine freedom. As a result, religious freedom is referred to as the first freedom. Hence, it must be respected and its purpose must be realized. "Every human has four endowments - self-awareness, conscience, independent will and creative imagination. These give us

[4] James Montgomery Boice, *Genesis: An Expositional Commentary 1-11*, vol. 1, (Grand Rapids: Baker Books, 1998), 88.
[5] Boice, *Genesis*, 90.
[6] Boice, *Genesis*, 90.
[7] Boice, *Genesis*, 91.

the ultimate human freedom... The power to choose, to respond, to change."[8] Frank Murphy aptly stated it, "Religious freedom is too sacred a right to be restricted or prohibited in any degree without convincing proof that a legitimate interest of the state is in grave danger."[9]

The Exodus: From bondage to bonding

Exodus is the story of the institutionalization of religious freedom. In Exodus, religious freedom is not only an individual perception of a vertical awareness, but also a social celebration in horizontal organization. But what is Exodus? Exodus is not a mere escape from Egypt through the Red Sea. Rather it is the transformative event that made Israel what Israel was created to be, the people of God. That is, Exodus is the making of a people, the demonstration of Yahweh's covenant faithfulness to Abraham, Isaac and Jacob. Hence, Exodus is the witness to the nature and works of Yahweh for his suffering people. Thus, Exodus has become the identity of Israel in relationship to her covenant keeping God, Yahweh.

In Genesis, we saw the free movement of God towards man, the object of his love. Now in Exodus we see the reverse free movement of Israel towards Yahweh, the subject of her worship. It is the movement of Israel, the people of God, from bondage to bonding, from the slavery of Pharaoh to the servanthood of Yahweh, and more specifically from enforced construction work to building a tabernacle unto the Lord.[10] Worship is a central theme of this book. The people of God move from lament to deliverance to praise and worship, the common liturgical rhythm of Israel's worship of Yahweh.[11] The theological trajectory of Israel's movement towards Yahweh in the narrative of Exodus is in harmony with the literary structure of the book and the verbal markers of the narrative. Moses

---

[8] Stephen Covey, *Brainy Quote*, accessed on July 25, 2017, https://www.brainyquote.com/quotes/quotes/s/stephencov138246.html?src=t_power.

[9] Frank Murphy, *Brainy Quote*, accessed on July 25, 2017, http://www.brainyquote.com/quotes/authors/f/frank_murphy.html.

[10] Terence E. Fretheim, *Exodus Interpretation: A Bible Commentary for Teaching and Preaching* (Louisville: John Knox Press, 1973), 1.

[11] Fretheim, *Exodus Interpretation*, 20-21.

devotes the first 24 chapters of Exodus to the making of a people for His name. The second half, Chapters 25-40, is devoted to making of a place for His glory. At the end of the book, we have both in place, the tabernacle amid Israel. The literary markers in the narrative furnishes this theological task of the book clearly. We see this, particularly, in Yahweh's express purpose for the Exodus that they may "sacrifice to the Lord our God" (Exod. 3:18; 5:3), "may serve me" (Exod. 4:23; 7:16; 8:1, 20; 9:1, 13, 10:13), "celebrate a feast to Me" (Exod. 5:1), "that I will take you for My people and I will be your God, that you shall know that I am the Lord your God" (Exod. 6:7). These verbal markers express the doxological purpose of the Exodus, appearing about eleven times in the course of ten plagues.

However, what is most relevant and instructive to this essay is the revelation of Yahweh's sovereignty within Exodus 4-19. How are we to make sense of the revelation of God's sovereignty in the interplay of such different factors in the central part of the first section? These four factors are the (i) obedient cosmic forces, (ii) Moses, the reluctant agent of God, (iii) Pharaoh, the stubborn opponent of divine purpose and (iv) the People Israel, numb with their oppression, bereft of any faith or hope in Yahweh for their deliverance.

First, creation in Exodus is the most obedient instrument of God. Nature is doing His will even in the moral and spiritual order, by carrying out God's judgment on Pharaoh and Egypt. What seems to be natural disaster in Egypt is nature's act of obedience—doing what they were created to be doing—in worship to the Sovereign Creator.

Second, Israel's phenomenal growth, the cause for Pharaoh's panic, is actually, "God's ongoing creation and blessing." Causally speaking, Israel's suffering in Egypt is the result of her growth spurred by Yahweh. From a theological perspective, this pressured situation is the divine mould in which Israel was to be shaped as the people of God. Israel is the passive participant, swept into Egypt from a scorching famine, multiplied in an arithmetic ratio in the fertile Goshen and now driven to despair under the weight of Pharaoh's demographic phobia. Suffering must shape our hope and not sap away our hope. Finally, Israel chose to serve Yahweh in the worst pressured condition of biblical history.

Third, the Moses/Yahweh dialogue is revelatory of divine sovereignty at its persuasive best. How does God persuade an unwilling heart? Moses' questions are met by God's self-revelation and his reluctance is met by God's heart for suffering Israel. Divine instrumentality does not imply human passivity. On the contrary, the exodus is the result of this dual agency revealing their compatibility and potentiality to accomplish the plan of God. Yahweh prevailed in transforming Moses, from a hesitant agent to the most dedicated leader of biblical narratives. The exodus is one of the greatest examples of the way God uses human agency in restoring particularly the religious freedom of a deprived and suppressed people.

Finally, we see a contrast. If the Lord was persistent with Moses to own His "creational" design for Israel, He was immensely patient with Pharaoh to prevent him from going through with his anti-creational schemes. Pharaoh deserved to bear the brunt of divine wrath for his persistence with "anti-creational" schemes. "Sin-judgment" scheme in the narrative of Exodus is not natural, inevitable, and impersonal. Instead, Yahweh is the personal sovereign ruler upholding his creational plan and the personal judge to execute judgment of the plagues on Pharaoh's Egypt. However, his wrath is not arbitrary but in consonance with his nature as outlined in Exodus 34:6-7. But why such display of divine wrath? "To deny people their human rights is to challenge their very humanity."[12] Probably, we can contextualize it to Exodus to say that to deny a people their human rights, particularly their right to worship freely, is to challenge the purpose and wisdom of their Creator whose image they bear.

Daniel: theistic convictions in pressure situations

Daniel is about the practice of religious freedom as a non-negotiable, a conviction founded on the solid rock, the sovereignty of Yahweh. It is about religious freedom in captivity in a foreign land and institutionalized persecution against God-fearing leaders in

---

[12] Nelson Mandela, *Brainy Quotes*, accessed on July 25, 2017, https://www.brainyquote.com/quotes/quotes/n/nelsonmand447259.html.

high places. The book is a message to the Jews in exile to trust in the Sovereignty of Yahweh, the ruler over the nations. How does Daniel communicate this theology? Daniel outlines how the Lord will direct history and rule over the nations, by bringing three oracles of prophecy in Daniel 7-12. But how can the Jews in exile trust this prophecy while they are living under Babylonian rule in a foreign land? Geography determines theology. It is one thing to declare from Jerusalem that Yahweh is the ruler of all nations but it is altogether a different proposition to declare Yahweh's rule over the nations, as an exile, from the citadel of the Babylonian kingdom. In order to establish the trustworthiness of God's sovereignty declared in these oracles, Daniel argues from six stories of individual experiences in Daniel 1-6, that God not only reigns in the lives of His exiled people but also controls the affairs of their captors, the Babylonians. There could not have been a better place and time for Daniel to declare this eternal truth of God. Daniel's use of the past individual experiences to establish the future international events has two present national implications. First, it is possible to prosper under a foreign rule because the Lord answers prayers and grants the needful (i.e. wisdom) even in difficult times. Yahweh still reigns. Second, life in exile often encounters challenges and urges to compromise with things contrary to the Law, promising lucrative opportunities or gains. Often, the voice of the majority is so overwhelming that any form of resistance seems futile. Rather it is tempting to abandon one's faith and accept the majority position as truth. Daniel's point is that living a life of non-compromising silent convictions is worth the risk. There is virtue in keeping the Law.[13] But how does one cope with sufferings that last so long? How does someone cling to his faith when the cost is such inhuman torture and painful death?

First, the story of Nebuchadnezzar's golden image and the fiery furnace give us a burning example of the painful reality of being a distinct minority. The three Jews are high officials under Nebuchadnezzar. But with one whimsical decision of Nebuchadnezzar, they lost their freedom to be Jews. Their being Jews is not a mere racial category but the identity of their ultimate loyalty.

---

[13] Donald E. Gowan, *Daniel*, Abingdon Old Testament Commentaries (Nashville: Abingdon Press, 2001), 48.

The story is first about the danger of unbridled power and the reward of unquestioning loyalty. Second, the story is about the risks of the non-negotiable convictions of a minority. Nebuchadnezzar demands obeisance before his idol and the three Jews found it non-negotiable on account of the first two commandments of the decalogue. There was no middle ground, even though Nebuchadnezzar was courteous enough to give them a chance reconsider their position. Their conviction was too strong for the threat of the nature of death—to be burnt alive—to have any effect on them. Their bold affirmation of Yahweh in response to Nebuchadnezzar's offer to reconsider matches word for word (Dan. 3:18). They simply refused to bow because they recognized no one greater than Yahweh, their God. They confessed that their God is able and yet their loyalty to Him was not dependent on their deliverance. The faith of the three Jews didn't have the insurance of a happy ending to the stories of their lives. In the face of death, they stood their ground, affirming the *atheism of force to be a fraud*. They served God because He was God, sovereign over kings and the forces of nature.

The painful story of being a minority is more glaring in Daniel's case. Even such close friendship with King Darius was not an insurance for his safety. History bears us witness that many powerful kings, like the friend of Daniel, have been checkmated by their powerful bureaucracy to suffer the pain of being a minority. As for Daniel, probably the temptation to compromise his time and mode of prayer was immense so that the king, his friend, will not be forced to choose between Daniel and his edict. The three Jews dared Nebuchadnezzar, who acted as an enemy, but Daniel risked his friendship with Darius, who was his friend. Why should Daniel open the window and pray? The Law of Moses did not require of him to pray publicly or visibly and, surely, he could have changed the mode of his prayers for the stipulated time, thirty days. The answer could be two dimensional: attitudinal and theological. First, it is the question of his conscience. By praying with an open window towards Jerusalem, Daniel neither wanted to display nor wanted to hide but to do business as usual, his practice of prayer. Would he pray differently because of his detractors? Prayer like any other mode of worship must be done with a clean conscience, not with reference to anybody but only with reference to God. Speaking about "freedom of conscience," Daniel "knew of no such term and was ahead of his time in thinking this way, but he understood the concept."[14] Mahatma Gandhi considered Daniel as one of the "greatest passive resisters that ever lived."[15] Second, praying with open window towards Jerusalem was theological. The decree of Darius (Dan. 6:7) seems to be a politically astute move to ensure the loyalty of a fractured people towards a new king. But the ulterior motive of the edict was to interrupt Daniel's commitment to the "Law of his God" (Dan. 6:5). Daniel could have devised a religious pluralism instead of his exclusivism, praying in a manner that would not discredit prayers offered unto Darius. Why did Daniel pray with open window towards Jerusalem? Probably the answer to this question is to be found in the "time." The seventy years of exile was at its fag end. The exile and Daniel's prayer were in accord with the warning and promise which God had given to Solomon at the dedication of the temple (Dan. 9:1-9). The temple of Solomon did not exist by then, but the promise of Yahweh did exist (1 Kings 8:27-30). Daniel's prayer was not directed towards a visible, tangible, and physical temple, for it didn't exist by then, but towards an unassailable promise of God even though his sovereignty was not visible.

Daniel realized early that despite his racial otherness, he is called to handle the affairs of the mighty Babylonian empire. Minority status never tempted him into isolation from the mainstream. Rather he used every opportunity for his political witness, a testimony unto his covenant Lord, Yahweh. That was his insurance for a life of success as a royal palace executive in the Babylonian and Mede-Persian empire. It had immense impact on Mahatma Gandhi, who called Daniel's open window prayer "soul force" of non-violent resistance, or *satyagraha*. Gandhi saw "Satyagraha in its purest form" in Daniel, when he threw open his doors in "defiance of the laws of Medes and Persians" which offended his conscience.[16]

---

[14] Gowan, *Daniel*, 101.
[15] Daniel L. Smith-Christopher, "Gandhi on Daniel 6: A Case of Cultural Exegesis," *Biblical Interpretation* 1 (1993): 326.
[16] Smith-Christopher, "Gandhi on Daniel," 326.

Esther: A beacon of light in a world without God

We see in the book of Esther full-blown religious intolerance and institutionalized persecution of a believing community. What was Esther's world like? Linda M. Day beautifully describes Esther's context: "What is revered and obeyed is the state, not God or priests or Torah. The physical is what is presented as important in this environment, not the spiritual; personal wealth, not personal piety. Earthly happiness rather than eternal happiness is the ideal."[17] Perhaps Vashti deemed the King's order degrading her personhood and followed her conscience to resist her drunken world although the price of her decision was costly. She, surely, can be a counter-cultural figure. Freedom can be very expensive but if the only option to it is *enduring enslavement* against your conscience, no price or risk is greater than personal integrity, dignity and freedom of conscience. The failure of Vashti is the backdrop for the presentation of the two main characters with actions in the book of Esther, namely Esther and Haman. How did they behave in their world, where God seemed to be absent? How should we conduct ourselves in this kind of a world today?

Esther was a powerless woman with no control over her destiny. She was carried like a dry leaf in the current of time from one stage to the other stage of her life. Before she realized it, she found herself in a golden cage, hiding her real identity for fear of discrimination. "History has shown that assimilation does not always safeguard one from harm in times of genocide; keeping silent does not necessarily protect."[18] But when it was time to act, she didn't shy away. Rather she took timely calculated risks, executing her plans wisely and patiently. She did the opposite of what queen Vashti did and yet, she got the result Vashti wanted—dignity for her womanhood in the world of (drunken) men. Vashti refused to come to the king when she was called but Esther went to the king without being called. Vashti refused to attend the king's wine party but Esther brought the king's wine party to her own privacy. Vashti was, probably, afraid of dishonour to her womanhood in the king's

---

[17] Linda M. Day, *Esther*, Abingdon Old Testament Commentaries (Nashville: Abingdon Press, 2005), 27.

[18] Day, *Esther*, 61.

wine party but Esther won freedom and dignity for herself and her people in her wine party for the king. In sum, Esther effected changes by means of relationality, not in isolation. She acted according to her wisdom and intuition and soon she accomplished what she wanted successfully. What a contrast is the life of Haman! If Esther controlled the king with the power of her love, Haman controlled the king with his love for power. Haman was a powerful man but he suffered social racism and prejudice because of his personal insecurities. His racial prejudice burned within him kindling the fire of ethnic cleansing. Probably the words of Mother Teresa are very appropriate for this context: "If we do not have peace, it is because we have forgotten that we belong to each other." Haman didn't realize that we cannot form a judgment or an image of a person based on one sight or one experience. We all belong to a network and in some way we are related to one another. Little did he realize that the cute queen will be related to Mordecai and she will be instrumental in their redemption and his own death. Haman missed a truth of life. Relating with a sense belonging, even beyond the boundaries of one's race and religion, can be an olive leaf, a touch of healing, bonding strange and diverse people into one community.

There are divergent views on the use of force or violence in the book of Esther. But this concluding section must be seen in its context. We must remember that violence was not the first choice of Esther. She, in fact, requested the revocation of Haman's decree. "[T]he motivational differences between the two decrees are as revealing as the similarities. Haman's edict was offensive in nature, promulgated because of ethnic hatred and avarice; Mordecai's counter edict sanctions self-defense, for the goal of self-preservation."[19]

Acts: non-negotiable exclusivity of Jesus' lordship

In the book of Acts, we find institutionalized persecution of a minority community for reasons such as hermeneutics, insecurity and anger with theology at its core.

First, persecution in Acts is opposition to Jesus Christ. Luke expresses this fact through his "witnessing-opposition" paradigm by

[19] Day, *Esther*, 141.

using the "opposition in the royal-enthronement Psalms" (Pss. 35, 37). Chan notes,

> In his description of the opposition scenes following the ascension of the Davidic Messianic Jesus (Acts 3–5), Luke lays out the theological foundation of opposition to the church: the cause of the persecution is the preaching of and witnessing to the name of Jesus in Jerusalem. The opposition to Jesus and his church will never stop unless the church stops bearing witness to the name of Jesus.[20]

Luke articulates the cause of the Sanhedrin's twin opposition of the apostles in Acts 3-5, as their anger leading to the rejection and murder of Jesus Christ (Acts 4:10-11; 5:30-31).

Second, Luke sees a correlation between the persecution of the Church and the suffering of Jesus Christ. How does he show this correlation? He articulates the correlation from the very lips of Jesus, the enthroned king (Acts 9:5). In other words, persecution of the Church is the persecution of the enthroned king. It is a participation in the continued persecution of Jesus Christ (Acts 5:41). Luke does this task by furnishing the similarities between the death of Jesus and Stephen. Chan continues:

> The parallelism between the passion of Jesus and the martyrdom of Stephen rests on the thematic correspondence of these two accounts. Both include: (1) a hearing before the Sanhedrin (Luke 22:66; Acts 6:12); (2) the announcement or sight of the Son of Man at God's right hand (Luke 22:69; Acts 7:55–56); (3) condemnation for blasphemy based on the testimony of the accused (Luke 23:26; Acts 7:56–57); (4) an execution outside of city (Luke 23:26; Acts 7:58); (5) the cry of "receive my spirit" (Luke 23:46; Acts 7:59); and (6) the cry for forgiveness of the persecutors' sin (Luke 23:34, "Father, forgive them, they do not know what they are doing"; Acts 7:60, "Lord, do not hold this sin against them").[21]

---

[20] Addson Wai-Ka Chan, "Opposition to the Davidic Kingdom in the Book of Acts Through the lenses of the Davidic Psalms," PhD diss., Deerfield, IL.: Trinity International University, 2016, 252-253.

[21] Chan, "Opposition to the Davidic Kingdom," 260-261.

Luke gives us here a step by step participation of Stephen in the suffering of Jesus Christ although not in any atoning sense.

Thirdly, Luke shows that the name of Jesus is at the core of this persecution. The name of Jesus is the core content of the apostles' preaching and it is also the unique and main cause of their opposition and persecution by the Sanhedrin (Acts 5:28; 7:52, 56). In fact, Acts 9:14-16 underlines the relationship of persecution and bearing the name of Jesus three times, two of which are in relationship to Paul's ministry, to carry the name of Jesus to the Gentiles, kings and children of Israel.

The exclusivity of Jesus' Lordship and the universality of the gospel are co-related. The apostles never saw preaching as a violation of the other's freedom; rather they saw the opportunity to hear the gospel at least once as their need and right (Rom. 10:14-15). The name of Jesus Christ is at the core of preaching the gospel. Since persecution of the witnessing church and the persecution of Jesus are correlated, the Church lives two dimensionally.

THEOLOGICAL STRANDS OF RELIGIOUS FREEDOM

In the light of the findings of the above study or analysis, we will construct three doctrines, namely, the doctrines of God, Christ and the church, which are foundational to human freedom in the worship of God.

Doctrine of God: A suffering Deity

The first and foremost biblical identity of God is "the Creator" (Gen.1:1). The masterpiece of His creation is man, the bearer of His image. The freedom and ability to respond to Him is the central piece of this divine creative design. Hence religious freedom is the first freedom. Religious freedom is not a freedom from God but freedom for God. Ultimately, man's true freedom is the vertical expression of his religious constitution. Hence, the free and responsible use of this divine likeness is the ultimate witness to the sovereign freedom of God the Creator. However, freedom from God is contrary to divine creative design, generating pain for God.

Any attempt to hinder this vertical freedom is greater cause for divine intervention to restore God's plan for man.

The doctrine of Christ: Suffering witness

Christ ushered in His Kingdom in the backdrop of Roman dominion and the parallel power house of the Sanhedrin. Bearing the name of Jesus Christ inevitably draws persecution. Christians endured persecution under the Jews and the Romans. But why? Because the gospel communicates with and corrects every culture it encounters—it is counter-cultural in every age. "Persecution is simply the clash between two irreconcilable value-systems."[22] The Lordship of Jesus Christ is exclusive, a non-negotiable. Hence, persecution is inevitable. Hence Jesus addresses those "persecuted for righteousness" as "blessed ones" for they belong to a "noble succession" (Matt. 5:11-12). Divine solidarity with these participatory suffering witnesses is invariably followed by divine sovereignty for he is not a by-stander. The created nature groans in solidarity as well with the suffering witnesses in tune with the sovereign suffering witness (Ex. 3:7-8; Chapters 4-19). Persecution of the witnesses is the persecution of Christ, a privilege (Acts 5:41) for the witnesses, the fellowship of his sufferings (Acts 9:5; Dan. 3:24-25; Phil 3:10).

The doctrine of the Church: Fiery transformation

Finally, the ultimate question of religious freedom: "Christ or Caesar?" How does a Christian function in a context of dual authority? Christ was trapped by the Jewish leaders to answer this question (Matt. 22:20-22; Mark 12:17). Jesus, in response, beautifully nuanced our vertical relationship of freedom in its horizontal expression. Dual authority, divine and human, is the God ordained plan for human well-being. Loyalty to God must define loyalty to Caesar, the human authority. The social and political life of man must be the horizontal expression of his religious experience of freedom. Bonhoeffer's "holy worldliness" seems to be a good attempt for a contemporary conceptual capture of Jesus' answer to this dilemma.

---

[22] John R. W. Stott, *The Message of the Sermon on the Mount,* The Bible Speaks Today (Downers Grove: InterVarsity Press, 1978), 52.

John Stott adds, "holy worldliness" should not be either "world affirming" or "world denying," but it must be "world challenging."[23] The Christian mind must be "trained, informed, equipped to handle data of secular controversy within a framework of reference which is constructed of Christian presuppositions."[24] Christian political activism is "world affirming." The Christian political witness must be "world challenging." It is a transformation of the self and the world: a fiery transformation.

THE CONTEXT AND CONFLICT OF RELIGIOUS FREEDOM IN ODISHA

The Odisha context

The State of Odisha is a triangle of topography—mountains, plains and the coast, inhabited by a demographic triangle of tribes, dalits and the Hindus. In addition, the Hindu thinkers see a triangle of Holy shrines—the Konark, the Lingaraj and the Jagannath Temples. The Tribals (22.1%) and the Dalits (17%) together constitute a formidable portion of Odisha's 43.73 million population. Religions and traditions flourish in Odisha's fertile soil of simplicity.

The conductor

Maharaja Rajendra Narayan Singh Deo was the last ruler of the princely state of Patna in Odisha before Indian independence in 1947. His Son A.U. Singh Deo writes about him,

> Rule and Law was to him as sacred as the Rule of Gods. He would never deviate from that path. I have come across cases where he has stuck to principle even at the risk of the ministry collapsing. A unique character, he had faith in destiny and great devotion to his preceptor. His personal experiences of the occult, and his belief in the philosophy of Karma, were awe inspiring.[25]

---

[23] John Stott, *Human Rights and Human Wrongs: Major Issues for a New Century* (Grand Rapids, Michi.: Baker Books, 1999) 41.
[24] Harry Blamires, *The Christian Mind* (Vancouver: Regent, 1963) 70.
[25] "Maharaja R. N. Singh Deo," accessed on July 25, 2017, http://rnsinghdeo.

He had a smooth transition into independent India, first as a Member of Parliament and then as the finance minister of Odisha. He went on to become the Chief Minister of Odisha, heading a coalition government, fishing in the troubled waters of the coalition culture of Odisha politics. He was astute and fearless in his decisions, checkmated his rivals and calculated electoral gains very well. He enacted the Orissa Freedom of Religion Act 1967, first of its kind in the country, in the very first year of his office as the Chief Minister. Second, he appointed an Enquiry Commission to probe into charges of corruption against all the three previous Chief Ministers, namely Biju Patnaik, Biren Mitra and Sadasiva Tripathy. These were two of his striking moves. These bold moves can be traced back to his uncompromising tenacity as described above and his political calculation to checkmate his opponents in a coalition political culture. Singh Deo seems to have assumed the unquestioned support of the Dalits from the Western plains of Orissa. So, he attempted to bolster the support he enjoyed from the Hindus of the East Coast through the Anti-Conversion Act and offered blows to shut out the secular Congress party, which was then in disarray. He projected himself as a clean politician and offered fresh air of stability to people gasping in the successive failures of coalition governments. Singh Deo's personality is clearly visible in these two early political moves. Political short circuit does bring bright light for a moment followed by a long stretch of darkness. He never got to become Chief Minister again, but his political calculations continue to be a thorn in the flesh for the innocent Christians of Odisha. It is baffling that the State Congress government under the stewardship of Janaki Ballhab Patnaik, framed the Rules to support this anti-conversion act. There is no apparent justification and explanation for the Congress government to have enacted the Freedom of Religion Rules 1989. We also find no rationale in their implementing the Freedom of Religion Act because it was against the values of the Indian National Congress. Unfortunately, Giridhar Gamang, under pressure from fundamentalist forces after the killing of Graham Staines, signed the Orissa Freedom of Religion Rules and made the Act operative in 1999. The greatest evil of our society is not evil itself as much as spineless leadership that

---

com/web/.

bows before evil. So, what are the consequences of this political haste and political opportunism?

The content: In letter and in spirit

First, the title ("Freedom") and language of the Act of 1967 ("force," inducement") don't give the impression of an enactment for an orderly function of a family but of a "paternalistic"[26] hedge around the supposed *weak links*, the Tribals and Dalits, who they think are naïve and gullible.

Second, the consequences spelt out for their conversion are not meant to express the severity of punishment but their strong opposition to conversion itself. The Act is not meant to curb "illegal" conversion, if there are any, but to bring to a grinding halt any kind of conversion. Conversion by nature, they think, is the undermining of their faith whereas Hinduism, for them, is the classical religion.

Third, the urgency of the enactment exposes the underlying presupposition that conversion is a violence against the very fiber of a community. So, the violence of conversion must be met with an equal force, a stringent law. Conversion, they think, destabilizes the tranquility[27] of a settled community so the Law is designed to preserve the status quo.

Fourth, the nature of the Act is centripetal at its core. The goal of the Act speaks clearly of their theological claim. The theological claim of the Act is that a religious faith is not an individual, private affair. A religious faith is a faith of the community. To embrace a different faith is to turn one's back on their community. It is a betrayal, lack of patriotism or nationalism. Graphically speaking, the Act has a very strong centripetal force to keep the myriad of Indian people groups tied up to the core, Hinduism.

Fifth, the Freedom of Religion Act of Singh Deo is a pneumatic non-return valve. A pneumatic non-return valve facilitates flow of air and liquid in one direction and blocks any return flow. Constitutionally, India is an avowed secular democratic republic.

---

[26] Ian Douglas Richards, "The Perception of Violence: Conversion in Post-Independence India," MA thesis, University of Calgary, 2004, 98.

[27] Richards, "The Perception of Violence," 100.

However, by sheer strength of numbers, Hinduism shares more space in the public sphere. The Odisha Legislative Assembly is one of the second or state level shrines of Indian democracy. And yet, through the enactment of this Act, Chief Minister Singh Deo officiated the unholy cocktail of Hindutva and democracy at the cost of minority communities and their religions. Anyone can enter Hinduism, but a hefty penalty is imposed on any conversion of Tribals and Dalits to religions other than Hinduism.

How does the study done in the first section of this paper respond to these underlying motivations and forces of the Odisha Religious Freedom Act?

First, it was the fruit of political haste, a half-baked cake. Singh Deo did not feel it necessary to even talk about the Bill. Just a reading of it was enough for him.[28] Narayan Sahu tried to persuade Singh Deo to do a soul search instead of *blaming other religions* and passing such a strong Bill. He candidly acknowledged the *real culprit* which needs to be dealt with: "We have oppressed them" through our "practice of untouchability."[29] Prasana Kumar Panda went a long distance to dissuade Singh Deo. This Bill is *against the freedom granted in the Constitution* of India. It *will cause pain* to "innocent people." Since "poverty and social inequality" are the reasons for these conversions this Bill to crack down on other religions will be a "negative and unsuccessful move," he argued.[30] Santosh Kumar Sahu warned that the Bill will have *national as well as international implications*. Hence, it must be discussed at length and all *religious*

---

[28] "Respected Deputy Speaker, it is 'unnecessary to speak anything special' about this Bill. I will only read the Odiya translation of the purpose and necessity of this Bill that is in English." "The Orissa Freedom of Religion Bill, 1967" *Orissa Legislative Assembly Debates* 3, no. 13 (December 20, 1967): 45.

[29] "First, it should be seen who are the ones that have changed their religion in our state and around India. Those who are poor, ignorant, uneducated, Scheduled tribes, scheduled castes and people from lower strata have changed their religion. The reason for this is that we have been regularly exploiting them. We hate them. Because of the practice of untouchability taking the advantage of poverty and ignorance, others have converted into their religions." "The Orissa Freedom of Religion Bill, 1967," 45.

[30] "There is freedom in India to preach one's religion. Therefore no one can be barred from preaching his religion. If people are intercepted for preaching religion my opinion is that it is the innocent people who will be probably punished." "The Orissa Freedom of Religion Bill, 1967," 46.

leaders must be involved in the deliberation, those who have a stake in it.[31] Sunaram Soren *questioned* the wisdom and necessity of the Bill in the *secular independent* Indian republic. He feared the *abuse of innocent believers* in the hands of *unscrupulous administrators*.[32] Singh Deo tried to assuage the fear of the Legislative member of Brajaraj Nagar who feared that it will *curb religious freedom such as propagating one's faith*. Singh Deo tried to pacify the member of Baripada who *questioned why* the Bill was being pushed through in *such a hurry*. None of those concerns were really addressed. Instead, Singh Deo had his way to pass the Bill.[33] How do we interpret the urgency and intensity of Mr. Singh Deo to carry the Bill through the house? Probably the definition of statesmanship by former Prime Minister A. B. Vajpayee is useful to answer the question:

> Royal Duty! This is a very meaningful word. I am abiding by this word. I am making efforts to abide by the meaning of the word. For the king and the ruler, there can be no distinction between his subjects neither on the basis of birth, nor on the basis of caste or on the basis of community.[34]

Prime Minister Vajpayee gave this message to Narendra Modi, the then Chief Minister of Gujarat, during whose stewardship the state witnessed unprecedented violence against the Muslim minority community. How much Singh Deo should have been aware of "Royal Duty" since he came from a royal lineage! Singh Deo, the architect of the Freedom of Religion Act, had been voted by the people of Odisha, not the people of just one community. His "Royal Duty" called for patience, equality and non-discrimination, particularly sensitivity towards the minority communities of the state.

---

[31] "Even though the motive of the Bill is lofty and its length is brief it is possible that the impact of the Bill be national as well as international. . . Secondly, it would have been good if we had passed the stopping of conversion or this Bill on religion having discussed it well and consulted the priests of different religions." "The Orissa Freedom of Religion Bill, 1967," 46.

[32] "Those who will implement the law and those who will administer it must be people of integrity. . . If they will not be honest there are many ways to take advantage from the religious faith of people." "The Orissa Freedom of Religion Bill, 1967," 47.

[33] "The Orissa Freedom of Religion Bill, 1967," 47.

[34] It is the translation of the author. A. B. Vajpayee, accessed on July 25, 2017, https://www.youtube.com/watch?v=x5W3RCpOGbQ.

As a devout Hindu, he may not have embraced religious liberalism, if not religious pluralism. At least as a statesman, he could have demonstrated political liberalism. In a country of so much diversity like India, religious freedom can never exist without liberal toleration. No one can have a right at the cost of another's right. The use of the word "Freedom" to entitle the Act doesn't hide the fact that it is a sectarian enactment. People are precious, whether they are a minority or majority. Life is the gift of God and the trust of life must be discharged with integrity and foresight. Instead of rushing through the legislative procedure, listening to those voices of wisdom would have spared lot of innocent blood and minority anguish. As the Chief Minister of the state, Singh Deo was to be the father and protector of the least and the last, the majority and the minority, in fact for all of Odisha, not of one community at the cost of the others.

India is emerging from a progress-resistant culture to a progress-prone culture. A progress-prone culture encourages religious pluralism in the public worldview:

> In these societies, religious pluralism allows conversion in-and-out of spiritual and social spaces… In progress-resistant cultures the index of worldview and civic pluralism maintains a persistently different configuration. The public worldview is sourced and shaped by religious monopoly.[35]

Second, freedom of religion is not a mere legal/constitutional issue. The freedom to believe and worship is essential to being human. Singh Deo's Religious Freedom Act looks like an electric fence to protect the simple and gullible against certain "religious poachers." At the heart of religious freedom is the freedom of conscience and the freedom of the mind if life's ultimate commitments are to be embraced truly and freely. Singh Deo's worldview betrays his low view of the Tribals and Dalits who need his legal fence. The Act is indicative that he does not consider the Tribals and the Dalits to be equal, free and reasonable persons. The crux of the matter is not what the Act is made to look like. Who are the beneficiaries

---

[35] Thom Wolf, "Progress-prone and Progress Resistant Cultures: Worldview Issues and the Baliraja Proposal of Mahatma Phule," *Contemporary Social Work* 1 (April 2007): 40.

of this Act: the Tribals and Dalits or the custodians of Hinduism? How do the Tribals and Dalits feel about the Freedom Act: relieved or trapped? First, are they fully human? The Tribals and the Dalits need human dignity and identity as normal reasonable human beings. Indian Religious Freedom Acts must define and distinguish "man" and "animal"; "deity" and "diet." Why impose an alien dietary ethos and a subsequent economic burden on them? Second, are they truly or fully Hindu? Their human rights, particularly their right to religious freedom, must be restored and protected. How will their ultimate longings of life be satisfied unless they have religious freedom to enter holy places and read their scriptures for themselves? This is their urgent need of religious freedom, which alone can restore their humanity: "For the truth is something which can be recognized only in freedom... Truth then disappears the moment that freedom is removed... Truth and freedom, then, are inseparable; each implies the other."[36] In fact, they need Singh Deo's legal protection from those religious zealots who take their lives when they enter religious shrines or when they act consistent with their dietary traditions and practices. Nelson Mandela, a victim of such elite subjugation, rightly said, "To deny people their human rights is to challenge their very humanity."[37]

Third, the Odisha Freedom of Religion Act is nothing but nuggets of negatives: "No person shall convert or attempt to convert, either directly or otherwise, any person from one religious faith to another by the use of force or by inducement or by any fraudulent means nor shall any person abet any such conversion."[38] This negative statute betrays Singh Deo's deep seated "demographic phobia."[39] Why this extraordinary protection of the Tribals and Dalits?

---

[36] Charles W. Foreman, "Freedom of Conversion: The Issue in India," *International Review of Mission* 45, no. 178 (April 1956): 192.

[37] "11 Top Quotes on Human Rights," accessed on July 25, 2017, http://unfoundationblog.org/11-top-quotes-on-human-rights/

[38] Orissa Freedom of Religion Bill 1967 in "Proceeding Other than Questions and Answers," vol. 3, no. 13. (Bhubaneswar: December 20, 1967), 46.

[39] "From about 1908 it was argued that untouchables numbered anywhere between 16 and 24 percent of the Indian populace. Part of this problem lay in the Government of India's hesitation in classifying certain groups of people as Depressed Classes, on the assumption that it would serve to stigmatize them. When the Census Commissioner for 1911 suggested that the Depressed Classes

The Hindutva movement is involved in a massive dilution project. There is a systematic and planned distortion of language and in the process, the corruption of history and truth. As for example, why should the word "Adivasi" (original dwellers) be substituted with "Vanwasi" (forest dwellers)? If they are Hindus, as the Indian census records will show, why should they be sanskritized, or initiated into Hinduism? Why should they exchange their animism for Hinduism? Why should such esteemed educational institutions like KIITS, Bhubaneswar, be involved in the systematic initiation of Tribal boys and girls into Jagannatha worship? But why this demographic phobia? Ian Douglas Richards explains the phobia with two reasons: First, "inclusion of the tribes and Scheduled castes with Hindus" provides "demographic advantage" over the non-Hindus. Second, this inclusion makes conversion into other religions "repugnant."[40] Thus, to them, the impact of conversion ranges from destabilization of the community to violence against it.[41]

With a thought provoking analysis of a catalogue of Indian Adivasis and their deities, Ebe Sunder Raj concludes that Adivasis are not Hindus, a fact that stands corroborated by the desperate attempts of the Brahmins to sanskritize the tribes into Hinduism. "The entire tribal population of India, which is non-Aryan by race and non-Brahminical by religion, never came, except in a very small number of conversions, under the Brahmincal religion, because of the geo-racio-religious isolation. The vast majority of them remain to this day in their non-Brahminical native tribal faiths."[42] Hinduism can neither offer true religious freedom to the Tribals and the Dalits nor let them enjoy it elsewhere. Rather they offer what Sathianathan Clark says, "a pseudo-Hindu identity" which helps

should be counted outside the Hindu fold, caste Hindus began to renew their interest in reclaiming untouchables for Hindu society. The steadily decreasing Hindu population (see Figure) was cause for alarm in light of the recent Morley-Minto reforms of 1909 that had guaranteed Muslims separate electorates." Anupama P. Rao, "Undoing Untouchability? Violence, Democracy, And Discourses of State in Maharastra, 1932-1991," PhD diss., University of Michigan, 1999, 43-44.

[40] Richards, "The Perception of Violence," 111.

[41] Richards, "The Perception of Violence," 116.

[42] Ebe Sunder Raj, *Conversion: A National Debate* (Delhi: Horizon Printers and Publishers, 2004), 136.

them to bring a divide between the Tribals and the Dalits as well as between the non-Christian Tribals/Dalits and Christian Tribals/Dalits. That's not all; the pseudo Hindu identity[43] is used as an incentive to recruit foot soldiers to persecute the converted Tribals and Dalits.[44] The demographic phobia of Singh Deo is spurred by the growing self-awareness of the Tribals and the Dalits. Deprivation and indoctrination are great tools of enslavement. But how can stringent laws and fear of severe punishment enslave a hungry mind in this age of information technology revolution? Let them be human!

Finally, it is understandable why the religious zealots of India detest secularism. The Freedom of Religion Act of Odisha is a classic brewing of the democracy-religion cocktail, just to their taste. Man is a religious being and we carry our religiosity into our workplaces daily. Hence, pure secularism is theoretical. However, without classical political liberalism, how can a diverse society like India survive? This enactment betrays a very narrow vision of a trustee of a plural society. The Odisha Freedom of Religion Act is a classic pneumatic non-return valve. It is designed only to cut off the exodus from Hinduism. "The Hindutva claim for reconversion and their opposition to people converting from one religion to another requires serious consideration. It is unconstitutional to impose rules on any form of conversion. At the same time, unrestricted freedom of religion to choose religion of one's own choice is the spirit of the Constitution."[45] The zealous practice of *Suddhi*, Sanskritization and Ghar Wapsi are not apolitical religious rites. The political hidden agenda of "Suddhi movement speaks more loudly than its words of denial" by its practitioners.[46] These are practices to close the door of

---

[43] Sathianathan Clarke, "Hindutva, Religious and Ethno-cultural Minorities and Indian-Christian Theology," 6, accessed on May 10, 2010, http://www.religion-online.org/showarticle.asp?title=2449. *[editorial note: when last checked on August 15, 2017, the web-link was inactive]*

[44] Chakravarthy Zadda-Ravindra, "Mission as Reconciling Presence: A Missiological Response to Hindutva," PhD diss. (Chicago: Lutheran School of Theology, 2015), 11.

[45] S. Robertson, "Freedom of Religion: A Human Rights Issue," (Bangalore: BTESSC, 2007), 15.

[46] James Forbes Scunarine, "Reconversion to Hinduism through *Suddhi*," PhD diss., Princeton, 1974, 108.

conversion from Hinduism. On the other hand, it is a way forward towards a monolithic nationalism. Thus, the Odisha Freedom of Religion Act is vindictive, biased and a punitive tool in the hands of the religious majority. When the law is at the service of the unaccountable majority subjects in office, the situation of minor objects is devastating.

Conclusion: Theological and Practical Reflections

Christianity is a missionary religion. It cannot do otherwise, without altering its very nature. Its mission is the outflow of its twin theological foundations. First, the Lordship Jesus Christ is exclusive and, second, his gospel is universal. How can it then address the issue of conversion, persecution and church planting so as to be consistent with its own nature and calling?

First, freedom of religion is intrinsic to human nature. The freedom to choose and to embrace the ultimate truth of one's conviction is fundamental to all religions. But conversion, in a centripetal society, is bound to create disassociation and conflict. However, it is acknowledged in such a society, as in India, that freedom of speech, freedom of the press, and freedom of religion all have double aspects: freedom of thought and freedom of action. Therefore, along with evangelism, education must be pressed to service that it may cultivate virtues like thinking and acting freely within the sphere of a community for the vertical expression of their freedom.

Second, religious minority and religious persecutions seem to be the unfortunate reality of our world. However, the minority tag must not lead a community to political alienation or isolation. The Church and the State are not exclusive to one another. Rather, Christian participation in political mainstream can be a persecution deterrent. However, our Christian response to persecution must go beyond political activism to Christian political witness. Christian witness as the salt of the earth and the light of the world is impossible with an isolationist mindset. It calls for convictions of divine sovereignty, commitment to contribute in the legislative and administrative affairs of the state, and to take risks like Daniel and Esther did.

Third, transforming lives and transforming communities are inseparable spectrums of Christian witnessing and must go hand in hand. Christian witnessing involves the proclamation (truth) as well as the practice (unity) of the gospel. The gospel to be true and total must be heard and experienced. How can they experience it unless they hear it in an atmosphere of freedom? When they hear the gospel, it must convince the mind, transform the heart, and minister to the body. Hence, when the gospel is holistic, the transformation is comprehensive and complete. William Temple has rightly stated, "The Church is the only corporate society that exists for the benefits of the nonmembers."[47] Benjamin Franklin seems to be very prophetic to the context of India today, "Without continual growth and progress, such words as improvement, achievement, and success have no meaning."[48] What is the need of the hour? India must shed its progress resistance and live progress-prone.

---

[47] William Temple, cited by Charles Smyth in *Cyril Foster Garbett* (Hodder and Stoughton, 1959) 106.

[48] Benjamin Franklin, accessed on July 25, 2017, https://www.brainyquote.com/quotes/keywords/growth.html.

Religious Freedom and the Church: Between Secularism And Religious Nationalism

John Arun Kumar[1]

"Between the devil and the deep blue sea" is an adage meaning dilemma, caught between undesirable situations. As far as religious freedom is concerned, the Indian Christian church and the universal Christian church are in just such a dilemma.[2] At both macro and micro levels, the church in India is caught between secularism and religious nationalism. Macro and micro levels are relative terms determined by the large contextual reference. In the international context, macro level refers to international level and micro level refers to local levels such as national level or state or town or village levels. In the national context, macro level refers to national level and micro level refers to state level or district levels. So on and so forth.

According to the Indian Constitution, secular India in principle grants citizens religious freedom, which includes the right to profess, practise and propagate one's religion. However, this religious freedom becomes contentious for some when aspects of inter-faith or inter-religious conversion become explicit, especially when people of other religions change their religion to follow Christianity. The issue of religious freedom and conversion has been a burning issue facing India, especially for minorities and the Church in particular, with the rise of Hindu right-wing Bharatiya Janata Party (BJP) between 1998-2004 and again most recently with its majority win in 2014. The BJP is a political outfit of the Rashtriya Swayamsevak Sangh (RSS), a group committed to the Hindu right-wing ideology. There are other Hindu right-wing ideological

---

[1] Dr. John Arun Kumar is a faculty and HoD in the Department of Study of Religions, SAIACS, Bangalore.

[2] In this paper, Buddhists, Christians, Hindus, Jains, Jews, Muslims, Parsis, Sikhs, and various tribes, are those who subscribe to their respective faith traditions and/or identify themselves as belonging to their respective faith communities.

groups and they are collectively referred to as the Hindutva³ Parivar (family of Hindutva). Reportedly Hindutva groups have increased their activities of (re)converting people to Hinduism, under their programme known as Ghar Wapsi (homecoming). Their special focus is to convert Indians belonging to other faiths, especially Christians and Muslims, to Hinduism.

Secularists and other religious groups have been concerned about these (re)conversion activities by Hindutva proponents. The media has engaged many *gurus* and politicians in India in debates and discussions on (re)conversion. During his visit to India in 2015, the US President Obama made a strong pitch for religious freedom amid this (re)conversion backdrop.⁴ Such appeals suggest that (re)conversion has gained global attention and response. In the wake of (re)conversion discourses, there is a broader discussion on various issues such as religious conversion per se, the passing of the Bill on religious conversions, human rights, religious rights, Uniform Civil Code, freedom of speech and a host of related subjects.

Globally, issues relating to religious freedom and conversion have become transnational religious issues calling for international response and action. Hence, the international efforts made to study the phenomena and to work out strategies to maintain peace and justice among various peoples of the world. Some of the agencies involved in this way, to name a few, are World Conference on Religions for Peace (WCRP), World Council of Churches (WCC), World Evangelical Alliance (WEA), and the Lausanne Movement. A review of these gives a broader socio-religious framework of understanding the issues related to religious freedom and conversion

---

³ Hindutva is a term first coined by Sarvakar and that has stayed on ever since as a title for a right-wing Hindu ideology and for Hindu right-wing groups and activities. This term is a combination of two terms, Hindu (an English term to refer to Hinduism) and, *tva* (a Sanskrit suffix to indicate quality). The combined term means "Hindu-ness" or "Hindu-ity." V. D. Savarkar, *Hindutva: Who is a Hindu?* (Bombay: Veer Savarkar Prakashan, 1923; 1969), inside coverpage.

⁴ ET Bureau, "Obama in India: Barack Obama Wraps Up Visit with Advice on Religious Tolerance," *The Economic Times,* January 28, 2015, accessed on August 16, 2017, http://economictimes.indiatimes.com/news/politics-and-nation/obama-in-india-barack-obama-wraps-up-visit-with-advice-on-religious-tolerance/printarticle/46036880.cms?utm_source=contentofinterest&utm_medium=text&utm_campaign=cppst.

in general, at macro and micro levels. I suggest that the issue of religious freedom and conversion in India needs to be located in this broader socio-religious framework of understanding at macro and micro levels, in order to work towards a way forward. The reason being that secular India acceded on April 10, 1979 to international covenants: International Covenant on Civil and Political Rights (ICCPR) and International Covenant on Economic, Social and Cultural Rights (ICESCR).[5]

As citizens, Christians have the right to pursue religious freedom and their identity, and that includes freedom to speak and practise the Christian faith. Christians have their part to play in handling of issues of religious freedom at both macro and micro levels as a part of their Christian calling and witness. Given the religious and political climate of today, Christians are increasingly curtailed in exercising their rights. This paper uses multiple methodological approaches from the fields of social science, and political and religious studies, to discuss this important issue.

Religious Freedom and Conversion

The international human rights law has been playing a key role in setting the benchmark. Robert Traer writes that the International human rights law found acceptance because it leaves open to the state to decide on state and religion relationships.[6] Various countries of the world, US, UK, the Middle Eastern countries, China, so on and so forth, have varied responses to issues of religious freedom and conversion as per their own constitutions and socio-religious contexts. Broadly, nations fall into at least two categories depending on state and religion relationships—whether the two are separate or together. Some countries have taken a secular stance

---

[5] National Human Rights Commission, India, "Core International Human Rights Treaties, Optional Protocols & Core ILO Conventions Ratified by India," *A Handbook on International Human Rights Conventions* (New Delhi, India: National Human Rights Commission, 2012) 25, accessed on August 16, 2017, http://nhrc.nic.in/Documents/Publications/A_Handbook_on_International_HR_Conventions.pdf.

[6] Robert Traer, "Nationalism and Religious Freedom," 1998, accessed on August 16, 2017, http://religionhumanrights.com/Culture/Europe/rf.nationalism.htm.

and kept religion separate; others have made a religion their state religion. Christian experiences around the world have been varied. Under these, Christians are facing nationalism of two types, secular nationalism and religious nationalism, that affects their religious freedom in practice.[7]

CHRISTIANS AND SECULARISM

History has demonstrated that the Protestant Christian concept of a gathered congregation of individual believers has shaped the development of provisions protecting freedom of religion or belief under International Law.[8] In all its forms, although secularism makes room for Christian presence and practice, it brings its problems and limitations on such presence and practice.

Broadly, Christians could be classified on the basis of their demography as majority and minority communities. In countries where Christians are a majority, further broad classification could be applied on the basis of the relationship between state and religion. For instance, in the US the state and church are separate, whereas in England the state Regent and the Church of England are together and in some European nations this is the case, in that the head of the state is also the head of the church. In Italy the head of the church is also the head of the state. Thus in these Christian majority nations, there are two models of operations evident. In many secular nations, religious institutions and their freedom are seen as contradictory. Here it is important to note that in such contexts, on the surface, Christians have been given freedom to practise and promote their faith. However, this religious freedom is called into question when some of their faith practices clash with the freedom and practices of others. Then, these issues are settled in secular courts, who decide which religious practices are *more free* to be practised. In countries where Christians are a minority, such as in India, Pakistan, Indonesia, Turkey, Bangladesh and some others,

---

[7] John Arun Kumar, "Christian Identity and Religious Pluralism in India: Conversion and the Hindutva Challenge to Indian Identity," in *Indian and Christian: Changing Identities in Modern India,* eds. Cornelis Bennema and Paul Joshua Bhakiaraj (Bangalore: SAIACS Press, 2011), 176-196.

[8] Traer, "Nationalism and Religious Freedom."

Christians are allowed to practise their religious traditions in varying degrees, yet there are stronger restrictions concerning mission and evangelism, especially to protect majority interests. However, there are hardly any restrictions or protections offered on Christians who choose or are forced to choose another religion over their own.

INDIAN CHRISTIANS AND INDIAN SECULARISM

Secularism in India is different from the general definition and practice of it, in that it recognizes religions. Having made a choice for such secularism, a part of India's experience with drafting her Constitution was guided by making provisions for her Christian communities to be included in the democratic nation. Due considerations were given to the fact that Christianity is inextricably linked to its religious imperative to propagate its faith.[9] The term "right to propagate" was understood to mean the same as "right to convert." However, the states within the nation are given the freedom to decide on state and religion relationships. This has resulted in the passing of anti-conversion laws in six states, and the remaining states may follow suit. In the Supreme Court verdict on Stanislaus vs. Madhya Pradesh, the judge interpreted the "right to propagate" to mean a right to preach one's tenets but not a right to convert.[10] Although India is a secular country, this has made life difficult for the Christian minority in those states, to freely practise their religious imperatives.

Both at macro as well as micro levels, Christians, whether they are a majority or minority under secular countries, are facing challenges that increasingly make their presence, living and practice very difficult.

---

[9] Constituent Assembly Debates, vol. 7, December 6, 1948. http://parliamentofindia.nic.in/ls/debates/vol7p20a.htm *[editorial note: when last checked on August 16, 2017, the web-link was inactive. Alternative link, accessed on August 16, 2017: https://indiankanoon.org/doc/1308071]*

[10] A. Ray, "Rev. Stainislaus vs State Of Madhya Pradesh & Ors" on January 17, 1977. Equivalent citations: AIR 908 (1977), SCR (2) 61 (1977)," Date of Judgment, January 17, 1977, The Supreme Court of India, https://indiankanoon.org/doc/1308071/, as it appeared on June 2, 2017.

CHRISTIANS AND RELIGIOUS NATIONALISM

As already noted, the international human rights law leaves open to the state to decide on state and religion relationships.[11] Traer says because of this it is possible for the governments to support a religion or two and thus become itself discriminatory.[12] On this he writes,

> International human rights law may well favor a "secular" state, as some religious critics claim, but it does not require it. Instead, international human rights law requires states to "prevent and eliminate discrimination on the grounds of religion or belief" and to "combat intolerance on the grounds of religion or other beliefs." International law names the evil as "discrimination" and "intolerance" rather than "establishment," allowing that some sort of "fair and tolerant establishment" of religion is possible. Put more precisely, it leaves open the question of special relationships between the state and one or more religious traditions to an evaluation of the effects of such relationships on religious freedom, rather than asserting in principle that any support for religion by a government will necessarily be discriminatory.[13]

I suggest international law that made room for secularism based on the principle of democracy also has made room for the state to have special relationships with one or more religious traditions. This feature has given rise to the dawn of religious nationalistic movements. It appears that the key feature of these movements is that they seek political control and rule over the state by using religion and by making use of the freedom the state has to keep state and religion together under the human rights law. In recent times in different parts of the world, there has been a rise in religious nationalism.[14]

For many in Central and Eastern Europe, religion is inextricably related to cultural and national heritage. Traer notes that the

---

[11] Ray, "Rev. Stalnislaus vs State."
[12] Ray, "Rev. Stainislaus vs State."
[13] Traer, "Nationalism and Religious Freedom."
[14] These have been researched and discussed extensively in Kumar, "Christian Identity and Religious Pluralism in India," 176-196.

Balkan war was the result of such nationalism.[15] He notes, "Most Orthodox churches identify strongly with a particular ethnic and cultural history that is represented concretely by a nation. Thus an Orthodox church expects the state that governs its nation to represent and protect the interests of the church."[16] Traer, discussing the Bosnian war, points out that although religious support for human rights in the midst of the Bosnian war was relegated to statements of remorse, there was support for human rights through inter-faith initiatives to achieve peace.[17] He notes that the religious leaders from the Serbian Orthodox, Croatian Catholic and Bosnian Islamic communities have been brought together through the World Conference on Religion and Peace in an inter-faith initiative to heal the wounds of the society and to support democratic government.[18]

Further citing the case of the Volga nations in Eastern Europe, Traer writes, "Nationalist movements in some of the newly independent political jurisdictions of Eastern Europe that were oppressed by Communist rule hope to use democratic government to recover indigenous religious traditions."[19] He notes other forms of nationalisms in that context: "In Chuvash, efforts by the Orthodox Church to establish itself as the national religion are being resisted by the Chuvash National Congress, whose members promote a return to pagan roots."[20] In India, Hindu nationalism has grown stronger.[21]

HINDUTVA

Traer's assessment, as noted above, seems to fit the Hindutva phenomena right from its inception in Indian history. Hindutva (the Hindu right-wing) activists claim that Hinduism was the religion of the land prior to the advent of other religions on Indian soil and they are against inter-religious conversions. In line with this, they

---

[15] Traer, "Nationalism and Religious Freedom."
[16] Traer, "Nationalism and Religious Freedom."
[17] Traer, "Nationalism and Religious Freedom."
[18] Traer, "Nationalism and Religious Freedom."
[19] Traer, "Nationalism and Religious Freedom."
[20] Traer, "Nationalism and Religious Freedom."
[21] See Kumar, "Christian Identity and Religious Pluralism in India," 189.

have increased their religious (re)conversion activities targeting mostly the recently converted to Christianity. At present Hindutva is becoming the dominant voice in India. On one of its websites, it asks that religious freedom be granted to Hindus to practise their religion in Sri Lanka. Whereas it advises against Indian Hindus exercising their religious freedom to opt for inter-religious conversions, saying such conversions are harmful. It pictorially portrays Christianity and Islam as religions using force and inducements to convert others. Christians are targeted increasingly by countries where forces of religious nationalism are in control of governments.

Hindutva influences the states where the Hindutva nationalist party is in power, and have imposed anti-conversion laws. This has resulted in disturbing the secular position of the country and has especially affected the minorities' right to religious freedom. In this context, it is worth noting how International agencies have responded to the issues of human rights.

INTERNATIONAL RESPONSE TO CHALLENGES UNDER HUMAN RIGHTS

By making room for the individual states to choose the type of state and religion relationships, the international human rights laws appear to have various problems. To note a few international agencies that are actively involved in addressing these: World Conference on Religions for Peace (WCRP), World Council of Churches (WCC), World Evangelical Alliance and Lausanne Movement.

World Conference on Religions For Peace (WCRP)

The World Conference of Religions for Peace is a multi-religious congress whose membership includes religious leaders from the Baha'i; Mahayana and Theravada Buddhism; Orthodox, Protestant, and Roman Catholic Christianity; Confucianism; Hinduism; indigenous faiths; Islam; Jainism; Reform Judaism; New Religions; Shinto; Sikhism; and Zoroastrianism.[22] It invites world religious leaders to participate in congresses to share their goals and

---

[22] For more information, see the website for "Religions and Peace," http://www.religionsforpeace.org.

contribute to world peace in the spirit of inter-religious cooperation.[23] WCRP has played an important role through its inter-faith initiatives in working towards a stable peace following the Bosnian war.[24] On this Traer observes, "Not surprisingly, leaders from... three religious communities have drawn on the teachings of their traditions to justify their support for human rights and for peace with their recent enemies."[25] Here we note that inter-faith initiatives have yielded support for human rights and for peace between those who were enemies based on their religious teachings. This is a welcome outcome towards achieving stable peace in spite of the international human rights' inherent feature to leave open the choice of relationships between state and religion to the state. However, the question of religious freedom and conversion is not the focus of WCRP and the church represented by the Vatican and WCC in the WCRP are busy promoting pluralism.[26]

World Council of Churches (WCC)

WCC, apart from promoting religious pluralism, has published a statement on religious freedom in the wake of the increase of intolerance towards minority religions in many parts of the world.[27] The statement is built on international human rights. It calls for the various states to act as per the UN Declaration on Human Rights. WCC launched a ten-year study project on religious conversion and has published its findings in its *Religious Conversion: Religion Scholars Thinking Together* (2015).[28] It covers contributions from religious scholars and leaders of Buddhist, Christian, Hindu, Jewish,

---

[23] http://www.religionsforpeace.org.
[24] Traer, "Nationalism and Religious Freedom."
[25] Traer, "Nationalism and Religious Freedom."
[26] Anna Halafoff, *The Multifaith Movement: Global risks and Cosmopolitan Solutions* (New York, USA: Springer Science & Business Media, 2012), 40-41.
[27] "Statement on the Politicization of Religion and Rights of Religious Minorities," Adopted by the WCC 10th Assembly as part of the Report of the Public Issues Committee, November 8, 2013, accessed on September 5, 2015, https://www.oikoumene.org,
[28] WCC, *Religious Conversion: Religion Scholars Thinking Together*, 2015, accessed on September 5, 2015, https://www.oikoumene.org.

and Muslim traditions on various issues relating to the nature, methods, and effects of religious conversion in the major world faiths.[29] It discusses questions on religious freedom, legal considerations, and the future for religious conversion.[30] It basically affirms an individual's right to convert and opposes forced conversions.

World Evangelical Alliance (WEA)

World Evangelical Alliance is an international evangelical forum that has membership of Christians from 128 countries. It has set up a Religious Liberty Commission (RLC) to promote freedom of religion for all people. WEA-RLC monitors religious liberty by conducting research through its wing, the International Institute for Religious Freedom (IIRF), which is a network of academicians and researchers from all continents.[31] It publishes WEA Global Issues Series highlighting various global issues. In the wake of attacks by religious fundamentalists in the US and in Europe, it has published under the series a book focused on religious fundamentalism.[32] The book suggests that the current fundamentalism ought to be understood in terms of militant truth claims, of which corresponding currents are found in all religions and worldviews.[33] It has published a report on anti-conversion laws in India.[34] The report highlights how the anti-conversion laws enacted in six states in India go against the international covenants supporting religious freedom signed by India. This report points out that there are more states that may follow suit in adopting such laws, both within India and in the neighbouring countries of India.[35] The continuing of such laws is going to work against freedom of human rights and

---

[29] WCC, *Religious Conversion*.
[30] WCC, *Religious Conversion*.
[31] http://www.iirf.eu.
[32] Thomas Schirmacher, *Fundamentalism: When Religion becomes Dangerous*, The WEA Global Issues Series, vol. 14, (Bonn: Culture and Science Publishing, 2013).
[33] Schirmacher, *Fundamentalism*.
[34] Tehmina Arora, *India's Defiance of Religious Freedom: A Briefing on 'Anti-Conversion' Laws*, IIRF Reports, vol. 1, no. 2, (February 2012), 14.
[35] Arora, *India's Defiance of Religious Freedom*, 14.

cause more communal problems. This report calls for action in repealing such laws. It notes that "India's civil society, judiciary, legislature and executive, as well as the international community, need to work towards the repealing or striking down of these laws as they threaten not only the Indian ethos of tolerance and communal harmony but also set a dangerous precedent for other nations in the area of religious freedom."[36]

Lausanne Movement

Lausanne Movement is another global evangelical forum which also addresses issues of religious freedom across the world under the banner Lausanne Global Analysis.[37] Like WEA, it periodically publishes the results of its analysis, thereby raising awareness about issues concerning freedom of religion in various countries.[38]

US response to religious freedom

The findings of the United States Commission on International Religious Freedom (USCIRF), largely based on the accounts of religious leaders of the minorities and non-government organizations in India, have led it to place India on its Tier 2 list of countries for the seventh year in a row.[39] Only time will tell how this will impact Christian minorities in India.

Overall, as noted above, international responses to the issue of religious freedom have been a bane and boon: a bane to minority communities in terms of becoming targets of violence in their local contexts and a boon to them in terms of some relief that international interventions bring, which in some ways help Christians survive locally. However, under religious freedom there is more stress given to peaceful co-existence than to exercise of freedom to practise evangelism and missions. Having noted responses by

---

[36] Arora, *India's Defiance of Religious Freedom*, 15.
[37] http://www.lausanne.org.
[38] http://www.lausanne.org.
[39] United States Commission on International Religious Freedom, Annual Report 2015, accessed 5 September 2015, http://www.uscirf.gov.

international agencies, we shall now turn to Indian responses to the challenges posed to religious freedom in India.

Response to Issues of Religious Freedom in India

In India, there have been responses from government and politics, judiciary, media, and religions.

Political responses by the government

As already noted, the Indian Constitution upholds secularism, where state and religion are seen as separate. However, much consideration was given to framing articles on freedom of religion. It is important to note that the presence of the Christian community and its religious imperative to propagate, played an important part in the discussion on the right to propagate as a part of the freedom of religion. As part of the discussion on the notion related to the "right to propagate," a discussion on the right to convert from one religion to another was also included. Conversions by influence, coercion, and fraud were opposed and at the same time room was made for individuals to exercise freedom of conscience and voluntarily choose to convert. In the former instance, the state could exercise the right to regulate such activity.

In both houses of parliament wherein the issue is debated, there is push for passing a national anti-conversion law by the Hindu right-wing nationalist party. Regarding issues of religious freedom and conversion in other countries, India has hardly shown any interest, especially under the BJP majority government.

Judiciary responses to religious freedom and conversion

Tehmina Arora in her report has reviewed the anti-conversion laws passed in the six states of India and has shown how they violate the spirit of religious freedom that India has committed to at international forums for human rights.[40] Since the Hindu right-wing nationalist party's recent victory in elections, there is a majoritarian

---

[40] Arora, *India's Defiance of Religious Freedom*, 15.

show of strength by Hindutva proponents through their organized (re)conversion programmes. Referring to experience with such legislation and its impact in Madhya Pradesh and Gujarat, Suhrith Parthasarathy, an advocate from Chennai, contends that these laws have inevitably been fraught with interpretive maladies that often strike at the root of our right to religious freedom.[41] Parthasarathy explains how the interpretation and use of the term "to propagate" in a verdict has impacted the subsequent verdicts on religious freedom and conversion. He writes concerning the Stanislaus case: "Justice Ray interpreted the word propagate, to mean to transmit or spread one's religion by an exposition of its tenets, but to not include the right to convert another person to one's own religion."[42] He notes Justice Ray's words:

> Article 25.1 guarantees freedom of conscience "to every citizen, and not merely to the followers of one particular religion… and that, in turn, postulates that there is no fundamental right to convert another person to one's own religion because if a person purposely undertakes the conversion of another person to his religion, as distinguished from his effort to transmit or spread the tenets of his religion, that would impinge on the freedom of conscience" guaranteed to all the citizens of the country alike.[43]

Parthasarathy observes that Justice Ray's reasoning is clearly conflating the issue. He argues that if "a person's right to propagate his religion does not include a right to freedom of speech aimed at seeking conversions, would not such a right be purely illusory?"[44] He draws on the observation by the constitutional law scholar, H. M. Seervai, in response, that

> …to propagate religion is not to impart knowledge and to spread it more widely, but to produce intellectual and moral conviction leading to action, namely, the adoption of that religion. Successful propagation of religion would

[41] Suhrith Parthasarathy, "Conversion and Freedom of Religion," *The Hindu*, December 23, 2014, accessed on May 29, 2015, http://www.thehindu.com/opinion/lead/conversion-and-freedom-of-religion/article6716638.ece
[42] Parthasarathy, "Conversion and Freedom of Religion."
[43] Parthasarathy, "Conversion and Freedom of Religion."
[44] Parthasarathy, "Conversion and Freedom of Religion."

result in conversion. Therefore, when a person converts to another religion, based on speech, which aims at producing such conversion, he or she is, in fact, exercising a general right to freedom of conscience.[45]

Parthasarathy assesses that Justice Ray's verdict has confused a person's liberty to exercise free conscience for another person's right to propagate religion and has produced damaging results.[46] He notes that the

> ...case relates to a fundamental, and more nuanced, issue of intervention by the state… and its courts… in religious affairs."[47] He explains that "Anti-conversion laws allow the state the authority to determine what constitutes an illegitimate inducement, and, in doing so, they create a slippery slope.[48]

Media responses

Media in general is engaged in giving wide coverage to political debates on religious freedom and conversion. Television media is abuzz with its shoot-and-scoot format on events concerning religious freedom and conversion. It has also engaged in debates on the issue involving commoners, social activists, and political and religious leaders. The media has engaged interviewing popular cine stars, *gurus* and politicians on the issue. One of the Hindu religious leaders who took the opportunity to speak for the Hindutva agenda is symptomatic of all such views.[49] Referring to the work of Jakob de Roover of Ghent University, Jaideep Prabhu, in his article, "Is Religious Conversion Really a Fundamental Right, or Can we Ban it?"[50] argues that truth claims create antagonism by its conversion

---

[45] Parthasarathy, "Conversion and Freedom of Religion."
[46] Parthasarathy, "Conversion and Freedom of Religion."
[47] Parthasarathy, "Conversion and Freedom of Religion."
[48] Parthasarathy, "Conversion and Freedom of Religion."
[49] "Ghar Wapsi, Beef Ban & Church Attacks: Unraveling The Truth," accessed on May 29, 2015, www.ishafoundation.org/blog/sadguru/masters-words/ghar-wapsi-beef-ban-church-attacks-unraveling-truth.
[50] Jaideep A Prabhu, "Is religious conversion really a fundamental right, or can we ban it?" *Firstpost*, September 8, 2014.

imperatives and it finds its place in multi-religious societies through secularism, whose roots are in Abrahamic faiths.[51]

Indian Christian responses

As already noted, the relationship of state and religion has its impact on the Christian world itself. This has evoked varied Indian Christian responses to secularism and right-wing nationalism. Here below I note some of the responses from Roman Catholic, Ecumenical, Evangelical, and other voices.

A. D. Mattam writes on religious freedom from a Roman Catholic perspective. He explains that "[r]espect for religions does not mean that one must accept in principle that one religion is as good as another. One can stick to one's own religious convictions, and peacefully practice the religion of his choice. But the same right is to be conceded to other people."[52] A. Edmond, a Roman Catholic Christian responding to Hindu fundamentalism writes, "Challenges and questions posed in front of any rational beings and every socially concerned person in India to immediately respond to ...the Hindutva...."[53] On the same website, he notes in one of his articles titled "Secular Counterpoint of Hindu Fundamentalism" that "Secularism (non-religious) and Hindu fundamentalism contradict each other...."[54] Further on this point he explains, "Secularism in India mainly means: no religion will be recognized as the state religion even that of the majority community, unity and equality of the people should be asserted regardless of religion and caste, no interference from the religious or state authority in individual's right to profess his or her own faith."[55] He writes his Indian Christian response,

---

[51] Prabhu, "Is religious conversion."
[52] A. D. Mattam, *Religions and Religious Freedom in India* (Delhi: Media House, 2009), 130.
[53] A. Edmond, "Responses to Hindu Fundamentalism," May 25, 2017, accessed 5 September 2015, https://sites.google.com/site/yeswereallycan/hindu-funadamentalism.
[54] Edmond, "Responses to Hindu Fundamentalism."
[55] Edmond, "Responses to Hindu Fundamentalism."

> I am convinced that our response as Indian Christians to Hindu fundamentalism is not to mainly condemn but to positively prove ourselves as more patriotic than the Hindu fundamentalists themselves. The Indian Church should question the anti-human aspects of Hindu fundamentalism through thoroughly getting inculturated [sic] into the customs of the local people. ... Surely, these positive approaches will concretely respond to the Hindu fundamentalism.[56]

Further he writes, "The Christians and Muslims should also give up every trace of superior-feelings over other religions in order to foster religious harmony in India."[57]

From an ecumenical point of view, Christian theologians such as J. R. Chandran, M. M. Thomas and others have written on religious freedom suggesting that consultative bodies for Christians should be set up at international and national levels on matters relating to Christians.[58] The National Council of Churches in India (NCCI) and its allied bodies seem to fulfil this role according to them.

The Evangelical Fellowship of India (EFI) represents many evangelicals and one of its roles has been to faithfully report Christian struggles and incidents of attacks on Christians.[59] This has been useful in bringing awareness about Christian minority problems faced in the country. These reports have helped the US religious freedom forum to look into the minority situation in the country which is highly influenced by the Hindutva politics at present.

M. T. Cherian, religion scholar, in his book *Hindutva Agenda and Minority Rights: A Christian Response*, has studied Hindu fundamentalism and its impact on secularism from 1947 to 1997.[60] He suggests that since Christians in India are a minority, we need to assume a minority viewpoint in our response to Hindutva.[61] He

---

[56] Edmond, "Responses to Hindu Fundamentalism."
[57] Edmond, "Responses to Hindu Fundamentalism."
[58] J. R. Chandran and M. M. Thomas Sapru, *Religious Freedom*, 1956.
[59] EFI Reports, 2014, http://iirf.eu.
[60] M.T. Cherian, *Hindutva Agenda and Minority Rights: A Christian Response* (Bangalore: Centre for Contemporary Christianity, 2007).
[61] Cherian, *Hindutva Agenda*, 266.

proposes that Christians should develop public theology through various engagements with the public.[62] He suggests that Christians could respond by asking questions to different "publics"—such as political public, economic public, academic public, religious public and legal public—in order to bring awareness and response.[63] He also suggests that Christians should also seek help from international forums for religious freedom and justice.[64]

Joseph M. Athyal, a religion scholar from Gurukul Lutheran Theological College, Chennai, in his article traces the conversion debate in history and discusses the Tambaram meeting to Hans Ucko to the Dalit perspective.[65] He says the Thomas-Newbigin debate is important to note on matters of conversion.[66] Because Christ relativizes all religions, he cannot be confined to any religion, and "Conversion of the marginalized people in India, however, was not confined to the Christian faith."[67] Athyal asks, "Can Christ-centered fellowships within other religions be a substitute for the organized church?"[68]

Abraham Vazhayil Thomas in his work *Christians in Secular India* writes that Christians in India have a role to play in politics as communities, churches and individuals.[69] The Supreme Court's definition of the essence of religion is to be understood for each religion as per its tenets and its claims. Hence it becomes tricky in a multi-religious context where there are fundamental differences in the tenets, to apply it meaningfully.[70] He further argues that Hinduism is not based on individual rights but on individual role and so it is at odds with secularism. He proposes that Christians

---

[62] Cherian, *Hindutva Agenda*, 309.

[63] Cherian, *Hindutva Agenda*, 303-308.

[64] Cherian, *Hindutva Agenda*, 311.

[65] Joseph M. Athyal, "The Conversion Debate in India: Tambaram to Hans Ucko to a Subaltern Perspective," (Chennai: Dharma Deepika, 2007).

[66] Athyal, "The Conversion Debate in India."

[67] Athyal, "The Conversion Debate in India."

[68] Athyal, "The Conversion Debate in India."

[69] Abraham Vazhayil Thomas, *Christians in Secular India* (Rutherford, N.J.: Fairleigh Dickinson University Press, 1974), 214.

[70] Thomas, *Christians in Secular India*, 214.

should play an active role in nation-building that seeks a national integration not on the basis of religion but on common humanity.[71]

Further Thomas writes that Christians have a special role to play as the second largest minority in India "to contribute toward furtherance of the ideals of the secular state and particularly of maintaining separation between religion and state and religious liberty as well as defending the legitimate rights of its disadvantaged members."[72] He cites examples from Europe—the 17th century Catholic minority and the Baptist minority in New England—and America where Baptists and Quakers and other religious minorities have played a decisive role in achieving this.[73] He further explains that in "any country inundated [sic] by a large religious majority the temptation is always present to throw away these ideals of secular state."[74] He suggests that Christians have to offer their service to others without the motive of evangelization.[75] And lastly he suggests that Christians should maintain inter-communication through its forum with the state for mutual understanding and cooperation.[76]

Arthur Jeyakumar's study on Indian Christian religious nationalism is about Christians who were nationalists and active in the freedom struggle of India.[77] He presents how the Memoranda were used by the British rule in India to keep missionaries and Indian Christians from participating in the national movement.[78] He notes that Christians should be engaged actively in nation-building rather than focusing on evangelism.[79]

In Nepal, which was counted as the only Hindu nation in the world until a few years ago, some pragmatic solutions have been worked out by Christians there, to face the problems posed by Hindu religious nationalism. A couple of solutions to note are: first,

---

[71] Thomas, *Christians in Secular India*, 214.
[72] Thomas, *Christians in Secular India*, 196, 214.
[73] Thomas, *Christians in Secular India*, 214.
[74] Thomas, *Christians in Secular India*, 214.
[75] Thomas, *Christians in Secular India*, 214.
[76] Thomas, *Christians in Secular India*, 214.
[77] D. Arthur Jeyakumar, *Christians and the National Movement* (Bangalore: Centre for Contemporary Christianity, 2009).
[78] Jeyakumar, *Christians and the National Movement*, 2.
[79] Jeyakumar, *Christians and the National Movement*, 2.

Christians there do not use the term conversion in their evangelistic activities. Second, many Christians do not practise child baptisms and wait to perform adult baptism for an individual who wishes to follow Christ, only after he or she has legally changed religion.[80] The Nepalese government has opted for secularism and like India believes in freedom of religion and so the government's new constitution is committed to protecting all religions.

Pursuing our religious imperatives as Christians, I suggest that we could apply a cognitive approach following Paul Heibert's critical contextualization model for doing missions in this context.[81] My SAIACS Academic Consultation paper (2010) focused on identity issues and there I chose to write on religious conversion.[82] Here, following suggestions of Kwame Bediako, we could learn and apply some of the ways from the life of the early church fathers as to how they handled identity issues amidst a situation similar to ours. Again in the next SAIACS Academic Consultation (2011), my paper was on being Christians in the public square, which related to religious freedom issues.[83] Here the suggestion was that following Max Stackhouse's analysis of Christians in public square and his suggestions, we reconsider Max Weber's ideas about the need for individuals to realize their political presence and to act responsibly to address the issues.

It is important for the Christian church and other minorities to oppose any imposition of anti-conversion laws, either at national or state levels.

Considering the changing Christian self-understanding in history, the question whether such change should not be conceived in the contemporary context of globalization and religious pluralism context as about identity. In his article, "Christian Identity and

---

[80] From my notes on informal talks with a friend from Nepal, now studying in India.

[81] John Arun Kumar, "Mission and Postmodernity, Neocolonialism and Globalization," in *Edinburgh 1910 Revisited*, Bangalore: CMS/ATS, 2010), 118-146.

[82] Kumar, "Christian Identity and Religious Pluralism in India."

[83] John Arun Kumar, "Transforming Motives: the Use and Misue of Religion with Implications for Indian Christian Involvement in the Public Square," in *Christians in the Public Square,* eds. Varughese John and Nigel Ajay Kumar (Bangalore: SAIACS Press, 2013), 64-79.

Theology of Religious Pluralism [TRP]" José María Vigil writing on religious pluralism and its effects, argues that the history of Christian self-understanding has changed based on historical contexts.[84] He writes, "If, when faced with liberation and Liberation Theology, many Christian churches felt challenged by alleged risks implicit in the field of ethics both in practice and in policy, now when faced with the actual reality of religious pluralism and TRP, churches feel challenged in their very identity and especially in the field of their theology. Religious pluralism questions their very identity." He further predicts, "The center of debate in coming years will be 'the Christian identity': 'this is 'Christian,' that is not'; up to a certain point one is 'Christian' but from there on one is 'un-Christian.'"[85] He observes that this debate concerning religious pluralism and inter-religious dialogue already actually exists.[86] "... Perhaps even 'a new identity'?"[87] "... Can we speak of 'one and the same Christian identity' as being common to all that we here have called 'readings' but that could also be called 'Christian Identities'? If we would wish to establish 'The Christian identity,' on just what would we base it?"[88] Further, he observes on Christian identity from synchronic perspective. He writes, synchronically speaking, it is not possible to speak of a real and unique Christian identity, even though "the institution" officially declares that there exists only one "Christian identity." The missionaries, professionally obliged to refer constantly to the Christian identity, objected: "Does a missionary imbued with an exclusive paradigm preach the same 'Christian identity' as a missionary imbued with an inclusive paradigm?"[89]

---

[84] José María Vigil, "Christian Identity and Theology of Religious Pluralism," trans Justiniano Liebl, in *Along the Many Paths of God–IV: Intercontinental Liberation Theology of Religious Pluralism,* ed José María Vigil, Luiza E. Tomita, and Marcelo Barros. (EATWOT, Ecumenical Association of Third World Theologians For this digital bilingual edition: EATWOT's International Theological Commission Cyberspace, March 2010, 107.

[85] Vigil, "Christian Identity," 107.

[86] Vigil, "Christian Identity," 107.

[87] Vigil, "Christian Identity," 107.

[88] Vigil, "Christian Identity," 107.

[89] Vigil, "Christian Identity," 107.

He suggests some possible shifts in the current theological development. He writes, "If, during the current theological transition, the great Christian majority were to pass from inclusion to pluralism, would it maintain its present Christian identity, or would it have changed substantially?"[90] He further observes that human religious identity has been dynamic; it changes constantly with the times.[91] From this premise he writes that the same identity did not exist throughout history and hence, religious identities are expected to continue evolving.[92] He further asks, "Do we maintain the Christian identity in the TRP, or have we breached its borders? Is it possible that different modes of understanding can fit within the same Christian identity?"[93] Based on the perspectives of religious pluralism on other religions, he further reflects on the Christian identity based on the idea that "Christians are chosen people of God and endowed with a position of priority in relation to other races and religions." On this he observes that in the self-understanding of other religions, each religion thinks the same and so in the religiously plural context, Christian claims become relative.[94] He further extends his argument to referring to the crisis of religion itself, and of "religions" in the recent discussions, and suggests that these "will move the question of Christian identity to a new and deeper level converting it into the very question of religious identity."[95] He explains that much of Christian identity depends on our understanding of religions and religion.[96] He observes based on the dating of human existence through scientific discoveries to being 40,000 years old and, religion being co-terminus with human development, the development of religions is much later. Hence, in light of this, he suggests that all religions including Christianity will again belong in the discussion on religious identity, which might impact the self-understanding of Christian identity.[97]

[90] Vigil, "Christian Identity," 107.
[91] Vigil, "Christian Identity," 107.
[92] Vigil, "Christian Identity," 107.
[93] Vigil, "Christian Identity," 107.
[94] Vigil, "Christian Identity," 107.
[95] Vigil, "Christian Identity," 107.
[96] Vigil, "Christian Identity," 107.
[97] Vigil, "Christian Identity," 107.

The suggestions above range from abandoning evangelistic and missionary mandate to focus on maintaining harmony and peace, or speaking up for preserving the religious mandate, and to be committed to nation-building and being prepared to lose Christian identity altogether. From the above Christian responses, we could cull out the following suggestions for Christians: affirm an individual's right of choice; religion is a private matter and there should be freedom for each individual without outside influence to choose the religion they would like to follow, and quietly pursue their faith without public ceremonies of conversion. Further suggestions are that Christians should work for the dignity of people, especially minorities; strive for unity among Christians; make sure Christian imperatives to propagate are given due place in the Constitution; engage in creative ways of following Christ within cultures in the face of opposition to religious conversion.

As already noted, various Christian groups and individuals affirm international universal human rights. Here we could suggest that the essential self-understanding of Christianity and its acceptance by others is at core of the discussion on religious freedom. At the core of the issues relating to religious freedom is the understanding of Christian identity. However, there are also speculations that this very identity could be lost in the light of new understanding of origins of religions, as expressed by a Christian scholar on religious pluralism.

What the world recognizes about Christians is clearly that Christians are inextricably related to their spirituality and committed to fulfil their religious imperatives, including evangelism and missions. It is the Holy Spirit, that Divine Wind, that opens up and paves the way in this world and helps us to walk the walk of faith, be faithful to God and be witnesses to the world.

Going back to the idiom, "Caught between the devil and the deep blue sea," or "Stuck between a rock and a hard place," if you like, we only have to look at a similar situation in the sacred history of Christians. The answer lies in faithfully following Christian spirituality that believes God has worked and will work on behalf of his people. The gospels record the words of Jesus as he prepares his disciples prior to his death and resurrection, offering guidance for a life without him in the world. The great commission is that as God sent Jesus so Jesus sends his disciples. However, the implication here is that they will have a separate and a new identity with Jesus in the world. Further, they will be targets of violence in the name of God, whatever the world (I suggest this could be seen as multi-religious world) makes God out to be. This is because the world does not know the Father or Jesus. The disciples are to faithfully disciple the world to follow Jesus. I suggest the term Ghar Wapsi itself needs to be redeemed as it is potentially useful for Christian evangelism, mission and ministry. The Hindutva term *ghar* (home) is used to refer to Hinduism, a religion. The Christian message is precisely a message of calling people to return home, not to a religion but to a restoring relationship with their heavenly Father, God, and to his people. It is God who does the conversion of individuals and people.

Freedom and Tolerance: A Muslim Perspective on Religious Freedom and Conversion

Farida Khanam[1]

INTRODUCTION

There is a heated debate on the issue of religious conversion, some being pro-conversion and others against it. This debate is based on a misunderstanding. Both the parties take conversion as proselytization, that is, one person attempting to change the religion of another person. But this concept of conversion is misleading. It portrays conversion as a bilateral issue, however it is not so.

To make one's choice is everyone's birthright. In modern times, this right of an individual has been established in the world as an international norm. Every person is free to choose his education, his job, his business, his life partner, and so is the case of religion as well. Religion is also a matter of individual choice. Just as in other matters a person has no right to intervene in another's domain, so it is in the case of religion. No one has the right to apply curbs to religious freedom.

According to the modern concept of human rights, it is everyone's internationally accepted right to choose his or her religion. It has been affirmed in the United Nation's Universal Declaration of Human Rights and accepted by all the nations of the modern world. The right to choose one's religion is also upheld by the Constitution of India.

Freedom of choice is not something to do only with religion. Human development fully depends on whether or not one has full freedom to pursue one's goals. In this way, freedom of choice is

---

[1] Dr. Farida Khanam was Professor of Islamic Studies at Jamia Millia Islamia in New Delhi. She is currently Chairperson of Centre for Peace and Spirituality. She has authored and translated several books on Islam such as *Islam and Peace*, *Life and Teachings of Prophet Muhammad* and *Sufism: An Introduction*. She is also the editorial director of the monthly journal, *Spirit of Islam*.

linked to every progress. In the absence of freedom, all progress will come to a halt.

Religious Conversion

Conversion in Islamic thinking is not synonymous with proselytization in the formal sense. It is an event which takes place in a person's life as a result of intellectual revolution or spiritual transformation. It is not simply leaving one religious tradition for another. What is meant by conversion is that the individual has discovered the truth after an exhaustive search for it and then, by his own choice, abandoned one religion for another.

But conversion, in its broadest sense, is a universal principle of nature. It is a historical process—healthy and inexorable—and attempting to put a stop to it would be like trying to put a stop to history itself. And who in this world has the power to do so? Conversion, in reality, is the birth of an entirely new entity resulting from the encounter between old and new schools of thought. This is a universal law established by nature itself.

The study of human history reveals that one process is always at work. Karl Marx had wrongly called this dialectical materialism. More rightly this is a dialogue-conversion process. That is, when two systems of thought clash with each other, an intellectual revolution ensues.

The conversion process is the only ladder to all kinds of human progress. That is, whenever any revolution of civilization has been produced or a human group has succeeded in performing some great creative role, it has always come in the wake of this same dialogue-conversion process.

There is no single form of this process. It can be religious or non-religious in nature. In the history of the last 1500 years, we find two major examples—one of religious conversion and the other of secular conversion.

The history of the Arabs provides the example of religious conversion. By 6th century CE, the Arabs were leading a confined tribal life under the idolatrous system. Then in the beginning of 7th century CE, Islam, the religion of monotheism, appeared. As a consequence, intensive dialogue began between the monotheists and idolaters. This dialogue assumed such an aggressive character that it came to the point of collision. As a result, a new way of thinking was born among the Arabs, which went on growing till it took the form of a great intellectual revolution.

This intellectual revolution, or this discovery of a new idea, resulted in the emergence of a new personality among the Arabs. In the words of a European historian, every one of them acquired such a revolutionary personality that their entire people became a nation of heroes. Within just fifty years, they brought about that historical event which is called by a historian "the miracle of all miracles."[2] In *The Making of Humanity* Robert Briffault (1876-1948) puts this in a nutshell: "But for the Arabs, the western civilization would never have arisen at all."[3]

Another example is that of the European Christian nations. After the crusades, a historical process extending several hundred years took place, when these nations too went through a conversion process. This conversion was secular rather than religious. Intense conflict took place between science and religion. One report of this conflict can be seen in the book *History of the Conflict Between Science and Religion* by John William Draper (1811-1882).

This encounter continued for several hundred years in the form of dialogue and conflict until a new intellectual revolution was produced within the European nations and they finally bade goodbye to the old and opted for the new. This revolution is known as the Renaissance. It was this revolution, which enabled the European nations to perform the greatest feat of history by emerging from the traditional age into the age of science. The truth is that the human mind is a treasure house of unlimited power. In normal situations, the human brain remains in a dormant state. It is only external shocks which awaken it, and the greater they are, the greater the intellectual revolution within man. This shock treatment produces in man what psychologists call brainstorming. This brings about a new intellectual change, a conversion that elevates a normal man to the level of superman, who is then able to perform great feats.

---

[2] Wahiduddin Khan, *Islam Rediscovered* (New Delhi: Goodword Books, 2005), 272.

[3] Robert Briffault, *The Making of Humanity* (London: George Allen & Unwin Limited, 1919), 190.

Religious conversion is only a small part of this whole process. When the dialogue-conversion process is set in motion it cannot have limits set to it. It is not possible to allow one kind of conversion and to prohibit another. Being a stormy process, it is boundless.

It must be appreciated that there are two major kinds of religious conversion—inner faith conversion and inter-faith conversion.

Now let us take an example of inter-faith conversion. There was a multi-lingual Bengali Doctor of Philosophy, Nishi Kant Chattopadhyaye, who, having first studied philosophy, then all major religions, faced intellectual confrontation with different faiths. Finally, he made an intellectual discovery, as a consequence of which he left his ancestral religion, Hinduism, in favour of Islam. His Muslim name was Azizuddin. He wrote a book, *Why I Have Embraced Islam*, which describes in detail the story of his intellectual development.[4]

Examples of inner faith conversion are several men and women who were born in Muslim families. Later on they threw away their family religion to turn into secularists or even atheists in some cases. However, sooner or later they approached a turning point in their lives, when they came back to Islam as sincere practising Muslims.

To sum up, conversion is a universal and inescapable law of nature. A study of psychology and history tells us that in order to give a new impetus to an individual or a group and to bring about a moral revolution, what is most effective is the sense of discovery. This feeling of having discovered some truth, which was as yet unknown, awakens all the dormant powers of the individual. This feeling turns an ordinary man into superman. It is such supermen who cross the ocean, who scale mountains, and who by their heroic character let history enter a new age. Today human history is once again facing a deadlock. History is once again in need of people who pass through this experience of a discovery. For such people, charged with new human power, will give a strong push to human history to enter a new and a better age.

---

[4] Wahiduddin Khan, *Conversion: An Intellectual Transformation* (New Delhi: Goodword Books, 2001), 20.

CONVERSION IN ISLAM

During his prophetic career in Makkah, whenever the Prophet saw a gathering, he would make a point of going to that place and address the people thus: "O people, say there is no God but God and you will attain God's grace."[5]

At first glance this was an invitation to people to change their religion. But the study of the Quran tells us that it was in actual fact an invitation to a transformation in thinking, instead of a change of religion in the simple sense.

In the first phase of Islam, some Arab Bedouins who had accepted Islam would just be reciting the *kalimah*, or the creed of Islam, while they had not undergone any change in character at a deeper level. The Quran admonished them in strong terms: "The Arabs of the desert say, 'We have believed.' Say to them, 'You have not believed yet; say rather, We have accepted Islam, for the true faith has not yet entered into your hearts'" (Quran 49:14).

From this we learn that conversion according to Islam means a thorough transformation of the person and not just a change of religion in the everyday sense.

The Quran refuses to give its seal of approval to conversions which are mere formalities. In ancient Madinah about 300 people had become Muslims by reciting the Islamic creed. Apparently, they even said their prayers and fasted, but they did all this in a hypocritical manner, paying only lip service: their inner state did not correspond to their outward pronouncements.

They claimed allegiance to Islam by word of mouth, but as regards the state of their hearts, the Islamic spirit was lacking. The Quran brands the "Islam" of such people as a falsity: "When the hypocrites come to you, they say: 'We bear witness that you are God's apostle.' God knows that you are indeed His Messenger, and God bears witness that the hypocrites are lying" (Quran 63:1).

---

[5] Abu Jafar Muhammad ibn Jarir al-Tabari, *The History of al-Tabari*, vol. 4, trans. W. Montgomery Watt and M. V. McDonald (New York: State University of New York Press, 1988), 93.

The Quran mentions about another group of 70 people who accepted Islam and said:

> Count us among Your witnesses. Why should we not believe in God and in the truth that has come down to us? Why should we not hope for admission among the righteous? (Quran 5: 83-84)

Religious conversion in actual fact is the result of a realization. When the individual's search for truth finds a convincing answer, his heart is intensely moved. His eyes are filled with tears. His whole existence is moulded in the hue of truth. It is then that he emerges a new and altogether different person, having undergone a transformation.

That is why the Quran uses no synonym for conversion. To express the act of conversion, other more meaningful words have been used. For instance, the *dawah* mission (the communication of the message to others) of Islam finds mention in the Quran in these words:

> A light has come to you from God and a glorious Book with which He will guide to the paths of peace those that seek to please Him. He will lead them by His will from darkness to the light; He will guide them to a straight path. (Quran 5:15-16)

Those who enter the fold of Islam after being influenced by their study of the Quran, have been thus described in the Quran: "Shall he then who knows that what has been revealed to you by your Lord is the truth be like him who is blind? But it is only the men of understanding that pay heed" (Quran 13:19).

According to this verse, the real conversion is one which has taken place when the convert is aware that he has entered the phase of gnosis and has left behind the phase of ignorance. That is why a tradition of the Prophet speaks of the period prior to Islam as a period of ignorance. Similarly, the difference between a believer and a non-believer has been alluded to in the Quran in the context of life after death:

> Can the dead man whom We have raised to life and given a light with which he may be guided among men, be

compared to him who blunders about in a darkness from which he will never emerge? (Quran 6:123)

This same reality has been expressed in different ways in the Quran, for instance, by the simile of the earth:

> When the rains come, the fertile earth blooms, becoming green with vegetation. Good soil yields fruit by God's leave. But poor and scant are the fruits which spring from barren soil. Thus we show our signs to those who render thanks. (Quran 7:58)

Then there is the parable of the tree:

> Do you not see how God compares a good word to a good tree whose root is firm with its branches in the sky, yielding its fruit every season by God's leave? God gives parables to men so that they may become mindful. But an evil word is like an evil tree torn out of the earth, and has no stability. God will strengthen the faithful with His steadfast word, both in this life and in the Hereafter. He leaves the wrongdoers in error. God accomplishes what He pleases. (Quran 14:24-27)

These verses from the Quran tell us the difference between one who has found the truth and one who has failed to do so. The latter is like the shrub growing on the upper surface of the soil: it is short-lived, either vanishing on its own or being pulled out, and is of no use to mankind. The former resembles a profitable, fruitful tree putting its roots deep down into the earth. It seems that it is for the earth and the earth is for it. Receiving sustenance from the earth as well as the atmosphere, it benefits people in many ways. Rooted as it is in the earth, it has a desirable and meaningful existence.

Religious Freedom in Islam

In 1948, the United Nations gave the world its Universal Declaration of Human Rights, a charter of what human beings in all walks of life could claim as theirs as a matter of fundamental human dignity. Article 18 of this declaration reads as follows: "Everyone has the right of freedom of thought, conscience and religion; this right includes freedom to change his religion or belief, and freedom, either alone or in community with others and in public or private, to manifest his religion or belief in teaching, practice, worship and observance."[6]

These ideas are exactly in accordance with the principles of Islamic teaching, for in Islam, man's intellectual development is firmly believed in, and any system which favours intellectual development will, of necessity, uphold freedom of thought. Without this it is impossible for there to be any fruitful development of the human personality.

But what is perhaps even more important is the Islamic concept of the predetermination of the course taken by all inanimate objects and by all of God's creatures, except man. Man is held to be born free while every other animate or inanimate object is subservient to God's will. There is nothing in the heavens or on earth which can decide upon the course of its own existence, this having been eternally predetermined while everything in the physical world—save man—must follow the path laid down by God; only man has been granted the freedom of choice and the power to take matters into his own hands, and make his own decisions.

Islam requires man to make his own quest for the truth. This is something of which he should be fully conscious and which he should impose upon himself as a matter of religious duty. This is the only way that true nobility of character can come into being. Externally given commands are meant for robots, not for fully mature human beings.

Real, alive, human beings cannot ever come into existence in an atmosphere of blinkered constraint. What truly moves the human psyche above all is the feeling in individuals that their achievements have been the result of their own personal deliberations. The opinions they have arrived at are their own. The beliefs on which they base their actions are the outcome of their own deep reflections. It is this freedom of choice that can lead to their being fully integrated personalities.

Here a few references to Islamic teachings will bear out the above contentions.

---

[6] "Article 18," *Universal Declaration of Human Rights*, December 10, 1948, Palais de Chaillot, Paris.

When Islam came into the world in 7th century CE, it was a time when religious persecution was prevalent, but it is noteworthy that it remained uninfluenced by the common practices of the time. Islam, running counter to the age, proclaimed religious freedom. Although a missionary religion, it was against any imposition of restrictions on human thought, which meant that there should be no forced conversion. In his book, *The Preaching of Islam*, Professor T. W. Arnold has gone into considerable detail to show that under Islamic rule, other religions were allowed full freedom. He writes, inter alia,

> ...for the provinces of the Byzantine empire that were rapidly acquired by the prowess of Muslims found themselves in the enjoyment of a toleration such as, on account of their Monophysite and Nestorian opinions, had been unknown to them for centuries. They were allowed the free and undisturbed exercise of their religion. The extent of this toleration – so striking in the history of the seventh century – may be judged from the terms granted to the conquered cities.'[7]

Compulsion impermissible

According to the Quran, "There is no compulsion in religion" (Quran 2:256). The verse of the Quran expresses the fundamental principle of Islam, according to which, if a person believes in the truth of something, he has every right to proclaim it as such, provided that he supports it by logical arguments. His task is complete once he has described his belief in the clearest possible way. But he has no right to compel others to accept it. Whoever accepts the truth does so for his own benefit and whoever denies it does harm only to himself.

Freedom for all

Likewise, the Quran states: "Say, the truth is from your Lord. Let him who will believe it, and let him who will reject it" (Quran

---

[7] Thomas Walker Arnold, *The Preaching of Islam* (London: Constable and Co. Ltd., 1913), 56.

18:29). This also clearly expresses the notion that truth is something which should be accepted or rejected by one's own decision, and not something which should be imposed upon one. The resulting belief is valid only as being the outcome of one's own conscious decision. It is the very negation of truth to force its acceptance upon unwilling or unprepared individuals. Truth can be accepted as such only when man's reason, his intellect, attests to its being so. The imposition by force of a truth to which one's reason fails to testify, brings about not the recognition of truth but the recognition of force. It is an insult to truth itself if people are bludgeoned into accepting it.

A preacher's mission is to convey the truth to the members of his congregation. And once he had done that, he has fulfilled his religious obligation. It is not part of his task to compel others to accept what he says. It is significant that in the Quran God thus admonishes the Prophet: "Remind them, for you are only one of the warners. You are not at all a warder over them" (Quran 88:21-22).

This shows how different are the respective roles of the preacher and his hearers. It is the task of the preachers to convey the word of God, but his hearers have the right to reject his message. The most that the preacher can do to convince his hearers that he brings them the truth is to offer them strictly logical arguments. He must never stoop to coercion. God has never given His preachers this right.

Respect for others' religions

Certain of the companions of the Prophet of Islam, in their zeal to propagate the new faith, began to abuse those who worshipped other gods besides God. But this incurred God's displeasure, and a verse was revealed in the Quran giving a commandment not to revile other people's faiths.

The freedom of religion advocated in the Quran can be explained as a policy of mutual benefit. If we want to have freedom for ourselves, the price we must pay is the granting of the same right of freedom to others. There can be no exclusivity about freedom if there is to be justice in this world. Only if we grant others their legal rights, will they be willing to reciprocate in like manner.

But if we abuse or coerce them, we should expect to have the same treatment at their hands. The result would be that there would be no religious freedom whatsoever, regardless of whether society were of only two or of multiple religious persuasions.

The fact that Islam is an upholder of religious freedom, in the fullest sense of the term, is so obvious that even those who are averse to it have not hesitated to testify to it. We shall quote here some instances which bear this out. After the defeat of Muslims in Spain at the hands of Christians, a royal decree was issued by Spain's Christian ruler, Philip II, ordering the forcible re-conversion of Spanish Muslims (Moriscoes) to Christianity. But the Archbishop of Valencia favoured the extreme step of expulsion rather than forced conversion and, in an account of the Apostacies and Treasons of Moriscoes, in 1602, in which he makes this recommendation to the king, he sets forth one of his principal reasons for wishing to banish the Muslims: "That they commended nothing so much as that liberty of conscience, in all matters of religion, which the Turks and all other Mohamadans, suffer their subject to enjoy."[8]

It is noteworthy that by the time of the last expulsion in 1610, over 500,000 people had been affected. Yet even the opponents of Islam could not but appreciate the religious liberty offered to all faiths under Islamic rule. Again in 7th century CE, on an occasion when fearful atrocities had been inflicted by Catholic Poles on the Russians of the Orthodox Eastern Church, Macarius, the Patriarch of Antioch, bewailing the cruel martyrdom of 70 to 80 thousand innocent souls, said, "God perpetuate the empire of the Turks for ever and ever! For they take their impost and enter into no account of religion, be their subjects Christians or Nazarenes, Jews or Samarians."[9]

Another remarkable example of religious tolerance was set by Uzbek Khan who was leader of the Golden Horde from 1313 to 1340, and who distinguished himself by his proselytising zeal. It was his mission to spread the faith of Islam throughout the whole of Russia, but although the Mongols were paramount in Russia for two centuries, they exercised very little influence on the people

---

[8] Imam-ad-Dean Ahmad, *Signs in the Heavens: A Muslim Astronomer's Perspective on Religion and Science* (Beltsville: Writer's Inc. International, 1992), 42.

[9] Arnold, *The Preaching of Islam*, 156-157.

of that country. T.W. Arnold, in his book, *The Preaching of Islam*, says that, "It is noticeable, moreover, that in spite of his zeal for the spread of his own faith, Uzbek Khan was very tolerant towards his Christian subjects, who were left undisturbed and even allowed to pursue their missionary labours in his territory."[10]

One of the most remarkable documents of Muhammadan toleration is the charter that Uzbek Khan granted to the Metropolitan Peter in 1313. He then goes on to give the highly specific details of this lengthy charter which gave every conceivable protection to Christians, their institutions, and their way of life. "Their laws, their Churches; their monasteries and chapels shall be respected; whoever condemns or blames this religion, shall not be allowed to excuse himself under any pretext but shall be punished with death." Arnold later points that these were no empty words and "that the toleration here promised became a reality may be judged from a letter sent to the Khan by Pope John XXII in 1318, in which he thanks the Muslim prince for the favour he showed to his Christian subjects and the kind treatment they received at his hands."[11]

A similar contrast was made in 1605 by Richard Staper, an English merchant who had been in Turkey as early as 1578:

> And notwithstanding that the Turks in general be a most wicked people, walking in the world of darkness....Yet notwithstanding do they permit all Christians, both Greeks and Latins, to live in their religion and freely to use their conscience, allowing them churches for their divine service, both in Constantinople and very many other places, whereas to the contrary by proof of twelve years' residence in Spain I can truly affirm, we are not only forced to observe their popish ceremonies, but in danger of life and goods.[12]

How far Islam goes along the road to religious freedom is made clear by an event which occurred in the Prophet's lifetime. The famous 8th century biographer, Ibn Ishaq, records how a delegation of Yemenese Christians came to see the Prophet of Islam and had a

---

[10] Arnold, *The Preaching of Islam*, 241.

[11] Arnold, *The Preaching of Islam*, 240-241.

[12] M. Epstein, *The Early History of the Levant Company* (London: George Routledge & Sons Ltd., 1908), 157.

long dialogue with him in his mosque in Medina, which went on until the Christians' hour for prayer. They then expressed a desire to worship there, according to their own rites, in this mosque which is considered by Muslims to be second in importance only to the Masjid-e-Haram in Mecca.[13]

Tradition has it that they were beginning their orations when one of the Muslims attempted to stop them from praying in the Christian way. But the Prophet intervened, and asked him to refrain from interrupting them, and they were thus permitted to complete their prayers inside the mosque.

The rights of others

Islam gives such serious consideration to religious freedom that it takes pains to avoid infractions of it which exist only in the realms of remote possibility. There is an incident in Islamic history which illustrates this point with great pertinence. Palestine having been conquered in 638 CE, Umar Faruq, the second Caliph, travelled to Palestine at the request of the Christians in order to finalize the agreements between them and the Muslims. T. W. Arnold in his book, *The Preaching of Islam*, relates how, "In company with the Patriarch, Umar visited the holy places, and it is said while they were in the Church of the Resurrection, as it was the appointed hour of prayers, the Patriarch bade the Caliph offer his prayers there, but he thoughtfully refused, saying that if he were to do so, his followers might afterwards claim it as a place of Muslim worship."[14]

He obviously foresaw later generations of Muslims might feel inspired to attempt to build a mosque on that very spot, thus setting up restrictions upon religious freedom. This discretion shown by Umar is all the more remarkable for his having been the ruler of Palestine at that time and, therefore, in a position to do anything he wished. A man with less insight and forethought would have regarded his praying inside the church as an apparently harmless event and one which could in no way be interpreted as depriving anyone of his rights. Umar, in fact, moved a stone's throw away,

---

[13] Frans Wijsen and Peter Nissen, eds., *Mission is a Must: Intercultural Theology and the Mission of the Church* (New York: Editions Rodopi B.V., 2002), 210.
[14] Arnold, *The Preaching of Islam*, 57.

and said his prayers at a discreet distance from the church. Muslims did indeed come to this city later on, and, as he had foreseen, they built their mosque at the exact point where he had said his prayers. The mosque exists to this day, but presents no obstacle to Christian worship.

It is true that in later times certain excessively zealous Muslims converted a number of non-Muslim places of worship into mosques. But such actions, far from being an application of the teaching of Islam, are to be deplored as deviations from it. Says Arnold, "But such oppression was contrary to the tolerant spirit of Islam."[15]

Islam, in actual fact, is the name given to teachings of the Quran and the Hadith, and the finest example of living up to this standard was set by the Prophet and his companions. The deeds of later generations, when judged by these primary criteria, will be seen to be sadly deficient in true Islamic spirit. Those who make no attempt to live up to the Prophet's example are in no way representative of Islam.

On the question of religious tolerance, everyone must be granted the right to present his thoughts, and to be given a quiet hearing. The truth is not something to be forced upon one, but something which one is gently assisted to go in quest of as a matter of personal discovery. In this respect, Islam is the greatest upholder of religious freedom.

In ancient Makkah, the Quraysh had placed the idols of all the tribes in the Kabah. Arab tribes from far off places came to visit the Kabah in order to venerate the idols. The Prophet of Islam used to go to the camps of these polytheistic tribes and call them to God. The details of his efforts are recorded in his biography. Once he visited the camp of the tribe of Banu Shayban ibn Thaalaba. He said to them: "'I call you to bear witness to the one God. For there is no god but the one God." The chiefs of the tribe rejected his call and said,

> We live on the border of Persia and the Emperor of Persia has taken an oath of allegiance from us that we will not

---

[15] Arnold, *The Preaching of Islam*, 77.

indulge in anything new (i.e. abide by the status quo) and that we will not welcome anyone who does so.[16]

The Prophet of Islam had called upon the tribe to engage in a purely non-political action, so why did they answer in this manner? The reason was that in ancient times religion was regarded as a matter for the state to decide. To believe in a religion or invite people to accept a new religion required the permission of the state. Propagating a new religion without such permission was equivalent to treason and as such could incur the harshest punishment. This is why we find cases of religious persecution in every country in ancient times. Religious persecution was resorted to in every part of the world. Religious matters depended wholly on the will of the king and no king was willing to give religious freedom to his people. That was why the propagation of religion was the most difficult of tasks.

After a long historical process, the age of religious persecution has been replaced with that of total religious freedom all over the world.

After World War II, when all the nations of the world came together to form the United Nations, their organization issued a Declaration, subscribed to by all in June 1948 known as the Universal Declaration of Human Rights. This charter accepted with greater force that "Every man or woman enjoys the right to opt for any religion according to his or her will, and may propagate it peacefully."[17] This Declaration was signed by all the nations of the world and was made part of the Constitutions of all the signatories. For instance, the Indian Constitution, written after 1947, included Article 18 in which every Indian citizen has been granted the freedom to practise and propagate his religion.

THE INDIAN TRADITION OF TOLERANCE

Tolerance is an integral part of India's tradition. One can say that tolerance is India's national identity. India has a long history of

---

[16] Muhammad Yusuf Kandhlawi, *The Lives of the Sahaba*, Vol 1, trans. by Abdul Hai (New Delhi: Idara Isha'at-e-Diniyat, 2009), 101-102.

[17] "Article 18," *Universal Declaration of Human Rights*.

the culture of tolerance. India is a multi-religious society. Almost all the major religions live in India in total harmony. One can say that India has proved to be a peaceful haven for different religions and cultures. In this sense, one can say that India is like a peaceful garden in which all kinds of plants and trees flourish. This is the identity of India. India is a composite society. According to the 2001 census, the demographics of India's population according to religion are: 80.5% Hindus, 13.4% Muslims, 2.3% Christians, 1.9% Sikhs, 0.8% Buddhists, 0.4% Jains, and 0.6% followers of other religions.

This composite nature of the Indian society is not by accident. It is directly due to the Indian way of thinking. According to the traditional way of thinking, India believes in plurality, or in the words of the great Indian leader Mahatma Gandhi, "the many-ness of reality." Hindus comprise the majority in Indian population. The Hindu religion is based on *advait vad*, that is, monism. Monism means that divine reality is one, manifested in different ways. According to this religious philosophy, the Hindus believe that everything in the cosmos is an *ansh*, or part, of divinity. They believe in the concept of an indwelling god, that is, every human being has a content of divinity. Due to this concept, the Hindu mind accords equal position to every man and woman. This is the genesis of the culture of tolerance in India.

The Bhagavad Gita is one of the holy books of Hinduism. It maintains that all paths lead to the same summit. It was this concept that was declared by the well-known Hindu thinker Swami Vivekananda (1863-1902) at the Parliament of the World's Religions in these words: "We believe not only in universal toleration but we accept *all religions* as *true*." (Chicago, September 11, 1893). It is a fact that Hinduism believes in religious pluralism. Almost all scholars of Hinduism, for example, Sri Aurobindo Ghose, Rabindranath Tagore, C. Rajagopalachari, and S. Radhakrishnan, have confirmed this concept of Hindu philosophy.

A practical example of this culture is narrated by Jawaharlal Nehru (1889-1964) in his famous book *The Discovery of India*, in these words: "In Kashmir a long-continued process of conversion to Islam had resulted in 95 per cent of the population becoming Moslems, though they retained many of their old Hindu customs.

In the middle nineteenth century the Hindu raja (ruler) of the state found that very large numbers of these people were anxious or willing to return *en bloc* to Hinduism. He sent a deputation to the pundits of Benares, the religious centre of India, inquiring if this could be done. The pundits refused to countenance any such change of faith and there the matter ended." According to the Hindu Pandits, this kind of conversion was not objectionable.

Due to this mindset, the authorities of the Hindu religion have given Islam a very honourable status. For example, Bhagavan Das (1869-1958) was a well-known scholar of Hindu religion. He was the author of a large number of learned works on philosophy and religion. He writes in his magnum opus, *Essential Unity of All Religions*: "The word *Islam* has a profound and noble meaning which is, indeed, by itself, the very essence of religion. Derived from *salm*, peace, shanti, it means 'peaceful acceptance' of God; calm resignation, submission, surrender."[18]

Acharya Vinoba Bhave (1895-1982) was one of the greatest advocates of the Hindu philosophy. He used to say that although he was born as a Hindu, but "*main hindu bhi hun, main muslim bhi hun, main Christian bhi hun*," that is, "I am a Hindu too, I am a Muslim too and I am a Christian too."

This Hindu formula means: "I am right, you are also right." In other words, it is based on mutual acceptance. From the point of view of theoretical theology, this concept may be debatable. However, in terms of pragmatism, it is of great value, because it gives an equal place to all religions and traditions under the same roof. It was this Indian principle that found expression in the political field as the Panchsheel Principle or the Five Principles of Peaceful Coexistence. This formula was propounded by the then Prime Minister of India Jawaharlal Nehru in 1954 under of the banner of the Non-Aligned Movement.

The different religions of India have their own distinct history of how they reached this land. As far as the religion of Islam is concerned, it first reached India toward the end of 7th century CE, that is, in the same period that is regarded among the three golden periods of Islam (*qurun-e-thalatha*). This first group of Muslim

---

[18] Bhagavan Das, *Essential Unity of All Religions* (Whitefish: Kessinger Publishing, 1994), 107-108.

Arabs came from Iraq by sea-route and settled in Kerala, a coastal state of India. Due to the above-mentioned Indian spirit, this group was hailed with respect. The Indians conferred on them the title of Mappila, which means a highly respectable person. Jawaharlal Nehru, in *The Discovery of India*, observes that when the Arabs came to India, they brought with them a brilliant culture.

Due to this reason, Islam found a very favourable atmosphere in India. In the beginning Muslims were just a small group, but now they comprise about 13% of the 1.2 billion population of India. An Indian scholar Tara Chand, an eminent scholar of Ancient History and Culture, has documented the advent and influence of Islam in India. His major contribution to Indo-Islamic culture and philosophy is the work *Influence of Islam on Indian Culture*. The book, which was first published in 1922, has become a classic on this subject for researchers and historians.

According to the Indian Constitution, which came into effect in January 1950, Muslims have equal rights of citizenship in every aspect and there is no discrimination at all on the basis of religion.

There are about one million Muslim masjids, *madarsa*s and various Islamic organizations in India at present. All these institutions are flourishing and working smoothly. There are numerous schools, colleges and universities freely run by Muslims. Muslims have a distinctive presence in every field of Indian society such as the government, administration, business, industry, education, social institutions, and so on. The President of India holds the highest office in the country. He is the head of the state and the first citizen of India. In the history of independent India, four Muslims have, to this date, held the office of the president. These were: Zakir Hussain (1967-1969), Mohammad Hidayatullah (July-August 1969), Fakhruddin Ali Ahmed (1974-1977) and A. P. J. Abdul Kalam (2002-2007).

The sound of *allah akbar* can be heard from the minarets of the Indian mosques in the same way as it is observed as a common phenomenon in Muslim countries. The writer of this article also runs an Islamic centre with complete freedom in the capital city of Delhi. The registered name of our centre is *al-markazul islami lil-buhooth wal-dawah*, that is, Islamic Research and Dawah Centre. Our mission is spread throughout India as well as abroad. We never receive the slightest problem from the Indian administration or the Indian people.

In the first quarter of the 20th century, the Khilafat of Turkey was under constant threat from the British Empire. It is interesting to note that in those days it was only in India that a movement, under the leadership of Muhammad Ali Jouhar (1878-1931), originated in support of the Turkish Caliphate. This movement received the full support of Mahatma Gandhi (1869-1948), who was the greatest Indian leader at that time. This phenomenon is also a testimony to the fact that there is no religious bias in India. Here all religions are given an equal place.

If there are some problems faced by the Muslim community in India, they are due to the law of nature and not on account of any kind of discrimination. Differences are a part of the law of nature. Thus, it is but natural that there are problems in every society, including a Muslim society. These kind of problems are normal and not worthy of any consideration. According to the law of nature, it is impossible to have a country which is totally problem-free, and certainly India is not an exception in this regard.

The ties of trade between India and Arabia existed from ancient times. And the first Muslim group that came to India in the 7th century CE was also part of this relationship. Moreover, India has a very special reference in the Hadith literature. According to a tradition, the Prophet of Islam is said to have declared that "he felt cool breeze of knowledge coming from the land of India" (*ajedo rih al-ilm min bilad al-hind*). Perhaps the Prophet of Islam, through inspiration, discovered the fact that India would be a better place for Islam in the later periods of history. In one of the traditions narrated by al-Nasai, the Prophet of Islam has predicted that in future, a Muslim group will emerge in India that will work for the spreading of the message of Islam.[19]

Swami Vivekananda is one of the most admired religious leaders of India. He was a great believer in Hindu-Muslim unity. Once he stated his concept in these words: "I see in my *mind's* eye the future perfect India rising out of this chaos and strife, glorious and invincible, with *Vedanta brain* and *Islam body*."[20]

[19] *Sunan*, Al-Nasai, Hadith No. 3175.
[20] Chaturvedi Badrinath, *Swami Vivekananda, the Living Vedanta* (New Delhi:

Due to this spirit of tolerance and mutual acceptance, Islam and Muslims found very favourable soil in India. For example, the Sufis generally came from Central Asia and settled in various Indian cities. They established *khanqahs* and tried to peacefully disseminate the message of Islam. The Sufis never experienced any obstacle from Indian society. They converted Hindus to Islam in large numbers and the latter did not object to this process. Jawaharlal Nehru noted that "conversions to Islam were group conversions."[21] According to the Hindu thinking, if a person peacefully carries out his mission, then it is non-objectionable. Some Western scholars maintain that Islam spread by force. However, the Hindu scholars have themselves rejected this notion. For example, Swami Vivekananda maintains this in one of his writings: "Why amongst the poor of India so many are Mohammedans? It is nonsense to say they were converted by sword."[22]

The above historical references explain how it was possible that the different groups of religion and culture have been living in harmony in India since long. How did the people of a nation that had so many religious beliefs live together from the past to the present with this diversity, without conflict? It was not due to any coincidence. But, it was due to the deep-rooted traditions of the Indian culture. The theoretical explanations of this phenomenon can be different, but it is a fact that this kind of tolerance is a great strength of India. It gives India a special place on the world map. In its article on "Pacifism," the *Encyclopaedia Britannica* has this to say about Mahatma Gandhi: "The most massive, comprehensive, and historically effective example of nonviolent activism is that of the movements unchained and organized by Mahatma Gandhi."[23] The case of Mahatma Gandhi is not an individual case; in fact, he was only a manifestation of India's spirit of peace and tolerance.

Penguin Books India, 2006), 270.

[21] Jawaharlal Nehru, *Discovery of India* (New Delhi: Oxford University Press, 1985), 265.

[22] Jerald D. Gort, Henry Jansen and H. M. Vroom, *Religion, Conflict and Reconciliation: Multifaith Ideals and Realities* (Amsterdam: Rodopi, 2002), 48.

[23] "Pacificism," *The New Encyclopaedia Britannica*, 15th ed., vol. 13, 1980, 850.

Khrist-Bhakta Model of Ecclesia

Cyril Kuttiyanikkal[1]

INTRODUCTION

In the recent past, the issue of religious freedom and conversion has come to the forefront. The re-energized call for Ghar Wapsi and the ban on entry of non-locals (read Christian missionaries) to Bastar villages of Chhattisgarh are but examples of the emerging religious atmosphere. It is regrettable that Christians are under constant attack for alleged conversion charges. Often, Hindu groups oppose the Church's social welfare programmes, portraying them as fraudulent means to lure poor people to Christianity. Christians are portrayed as anti-nationals adamant on destroying cherished Indian values and Hindu religion and culture. Now an atmosphere is being created, where the tiny Indian Christian minority's existence and the very purpose of their mission are doubted, and the preaching of the *good news* as well as the life of the missionary are targeted.

Although we do not fall a prey to this false propaganda, and we do not need anyone's certificate to prove our patriotism and our contribution to nation-building, it seems true that the Christian ecclesial model visible, lived and presented to India is against the religious ethos of the country. Therefore, the contemporary politico-social context of India is an opportunity for Christians not only to adjust few policies and practices but to fundamentally rethink what it means to be Christians and what model of church is being practised.

Therefore, first of all, I would like to present a different model of being a church in India.[2] The ecclesial model which I call the

---

[1] Dr. Cyril Kuttiyanikkal is Professor of Systematic and Practical Theology at Samanvaya Theology College, Bhopal. He is also the secretary to the Commission for the Doctrine of the Bishops' Conference of Chhattisgarh region. Some of his publications include *Khrist Bhakta Movement: A Model for an Indian Church?* (2014), and *Fortress of Solitude* (2017).

[2] I will be presenting from a Catholic perspective.

"*asram*-based charismatic model" and which lies underneath the Christ-devotee[3] movement will be presented in a nutshell. I will not be spending much time presenting the current state of affairs. Instead, I will be limiting myself to presenting the data necessary for further discussions as well as for providing a roadmap for the way ahead. Thereafter, I shall discuss why this model is different and what its implications are for the church in India, with a specific focus on the relationship between religious freedom, baptism and conversion. I will be dealing with the specificities of this movement in the context of India, where a negative attitude is prevalent against Christians. Finally, I shall conclude with some questions the movement has to face.

The *asram*-based charismatic model of Ecclesia

The *asram*-based charismatic model of church is emerging from the context of the Christ-devotee movement. Therefore, it is important that first of all we identify and demarcate the Christ-devotees and take stock of this movement with its *sitz im leben*.

Who are Christ-devotees?

Christ-devotees (or *Khrist-Bhaktas*) are mainly Hindus[4] belonging to all caste[5] groups and who hail from rural, semi-urban and urban areas of Varanasi and Uttar Pradesh in India, and who live culturally as Hindus and spiritually as Christians, and lead a life of Christian

---

[3] I shall be using both the English term "Christ-devotee" as well as the Hindi term *Khrist-Bhakta* interchangeably.

[4] There are also some people belonging to other religions.

[5] The original term is *varn*, though in general it is called as caste. The term caste is equivalent to the Sanskrit term *jati*, used in the Indian sub-continent to refer to "race", "breed", or "lineage." *Jatis* are the sub-divisions of the four basic *varns*. The numbers of *jati*, including sub-castes, is numerous and cannot be counted, as their number grows even today. There are four *varns* (Brahmans, Ksatriyas, Vaisyas and Sudras), or five when those outside (*Pancama*) are included as a category. Both *varn* and *jati* are hierarchical orderings. The ranking among the four *varns* is fixed, while *jati* has a lot of fluidity. In general, the *Brahmans* rank as highest and the so-called "untouchables" rank as the lowest. It is impossible to rank the *jatis* on a single scale of highest to lowest.

discipleship without discarding their Hindu religio-cultural identity. They remain a part of Hinduism in a social and cultural sense, but in a spiritual sense they are followers of Christ. Although they are not baptized as Christians, they practise faith in Christ radically.

The beginning and spread of the movement

This movement had a humble beginning. Their numerical strength was only a handful in the early 1990s, when it started. And geographically they were limited only to Banaras, especially around the villages of Matridham *asram*. The Matridham *asram* stands at Chandmari, which is just 7 km (north-west) from Varanasi railway station on Sindhora road, Uttar Pradesh. Generally called Banaras, Varanasi is called the religio-cultural capital of India. This city has become a meeting point for various religious movements. The Christ-devotee movement has also grown and spread in the sub-urban and surrounding areas of Varanasi. The movement spread around the *asram* and grew enormously (and is still growing) and has taken on the form of a movement, now called the *Khrist-Bhakta* or Christ-devotee Movement. From a handful of people in 1993, it has grown to 50,000 to 60,000 devotees.[6]

THE CHRISTIANITY OF THE CHRIST-DEVOTEE MOVEMENT

The outward expression of Christianity of the *Khrist-Bhakta* movement is visible on three levels: at the common gathering at the Varanasi *asram*, at the village level gathering at house prayer meetings in villages and at the family level.

A majority of the Christ-devotees (3,000 to 4,000) gather on Sundays and second Saturdays for a prayer meeting called *satsangh*. These prayer meetings last for three to four hours, and includes preaching of the word of God, intercessory prayers, adoration, praise and worship and singing of *bhajan*s, etc. In these charismatic prayer gatherings, physical healings and miracles occur by the power of the Holy Spirit and in the name of Jesus Christ.

---

[6] More details about *Khrist-Bhakta* movement can be found in C. J. Kuttiyanikkal, *Khrist Bhakta Movement: A Model for an Indian Church?* (Munster: Lit Verlag, 2014). Most of the descriptive part is adapted from this book.

News about the miraculous healings and incidents are spread by word of mouth. In turn, many others also throng to receive similar blessings. Not only those who intend to become devotees, but also onlookers are attracted to the movement. However the receptions of blessings lead many of them to deeper faith in Christ and make them sometimes his messengers as well.

Those in the *asram* who preach to them the Word of God do not demand their transference from one religion to another religion, but they focus on the need for the conversion of hearts to Christ. Since the devotees are not forced to change their religion and the preachers focus not on proselytization but on the conversion of heart to God, more and more people from all walks of life have come forward to publicly express their faith in Christ. This has also silenced the Hindu fundamentalists, who were on the lookout for the Christian preachers in the beginning.

On a second level, they also gather in the villages under the guidance of an *agua* (leader) for a weekly prayer meeting at noon. These gathering are generally of small size, sometimes with just 10 to 15 women, and other times, in certain villages, from 30 to 50 people. Additionally, those who wish to become devotees also join these gatherings and ask for prayers. Some devotees, who are not able to go to the *asram* due to either objection from families or some other reasons like sickness, also attend the village meetings.

On the third level, there is also something called the practice of family prayer. Before becoming *Bhaktas*, they did not have any ritual similar to a family prayer. Many of them had a family deity placed in one room where they offered *puja* to the deity. Once they became Christ-devotees, they took the family deity to the *asram* "to be buried under the cross of Christ" and now keep the picture of Jesus or other Christian symbols at home. After becoming devotees of Christ, all the family members gather for the family prayer, which is done mostly in the evening. It includes lighting of the lamp, intercessory prayer, the Rosary, sometimes reading from the Bible, *bhajans*, praise and worship. The prayer is concluded with the *arti*. The more devoted spend one or two hours in prayer.[7] It is the women who mostly lead the prayer and perform the *arti*.

---

[7] People like Shanta Prasad spend three hours in prayer, with longer time for reading the Bible.

Special and occasional prayers

The Christ-devotees have some special and interesting devotions too. Some of those devotional practices are unique to the Christ-devotees while some they share with the other Christians. Even when the devotions are common to other Christians, the manner in which they are practised is unique to them. These special devotions tell us much about their way of understanding and celebrating their faith in Christ. Some of them are annual celebrations, while some are monthly and even daily.

The Christ-devotees learn about Christianity during intense three-day monthly retreats. These retreats are normally attended by some 200 devotees and are occasions for them to live together and learn about Christian worship and living. They also have the an annual charismatic convention attended by a larger crowd of about 10,000 people. Their Lenten and Holy week celebrations are so intense that even traditional Christians are inspired by their faith practices. They spend practically the whole three days in prayer. Similarly, they celebrate the whole Christmas night more earnestly than traditional Christians. They also celebrate *Gurupurnima,* when they pay homage to their eternal *guru* Jesus and honour their human *guru* in the *asram*.

The role of fasting, penance, several kinds of *mannath*s, shaving of hair etc., are optional devotional practices. They adore Jesus and intercede for others too. The Word of God is repeated as the source of life. Even the illiterate have learned to quote the Bible. They take home holy water and blessed oil, and these are used as holy medicines against all kinds of diseases and ailments for humans, animals and even crops.

THE SPIRITUAL EXPERIENCES OF THE CHRIST-DEVOTEES

Remember that the general Hindu public who comes in contact with the charismatic form of prayer, that too in a large gathering of about 4,000 to 5,000 is wonder-struck by the very atmosphere—the vocal prayer, singing and praising. Add to it their intense desire and yearning for cure from prolonged illness, which in turn adds impetus to their craving for miracles, and they are sure to experience the healing touch of Jesus. Many people come to the prayer meetings as the last resort, having spent all their money and time on different village doctors and sorcerers. It is also true that not everyone comes with a spiritual quest. Many people come for the first time out of curiosity. Others come to get cured. Since the news about the miracles happening in the *asram* spreads, many people come to get freedom from evil spirits, while some others come to get cured from physical ailments, etc. But once they come to the *asram*, they are captured by the atmosphere, prayers, preaching, miracles, etc. There are cases of those who came only out of curiosity but became a devotee the very first time and then an *agua* not long after. They experience the grace of God in various forms.

Miracles, cures, witnesses, and freedom from evil spirits

Many people suffer from various kinds of problems and illnesses and have either less means to access medical treatment in time, or the treatments have not yielded any result, or the problems of life are such that they do not see any solutions. Mostly people turn to witchcraft or sorcerers, who are called *ojhas*. *Ojhas* collect money and materials like chicken, liquor, etc., and go on with their witchcraft, while the suffering remains. There are also instances when medical treatment for long periods have not resulted in any cure. Hence, people are desperate for cures of their ailments. When they hear about the miraculous cures happening in the *asram*, they flock to it. People who are suffering are eager to get cured and, as they take part in the prayers and healing services, they often get cured miraculously. They may come to the *asram* just for the sake of physical cure. However, once they get cured, the experience of the cure encourages them to become *Khrist-Bhaktas*.

Expressive prayer: communitarian and charismatic

For the Christ-devotees, expressive prayer and community prayer is something new. In Hinduism, prayers are mostly offered silently by individuals. Even when there is a gathering in the temple, each person approaches the deity individually. In the *asram*, the Christ-devotees are taught to pray loudly, as one family and for one another.

The charismatic form of prayers said aloud and in community are new experiences for them. It seems that the charismatic method of prayer and preaching of the Word of God leads them to a different level of spiritual freedom and inner healing. They seem to experience the power of the Spirit during the *satsangs*. The people who are afflicted by poverty, social oppression, and physical and psychological problems, find solace in these prayer meetings. The physical and psychological healing that is happening during prayer adds to their devotion and faith. They are also freed from various superstitions and bondages, which leads to peace in their personal and family lives.

The Ecclesiology of the *Khrist-Bhakta* Movement: *Asram*-Based Charismatic Model

In order to unearth the implicit ecclesiological dimensions, I have made an exploratory and explicatory study into the nature, structure, and working of the *Khrist-Bhakta* movement. The questions of whether, to what degree, and in which respects this movement can be called a model for Ecclesia are still unresolved. However if judged worthy of consideration, then it presents a hybrid model, stemming from the meeting of a charismatic form of Christianity with a cultural and rural form of Hinduism. It is true that the *asram* model was seen as copying the Hindu way of life or rather "aping" the *Brahminic* elements for Christianity. However what is happening in this model is something quite different. The *asram* model in this movement is not limited to *asram* but supplemented by the charismatic model, which focuses on the "laos" or the people's devotion. Hence I have qualified this model as *asram*-based charismatic model.

The type of Christianity practised by the *Khrist-Bhaktas* is the catholicized charismatic form of Christianity furnished in the context of the *asram*. This form of Christianity has found a way to their hearts and minds, captured their imagination, and seems to fulfil their religious needs. It has thus become the meeting point between Hinduism and Christianity. The devotees are appropriating it into their cultural world. Therefore, their religious expressions have features of these charismatic elements as well as their original culture.

This combination is a unique form, which, ecclesiologically, shows a christological as well as a pneumatological character in many of its expressions. Christology and pneumatology are also the constitutive elements or the roots on which this movement has grown. The other aspects can be considered as the results of the pneumatological and christological emphases. Moreover, the *satsangs* in the *asram* and the prayer meetings in the villages are contexts and occasions for encountering the divine in Christ and Spirit.

The movement is centred on the Matridham *asram* and the concept of the *asram* came from Hinduism. The very concept of the *asram* with its implications is something new to the church. Avery Dulles speaks about the capacity of models to lead to new theological sights when used in an exploratory or heuristic way.[8] The *asram* model leads one to focus on the spiritual aspects of Christianity. Its openness invites people of all religions and cultures. Its simplicity attracts ordinary people to Christianity. Christianity thus becomes a symbol of spirituality and communion for people of all religions, all cultures, and all economic standards.

The leaders who live in the *asram* and guide the movement are Christians while the devotees are mostly Hindus. The religious practices of *Khrist-Bhaktas* come from the charismatic form of Christianity as presented to them. What is emerging is a mosaic of Hinduism and Christianity, making the devotees both Hindus and Christians at the same time.

THE SIGNIFICANCE OF THIS MODEL

It can be stated that the church actualizes itself most fully in the worshipping assembly.[9] According to Yves Congar, the church first of all is the fellowship of persons in communion with God and with one another; at the same time, the church is also the means by which this fellowship is accomplished and maintained.[10] The

---

[8] A. Dulles, *Models of the Church: A Critical Assessment of the Church in All its Aspects* (Dublin: Gill and Macmillan,1976), 24.

[9] R. Haight, *Christian Community in History* (New York/London: Continuum, 2005), 465.

[10] G. Flynn, *Yves Congar's Vision of the Church in a World of Unbelief* (Aldershot: Ashgate Publishing Ltd, 2004), 80-95.

Khrist-Bhakta movement is contributing to these two aspects. The worshiping assembly of the devotees, which bind those people together, who are otherwise divided by caste-hierarchy, is a sign of communion with God and one another and, at the same time, is a means for accomplishing and maintaining fellowship.

The implications from stressing the charismatic elements, especially the Christo-pneumatology and the composition of the movement, can lead us to new theologico-ecclesiological meanings. Normally, the *asram* is considered as a place for higher *varnas* and for people of higher levels of spirituality (*Jnana marga*). However, the stress on charismatic elements has brought the ordinary people and the high spiritually-oriented people under one umbrella.

The most important significance of the *asram*-based charismatic model of the Christ-devotee movement is its ability to exploit the gap emerging from the Hindu understanding of religion and social community, together with the Christian understanding of faith. The Hindu understanding offers possibilities for a Christ-devotee to remain within the community and culture without legally changing the community, while accepting Jesus as the only Lord and saviour. It allows a devotee to remain faithful only to Christ and remain Christian on a spiritual level, while allowing sufficient freedom on the social level. The success of this model in negotiating the boundaries of both Hinduism and Christianity should be noted against the earlier attempts to find a theological base on human rights as noted by Sebastian Kim in this present volume.[11] Kim notes that the Christian argument on religious freedom and human rights was not effective in the debate with Hindus. Therefore he believes that an alternative model is required. The Christ-devotee model promises to be an alternative model conducive to Indian ethos.

Other significances

a) The spreading of faith in Christ in this model is from below and that too by the devotees themselves who have experienced the healing touch of Christ.

[11] Sebastian Kim, "Religious Freedom, Minorities and the Concept of Religion," in the present volume.

b) It witnesses to the fact that Christians are not adamant on destroying any culture and opens up the possibility of the emergence of an Indian form of Christianity. This model is an answer to the new fellowship, as hoped by A. S. Dasan and Nalini Xavier in the present volume: "...wherein all could take part transcending/sublimating all our religious and cultural particularities into a unification of aesthetics and sensibilities, godly and earthly at the same time which could reflect and manifest the glory of existence against all forms brutality in the name of religion."[12]

c) It safeguards the Christian mandate of proclaiming faith and preaching the Word of God, thereby spreading the message of Christ without hindrance and threat to the Indian culture.

d) The multi-caste/*varn* composition of the community of the *Khrist-Bhaktas* is a contribution of Christianity to Indian society, although the road ahead is longer.

e) The model of the *Khrist-Bhakta* movement does not project the Christians as anti-nationals but as fellow-pilgrims. This will open up new frontiers in the mission in India and elsewhere.

CONVERSION, BAPTISM AND RELIGIOUS FREEDOM IN THE CONTEXT OF THE KB MODEL

Jude Jacques says, "In achieving various goals, problems can be identified which need to be solved in order to achieve the goal. If we really understand the problem, the answer will come out of it, because the answer is not separate from the problem."[13] What is the crux of the real problem that we face today? On the one hand, the Christians have the divine mandate of proclaiming the gospel and the question of the freedom of spreading one's religious faith in India, while on the other hand there is the persistent opposition to this Christian right by several groups. Now why is it that so many Indians, in a country known for its religiosity, oppose Christianity? Why is that the conversion to Christianity is opposed in India with

---

[12] A.S. Dasan and Nalini Xavier, "Consequences of Globalization and Contours of Democracy, Freedom, and Faith in the Indian context," in the present volume.

[13] Jude Jacques, *The Fundamental Fair Pack: Government Reforms 101* (Bloomington: Author House, 2011), 76.

all possible rules and regulations? There can be several reasons like, political, cultural, sociological, religious, or even selfish reasons and motives. However, it is a fact that the churches in India come across to the people as an European entity.

Looking back one can notice that during the modern missionary movement, most of the missionaries believed in the inner and outer correlation between western culture and Christianity. The missionary activity included both the spreading of the Gospel and the spreading of civilization. This mixture of faith and civilization, evangelization and civilizing activities, affected almost everywhere.[14] Therefore, while spreading the Christian message, they indirectly spread western culture as well. According to Horst Gründer, the role of missionaries in spreading western culture was highly significant, as the missionaries thought of their effort as a spiritual conquest and thus became what he calls "the most militant advocates of European culture."[15] Most of the European missionaries believed in the superiority of their culture, civilization, and, above all, their religion.[16] Biblical conceptions of space and time remained the standard for them. Hence, travelling to non-European cultures was compared to travelling backwards in time, to an era of primitive simplicity. European culture was regarded as characterized by artifice and deliberations while cultures other than European were regarded as literally decomposed or inferior. In the same way, any religion other than Christianity was considered diabolic and based on instinct and intuition.[17] The missionaries considered themselves as the bearers not only of a superior religion, but also of a superior culture.[18] Therefore, by way of baptizing, the missionaries were

---

[14] C. Baldi, "The Mission of the Church: To Gather into One the Scattered Children of God" in *Catholic Engagement with World Religions. A Comprehensive Study*, eds. K.J. Becker and I. Morali (New York: Orbis Books, 2010), 287.

[15] H. Gründer, "Christian Mission and Colonial Expansion: Historical and Structural Connections" *Mission Studies* 12 (1995): 22.

[16] D. Hempton, *The Church in the Long Eighteenth Century* (London/New York: I. B. Tauris, 2011), 20. The local measuring units, the local calendars, and the local understanding of seasons were abolished and replaced with European standards.

[17] A. Pagden, *European Encounters with the New World: From Renaissance to Romanticism* (New Haven: Yale University Press, 1993), 150.

[18] C. R. Boxer, *The Church Militant and the Iberian Expansion* (Baltimore-Londers:

trying to integrate the natives into the European cultural complex.[19] They believed that they were doing a noble thing by spreading Christian civilization to all peoples. According to Kuncheria Pathil,

> The new churches in the colonies were not exactly new "local churches," but extensions of the colonizing churches.... Baptism thus became not only a symbol of a religious conversion, but also of a cultural conversion to the European or western ways and customs.[20]

In general, baptism in the eyes of Hindus is not primarily a sign of commitment to or faith in Christ but rather as a sign of discarding one's own culture and community.[21] The Hindu understanding of baptism stems from their understanding of religion, community, and culture. Hindus grasp the very idea of religion differently. They perceive religion inherently as a way of life adopted by community, and not as a religion.[22] Being a Hindu is primarily a matter of maintaining one's cultural identity and fulfilling one's duty (*dharma*) pertaining to one's caste and stage of life. It is not based on professing any definite creed. Remaining within the group and fulfilling one's duty, a Hindu is free to worship according to the religious beliefs of one's choice. On the spiritual level, a Hindu is free to believe in what he likes; on a social and cultural level, he is not. Spiritual allegiance to Jesus Christ, however intense it maybe, is not regarded as a stain on a person's standing as a true Hindu.[23] As S.

The Johns Hopkins University Press, 1978), 39.

[19] Peter C. Phan clearly exhibits this mentality by the example of the 17th century translation of the Vietnamese interpreters of the question in the baptismal rite: "Do you want to become a Christian?" as "Do you want to become a Portuguese?" See P. C. Phan, "An Asian Christian? Or a Christian Asian? Or an Asian-Christian? A Roman Catholic Experiment on Christian Identity" in *Asia and Oceanic Christianities in Conversation: Exploring Theological Identities at Home and in Diaspora*, eds. H.Y. Kim, F. Matsuoka and A. Morimoto (Amsterdam/New York: Rodopi, 2011), 62.

[20] K. Pathil, "New Ways of Being Church in Asia" in *Third Millennium* 1 (1998): 9. One of the priorities of the missionaries at that time was planting of churches in the non-Christian world.

[21] For more details, see Sebastian Kim's article in this present volume.

[22] E. D. Devadason, *Christian Law in India: Law Applicable to Christians in India* (Madras: DSI Publications, 1974), 342-345.

[23] H. Staffner, "Conversion to Christianity Seen from the Hindu Point of View"

Radhakrishnan says, "Hinduism is more a way of life than a form of thought. While it gives absolute liberty in the world of thought, it enjoins a strict code of practice. The theist and the atheist, the sceptic and the agnostic may all be Hindus if they accept the Hindu system of culture and life."[24] For them, what is essential for one's soul is conversion from the baser to nobler sides of one's personality and not from one religion to another.[25] A Hindu can remain a genuine Hindu even if he worships none of the Hindu gods. He is aiming for personal spirituality rather than one concerned about religious systems.[26]

In contrast, Christianity as a religion is well organized.[27] However, we cannot speak of a Hindu religion in the sense in which we speak of the Christian religion. The difference can easily be grasped by comparing the situation of expulsion of a person in Hinduism and Christianity. If a Christian is expelled from his church, another group may be ready to accept him because organized religion cannot exercise its influence beyond the limitations of religion. In Hindu society, an ex-communicated person has either to repent and return or to leave that society and village.[28] In the religious sphere, freedom is given to the individuals while it is required of the people to subordinate themselves to the status quo of the social structure.[29]

in *Evangelization, Dialogue and Development*, ed. M. Dhavamony (Roma: Universita Gregoriana Editrice, 1972), 236.

[24] S. Radhakrishnan, *The Hindu Way of Life* (London: Unwin Books, 1956), 55.

[25] T. M. P. Mahadevan, "The Christian Image in India" in *Debate on Mission: Issues from the Indian Context*, ed. H.E. Hoefer (Madras: Gurukul Theological College & Research Institute, 1979), 302.

[26] D. Bharati, *Living Water and Indian Bowl* (Delhi: ISPCK, 2004), 49.

[27] Christianity holds to certain essential articles of faith. The Christian faith can be inserted into any social or cultural life of a people in any part of the world. It can take flesh in any society while maintaining its essentials of faith.

[28] Bharati, *Living Water and Indian Bowl*, 48. Here one might point out that on the social level Hinduism behaves as totalitarianism, while leaving the religious sphere free. Any kind of totalitarian system invites a critique of the gospel.

[29] Brahamabandav Upadhyaya had made the distinction between *samaj dharma* (way of life) and *sadana dharma* (means or way of salvation). Being a Christian by religion means the following of a certain way of salvation, accepting Jesus Christ as the way to God, our Father. A human being is Christian precisely because he follows the Christian way of salvation. In Hindu terminology, this

Today, when we speak of conversion, what is grasped by a Hindu and a Christian is fundamentally different. The Hindus grasp the very term religion differently. "The word 'religion' is not a native category," says Jonathan Z. Smith. "It is not a first person term of self-characterization. It is a category imposed from the outside on some aspects of native cultures. It is the others... who are responsible for the content of the term."[30] Often the term *dharma* and religion are used interchangeably. The word *dharma* has quite a different meaning from what people in the West understand by religion. Nicholas Lash shows how the English-speaking people in 19th century had presumed that there must be some word in every language that corresponds to the sense in which the word "religion" is used. He says that, as a result, the word *dharma* was mistranslated as "religion," which guaranteed the intractable misunderstanding between Indians and English-speaking Westerners.[31] Hindus use the term *dharmantar* (change of *dharma*) to denote the conversion of Hindus to Islam and Christianity. In addition, they consider that there is nothing spiritual about *dharmantar*; it is only proselytism. Hindus do not object if their members undergo a change of heart and believe in Jesus Christ. However, they object to the change of

---

means that the Christian religion is a *sadana dharma*. But the Christian religion is not a distinct *samaj dharma*: it does not prescribe any distinct way of life as regards social customs, diet, inter-dining, ritual purity, etc. Being a Hindu, on the other hand, does not mean following any specific *sadana dharma*, any specific way of salvation. A Hindu is free to choose any *marg* or way of salvation, i.e., *sadana dharma* that appeals to him although he is bound by the *samaj dharma*, by rules regarding diet, ritual purity, and various forms of social behaviour. For further details, see Staffner, "Conversion to Christianity," 241-243.

[30] J. Z. Smith "Religion, Religions, Religious" in *Critical Terms for Religious Studies*, ed. M. Tylor (Chicago: The University of Chicago Press, 1998), 269. It has to be remembered that the term "religion" became established as a generic term applicable to various "religions" only in the early modern age as a result of a development lasting centuries starting from Cicero. Only in David Hume (1711-1776) did it finally attain this meaning. Hegel and Schleiermacher established the term in its modern day sense. See for more details, P. Henrici, "The Concept of Religion from Cicero to Schleiermacher: Origin, History and Problems with the Term" in *Catholic Engagement with World Religions: A Comprehensive Study*, eds. K.J. Becker and I. Morali (New York: Orbis Books, 2010), 1-20.

[31] N. Lash, *Holiness, Speech and Silence: Reflections on the Question of God* (Aldershot: Ashgate, 2004), 12.

dharma. Hindus do not consider conversion as something that is related to the spiritual sphere but as "the step by which a person changes his social community."³²

Thus, in the context of India, as M. M. Thomas has pointed out, baptism is not seen primarily as a sign of incorporation into Christ but as a sign of proselytism into a socio-political-religious community involving rejection of their socio-political-religious communities.³³ It is a social and a civil event.

By baptizing a Hindu person as Christian, he/she ceases to be a member of the Hindu community.

> Far from being purely a spiritual event, a spiritual rebirth, baptism implies the changeover to and the renunciation of a person's social community in favour of a new and different social group—a step that is not only alien to the Hindu mind but also fraught with far-reaching legal and social consequences.³⁴

Because of baptism, the convert is, socially speaking, considered as an outcast from his social group and family. He is forced to leave his joint family and has to find his own property and an independent family. This change legally brings him or her under Christian Personal Law and affects matters such as succession, marriage, maintenance, guardianship, and adoption.³⁵ The British introduced the Christian Personal Law, which is regarded by many as a European law. Therefore, the convert to Christianity changes from Hindu Personal Law (read as being Indian) to Christian Personal Law (read as being European). Thus, a convert changes over from one social group to another legally and he/she has to follow the laws regarding marriage and inheritance of the community to which he/she has moved.³⁶

---

³² Staffner, "Conversion to Christianity," 237.

³³ M. M. Thomas, "Baptism, the Church and Koinonia" in *Some Theological Dialogues*, ed. M. M. Thomas (Madras: The Christian Literature Society, 1977), 115.

³⁴ Staffner, "Conversion to Christianity," 235.

³⁵ J. Saldanha, *Conversion and Indian Law* (Bangalore: Theological Publication in India, 1981), 115. Conversion affects the cohesiveness and unity of the Hindu family and community.

³⁶ See more discussion on the formation and development of Christian

Accordingly, any Hindu who accepts the Christian faith and is baptized, ceases to be a member of his social group and family. He loses his right to inheritance, any privileges meant for his caste, like reservation in jobs, and cannot be ruled by the Hindu Personal Law. Thus, although Christians regard baptism purely as a spiritual and a religious event, it is seen and understood in India as a social and a legal event, with its economic and cultural consequences.

Understanding the Hindu view on baptism does not necessarily call for accepting their view on baptism. The crux of the problem is the heterogeneous understanding of baptism. Christians and Hindus have a different understanding of religion, community, and culture. Christians are inclined to project their notion of religion on Hinduism though it does not fit it, while Hindus are inclined to project their notion of the spiritual path on Christianity though it does not fit it.[37] Christians do not intend the negative social, legal, and communal consequences of baptism. They do not intend to break up the community by baptism but want the community to grow spiritually and be united in the name of Christ. Christians stress the spiritual level while allowing sufficient freedom on the social level. Hindus oppose the social aspect of baptism, while leaving freedom on the spiritual level. This distinction paves the way for some possibilities of mutuality between Hinduism and Christianity.

This distinction opens up the possibility of having a synthesis of Hindu social life and Christian spiritual life. This possibility is negotiated and materialized in the *Khrist-Bhakta* movement, albeit the new problems it brings with it. The most important problem is related to baptism and membership. In this movement, people do not consider baptism as a sign of faith but as a sign of betraying the culture; it has to be either replaced/substituted or discarded, as it was the case with circumcision.

Conclusion

There are some real issues left unresolved which would require further scholarly discussion, until this movement can be considered a

Personal Law and its interpretations by the Supreme Court in the present volume (Sebastian Kim and Tehmina Arora).

[37] Staffner, "Conversion to Christianity," 247.

full-fledged model of ecclesia. I shall briefly present some of them in a nutshell:

a) Is accepting the gospel, the desire for communion with Christ and a life of discipleship enough for someone to be considered as a member of the Church? Can there be a church without baptism? Can there be a church without boundaries?

b) Although they practise much of Christian devotion, the Hindu concept of creation together with its worldview, might still be working on the horizon of the devotees. Questions can also be raised about their Hindu worldview with its lack of social commitment, which may not go hand-in-hand with the Christian commitment to human dignity and society.

c) Every new movement needs some kind of boundaries and rules to sustain it and to exclude potential free riders and doubters, although these rules must be sufficiently low not to drive away those who are willing to take the faith seriously. However this *asram*-based charismatic model of church lacks boundaries, such as initiation ceremonies, rules or mechanisms to sustain itself, which in turn encourages "shoppers."

d) On the one hand, this movement is growing day-by-day, but on the other hand, many devotees are deserting it. History teaches us that not many movements succeed to generate enough energy to outlive the initial enthusiasm.[38] This movement also has the weakness of becoming a haven for short-term religious sojourners.[39]

e) Although many devotees are attracted to the charismatic prayer and its experiences, as time goes by, it is no longer appealing to many of them. It also encourages too much emotionalism, claims

---

[38] Rodney Stark shows that only one out of 1,000 new religious movements will attract 100,000 followers and last for as long as a century. R. Stark, "Why Religious Movements Succeed or Fail: A Revised General Model" in *Cults and New Religious Movements: A Reader*, ed. L. L. Dawson (Malden/Oxford: Blackwell Publishing Ltd, 2003), 259.

[39] A study on new religious movements done by Frederic Bird and Bill Reimer reveals that many members are short-term members. They point out that the group called Family had 57,000 members but, after 25 years, their numbers had come down to 3,000. See for details, F. Bird and B. Reimer, "Participation Rates in New Religious and Para Religious Movements" in *Journal for Scientific Study of Religion* 21 (1982), 1-10.

of direct revelation from God, and encourages literal interpretation of the Bible.

f) The leaders have different and unique roles, each representing critical contributions to the collective action. This requires coordination and synchronization among members and integration of their contributions to achieve team goals.[40] According to Ralph Stacy, an expert in management, any successful organization requires leaders to strongly share the same values and same vision of the future and work in harmony.[41] There is an absence of clear vision about the future of the movement among the leaders who are involved in the movement.

g) The formation of the *Bhaktas* into a new community has not broken the central caste/*varn* barrier yet. Although there are some glimpses of such changes, other issues show that community formation is not in full swing. Christ-devotees have not been able to enter into any inter-*varn* marriage, which is a sign of communion.

h) India is a country where plenty of *guru*-directed movements have appeared and died, and not many new religious movements were able to draw many people or sustain themselves for over hundred years. It is possible that the stress is diverted from Christ to the human *guru* in the *asram*.

i) Syncretism, when considered as a negative concept, is also happening. The movement is mixing elements from both Christianity and Hinduism. On many occasions, new devotees listen to other devotees and their interpretation of Christianity. What the new devotees believe may not be what the Church teaches, but can be the interpretation and assimilation by the devotees themselves. Since the gathering is large and no personal attention can be given, an indiscriminate mixing of religious belief and practice is possible.

---

[40] S. J. Zaccaro, A.L. Rittman and M.A. Marks, "Team Leadership" in *The Leadership Quarterly*, 12 (2001), 457. Collaboration points to reduction of autonomy which the priests do not want to give up. For the details on the importance of collaboration, see J. Van Diggelen, J.M. Bradshaw, M. Johnson and others, "Implementing Collective Obligations in Human-Agent Teams Using KAoS Policies" in *Lecture Notes in Computer Science* 6069 (2010): 37-52.

[41] R. Stacey, *Strategic Management and Organisational Dynamics* (London: Pitman publishing, 1993), 18.

Religious Freedom and Conversion in Sri Lanka: An Analysis

G. P. V. Somaratna[1]

INTRODUCTION

The United Nations regards freedom of religion as a basic human right. Its Universal Declaration of Human Rights states, "Everyone has the right to freedom of thought, conscience and religion; this right includes freedom to change his[2] religion or belief, and freedom, either alone or in community with others and in public or private, to manifest his religion or belief in teaching, practice, worship and observance." The UN's Human Rights Committee, commenting on the International Covenant on Civil and Political Rights, declared in 1993 that Article 18 "protects theistic, non-theistic and atheistic beliefs, as well as the right not to profess any religion or belief."[3] The Government of Sri Lanka is a signatory to these Resolutions of the UN.

It also stated that "the freedom to have or to adopt a religion or belief necessarily entails the freedom to choose a religion or belief, including the right to replace one's current religion or belief with another or to adopt atheistic views." Signatories to the convention are barred from "the use of threat of physical force or penal sanctions to compel believers or non-believers" to recant their beliefs or convert. Despite this, minority religions are still persecuted in many parts of the world.

---

[1] Dr. G. P. V. Somaratna has been professor of Modern History, University of Colombo and is presently Research Professor of Colombo Theological Seminary. He specializes in the History of Theravada Buddhism and Culture.

[2] In this paper, "his" would mean "her" as well.

[3] ICCPR Article 18, CCPR General Comment 22, July 30, 1993, accessed on July 15, 2015, http://www.minorityrights.org/3273/normative-instruments/ccpr-general-comment-22-300793-on-iccpr-article-18.html. *[editorial note: when last checked on August 16, 2017, the web-link was inactive]*

Sri Lanka

Sri Lanka is a democratic republic. It is a multi-ethnic and multi-religious nation-state. According to the 2011 Census, 70.19% of Sri Lankans were Theravada Buddhists, 12.6% were Hindus, 9.7% were Muslims and 7.4% Christians.[4] Christians are inclined to be concentrated in the Western Province and the Mannar district; Muslims are scattered in all urban areas of the country with a high concentration in the southern area of the Eastern Province; the Northern Province and some sectors of the estate areas of the central highland are Hindu. Most members of the majority Sinhalese community are Theravada Buddhists. Most Tamils, the largest ethnic minority, are Saivite Hindus. Most Muslims are Sunnis and speak the Tamil language. Almost 80 percent of Christians are Roman Catholic; other Christians are Protestants belonging to various denominations. It is reported that evangelical Christian groups have experienced a phenomenal growth in the last three decades, although their gains are not reported in the census reports. The Christian community cuts across all ethnic lines while other religions are associated with a particular ethnic community. These demographic factors have a close correlation with religious conversion as there is a tendency to disturb ethnic connections with religious affiliations in Sri Lanka. However, the Government of Sri Lanka theoretically respects religious freedom. The country's Constitution and other laws protect religious freedom.

Buddhism and religious freedom

The idea of religious freedom is not alien to Sri Lanka's major religion, which is Buddhism. Buddhism is regarded as one of the most liberal and tolerant religions in the world. As such, religious freedom as a concept has not been contested in the history of Sri Lanka. Disputes caused by the lack of religious freedom were alien to Sri Lankans before the arrival of the Portuguese in the 16th century

---

[4] 6.1% of the Christian population is Roman Catholic and 1.3% are other Christian categories. The latter is divided among a large number of denominations, both mainline and charismatic.

CE, with their exclusivist Roman Catholic form of propagation of Christianity.

The Sinhalese royalty, upto its termination in 1815, patronized other religions while giving a prominent place to Buddhism. Buddhist temples have had a place within their precincts, to worship Hindu gods. Siva temples that the Cola invaders built in Polonnaruwa remained centres of worship even after the Colas were driven out from the country.[5] The kings of Kandy gave asylum to the Muslims who were expelled by the Portuguese from their territory in 16th century CE. They settled in large numbers in the eastern part of Sri Lanka. In the second half of 17th century CE, when the Dutch Protestant rulers expelled the Roman Catholic priests from the Dutch-held area of the country, the king of Kandy allowed them to settle in his kingdom. Later in 18th century CE, the Buddhist king of Kandy intervened to get the release of Catholic priests incarcerated by the Dutch.

Religious intolerance has its roots in exclusivity—believing that only one religion can offer salvation and that there is no alternative available. The Catholic missionaries of the Counter Reformation era could only see other religions as evil. On the other hand, Buddhism is an inclusivist religion. Therefore while their own set of beliefs was regarded as absolutely true, other sets of beliefs were treated at least as partially true. Buddhism has been able to combine a missionary zeal with this tolerant attitude. Buddhist scholars have said that, "Not a drop of blood has been shed throughout the ages in the propagation and dissemination of Buddhism in the many lands to which it spread; religious wars either between the schools of Buddhism or against other religions have been unheard of. Very rare instances of the persecution of heretical opinions are not lacking, but they have been exceptional and atypical."[6] The activities of extremist Buddhists in the recent past have eroded the validity of this statement.

---

[5] The Cola rule lasted from 1017 to 1070 in Sri Lanka, with the exception of the southernmost parts of the country.

[6] K. N. Jayatilleke, *The Buddhist Attitude to Other Religions* (Kandy: Buddhist Publication Society, 1966).

Around 1850 Daniel Gogerly, a Methodist missionary, noted: "Until Christianity assumed a decidedly opposing position, even the priests looked upon that religion with respect, and upon its founder with reverence. I have seen it stated in a controversial tract, written by a Buddhist priest of Matura not fifteen years since, that probably Christ in a former state of existence was a god residing in one of the six heavens (a position which they represented Gotama as having occupied immediately previous to his birth as Buddha); that animated by benevolence he desired and obtained a birth as a man, and taught truth so far as he was acquainted with it. That his benevolence, his general virtue, and the purity of his doctrine rendered him worthy of reverence and honour. If, therefore, the supremacy of Buddha and the absolute perfection of his system were conceded, they saw nothing inconsistent in respecting both systems - Buddhism as the perfection of wisdom and virtue; Christianity as an approximation to it, though mingled with errors."[7]

Conversion

Religious conversion is a general term that applies to all changes that involve a transformation from one religious belief system to another. From a theological point of view, conversion to Christianity can be considered as an intensely personal affair. It is a transformative event in the life of the individual. It is a change in a person's religious affiliations. Ideally, religious conversion is a matter of personal choice. It is guaranteed as a fundamental right in the Constitution of Sri Lanka.

Usually converts display change of habits in agreement with the new faith. From this point on, the convert is expected to be faithful and committed to his new religious orientation, leaving behind past habits and practices that contravene the new faith. This sudden and complete change can be noticed by their neighbours and colleagues with apprehension. Converts from Buddhism have said that they were attempting to deal with life's mysteries, the meaning of life, the meaning of death and tragedies. Evangelical

---

[7] James Emerson Tennent, *Christianity in Ceylon* (London: John Murrey, 1850), 240.

Christian converts have stated that they became Christian because of some tangible experience related to Christian faith in their life.

Legal provisions regarding conversion as depicted in the Constitution of 1978

In the third chapter of the Constitution of Sri Lanka of 1978 defining Fundamental Rights, Article 10 mentions that "Every person is entitled to freedom of thought, conscience, and religion, including the freedom to have or to adopt a religion or belief of his choice."

Its article 14 (1) (e) states that "Every person is entitled to the freedom either by himself or in association with others, and either in public or in private, to manifest his religion or belief in worship, observance, practice and teaching."

Article 15 places checks on the exercise of Fundamental Rights. Article 15 (4) states that the Fundamental Rights declared by Article 14 (1) (e) "shall be subject to such restrictions as may be prescribed by law in the interests of racial and religious harmony or national economy."

Article 15 (7) indicates that the Fundamental Rights declared in Article 14 "shall be subject to such restrictions as may be prescribed by law in the interests of national security, public order and the protection of public health or morality, or for the purpose of securing due recognition and respect for the rights and freedoms of others, or of meeting the just requirements of the general welfare of a democratic society."[8]

Conversion and politics

In Sri Lanka, conversion means much more than a change of personal religion. The issue of conversion has become very much a political matter. It has become a topic far from a personal concern. Conversion of Buddhists to Christianity alters the social boundaries that make up the Sinhalese-Buddhist identity. The emphasis given to conversion among Christian evangelical groups carries with it certain institutional efforts which have political implications.

---

[8] Anton Fernando, "Conversion and the Law," *Living Faith* 5, no. 1 (2004): 17-26.

Therefore, it has become a public affair because local as well as external forces have got involved in it. One may notice that the current conflict over conversion has collided with the identity of Sri Lanka as a multi-ethnic and multi-religious state.[9]

Anthropologists have stated that religious conversion is a complex matter. Conversion is not simply a sudden moment of insight or inspiration. It is a change of individual consciousness together with social affiliation, mental attitude and even physical experience. The unfolding of this change in one's cultural setting would cause irritation to the neighbourhood, which is used to seeing that person in their cultural milieu. Emergence of newly formed pockets of Christians in hitherto predominantly Buddhist areas has alarmed those who treat Sri Lanka as a Buddhist nation and hold to the opinion that the Sinhalese are Buddhist. Most Buddhist nationalists believe that Buddha designated Sri Lanka as the repository of pure Buddhism and therefore that Sri Lanka belongs to the Buddhists, who are Sinhalese.[10] Many Buddhist leaders have reiterated that the link between the Sinhala race and the Buddhist religion is inseparable.[11] Sri Lankan historian K. M. de Silva states: "In Sinhala language, the words for nation, race and people are practically synonymous, and a multi-ethnic and multi-communal nation or state is incomprehensible in the popular mind. The emphasis on Sri Lanka as the land of the Sinhala Buddhists carried an emotional popular appeal, compared with which the concept of a multi-ethnic polity was a meaningless abstraction."[12] This is a misguided but a popular notion held by most Sinhalese Buddhists. Sinhalese Christians, let alone the Tamil minority, are offended by the inter-changeability of "Sinhalese" and "Buddhist."

---

[9] Rosalind I. J. Hackett, *Proselytization Revisited: Rights Talk, Free Markets and Culture Wars* (London: Routledge, 2014), 199.

[10] Jason Stone and Neil DeVotta, *Sinhalese Buddhist Nationalist Ideology: Implications for Politics and Conflict Resolution in Sri Lanka* (Washington: East West Center, 2007), 29.

[11] Mahinda Deegalle, "Politics of the Jatika Hela Urumaya Monks: Buddhism and Ethnicity in Contemporary Sri Lanka," *Contemporary Buddhism* 5, no. 2 (2004): 87.

[12] K. M. De Silva, *A History of Sri Lanka* (London: C. Hurst and Company, 1981), 35.

Unethical conversion

Sinhalese Buddhists have been alarmed by the recent appearance of evangelical Christian churches all over Sri Lanka. The Buddhist leaders have found it difficult to understand the reasons for these conversions. Previous conversions of Sinhalese to Christianity took place in the colonial era. The census reports of the country from 1946 showed a clear fall in the percentage of Christians in the total population in the country. Therefore, some critics have prophesied that Christianity would eventually disappear from Sri Lanka. However, the recent wave of conversions do not fall into the category of conversions of the colonial era, where material advantage was one of the causes for conversion. Therefore, the Buddhists have speculated several reasons for this phenomenon and undertaken some remedial solutions.

Buddhist organizations have accused Christian evangelists of offering material benefits to Buddhists to embrace Christianity. The accusation is that Christian evangelists exercise "force, coercion, allurement, fraud or other unethical means" to convert Buddhists to Christianity. According to the Buddhist critics, the methods used in the procedure of conversion are similar to advertising. The accusation is that their targets are the poor, the unemployed, the sick, the bereaved, children and young adults. Material inducements such as houses, clothes, food, money, etc., are offered to the poor and also the needy. They have accused Christians of employing physical violence, chasing monks out of their temples, threatening monks with bodily harm, destroying the Buddhist heritage, and of sending paid workers to destroy Buddhist archaeological sites and rob temples. These statements have not been substantiated with evidence; yet they have created a negative attitude among the Buddhists, who accept these rumours without verification. In the recent past, Buddhists have coined the expression "unethical conversion" to express their disapproval of the conversion of Buddhists to Christianity.[13] Christians have denied all these accusations as malicious fabrications. Independent observers have stated that

---

[13] "Tactics and Strategies of Unethical Conversion," August 7, 2015, accessed on August 16, 2017, http://www.lankaweb.com/news/items/2015/08/07/tactics-and-strategies-of-unethical-conversion/comment-page-1/.

Christians are an insignificant minority in the villages in Sri Lanka, which are dominated by Buddhists, Hindus, Muslims or Roman Catholics. Hence they are unable to carry out such hateful actions even if they desire to do so.

Anti-conversion debate

Buddhist agitation against Christianity goes back to the latter part of 19th century. Before 19th century, many of those who embraced Christianity did so for material benefit, out of fear or with coercion. Buddhists have cited the atrocities committed by the Portuguese (1505-1658) to convert Sri Lankans to their faith, and the Dutch (1658-1796) intolerance of non-DRC religions, to prove that Christian evangelism continues to be associated with material inducements. However, it was no longer necessary to embrace Christianity for those reasons in 19th century CE as the British Government (1796-1948) was liberal and tolerant of all religions. The colonial connection of Christianity continued and many, especially the elite, were benefited by their association with the British administration, until the granting of universal franchise for an electoral process to select leaders for the new State Council in 1931.

Ever since the onset of the Buddhist resurgence in 19th century, the idea that the Sinhalese are Buddhists has been repeated by successive generations of Buddhist leaders.[14] Since the 1980s Buddhist fears about losing their grip on their motherland were caused by two reasons. One was the Tamil militant movement demanding a separate state within the island, which escalated into a full scale civil war in 1983. The second was the spread of Christianity among the Sinhalese villagers without any political support. This led to a debate among Buddhist leaders on the issue of religious conversion, eventually having an impact on the politics of the country.

---

[14] Kitsiri Malalgoda, *Buddhism in Sinhalese Society 1750-1900: Study of Religious Revival and Change* (Berkeley: University of California Press, 1976), 232-242; DeVotta, *Sinhalese Buddhist Nationalist Ideology,* 40.

Conversions

Many evangelical groups and churches have moved to establish indigenous churches to spread their faith. The numbers of converts have increased in recent years. These churches are led by local pastors without foreign supervision. This phenomenon is interpreted, without any evidence, as a programme that has the backing and funding of foreign governmental and institutional support, such as the Vatican, NGOs, and evangelical organizations. There is a perception that Christian expansion due to conversions is disturbing the solidarity of Buddhist villages.

Organized Opposition to Conversion

The contemporary debate over conversion in Sri Lanka has its origins in the 1980s, when new charismatic groups began actively working among Buddhists in various parts of Sri Lanka. The convergence of anti-Christian views took a new turn as a result of the sudden death of Gangodawila Soma Thera in December 2003 in Moscow. This death sparked a new and vigorous campaign against Christian evangelism. Soma had been critical of Christian organizations distributing aid in Sri Lanka.[15] It was speculated that Christian evangelicals poisoned him. Subsequent to this rumour, a period of arson and acts of vandalism against Christian churches followed. Another result was the formation of a political party with a Buddhist agenda and led by monks. It subscribed to Sinhalese Buddhist nationalist ideology, with implications for politics in Sri Lanka.[16] The anti-conversion debate was spearheaded by the Buddhist political party known as *Jatika Hela Urumaya* (JHU). The JHU is a party of Buddhist extremists including some monks, who aspire to lead the country politically by contesting parliamentary elections.

JHU monks continued the rhetoric of Soma Thera. They were instrumental in presenting a Bill called "The Prohibition of Forcible Conversion of Religion" to the Parliament. When that proposal was rejected by the Supreme Court, the governing party drafted a Bill

---

[15] Hackett, *Proselytization Revisited*, 200.
[16] DeVotta, *Sinhalese Buddhist Nationalist Ideology*, 29.

known as the Protection of Religious Freedom Act. The Supreme Court objected to it on the argument that the contents of the Bill were unconstitutional.

There were other individuals and groups working to combat unethical conversion. Books were published criticizing evangelical Christians. Posters appeared in the main roads of several cities accusing evangelical Christians of acts of unethical conversion. The short-lived monthly Buddhist newspaper, *Buddhist Times*, continuously published articles denouncing and reporting instances where Christian evangelicals and NGOs had supposedly engaged in "unethical conversions."

The perception of the Sinhala Buddhist nationalists is that evangelical Christian proselytism is a threat to the longstanding cultural traditions of the nation. They have been alarmed by the appearance of evangelical churches all over the country, attracting a first generation of Christians from the poor and underprivileged communities. They purposely ignored those from educated and professional cadres who have embraced Christianity. Evangelicals were accused of encouraging people to sever ties with their local customs and relationships.

The most vociferous group of monks who oppose conversion to Christianity are the non-Siyam Nikaya[17] monks who depend on the devotees for their daily subsistence. Anyone leaving Buddhism is considered as a threat to their sources of support. There is paranoia of the possibility of many others following the path taken by converts to Christianity. The JHU and other Buddhist extremist groups held rallies all over the country to incite villagers against Christian evangelists in their midst in 2004 and 2005. These resulted in violence and arson in many places. As local and international religious groups as well as human rights agencies banded together to challenge the JHU policy on conversion, the accusation was made that there was an international conspiracy against Buddhism.

---

[17] The monks of the Siyam Nikaya are confined to the "high-caste," which is the Goyigama (farmer) caste in Sri Lanka. The other two *nikayas* (Orders) are Amarapura and Ramanna. The Amarapura Nikaya monks are "middle-caste" members. They belong to the Karawa, Salagama, and Durava castes. Each of these castes is a sub-nikaya of the Amarapura Nikaya. The Ramanna Nikaya has all castes from the "lowest" to "highest" castes.

Legislature

Some members of the Sri Lankan Parliament made many attempts to pass a Bill named "Unethical conversion." It was viewed as a blatant violation of religious freedom by minority groups. In the first instance in 2004, the Anti-Conversion Bill, spearheaded by the JHU, was shelved by the Chandrika Kumaratunga Government in the face of local and international pressure.[18] A second Bill titled "Prohibition of Forcible Conversions" was tabled in 2009 during the Rajapaksa Government. The provisions of the Bill criminalized any act to convert or attempt to convert a person from one religion to another religion by the use of force, fraud or allurement. Those found guilty could be imprisoned for upto seven years and/or fined up to Rs. 500,000. The Rajapaksa Government did not proceed with the Bill due to international pressure.

Critics of conversion have used expressions like "forced conversion," "proselytism" and "unethical conversion" to explain Buddhists embracing Christianity in the modern era. Some writers in the Buddhist camp have asserted that religious conversions result from a process variously called mind-control and brain-washing. But little or no evidence exists to support such presumptions. Christianity is also accused of being a handmaiden of colonialism, even though this is the post-colonial era.

The challenge to conversions to Christianity has come predominantly from Buddhists, although other religions are also affected by conversions to Christianity. The obvious reason is that they form the majority community in the land. Christian ministers, as well as the people that they converted to Christianity, have been the target of persecution, at times to the point of being martyred for their faith. According to the International Society for Human Rights, up upto 80% of acts of persecution in Sri Lanka, which are directed at people of the Christian faith, have come from the Buddhists.

When President Rajapaksa did not allow the Bill to be placed before Parliament in 2009, the Buddhist lobby took several actions. They sought a decision on the issue from the Supreme Court. It was mainly to create a public awareness of the proposed Act. At

---

[18] "Prohibition of Forcible Conversion of Religion (Private Member's Bill)", *Gazette of the Democratic Socialist Republic of Sri Lanka*, May 28, 2004, part 2.

the same time, the desire was to show to the public that there was "illegal action" taking place in the country by Christian evangelists. Although the Buddhist extremist group is a small minority, their views on anti-conversion became widespread among the Buddhists. Many of them offered silent and non-violent support to these views. Therefore the Anti-Conversion Bill almost reached the approval of the Parliament. It was an unwavering stand taken by the President that averted the passing of this Bill.

International interference

The politics of conversion in Sri Lanka is not totally local. Sri Lanka's socio-economic milieu is influenced by the global village interfering in national matters. Powerful international interests are represented by NGOs and foreign governments. They have shown their interest in the anti-conversion debate. Their political and cultural interests have a stake in the conversion debate in Sri Lanka. Most NGOs are supported by foreign funds and benefited by human rights organizations and multinational agencies. World Vision received ruthless harassment when the Buddhist militia went on a rampage against Christian NGOs in the wake of the Anti-Conversion Bill in 2004.

On several occasions, US embassy officials conveyed US Government concern about the lack of religious toleration and requested that the Government arrest and prosecute the perpetrators of religious violence.[19] A small state like Sri Lanka finds it hard to limit foreign influence in their internal affairs. International human right organizations want to ensure that the state respects and guarantees internationally recognized rights to all religious communities. Nevertheless international organizations have been silent on the issue of proselytism. Against this background, Buddhist nationalists are becoming frustrated by the constraints they face to protect Buddhist hegemony. They feel that they are trying to preserve the integrity of Sinhala Buddhist culture in the face of Western forces.

Buddhists have also wished to use international pressure to win support for their cause. It is reported that in September 2004 Buddhist monks from the *Jatika Hela Urumaya* (JHU) party launched

---

[19] U.S. Department of State, *Sri Lanka 2012 International Religion Report*, 2012.

an international campaign to win support for the proposed Anti-Conversion Bill in Sri Lanka. The monks met with representatives at the United States, United Kingdom, Canadian, Indian, Australian, French and German embassies in Sri Lanka, according to local press reports.

Buddhist view

The fear of alleged foreign involvement to disrupt the country had increased during the civil war which lasted from 1983 to 2009. Buddhist nationalists accused some Christian NGOs of aiding Tamil separatists.[20] In 1991 the Government appointed a commission to enquire into allegations regarding the use of NGO funds detrimental to the Government. Christian organizations, such as the Assemblies of God, were also questioned by the commission. The charismatic Buddhist leader, Gangodawila Soma Thera, often denounced Christian NGOs for "bribing the poor inhabitants" of the country with aid to win them over to the Christian faith.[21] He stated that Christian NGOs, like the colonialists in the past, were resorting to bribing Sinhala Buddhists with material inducements, consistently converting them to Christianity.[22] The allegation was that the ultimate aim is to establish a Christian Government in Sri Lanka.[23] These allegations, however imaginary, created paranoia among the Sinhala Buddhists in the period soon after Soma Thera's death.

---

[20] Tessa J. Bartholomeusz, *In Defense of Dharma: Just War Ideology in Buddhist Sri Lanka* (London: Routledge Curzon, 2002), 88.

[21] Stephen C. Berkwitz, "Recent Trends in Sri Lankan Buddhism" *Religion* 33, no. 1 (2008): 57-71, 92; Gangodawila Soma, *Misaditu Handa*, ed. Indu Perera (Colombo: Dayawansa Jayakody and Company, 2001), 75.

[22] Gangodawila Soma, "Sudda Langa Konda Namu Upasaka Chandalayo" (Self-righteous Outcastes Who Bent Their Bodies Before The White Man), *Janavijaya* (June 2, 2004), 5.

[23] Chamika Munasinghe, ed., *Ape Dharma Katikavatha* (Colombo: Dayavansa Jayakody and Company, 2004), 28.

Threat perception

By way of reacting to this perceived threat, there has been a wave of incidents since the 1980s in various parts of Sri Lanka, mostly led by some militant Buddhists, including monks. They were organized by several associations such as *Vira-Vidana*, Success, *Dharmayatra* and many other small groups. Political parties such as *Sihala Urumaya* (Sinhalese Heritage) and *Jatika Hela Urumaya* (Sinhalese National Heritage) also were active in taking action to restrain the growth of Christianity. Buddhist militia led by *Bodu Bala Sena* ("Buddhist Power Force," BBS) were instrumental in attacking Christian and Muslim religious places of worship in the last decade. The culmination of this was the recent rise of anti-minority movements, often with the clandestine support of powerful leaders of the Government in power, in the 2010s. This has tarnished the image of Buddhism as a peaceful religion.

Religious freedom is taken for granted as a human right in Sri Lanka. Advocacy of religious freedom is not popular. Yet the impracticability of implementing religious freedom in a pluralist society like Sri Lanka is seen in everyday occurrences. There is a real fear that the religious freedom that the nation has in its law books seems to fail to defend the rights of the minorities. For over a million Sri Lankan workers, who have worked in the Islamic states in the Middle East, where adherence to Islam is enforced by the state and non-Muslims are discriminated against, have been influenced by the religious intolerance found in those countries. These workers also have helped to create an intolerant attitude among opinion makers.

Government officers

The Registrar of Companies refused to give legal registration to three Christian organizations during the Rajapaksa regime. They are *Senehase Doratuwa* (Door of love), New Wine Harvest Ministries and Provincial of the Teaching Sisters of the Holy Cross, even though they did not violate any laws of the country.[24] In order to receive legal standing and rights, all religious institutions have

---

[24] Fernando, "Conversion and the Law," 26.

to be incorporated under the Companies Act. When Christian organizations seek to incorporate an institution, with a view to establishing charitable and humanitarian work and receive voluntary funds, they do not intend to violate the laws of the country. Such actions by the Government necessarily violate basic human rights guaranteed by the UN.

CHRISTIANS ARE PRESENTED AS CULPRITS

As mentioned earlier, there is legal provision in the Constitution of Sri Lanka to support the rights of the minorities. However, the exercise and operation of the fundamental rights declared and recognized by Articles 10 and 14 (e) in the Constitution are nullified by clause 14 (4) which states: "The exercise and operation of the fundamental right declared and recognized by article 14 (1) (e) shall be subject to such restrictions as may be prescribed by the law in the interest of racial and religious harmony or national economy." Article 10 of the Constitution grants freedom of religion with provision for the freedom to adopt a religion or belief of one's choice. The word "choice" implies the voluntary adoption of another religion of a person's selection. Article 14 (1) (e) allows every citizen, either by himself or in association with others, to manifest his religion or belief in worship, observance, practice and teaching. The freedom to preach and convert others is subject to restrictions specified in Article 15. There are other restrictions which could be used by the State to limit the exercise of the right to propagate and effect the change of the religious beliefs of others (Article 15 (7)). It could be on the grounds of public order, national security and the protection of public health and morality. In addition, it could be in order to secure due recognition and respect for the rights and freedoms of others and of meeting the just requirements for the general welfare of a democratic society.

This part of the Constitution has been used to restrict the activities of evangelical Christians in many places. The Buddhist militia, with the help of some village riffraff, have come to attack churches. When a complaint is made at the police station, the offending party is normally warned. The Buddhist militia-men do not back down at the police warning but repeat their actions, making it necessary for the Christian pastor to go to the police station several times to make his complaint. This creates the impression that the pastor who makes the complaint repeatedly is the cause of disruption of the peace. As a result, several churches have been asked to wind up their activities, as they are treated as the party disturbing peace and harmony in the village.

Aiding this predicament, two circulars entitled "Building of New Religious Places" were sent by the Secretary of the Ministry of Religious Affairs and Moral Upliftment dated September 10, 2008, and October 16, 2008, addressed to the Inspector General of Police, indicated that no religious building should be permitted without formal authorization of government agencies and that any building set up without permission should be stopped. Copies of the circulars were sent to all relevant departments for action.

When a Christian applies to the Department of Religious Affairs for permission to build a church, the application is first sent to the Provincial Secretariat, next to the Local Government authority, and finally to the village headman. The latter will consult the other religious leaders in the village as to whether to grant permission or not. Villages in Sri Lanka are either predominantly Buddhist, Hindu, Muslim or Roman Catholic. The religious leaders of any of these villages would not be amenable to the setting up of a new church from any denomination different from theirs. The Government that sent this circular is well aware of the difficulties that it would cause to new Christians. However, the impression created is that a democratic procedure is followed. The reply from the village headman would go in this manner to the Ministry of Religious Affairs, which could use it if there are any objections to the restriction of the building of new churches. In fact the permission of the Ministry of Buddha Sasana is needed even to set up a religious symbol. These rules and regulations still remain.

The Government of Sri Lanka launched a special police unit in April 2014 to address "rising religious tensions between Christians, Muslims and the Buddhist majority." The new department was to work under the Ministry of Buddha Sasana and Religious Affairs. Yet Christians and Muslims continued to report rising instances of attacks by Buddhist extremists.[25] Although the Constitution says

[25] "Sri Lanka launches police team to tackle religious disputes," April 28,

that there is freedom of religious belief, the Buddhists have used other clauses of the same Constitution to restrict religious freedom.

Violence

The Constitution and the laws of Sri Lanka, as well as international agreements that successive Sri Lankan Governments have signed, grant legally enforceable rights to those whose religious freedom is injured. However, news reports in Sri Lanka repeat stories of conflicts which show that these injunctions are not followed to the letter of the law.

There are instances where local authorities fail to respond effectively to the attacks on members of minority religious groups. Sporadic violent attacks on Christian churches by Buddhists and some societal tension due to ongoing allegations of forced or "unethical" conversions continue. The police are expected to provide protection for minority groups under harassment, but in some cases local police officials are reluctant to take legal action against individuals involved in these attacks. Incidents of the destruction of places of worship by Buddhist monks have aggravated religious tensions. Since 2013 the Sinhala Buddhist group *Bodu Bala Sena* (BBS)[26] has become active in organizing violent attacks on minority religious groups. In most cases the police have not been helpful in stopping violence against Christians and Muslims.

The number and scale of attacks became reportedly fewer since the change of the presidency in January 2015. The United States Commission on International Religious Freedom has announced that abuses against religious minorities have diminished since M. Sirisena became President. However, there are continued reports of sporadic attacks on minority religious groups backed by the Buddhist lobby. According to the NCEASL in the year 2016 there were 7 churches in several places in the country, which have been

---

2014, accessed on August 16, 2017, http://www.ucanews.com/news/sri-lanka-launches-police-team-to-tackle-religious-disputes/70806.

[26] The *Bodu Bala Sena* (Buddhist Power Force) which contested the national elections held on the August 17, 2015 under the name *Bodu Jana Seva* (Service for Buddhist People) did not even receive a total vote of .01 percent in the country.

forbidden to build their churches and told to discontinue their worship services by the government authorities.

Societal abuse

Incidents such as the destruction of places of worship by Buddhist monks have exacerbated religious tensions. Although the Government publicly endorses religious freedom, there were reports of covert abuses of religious freedom by the governing party before 2015. Many evangelical Christian groups have reported incidents of discrimination in the provision of services by governmental authorities. Authorities have been reluctant to investigate or prosecute those who are responsible for attacks on churches. Evangelical Christian denominations have often encountered harassment and physical attacks on property and places of worship by local Buddhists, led by monks who were opposed to conversion. These disturbances have not been confined to gatherings for religious worship. There are reports of disruption of life cycle rituals such as burial, wedding and baptism, as well as house visits of pastors and other gatherings.

Several smaller congregations were denied permission to register with the Ministry of Buddha Sasana and Religious Affairs as churches during the year 2012, reportedly because they were not members of the National Christian Council (NCC). This prevented them from obtaining authority to solemnize marriages. The National Christian Council, an umbrella organization representing "traditional" Protestant churches, coordinated action relating to the safety of Christians, often with the National Christian Evangelical Alliance of Sri Lanka (NCEASL), which represents the newer denominational churches. The Government reportedly used membership of the NCC as an administrative obstacle to give attention to newer denominations. Local authorities sometimes did not want these evangelical groups operating in their districts, and made use of allegations of so-called "unethical" conversions, and pressure by local Buddhist groups.

Noise factor

Government authorities have described these attacks on churches as random incidents and blame evangelicals for the harsh reaction of the neighbourhood, who are provoked by the noisy congregations. It is a local neighbourhood reacting to what it considers as a disturbance.[27] However, the fact of the matter is that the Government's lax attitude, evident in the statements made by its key interlocutors, tends to embolden the Buddhist zealots and foster further attacks. The absence of convictions itself fosters a climate of impunity which begets further attacks. Christians continue to be monitored and threatened by Buddhist monks, sometimes accompanied by mobs.[28] However, the noise factor at evangelical worship services has been a cause of irritation to the public. Many churches make it a point to acquire drum-sets and electric guitars. Their music is amplified with the help of a public address system, even though the number of believers gathered for worship may be less than twenty.

Religious education

All schools in Sri Lanka follow the Department of Education curricula on the subjects offered at General Certificate of Education (Ordinary Level) classes. Religion is a compulsory subject in the core curriculum in the public schools. Children are allowed to choose to study Buddhism, Islam, Hinduism, or Christianity. Students who find that their religion is not taught in the school are allowed to pursue religious instruction outside the public school system. Religion is obligatory for the GCE O/L exams. Many government schools with small numbers of Christian students have been hampered by the absence of teachers available to teach Christianity in classes. Therefore many Christian children have been required to attend the Buddhist religion classes. The difficulty

---

[27] Michael Roberts, "Noise as Cultural Struggle: Tom-Tom Beating, the British and Communal Disturbances in Sri Lanka, 1880s-1930s," in *Mirrors of Violence: Communities, Riots, Survivors in South Asia*, ed. Veena Das (Delhi: Oxford University Press, 1990), 240-85.

[28] https://www.opendoorsusa.org/christian-persecution/world-watch-list/sri-lanka/.

of Christian children is that these classes are not confined to the teaching of theory. The children are expected to take part in Buddhist ceremonies conducted in the school. There are also reports of government schools refusing to enrol Christians on the basis of their religion. Although the law makes it necessary for all children from the age of 6 to 14 to attend school and that the child should be given admittance to the nearest school to the child's home, this is overlooked by some principals of schools with impunity. The children of new converts have been harassed by their teachers of Buddhism, who are often Buddhist monks. In June 2014, it was reported that a 14-year-old Catholic student attending a Buddhist school was beaten by his teacher, a Buddhist monk, in the Kandy district.[29] During a Buddhism class, the boy was called upon and questioned on Buddhist history by the monk teacher. In response to the boy's lack of knowledge of Buddhism, the monk reportedly struck him. The boy was subsequently hospitalized for four days. The father filed a complaint with the police, but the authorities had not begun any action even by the end of the year. The normal pattern for parents as well as the students is to accept these abuses because of the possibility of further jeopardizing their education in schools.

The fact that there are one or two students seeking Christianity for O/L classes means that there are Christian congregations in the area. One cannot expect the Government Department of Education to set aside a teacher for one or two students. If such a teacher is appointed, that teacher would not have the required number of periods of teaching in the time table. In fact teachers who were trained for teaching Christianity have opted to teach other subjects in many schools because of the inadequate number of Christian pupils. It is unfair to expect the Government to provide a separate teacher for one or two students. Therefore the churches have been allowed to teach and evaluate the syllabus in their own Christian Sunday schools and to send the marks to the Department of Education, which would be counted as valid for assessing school term tests. However, very few churches have made use of this option.

Protestant Christian churches have not come out with a plan for teaching Christianity to school children even half a century

---

[29] This is only an example. These kind of incidents are too numerous to list.

after the nationalization of Christian schools. They have been given permission by the Government to provide Christianity classes in their own churches. Therefore one cannot blame the Government completely for the neglect of teaching Christianity to Christian children.

Christian Use of Anti-Conversion Act

Some Christian groups with international connections have made much use of the incidents of sporadic attacks on churches as a chance to win the sympathy of foreign supporters to raise funds. According to Open Doors International, NCEASL documented 45 incidents of religious persecution between January and May 2013, a steep increase from 2012's total count of 52.[30] Another report of the same organization shows some pictures of people in various areas with the statement, "You can change the lives of persecuted Christians by meeting their greatest needs. Donate today to help make an eternal difference."[31] NCEASL reported that "Sri Lanka saw six cases of religious persecution in the month of June alone, all of which took place in the districts of Hambantota, Batticaloa, Kegalle, and Kalutara." Another group known as "The Christian Consultation of Sri Lanka" based in a suburb of Colombo, stated, "Sri Lanka plans to establish itself as a racially-pure Sinhala-Buddhist country." These and other web publications of the parties interested in raising funds have made full use of international sympathy for minority rights. The so-called grievances of ethnic minorities and religious minorities have been utilized with great finesse in recent years to raise funds. Worse, the funds do not always go to where the need is.

Faults of Christians

Evangelical Christians also have contributed in many ways to create problems for themselves. When there are 10 believers in

---

[30] "Six Incidents of Religious Persecution in Sri Lanka," July 3, 2013, accessed on August 16, 2017, http://dbsjeyaraj.com/dbsj/archives/22349.
[31] http://www.opendoorsusa.org/christian-persecution/world-watch-list/sri-lanka/.

their church, they pretend to show 50. Some of the new evangelical groups have let their zealousness override common sense and discretion. Their bold attitude when proselytizing has led to predictable howls of outrage from Buddhist nationalists.[32] Many evangelicals have conducted themselves conspicuously and with little regard for Buddhist sensibilities. They have destroyed statues of Buddha and denigrated Buddhism in their sermons, churches and home cell meetings. Some of them have been accused of providing people with money, jobs, clothing, food rations, electrical items, access to education in international schools, with the hope of gaining converts. This has led to rumours that the missionaries from these groups have dishonest motives. These tactics have contributed to the attribution of the label of "unethical conversions."

Christian reaction

In 2005, NCEASL requested its Canadian brethren to write letters to the Sri Lankan High Commissioner in Canada and the Canadian Department of Foreign Affairs to protect the country's Christians and prevent the enactment of the Anti-Conversion Bill.[33] It indicated the potential implications of the anti-conversion legislation. It lobbied the United States Congress, American evangelical groups, the European Union and South Korea, on whom the Sri Lankan Government depends for aid. These activities further boosted the view of some Buddhist leaders that the foreign hand is there to undermine the integrity of the nation. Therefore, the JHU went a step further by proposing a constitutional amendment, making Buddhism the state religion in Sri Lanka.

Christian explanation

Christians on the other hand, quoted history to prove the legitimacy of their existence in the country. The existence of a robust Nestorian Christian church from 5th century CE onwards in the ancient kingdom of Anuradhapura is a fact. In addition, Roman

---

[32] Neil DeVotta and Jason Stone, "Jatika Hela Urumaya and Ethno-Religious Politics in Sri Lanka," *Pacific Affairs* 81, no. 1 (2008): 31-51.

[33] *Sunday Times*, July 31, 2005.

Catholic Christianity has been in Sri Lanka for over five hundred years. Protestants have also existed in the country since the 17th century. On the other hand, Buddhists have asserted the Buddhist hegemony of the land by using the ancient chronicles. However, these arguments from history are of no help to counter the perceived grievances of both sides.

Conclusion

Respect for another person's beliefs is one of the hallmarks of a civilized society.[34] As mentioned in this paper, most persecution and hindrance to religious freedom has come from the Buddhist majority. The Buddha's teaching that Theravada Buddhists profess to follow clearly says that "it is not for religion to compel which is to be taken up voluntarily nor undertaken under duress."[35] Buddhist militants seem to have disregarded this well-known teaching of the Buddha.

Freedom of religion is a major triumph of democratic society. There is a need to respect the diverse opinions and beliefs that guide the conscience and give direction to the lives of all members of society. In a democracy, every citizen has certain internationally recognized basic rights that the state cannot take away from them. "Everyone has the right to have their own beliefs, including their religious beliefs, and to say and write what they think." However, in Sri Lanka, the issue of conversion is far from a strictly personal affair. It has become intensely politicized to the benefit of the majority who control the democratically elected Parliament.

Conversions modify socio-religious boundaries and the make-up of religious communities, causing the transfer of one's allegiance to a different group. The problem is the balance between the protection of local cultural traditions and norms and the protection of the rights of religious minorities to practise their faith, without the interference of the state to limit their activities. The globalization which Sri Lanka in undergoing now is more than an economic

---

[34] Ian Leigh and Rex Ahdar, *Religious Freedom in the Liberal State*, (Oxford: Oxford University Press, 2013), 1.

[35] *Kalama Sutta: The Buddha's Charter of Free Inquiry*, trans. Soma Thera (Kandy: Buddhist Publication Society, 1981), 2.

movement. The open economy is not only competitive in the economic sphere but even in the religious and cultural spheres as well. In Darwinian terms, it is the survival of the fittest. Buddhism or any other religion cannot create for itself an artificial hedge of protection.

Populism and democracy are two concepts that are found in the field of political science. Although these two appear to be similar on the surface, researchers have indicated that populism often can be antithetical to true democracy. Populist politicians have emerged in Sri Lanka with promises of working for the people in opposition to a perceived group of opponents. They have used democratic institutions for personal benefits in the garb of helping certain groups gain a majority of votes. History shows that Sri Lankan populist leaders have used the ideals of democracy to rouse the masses with rhetoric to gain the popular vote. The populist leaders have acquired more and more power and have subverted the very tools of democracy, such as elections, to consolidate their authority and eliminate dissenting voices. This has led to ethnic and religious intolerance and violence against those seen as outsiders by the major citizenry. Bandaranaike used populist rhetoric with the promise to make Sinhala the only national language ("Sinhala only") in 1956, thereby distancing the minority groups. In the sixties, Christians were reduced to a state of a beleaguered minority when most of their avenues of social influence were removed. The Constitution of 1972 modified the clause that guaranteed minority rights in the Soulbury Constitution. The Constitution of 1978 increased the power of one man who holds the executive presidency. Attempts to bring in legislation to prevent conversions from one religion to another can be one more effort in that direction. Judging from the behaviour of the populist leaders in Sri Lanka, using democracy to gain votes by any means available, they would always find scapegoats in minorities like Christians, who are unable to react effectively in a threatening situation caused by the majority.

Bollywood Spirituality and Audience Desires: Exploring the Theme of Religion and Conversion Through a Study of Popular Hindi Films

Nigel Ajay Kumar[1]

INTRODUCTION

In the 1994 box office hit *Krantiveer*, there is a scene where communal tensions break out in a *basti*. The central hero, Pratab (played by Nana Patekar), confronts a Muslim man who is angry with Hindus for killing his family. Pratab smashes his own finger with a stone and does the same to the Muslim man, mixes the dripping blood onto his palm, and asks, "Now tell, which blood is Hindu and which blood is Muslim? If the Heavenly Maker did not differentiate between Hindu and Muslim, then who are you to differentiate between the two?" Hearing that, the Muslim man relents and apologizes for being led astray. Of course no one told the scriptwriters that in all likelihood there would be differences in their blood group, and certainly in their DNA. But that logic did not stop the film from becoming a huge success, winning the Filmfare and National Awards, and even being granted "Tax free" status in many parts of India for its message of communal harmony.[2]

Rather than critique the obvious lack of coherence or liberal use of sentimentality in such films, a recent scholarly trend has been to appreciate the uniqueness and value of Bollywood[3] films.[4] This

[1] Dr. Nigel Ajay Kumar teaches Theology at SAIACS. He is the author of *What is Religion?: A Theological Answer* (Pickwick, 2012; SAIACS Press, 2013).
[2] A tax free status is given to a film that helps towards nation building, urging Hindus and Muslims to be united.
[3] While the word "Bollywood" is often spoken of in a condescending or dismissive manner, in this article the word "Bollywood" is used as a shorthand for the Mumbai-based film industry that produces popular films. Similarly, I use the word "movies" as synonymous with "popular cinema."
[4] A few examples being, Vamsee Juluri, *Bollywood Nation: India Through its Cinema* (New Delhi: Penguin, 2013); Ajay Gehlawat, *Reframing Bollywood: Theories of Popular Hindi Cinema* (New Delhi: SAGE India, 2010); Vinay Lal

move is related to the recognition that popular culture is a useful tool to understand culture.[5] It is acknowledged that popular Indian cinema gives us a window into Indian culture in a way that is a necessary corollary to other typical ways to understand the Indian mind.[6]

Several scholars approach popular Indian cinema as a "contemporary political document"[7] as they prioritize the "ideological dimension of film form" to explain its affirmation of traditional authority or promote its subversion.[8] In contrast, there are Indian film theorists who adopt the position of a "fan" and revel in a subjective vision of India that a Hindi movie audience provides.[9] Others take a more descriptive approach and focus on the history, form and structure of Indian cinema, highlighting how the industry and the unique Indian way of expressing itself has for instance the "ability to withstand change and adapt to it."[10] Whether we adopt a textual (focus on the film), ideological/historical (focus on the message) or a viewer/reader orientation (focus on the audience), the need to examine Hindi movies to better understand India is warranted. Dwyer correctly asserts that Indian cinema offers "the most reliable

and Ashis Nandy, eds., *Fingerprinting Popular Culture: The Mythic and the Iconic in Indian Cinema* (New Delhi: Oxford, 2006); and Ravi S. Vasudevan, ed., *Making Meaning in Indian Cinema* (New Delhi: Oxford, 2000).

[5] For a discussion of the value of popular culture for understanding (religious) society, see the various essays in Gordon Lynch, ed., *Between Sacred and Profane: Researching Religion and Popular Culture* (London: I. B. Tauris, 2007).

[6] For instance, Lal and Nandy suggest that social sciences are limited in explaining "public sentiments" especially in the midst of the battleground between traditional and modern, global and local, myth and fantasy. Lal and Nandy, "Introduction" in *Fingerprinting Popular Culture*, xxiv. See also M. Madhava Prasad, *Ideology of the Hindi Film: A Historical Construction* (New Delhi: Oxford India Paperbacks, 2013). Prasad makes the point that the need to focus on cinema is not merely an occasional addition to the traditional fields of anthropology, sociology etc, but rather the study of cinema can "only be ignored at the risk of a serious misreading of its cultural significance." Prasad, *Ideology of the Hindi Film*, vii.

[7] Vasudevan, "Introduction," in *Making Meaning*, 2.

[8] Vasudevan, "Introduction," 23.

[9] Juluri, *Bollywood Nation*, 5.

[10] See Mihir Bose, *Bollywood: A History* (New Delhi: Lotus Collection, 2006), 362.

guide to understanding the nation's dreams and hopes, fears and anxieties," especially by providing a glimpse of how the "escapism and entertainment" of Bollywood functions to help Indians "think about life and the world."[11]

In view of the possibility that popular cinema helps in the better understanding of India, my current investigation into popular Hindi cinema is not an end in itself.[12] I assert an impossible-to-prove statement: the average middle-class, middle-caste, urban, Hindi-speaking Indian is against religious conversion.[13] To justify this, I use popular Indian Hindi cinema. I am motivated by the view that Christians, arguing for religious freedom and conversion in India, need to be aware of the battleground for ideas which takes place not just in legal courts or government buildings, or even in theological forums, but also in and through popular media. My thesis is that, to establish a workable proposal for religious freedom and conversion in the Indian context, we need to be mindful, perhaps more mindful than we have been, about how (we) Indians think about religion and conversion as expressed in what we choose to watch most. To establish this thesis, I adopt an ideological approach to Indian cinema, but one that takes into account the reader's participation in the process of constructing ideology. I then look at some (recent) popular Hindi films as a case study to show how this connection plays out on the theme of religion and conversion. Finally, these observations lead to a preliminary proposal for an alternative engagement with the topic of religious conversion in India.

---

[11] Rachel Dwyer, *Picture Abhi Baaki Hai: Bollywood as a Guide to Modern India* (Gurgaon: Hachette, 2014), 7.

[12] I admit that Indian television has an equal or possibly a greater impact on popular Indian culture, but a study of television programming is currently outside the scope of this paper.

[13] I put the qualifiers because I understand that popular cinema aims at the universal middle and tends to miss out on the large subaltern base that is either a victim of its projection, or excluded from its thought. Several subaltern studies have emerged, though Gehlawat provides helpful insights to the question of subalterns and Bollywood in his chapter 3, "Can the Bollywood Film Speak to the Subaltern?" Gehlawat, *Reframing Bollywood*, 53-83.

Approaching Popular Cinema as Maker-Audience Participation

There is a sense where cinema is a "transcultural phenomena," having a "capacity to transcend 'culture'... and engage audiences in ways independent of their linguistic and cultural specificities."[14] Nevertheless, when approaching Indian cinema, we must also be attentive to Indian film theorists who clarify that Indian cinema is not in some evolutionary stage of universal cinema, as if to suggest that it is lagging behind. Which is to say, Indian cinema is unique and should not be assessed in terms of some Western or Eurocentric standard of what makes a film good. For instance, celebrated French film critic Jean Mitry urges that, among other things, for cinema to be considered authentic cinema it must be explored within its own cinematic language and not be enthralled by the styles of over-expressionism, abstraction or even theatre.[15] Indian popular cinema in contrast has been known for its reliance on theatre, and seems to be rooted in over expressionism. In speaking of an Indian aesthetic, Shohat and Stam point to the lasting influence of the unique 2000-year tradition of theatre in the Indian region that "tells of the myths of Hindu culture through an esthetic [sic] based less on coherent character and linear plot than on subtle modulations of mood and feeling (rasa)."[16] For Gehlawat, Bollywood films are a "hybrid art form" that blend "theatrical and cinematic elements as well as First World and Third World cinema methodologies" to create an assortment of musicals and melodrama, to create a *masala* that "has previously been belittled in the theorization of Bollywood."[17] Indian movies are unique and deserve to be seen in their own terms.

However, when it comes to popular cinema, there are also certain transcultural similarities. In terms of the relation between popular cinema and culture, there are two dominant ways a movie

[14] Rey Chow, "Film and Cultural Identity," in *The Oxford Guide to Film Studies*, eds. John Hill and Pamela Church Gibson (New York: Oxford University Press, 1998), 169-175.

[15] See chapter 7, "Jean Mitry," in *The Major Film Theories: An Introduction*, ed. J. Dudley Andrew (New Delhi: Oxford, 2008), 205-206.

[16] Ella Shohat and Robert Stam, *Unthinking Eurocentrism: Multiculturalism and the Media* (London: Routledge, 1994), 295.

[17] Gehlawat, *Reframing Bollywood*, xiii.

functions in society. The first is to emphasize the effect popular cinema has to shape culture. The second is to see how culture shapes popular cinema. In either case, the audience has a role to play, either as the spectator or as an active participant who is more than a spectator.

In discussing the cross-cultural film-making process in Hollywood, James Morrison offers how popular movies have "parallel aims and aspirations...as social and economic institutions."[18] Morrison notes how such films elicit "cinematic pleasure" which results in "self-generation" of economic activity, where the audience buys tickets so that more such films can be made.[19] To ensure the smooth functioning of this structure, Morrison adds that the film industry produces "regulatory mechanisms to render their products not only recognizable but desirable" by making them follow popular identifiable forms/styles, coupled with mammoth marketing campaigns.[20] For Morrison, this regulation is not simply economic but also social, in that the industry shapes culture towards having a "large-scale aesthetic desires, mass fantasies, widely accessible mythologies."[21]

In the Indian context, Prasad highlights the economic relation between the Mumbai film industry and its ideology, arguing that film-makers in India are not interested in "narrative coherence."[22] Nevertheless a certain homogeneity in Hindi films is achieved through several formulaic aspects of film-making that must be included, such as movie-stars, music, locations, to guarantee economic results across the country.[23] Evidently, here the audience functions only as consumer (spectator), while the ideological constructions occur behind the film production process.

Nevertheless, certain film theorists argue that the audience, especially the Hindi movie audience, is not entirely passive. There is an aspect where the audience constructs its own identity in viewing

---

[18] James Morrison, *Passport to Hollywood: Hollywood Films, European Directors* (Albany: State University of New York Press, 1998), 6.
[19] Morrison, *Passport to Hollywood*, 6.
[20] Morrison, *Passport to Hollywood*, 6.
[21] Morrison, *Passport to Hollywood*, 6.
[22] Prasad, *Ideology of the Hindi Film*, 29-51.
[23] Prasad, *Ideology of the Hindi Film*, 42–45.

popular cinema, and in turn the film-makers match the adapted realities of audience to stay viable economically.[24]

In popular Indian cinema, it is readily acknowledged that the movie-watching public gets what it wants; demand determines the supply. To illustrate this, one can point to how Bollywood superstar Salman Khan often asks for script re-writes if he feels that his audience will not relate to it.[25] For instance, he asked the scriptwriters of the 2012 superhit *Ek Tha Tiger*, to change the scene of him running after the a "group of villains" to them coming to him. Reason: "since his fans would not like to see him chasing the bad guys."[26] More recently, Salman Khan rejected celebrated author Chetan Bhagat's first draft for his 2014 movie *Kick*, because it was not "commercial" enough.[27] If we can extend this to general *movie*-making, the makers of popular cinema must always be mindful of what the larger audience wants, and aim to give it to them.[28]

Dasgupta explains the role of the audience by bringing together the concepts of the "master narrative" (of cinema) with the "self-construction of individuals."[29] Dasgupta asserts that while

[24] For instance, see E. Deidre Pribram, "Spectatorship and Subjectivity," in *A Companion to Film Theory*, eds. Toby Miller and Robert Stam (Blackwell Publishing, 2004), 146-164. In that chapter, Miller and Stam show three dominant ways of viewing the audience, ending with the proposal to bring the audience to the forefront of culture analysis.

[25] Some of the sources for this point come from various gossip-oriented news magazines and internet portals, their lack of academic credibility, being understood. However, what is noteworthy is that assuming, as is often the case with superstars, that any reporting of the news is approved by the Star's PR team, Salman Khan most likely wants his fans (and the larger community) to know that he re-writes the scripts keeping them in mind.

[26] Smitha, "Salman Khan changes the Script of Kabir Khan's *Ek Tha Tiger*," *FilmiBeat*, February 13, 2012.

[27] Which is to say, it would not appeal to his fan-base and make the money that usually his movies would make. Mehul S Thakkar, "Salman Khan Rejects Chetan Bhagat's Script," *Mumbai Mirror.* March 14, 2013.

[28] We see this even in Hollywood, that often makes movies that aspire to be blockbusters not just thinking of the Domestic US audience but also the International and particularly Chinese audiences. Billion dollar earner *Transformers 4: Age of Extinction* being a case in point, where a third of the movie takes place in China.

[29] Probal Dasgupta, "Popular Cinema, India, and Fantasy," in *Fingerprinting*, eds. Lal and Nandy, 4.

"popular cinema holds the key to the self-world equation in our times," which is to say that the "master narrative" exerts influence on the "self-construction," the audience is not a mere spectator.[30] The audience of popular cinema is constantly aware of the "performed nature of the spectacle" so that "you know you are not seeing reality, and the way your complicity is elicited ensures that you know that the spectacle appeals to you by bringing your fantasies and desires directly into play."[31] Thus, in agreeing to participate in the fantasy, the audience wilfully enters its own fantasies and imagined selves.[32]

Sudhir Kakar, while stating that he intends no value judgement, provides what initially reads like a scathing critique of the psyche of the Indian audience. Taking on the concept of fantasy in Hindi cinema, Kakar calls it adult daydreaming, and goes on to hypothesize that Indians, more than other cultures, are closer to the "child's world of magic" providing, through the cinema, a "regressive haven for a vast number of our people."[33] Whatever our view of this position may be, Kakar makes the important point that Indian movie audiences are participant in the movie making project: "I regard the Indian cinema audience not only as the reader but also as the real author of the text of Hindi films."[34] For Kakar, the visible creators, like the directors or scriptwriters are "purely instrumental and akin to that of a publisher who chooses, edits, and publishes a particular text from a number of submitted manuscripts."[35] Kakar notes that,

> The quest for the comforting sound of busy cash registers at the box office ensures that the filmmakers select and develop a daydream which is not idiosyncratic. They must intuitively appeal to those concerns of the audience which are shared; if they do not, the film's appeal is bound to be disastrously limited. As with pornography, the filmmakers

---

[30] Dasgupta, "Popular Cinema, India, and Fantasy," 9.
[31] Dasgupta, "Popular Cinema, India, and Fantasy," 13.
[32] Dasgupta, "Popular Cinema, India, and Fantasy," 21–22.
[33] Sudhir Kakar, *Intimate Relations: Exploring Indian Sexuality* (New Delhi: Penguin India, 1989), 28.
[34] Kakar, *Intimate Relations*, 28.
[35] Kakar, *Intimate Relations*, 28.

> have to create a work which is singular enough to fascinate and excite, and general enough to excite many...the filmmakers repeat and vary the daydreams as they seek to develop them into more and more nourishing substitutes for reality.[36]

Yet Kakar's intention is not to diminish the importance of fantasy even as he posits a connection between fantasy and wish fulfilment. For Kakar, fantasies are not escapes from reality, rather they are journeys into another layer of reality, namely psychological reality.[37] In that sense, "the Hindi film demonstrates a confident and sure-footed grasp of the topography of desire."[38] The film stories "beneath the surface...add surprising twists to the conscious social understanding of various human relationships in the culture."[39]

Rachel Dwyer says something similar, albeit more sympathetically. She elucidates on how popular Hindi cinema represents the aspirations of the viewing public. For Dwyer, Hindi cinema provides "a way of understanding how some of contemporary India's people see themselves and their country's changing culture through the narratives, images and music of the films."[40] Yet that is not all because the removal of realism in Hindi cinema, in favour of heightened fantasy, aids in the creation of "imaginary worlds which allow ways of reflecting on how the new India could or should be."[41]

Dominant Themes of Indian Cinema

While audience research for popular Indian cinema is limited—and so none of the above statements by film theorists about Indian culture are proved beyond certainty—it remains crucial. Understanding popular cinema not only helps us see how the audience interacts with the filmic fantasy, or how the filmmakers adapt their "products" to suit public consciousness, but we potentially gain insight into who the watchers are by identifying the beliefs, values

[36] Kakar, *Intimate Relations*, 28–29.
[37] Kakar, *Intimate Relations*, 30.
[38] Kakar, *Intimate Relations*, 30.
[39] Kakar, *Intimate Relations*, 30.
[40] Dwyer, *Picture Abhi Baaki Hai*, 255.
[41] Dwyer, *Picture Abhi Baaki Hai*, 255.

and desires that they deem important. Scholars of popular cinema thus arrive at a sense of how Indians think, by identifying prominent themes in such films to form an ideological link between the movies and the society for which they are made. The more popular a theme, the deeper the connection with what the audience generally accepts. The presupposition is that for popular movies, people watch what they want to watch, and so the film's ideology will not be too opposed to general sentiment.

Juluri identifies four significant themes that govern Bollywood cinema: God, country, home and world. Dwyer adds cultural diversity and emotions to that list. Certainly "country" or "nationhood" is one of the biggest themes that have been explored through the history of cinema in India; from nationalist inclinations to the more recent fascination with displaced (read, NRI) identity.[42] It reflects the audience who continue to be fascinated and/or conflicted by what constitutes "India" in the midst of its colonial history and also its current diversity. "Family" or "home" too make the list of significant themes as several films, especially in the 1980s, feature domestic issues as the central space for conflict and resolve. A related, and significant sub-theme, is romance, where the lead up to marriage is the obsession of hundreds of plots. A more recent development allows for films to explore love, after and within marriage.[43] However, arguably, one of the most significant themes of Indian cinema, is God,[44] or religion, and to that we now turn.

THREE CASE STUDIES: *OMG–OH MY GOD*, *PK* AND *DHARAM SANKAT MEIN*

In this section of the paper, we explore the religious ideologies that govern the making and watching of popular cinema, examining three recent popular Indian films that explicitly address religion, to show that their vision is not simply a reflection of the film-maker's

---

[42] Of the several examples, *Swades* makes the issue of Indian identity for a non-residential Indian (NRI) one of its central themes.

[43] Films like *Chalte Chalte*, *Rab Ne Bana Di Jodi*, and *Vivah*.

[44] Juluri calls God "the single biggest concern for Indian cinema." Juluri, *Bollywood Nation*, 15.

ideology, but also the expression of the voice of the movie-watching audience that prefers these narratives.

OMG–Oh My God (2012)

OMG – Oh My God tells the story of man, Kanji Bhai (Paresh Rawal), who cannot get an insurance claim because the earthquake that destroyed his shop is deemed an "act of God." So, he sues God for his loss, or, as depicted in the movie, God's "collection agents." Most of the film features the trial where God (and his representatives) are put on trial. The twist comes when God as Krishna (Akshay Kumar), comes to Kanji disguised as a human and befriends him. At the trial, Kanji proves that God is the cause of all natural calamities, but as he disavows God in public, he goes into a coma. After a month, he is healed by Krishna, and Kanji realizes that God truly exists.

A key dialogue in the film takes place as Krishna (Akshay Kumar) reveals how he dislikes "exchange offer" religiosity. What Krishna wants is belief and devotion. Krishna even states that he only made humans, but humans made religion. Kanji then comes to know that while he was in a coma, Kanji is now proclaimed to be a god, and idols and temples (and a new religious empire) have been built around his name. Kanji realizes that he himself must break this idolatry.

As he goes to destroy the temple built to honour him, he tells the people (who quietly and patiently listen while rousing music plays in the background) that God does not live in temples, but lives in our hearts. The God-figure, Krishna, nods in the background. Eventually as the main exploiter of religion is defeated and leaves, he tells Kanji that he is not finished and soon another *ashram* will sprout up because the people are not "God-loving," they are "God-fearing." The film ends with a quote from the Gita, asking the readers not to fear.

It must be noted that *OMG* makes critical remarks about religion, but never fully moves away from religion. It relies on several quotations of the Gita, urging true readings that get the correct interpretation. There are also several places, but especially in the end, where religious music is interloped with the final anti-religious point. The audience, while being told that only faith is needed, are also given a picture of a "real" God who is there, but not contained in a human form, a common Hindu belief.

Similarly, at no point is *OMG* giving the movie watcher a radically new message. In fact, it only reinforces previously held cultural beliefs that spirituality is more important than temple or ceremonial worship.[45] There are parallels with the popular Bhakti religious traditions, which do not destroy religion, but find deeper meaning within it. Yet the way the film is made, it is evident that the audience is in on the "joke." While they are taken along in the narrative, they are not being told something counter-cultural, but they are being told something that many Indians would naturally believe. The message sounds counter-cultural, but it is very much within the cultural norm in India.

PK (2014)

PK tells the story of an alien (Aamir Khan), who is called PK on earth because he acts so strange that people think he is drunk, "*peekay.*" PK comes to earth on an exploratory mission, looking like a human but naked. He has a device that helps him return back to his home planet. However, that device is stolen and someone tells him that only God can help him find what he desires. So PK goes in search for God, so God can help him find his lost device. To find God, PK goes to the various religious institutions on earth, including temples, mosques and churches.

After an intense search, he comes to realize that the religious institutions have got it all wrong and their prayers are not being answered, because they are dialling the "wrong number" of God. In a key moment in the film, after a (providential) news programme that allows PK to state his views, the *masses* join in their protest against the "wrong numbers" of various religious institutions. It is a "wrong number" they say, when the way an institution says is the way to reach God, does not seem to be the right way.

Similarly, the theme of nakedness plays a significant role throughout the movie. PK's point is that religions are like garments

---

[45] This article began with an example of *Krantiveer*, which two decades ago made a similar point, that true religion is not limited to that which can be seen.

that you can wear or change, regardless of what you like. However, the essential person, as created by God, remains the same. God, PK reveals, does not make a person a Hindu or Muslim or Christian when humans are born. These labels, or clothes, are put on the "newborn baby" and given priority.

Finally, PK finds his device and returns to his own home with happy (and sad) memories of the planet.

PK, like *OMG*, plays it safe by being most critical of Hindu *guru*s, rather than Hinduism, or Islam itself. In the social situation of India, where anger against religious misrepresentation can lead to riots, the media is expected to be responsible and non-inflammatory. *PK* thus even begins with a verbal disclaimer, as well as a written disclaimer in three languages, that there is no ill-feeling meant towards any religion. The decision to be critical of Hindu *guru*s, rather than Hinduism, toes the line of the critique of those who interpret the truth, or institutionalize truth, while the truth remains pure.

Like *OMG*, *PK* stays within the religious framework while critiquing religion. The "truth" that God exists, is never questioned. Similarly the music, especially the *"Bhagwan hai kahan re tu"* song, is very much within the search-for-God theme as expressed through Bhakti and even Sufi traditions.

Furthermore, also like *OMG*, *PK* does not say anything new theologically. As a film, it is unique in its plotline, but in its message about God, it stays true to the popular Hindu tradition that asserts that all gods are essentially the same; there is only one God though there are many expressions of him. This message, as we can see, is largely palatable to the target audience and the audience is in on the critique, agreeing with PK's critique of abuse of religion.

Dharam Sankat Mein (2015)

More recently, *Dharam Sankat Mein* follows similar messaging, with a unique plotline. Dharam Pal (Paresh Rawal) is a secular Hindu. As a typical secular Hindu, he is critical of Muslims and makes derogatory statements about them, including of his Muslim neighbour. Also at this time, his son, who wants to marry the daughter of a devotee of a Hindu *guru*, wants Dharam Pal to become more visibly religious so that his future father-in-law will approve of the marriage. During this, Dharam Pal comes to realize that he was adopted, but not just that, he had been born to Muslim parents. When tracing his Muslim father, who it is revealed had lost his child in difficult circumstances, he finds him on his deathbed, longing for his lost son. However, the Muslim *mullah* does not allow him to see his father because he is a Hindu and insists that he must learn to look like a Muslim in front of his religious Muslim father, because otherwise his father would be hurt to see that his son is still (spiritually) lost.

This leads Dharam Pal to go through the motions of learning about Hinduism and Islam, and humorous scenes of ways of worship, ways of speaking, and ways of praying are compared side by side, obviously as a critique of the outwardly differences of religions, who seem, at the end of it, to be doing the same thing.

Desperate to meet his father and frustrated by his lack of progress, Dharam Pal pretends to be a Muslim and enters the mosque disguised as a Muslim. In doing so, he is caught by a Hindu mob, and so Dharam Pal, forced to prove that he is a Hindu, burns the Muslim cap he was wearing in public. That is revealed to the Muslims, who file a court case against him for disrupting religious sentiments. Dharam Pal's Muslim neighbour comes to his rescue and defends him.

At that time, when it is discovered that Dharam Pal is actually a Muslim by birth, the Hindu *guru* denounces the wedding of Dharam Pal's son because there is non-Hindu blood in his lineage.

Dharam Pal's father dies without seeing his son in person, though he does get to see his photo (dressed as a Muslim) before he passes away, we assume, in peace. Dharam Pal gets to be one of the pall-bearers during his father's funeral.

Dharam Pal then confronts the *guru* in his *ashram* (providentially no one attacks him or calls the security to stop him), by asking whether he ceases to exist as himself, be he a Muslim or a Hindu? But since that logic is not enough, he reveals that the *guru* before him is actually a Sikh by birth, and a famous singer who was caught trafficking women but escaped prison by creating a new identity. The masses following the *guru* denounce him, and the marriage can now finally take place.

Unlike *OMG* and *PK*, *Dharam Sankat Mein* was not a commercial success. However, it is included here because like popular cinema, it attempts to give the audience what it wants, and is thus an example of film-makers trying to cash-in on the audience's desire for films that critique religion. It did not succeed commercially, and yet, it is part of the collective popular cultural voice that represents the people and also influences the people.

In *Dharam Sankat Mein*, there is a much more direct attack against conversion, where the Muslim neighbour, who happens also to be a lawyer, challenges the Muslim *mullah* who filed the case, by threatening to counter-sue him for trying to convert *Dharam*. In that scene, rather than focus on the case at hand, or even argue that conversion has positive value, the *mullah* backs down in fear and says that he was not trying to convert. Similarly, in the final scene of the movie, Dharam Pal's daughter introduces him to her (boy) friend "Peter," an obvious reference to a Christian, and the film ends with the father telling his daughter and Peter not to tell him to go to church or light candles. The depiction clearly suggests that conversion is wrong or unnecessary. Once again, this message is familiar to the Indian movie-watching public, who would have heard this message over and over again in their movie-watching history.

Case study results

Some could argue from these movies, the first two being highly successful, that film-makers are reflecting an ideology, influenced by Brahminism or the Vedas, that is being ideologically forced onto the people. However, in view of the theoretical discussions before, it is unfair to suggest that Indian movie watchers are simply passive. They are constructing their own identities, participating in the narratives, and also determining the output, partly because economics mandate the kinds of movies the general public wants to see, but also because the desires to see a certain kind of film are shaped by ideological self-constructions and social aspirations. Considering that none of the above films are "art" cinema,[46] it is safe to assume that some audience preferences would have been sought

---

[46] The films that need not consider the "audience" but are made almost purely from the director's creative vision.

while planning the films. The message depicted is not simply the film-makers' vision, but is also a regulated voice that the audience and society want to hear. Further, while in reality, a Hindu or Muslim may not even practise the message of the film, the popular films represent the "aspired" belief of the people, something like a preferred reality that is closer to fantasy, where the reader desires to dwell in.

One wonders: if India was a Muslim dominant nation, what our popular ideological cinematic preferences might be? However, being a Hindu dominated nation, it is natural, and to be expected, that the dominant cinematic voice, as determined by the culture, will be pluralistic. To state it more systematically, assuming that popular ideologies are reflected in Hindi movies, not simply as truths of what the audiences believe, but values towards which they aspire, then the governing fantasy/desire is for at least three significant ideologies concerning religion.

The first ideology is that of a single and universal God, who stands above various religious projections. We saw this in all three examples, including the one first shown in the introduction, where God is depicted as being above Hindu and Muslim (and Christian) projections. Juluri states how this belief in one God may seem strange in a land where plurality is celebrated, however Indian cinema has "stayed true to a deeper sensibility in Hindu philosophy" where God can be many, and yet one.[47] The point to be noted is that the oneness of God, an abstract concept in popular thinking where household gods dominate, and multiple religions are evident, the common movie watcher aspires for the ideal belief that there is a greater truth beyond what is visible. That greater truth of oneness of God, expressed by regular people as an ultimate desire, is expressed naturally and without question in popular Hindi cinema.

The second ideology that governs the representation of religion in Hindi movies is the political and ethical implications of the claim of God's oneness. Here, the idea of nation is combined with the idea of one-God, which means all Indians are one (not just our gods), and also that we are meant to work together and not be in conflict. This socially uplifting message can be thought of as top-down, but it is also fair to assume that this is a commonly held

[47] Juluri, *Bollywood Nation*, 20-21.

belief of the people. The message is that we must not live in "hate" or exclusion, but rather in love, mutual tolerance and acceptance.

The third ideology, and in seeming contrast to the second but actually an extension of it, is that spirituality is a private affair. Previously, the oneness of God had political and social implications. However, here, the call for spirituality is limited to the home, personal and even the inner world of the individual. The natural result is that external expression of religion is considered imperfect or in the wrong direction, and knowledge and wisdom that God is above institutional religiousity, is the way to truth. In view of this, conversion from one visible projection to another is deemed as unnecessary, since externals of religions mandated by the institutions are limited in their understanding of God. Simply changing religion does not change the essential issue, one may say, and the truth is to find God outside these religious labels—in nakedness.

This last point in particular has implications for our topic at hand, because this must be seen not as imposed ideology onto the Indian audience, but rather a representation of the belief of the people. Any desire to "change" this belief, cannot be done simply by introducing a law that mandates religious freedom to convert, but to challenge these fundamental views held and cherished by a vast majority of Hindi speaking Indians.

Conclusions and Implications

It is not surprising, therefore, that actual genuine conversion is hardly ever featured as a theme in Hindi cinema; and it possibly never will be.[48] This is not only because conversion from one religion to another is too controversial to be represented, but because it is not a "popular" topic for a culture that feels that conversion is manipulative at worst or unnecessary at best. Thus, as I asserted in the beginning, the main audience of popular Hindi movies, and that is a lot of Indians, do not want conversion. Thus, any approach in India about religious conversion must be aware of how

---

[48] One must also be aware that actual genuine conversion may not have been seen even in western popular cinema, though there could be examples of individuals (not central characters) changing their religion, like in *Amistad*.

almost universally, it will be met with suspicion, derision and even opposition.

For Christians, trying to get Indians to accept conversion as acceptable and a fundamental right, they must also come to terms with the idea that Indians may not think it is a fundamental right; instead they may view it as divisive to their cherished beliefs and values. How then could we tackle this challenge: to help India see the Christian view of "conversion," as acceptable, fitting within cultural codes, and a necessary basic human and godly right?

Instead of providing a list of possible suggestions, I end this article with a possible movie idea; a story to be proposed to the media, so to speak. This, within the popular medium, that could potentially help get the Christian message across.

The story begins with a focus on a happy-go-luck non-religious Hindu Hero (and he must be Hindu) who does not care about religion. However, when his neighbour (friend) along with the family become Christians, things start getting difficult. This neighbour/friend is harassed and even his family's life is threatened. The Hero is forced to choose to take sides and begins to protect the newly Christian family. In the process of multiple physical fights with assailants, it is discovered that there is a political conspiracy afoot caused by some political opportunists, who want to spark communal tensions in the so-far peaceful area for political gains.

In the near to closing scenes, the Hero facing people's unrelenting opposition (and failure to see the bigger picture), makes a stirring speech to the crowd. He says that if the dominant religious community had so much faith in their religion, why are they so afraid if a person chooses to change his faith. He affirms that the search for faith is the mark of the true Hindu and we can choose whichever path we want to take.

The Hero also "scolds" the family that became a Christian for becoming liberal in customs and cutting themselves off from Indian culture. The Hero will talk about how dressing like an Indian is important and we should not need to adopt western cultural values. The Christian family that compromised in this way, would hang its head in shame, like the rest of the crowd.

In the final scene, the Hero, almost defeated, gains spiritual power from the prayers of the newly religious, and he defeats the main villain. Finally, the Hero returns to his own context, having dealt with the conflict and having been confronted with the view that without God he could not have won. And yet he maintains a certain distance, with humour, by giving his temple-God a wink, and lives to fight another day. The End.

The strength of this story is that it shows a Hindu protecting the rights of religious conversion and perhaps, for the Indian context, having a top star promoting that message is the best a Christian movie-maker can do. However, the hope is also to tap into the lesser known beliefs of the majority Indian people, that protection of the weak and the freedom to choose your own religious path, are also ideals and desires for society in India.

www.ingramcontent.com/pod-product-compliance
Lightning Source LLC
Chambersburg PA
CBHW022001160426
43197CB00007B/215